Learning Keyboarding
and Word Processing
with Word 2000

Cynthia Belis
Shirley Dembo

To Our Families

A special thanks to our husbands, Harold Dembo and Stephen Belis, who have patiently given us encouragement and support while they watched us work at the computer long into the night, and to our children, Craig and David, for their input, understanding and everlasting patience.

We also wish to thank Adrienne Frosch, Helen McClenahan, Rochelle Pollack and Gloria Jackelow for all their support during the development of this book.

A special, loving thanks to our mothers who were always there with their love, encouragement and patience that will never be forgotten.

Managing Editor	English Editor	Technical Editors	Design and Layout
Jennifer Frew	Emily Hay	Trent Harris	Elsa Johannesson
		Janet Madden	Adrion Smith
	Editorial Assistants	Jan Snyder	Paul Wray
	Emily Hay		
	Jacinta O'Hallaran		**Illustrations and Art Work**
			Amy Capuano

TABLE OF CONTENTS

TABLE OF CONTENTS

TABLE OF CONTENTS

iii

TABLE OF CONTENTS

TABLE OF CONTENTS

TABLE OF CONTENTS

ABOUT THIS BOOK

LEARNING TO TYPE WITH MICROSOFT® WORD 2000 will teach you how to type without looking at the keys, while at the same time teach you how to use Microsoft Word 2000 for Windows.

Each of the 40 lessons contained in this book consists of both typing instruction and Word 2000 computer concepts. All the alphabet keys are taught in the first eight lessons. Warm-up and review exercises are provided to reinforce both word processing and keyboarding skills. Lessons 10-40 provide timed writings along with a calculating ruler to enable you to gauge your current typing speed. In addition, the final lesson of the book is devoted to practice drills that will continue to build speed and accuracy.

Word 2000 concepts are taught using step-by-step instructions and are applied in exercises which create simple documents, letters, tables, lists, flyers, reports, and newsletters.

After completing the 40 lessons in this book, you will be able to use the basic features of Word 2000 to touch type and create most documents on the computer that you would have only previously been able to create with pen and paper.

HOW TO USE THIS BOOK

Each lesson contains the following parts:

Keyboarding Goals

Introduce new keys or keyboarding concepts for touch-typing.

Word 2000 Goals

Explain the word processing concept or feature that relates to the exercise.

Exercises

Allow you to practice the word processing and/or keyboarding concept that was introduced.

Timed Writing

Enables you to calculate your current typing speed.

Mouse/Keystroke Procedures

Outline the keyboard shortcuts for each Word 2000 concept taught in that lesson.

BUILD SPEED AND ACCURACY

The final lesson contains a variety of drills that focus on specific techniques for building speed and accuracy through:

- Keyboard reaches
- Letter combinations
- Common words and phrases
- Progressive speed drills

Though this is the final lesson in the book, these exercises can be used at any time once the alphabet keys have been learned.

AUTOMATED TYPING PROGRAM ON CD-ROM

THE TIMINGS FOLDER contains the DDC Edition of a program called ***All the Right Type*** (designed by Ingenuity Works Inc.). The program contains a TESTING CENTER, which houses the DDC Timed Writings that correspond with the Timed Writing section in Lessons 10-40. The program allows you to set the speed and timing goals that you desire. Each lesson in the program is correlated to a lesson in the text and numbered accordingly.

- OPTIONAL UPGRADE TO ALL THE RIGHT TYPE: A full feature version of the program is available from Ingenuity Works Inc. at a special DDC upgrade price (800-665-0667 or Fax 604-431-7996). That version contains a RECORDS LIBRARY, which provides a report of all tests taken to date, as well as a SKILL BUILDING and PRACTICE PAVILION area containing additional materials that can be accessed after new keys are learned.

INSTALL AUTOMATED TYPING PROGRAM

System Requirements

Software	Windows 95, Windows 3.1 (or higher), or Windows NT 3.51 (or higher)
Hardware	386/33MHZ or higher (486 or higher recommended), 8 MB RAM, 256 color monitor, and CD-ROM Drive
Disk Space	10 MB available hard disk space for a "Typical" installation.

1. Click **START** on the desktop, Click RUN and then type: **(CD-ROM drive letter):\TIMINGS\SETUP**.
2. Click **NEXT** twice to proceed to the Choose Directory Location screen.
3. Click **NEXT** to accept the default directory (or click **BROWSE** to select another directory) for installing program files. *Note: TYPICAL is recommended for most users.*
4. At the Setup Type screen, click a setup option based on your system needs and click **NEXT**.
5. At the Select Program Folder screen, click **NEXT** to accept the default folder (or select another folder) for storing the program icons.
6. At the Setup Complete screen, click **FINISH**.

START AUTOMATED TYPING PROGRAM

NOTE: Steps 3, 6, and 7 are only necessary the first time you log into the program or if you wish to make any program adjustments.

1. If program and program icons were installed to the default locations, click **START** on the desktop, click **PROGRAMS**, then click **All the Right Type DDC Edition.**
2. When the introductory screen appears, click anywhere to continue.
3. At the Sign On screen, click **EDIT USERS**, then click **ADD**, type your name, click **OK**, and then click **DONE** to add it to the program.
4. Click your name in the User list and click **SELECT**.
5. Click **CONTINUE** at the welcome screen.
6. Click **Options** on the menu bar and select **Set Options**.
7. **TO SET A SPEED GOAL:**
   (a) Click **Speed Goal.**
   (b) Select a speed goal from the drop-down list and click **OK**.
   NOTE: The User Prompt option allows you to manually adjust the speed goal for each exercise with out returning to the Options screen.
   OR
   TO SET A TIME GOAL:
   (a) Click **Timed Writing.**
   (b) Select a time goal from the drop-down list.

*NOTE: The **User Prompt** option allows you to manually adjust the timing goal for each exercise without returning to the Options screen. However, the User Prompt option does not enable you to select 30-second timings, whereas the Timed Writing drop-down option does.* **THE TIMED WRITING, USER PROMPT OPTION IS THE RECOMMENDED SETTING FOR THIS PROGRAM.**

8. At the FACULTY OF A.R.T. main campus screen, click the **TESTING CENTER** to access the timed writing exercises that accompany this book.
9. Double-click the exercise for which you wish to be timed.
10. Follow the online instructions.

NETWORK VERSION OF AUTOMATED TYPING PROGRAM

A network school version is available as a separate purchase from DDC Publishing. The network version allows you to install the program on an unlimited number of computers in your computer lab. It also provides the ability for instructors to view and monitor each student's progress and the ability to create timed writings tests from external documents. To order the Network version, contact DDC Publishing at 800-528-3897 and ask for Customer Service. The price of the Network version is $250. (Catalog number Z55CDSL)

TEACHER'S MANUAL

While this book can be used as a self-paced learning book, a comprehensive Teacher's Manual (Catalog number Z55TM) is also available. The Teacher's Manual contains the following:

- Lesson goals
- Related vocabulary
- Points to emphasize
- Exercise settings
- Solution illustrations

SOLUTION AND DATA FILES ON CD-ROM

Solution and data files can be purchased separately from DDC (Catalog number SLZ55). The solution files can be used to compare students' work with final solutions. Data files can be distributed to students who have missed the previous class.

TEST BANK

Tests correlated to each lesson come in a 3-ring binder and can be duplicated and distributed to students. (Catalog number BTZ55)

LOG OF EXERCISES

LESSON	FILE NAME	PAGE	SOLUTION FILE
Lesson 3	LES3	28	
Lesson 4	LES4	29	-
Lesson 5	LES5	38	-
Lesson 6	LES6	45	-
Lesson 7	LES7A	52	-
	LES7B	55	-
Lesson 8	LES8	59	-
Lesson 9	LES9	65	-
	LES9A	69	-
	L09TIME	72	-
Lesson 10	LES10	73	-
	L10TIME	81	-
Lesson 11	LES11	82	-
	LES11A	88	-
	L11TIME	92	-
Lesson 12	LES12	94	-
	LES12A	99	-
	L12TIME	100	-
Lesson 13	LES13	102	-
	RAINBOW	109	S13RAINBOW
	ASTRONAUT	110	S13ASTRONAUT
	L13TIME	111	-
Lesson 14	LES14	113	-
	INPUT	115	S14INPUT
	DEBATE	117	S14DEBATE
	L14TIME	120	-
Lesson 15	LES15	121	-
	SITES	124	S15SITES
	PRESENT	126	S15PRESENT
	L15TIME	129	-
Lesson 16	LES16	131	-
	SAND1	133	S16SAND1
	INTERVIEW	135	S16INTERVIEW
	CRIME	138	S16CRIME
	SAND2	140	S16SAND2
	L16TIME	141	-
Lesson 17	LES17	143	-
	INPUT	144	S17INPUT
	PENCIL	146	S17PENCIL
	REPTILES	148	S17REPTILES
	L17TIME	150	-
Lesson 18	LES18	152	-
	RAINBOW	154	S18RAINBOW
	SAND2	156	S18SAND2
	INPUT	158	S18INPUT
	L18TIME	160	-

LOG OF EXERCISES

LOG OF EXERCISES

DIRECTORY OF DOCUMENTS

LESSON 1

- Start Word Using the Mouse and Taskbar
- Identify Word Screen Parts; Use Minimize, Restore and Close Buttons
- Customize Menus and Toolbars • Change Default Font Size
- Close a Document • Exit Word

GOAL 1: Start Word Using the Mouse and Taskbar

- Microsoft Word 2000 is a **word processing software program**. It displays on a computer screen what is being typed into the computer program. Word 2000 features make it easy for you to make changes to your typewritten work and, when you are ready, print a copy of what appears on the screen.

- To start Word 2000, you must first learn to use the mouse.

- You must use the **mouse** to access many Word features and tasks. The mouse allows you to communicate with the computer.

- When the mouse is moved on the table or desk, the mouse pointer moves on the screen at the same time.

- The mouse pointer changes its shape depending on what it is pointing to on the screen. The mouse pointer will not move if the mouse is lifted off the table or desk.

- A mouse commonly has a left and a right button. Throughout the course of this text, you should use the **left mouse button** when instructed to click unless instructed in italic type to do otherwise.

- The following words are used throughout this text to describe how to use the mouse:

Mouse Action	Definition
• **Point to**	Move the mouse (on the table or desk) so the mouse pointer touches a screen element.
• **Click**	Point to something on the screen and quickly press and let go of the **left** mouse button.
• **Right-click**	Point to something on the screen and quickly press and let go of the **right** mouse button.
• **Double-click**	Point to something on the screen and press the **left** mouse button two times in a row quickly.
• **Drag**	Point to something on the screen and press and hold down the **left** mouse button while moving the mouse.
• **Slide**	Move the mouse on the table or desk.

LESSON 1

Start Word

- After you have turned on your computer, you will see the first screen. This screen is called the **desktop**. Word may be started as follows.

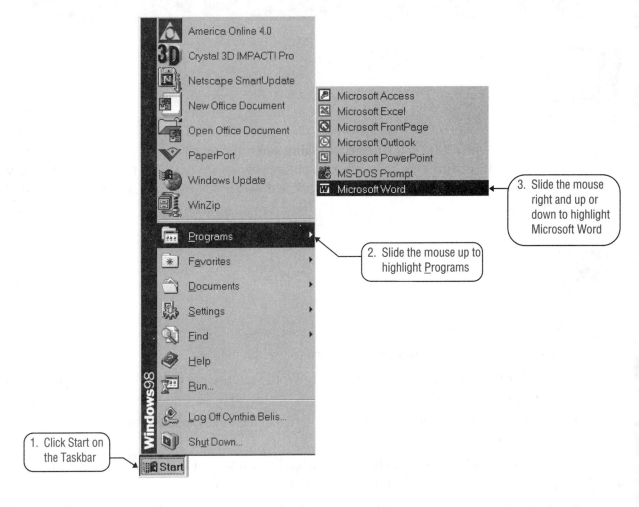

Exercise 1
Start Word

1. Click Start on the Taskbar.
2. Click Programs.
3. Click Microsoft Word.

GOAL 2: Identify Word Screen Parts; Use Minimize, Restore and Close Buttons

■ Once you start Word, a blank document automatically appears on the screen. The illustration below shows descriptions of Word screen elements.

■ Word 2000 opens with the Standard and Formatting toolbars on one row. However, if you have a previous version of Word installed, your document screen may differ from the following illustration.

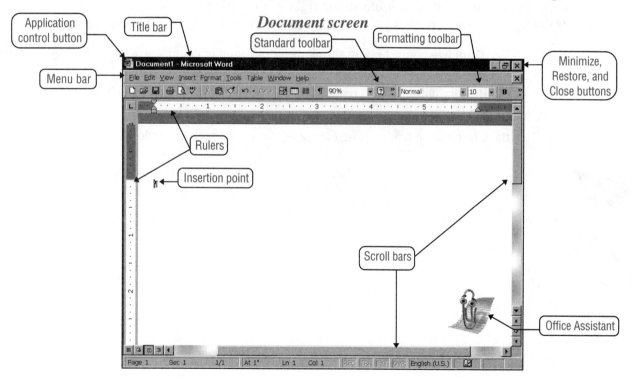

• **Title bar**	Lists the name of the document and the software program (Microsoft Word) next to it. The Minimize, Restore and Close buttons appear on the right of the Title bar. These buttons will be explained on the next page.
• **Menu bar**	Contains a list of menu items to help you operate the program. When a menu item is chosen, a drop-down list appears with more options.
• **Standard toolbar**	Contains buttons that you can click to quickly use some of Word's common menu commands.
• **Formatting toolbar**	Contains buttons and boxes you can click to use common formatting features.
• **Horizontal ruler**	Appears below the Formatting toolbar and shows the left and right margins.

•	**Vertical ruler**	Appears at the left of the screen and shows the top and bottom margins.
•	**Insertion point**	Indicates where you are located in a document. If it is displayed at the end of the document, it is also called the End-of-Document marker.
•	**Office Assistant**	Provides help for completing Word tasks.
•	**Scroll bars**	Allow you to see parts of a document that are not currently visible on the screen.
•	**Taskbar**	The Taskbar displays the programs that are currently open.

Use Minimize, Restore and Close buttons

- When you start Word 2000, you will see a set of buttons at the top right of the Title bar (note the illustration on the previous page). This set contains the **Minimize**, **Restore** and **Close** buttons and controls the document window. When only one document is open, its Close button appears on the Menu bar.
- A new document window usually opens at its maximum size. You can control the window size by choosing one of the three buttons to the right of the Title bar.
- If the Restore button is clicked, it is replaced by a new button, the **Maximize** button.

  - Click the **Minimize** button ▬ to shrink the application or document window to an icon, which displays at the bottom of the screen.
  - Click the **Restore** button ⬚ to reduce the size of the application or document window.
  - Click the **Maximize** button ☐ to return the application or document window to its maximum size.
  - Click the **Close** button ✖ to close the application or document window.

Exercise 2
Change Window Size

1. Click the Document Restore button at the right of the Title bar.
2. Click the Maximize button at the right of the Title bar.
3. Click the Minimize button at the right of the Title bar.
4. Click the document button on the Taskbar to restore the document window to its previous size.

GOAL 3:   Customize Menus and Toolbars

- As you work with Word, the program recognizes the menu commands and the toolbar buttons you use most often and saves these as your personalized settings. These settings are displayed on the menus and toolbars and are constantly updated as you work.

- For the purposes of this book, it is necessary to keep the menu commands and toolbar buttons uniform. Therefore, you will need to disable the customize options.

- Follow these steps to disable the Customize feature:
  1. Click Tools menu.
  2. Click Customize to access the Customize dialog box shown below.

Customize dialog box

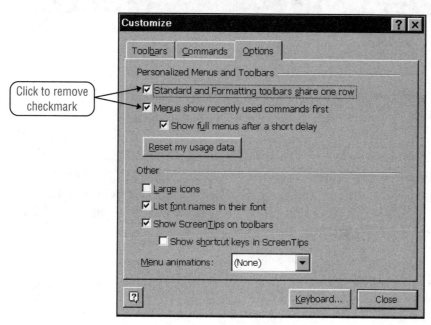

  3. In the Customize dialog box, click the Options tab if it is not already selected.
  4. Click to remove the checkmark from the following items:
     - Standard and Formatting toolbars share one row
     - Menus show recently used commands first
  5. Click Close.

Exercise 3
Customize Menus and Toolbars

1. Click <u>T</u>ools menu.
2. Click <u>C</u>ustomize.
3. Click <u>O</u>ptions tab.
4. Click "Standard and Formatting toolbars <u>s</u>hare one row" checkbox to remove the checkmark.
5. Click "Me<u>n</u>us show recently used command first" checkbox to remove the checkmark.
6. Click Close.

GOAL 4:   Change Default Font Size

- Every time Word 2000 is started, a new document opens with the same font, font size, margins and line spacing settings. These settings are referred to as default settings. Word's default font size and font is 12 point Times New Roman; however, you may have a different default font size due to a previous installation of Word. **You must change the default setting to 12 point so your work will match the exercises in this book.**

Font dialog box

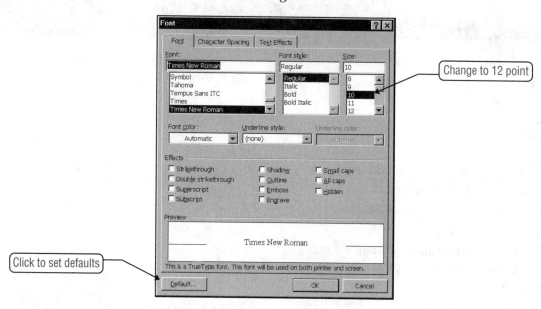

- Follow these steps to change the default font size to 12 points:
    1. Click Format menu.
    2. Click Font to access the Font dialog box illustrated above.
    3. In the Font list box, click the down arrow and select Times New Roman.
    4. In the Font style list box, click Regular.
    5. In the Size list box, click the down arrow and select 12.
    6. Click the Default button.
    7. Select Yes when asked to change the default setting to Times New Roman, 12 point.

Exercise 4
Change Default Font Size

1. Click Format menu.
2. Click Font.
3. Select Times New Roman from the Font box.
4. Select Regular from the Font style box.
5. Select 12 from the Size list box.
6. Click Default button.
7. Select Yes when asked to change the default to Times New Roman, 12 point.

LESSON 1

GOAL 5: Close a Document

- When you have completed your work, you should close your document. You can "throw it away" or you can save it for later use.

- Two ways to close a document without saving it are:
  1. Click File menu.
  2. Click Close from the drop-down menu.
  3. Click No when Word asks if you wish to save your document.

  OR

  1. Click the Close button (the X at the right end of the Menu bar).
  2. Click No when Word asks if you wish to save your document.

Exercise 5
Close a Document

1. Click File menu.
2. Click Close.
3. If prompted to save the document, click No.

8

GOAL 6: Exit Word

- ■ When you have closed all open documents, you can close the application by doing the following:
  - • Double-click the Application Control button .

OR

  - • Click the Close button ☒ on the Title bar.

OR

  1. Click File menu.
  2. Click Exit.

Exercise 6
Exit Word

  1. Click File menu.
  2. Click Exit.

MOUSE/ KEYSTROKE PROCEDURES

Start Word

1. Click **Start**
   button 🏁 Start .... Ctrl + Esc
   on Taskbar.
2. Click **Programs**....................... P
3. Click **Microsoft Word**.............. ✓↵

Change the Default Font

1. Click **Format** menu .... Alt + O
2. Click **Font**................................. F
3. Click **Font**................................ Alt + F
4. Click **Font style**............... Alt + Y

5. Click **Size**........................ Alt + S
6. Click **Default**.................... Alt + D
7. Select **Yes**............................... Y
   when asked to change the default
   font to Times New Roman, 12 point.

Close a Document

1. Click the **Close** button ☒.
2. Click **No** .... N
   when asked to save a document.

OR

1. Click **File** menu .... Alt + F
2. Click **Close** C

3. Click **No** .... N
   when asked to save a document.

Exit Word

Double-click **Application Control**
button 📄.

OR

Click the **Close** button ☒ on the Title bar.

OR

1. Click **File** menu .... Alt + F
2. Click **Exit**................................. X

LESSON 2

- Get Started with Word • Introduction to Home-Row Keys
- Learn F and J Finger Keys, Spacebar and Enter
- Move the Insertion Point • Change Zoom Option

GOAL 1:   Get Started with Word

- Once you start Word, you are ready to begin typing in the document window. Note the blinking vertical line. It is called the **insertion point**. It tells you where your typing will appear. As you type, the insertion point will move to the right.

Insertion point in document window

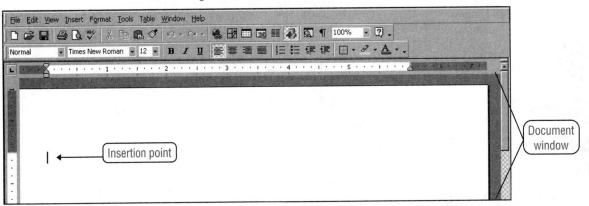

- Word contains **AutoCorrect** features that automatically correct certain typing errors. These automatic corrections will interfere with the typing of many of the exercises contained in this text. Therefore, it is necessary to turn the AutoCorrect features off.

- Follow these steps to turn off the AutoCorrect features:
  1. Click Tools menu.
  2. Click AutoCorrect.
  3. Click each AutoCorrect check box to remove the checkmarks and deselect the options.
  4. Click OK.

AutoCorrect dialog box

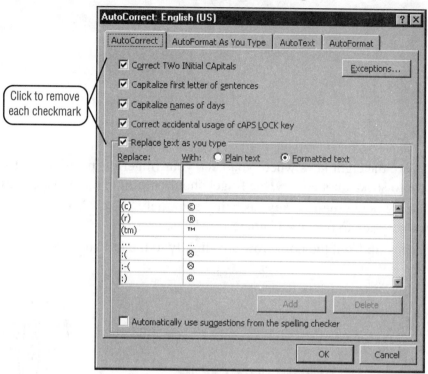

Click to remove each checkmark

Exercise 1
Turn Off AutoCorrect Features

1. Click Tools menu.
2. Click AutoCorrect.
3. Click each checkbox to deselect each option.
4. Click OK.

GOAL 2: Introduction to Home-Row Keys

- The **home-row keys** are the eight keys where you keep your fingertips positioned. Every time a finger leaves this row to strike another key, the finger should return to the home position quickly.
- Think of all keys that are not home-row keys as being extremely "**hot**." You will want to hit them with quick motion to get back to the "**cool**" home-row keys.
- Notice that most reaches **up** from the home row are slightly to the left and most reaches down are slightly to the right.

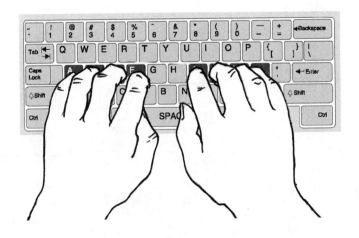

Exercise 2
Home Row Placement

1. Place your left hand on the keys as instructed below. Refer to the keyboard illustration on the previous page for correct placement.
   - pinky on the **A**
   - ring finger on the **S**
   - middle finger on the **D**
   - index finger on the **F**
     *Note: There are raised dots or dashes on the **F** and **J** keys so you can "feel" the correct placement of your **F** and **J** fingers without looking down at your fingers.*
2. Take your left hand off the keyboard.
3. Look at the keyboard and place your left hand back on the home-row keys.
4. Repeat Steps 2 and 3 twice.
5. Take your left hand off the keyboard.
6. Put it back without looking at the keyboard.
7. Check the keyboard illustration on the previous page to see if you placed your fingers correctly.
8. Repeat Steps 5 and 6 twice.
9. Take your left hand off the keyboard.
10. Place your right hand on the keys as instructed below. Refer to the keyboard illustration on the previous page for correct placement.
    - pinky on the **;**
    - ring finger on the **L**
    - middle finger on the **K**
    - index finger on the **J**
11. Take your right hand off the keyboard.
12. Look at the keyboard and place your right hand back on the home-row keys.
13. Repeat Steps 11 and 12 twice.
14. Take your right hand off the keyboard.
15. Put it back without looking at the keyboard.
16. Check with the illustration to see if you placed your fingers correctly.
17. Repeat Steps 14 and 15 twice.
18. Take your right hand off the keyboard.
19. Practice putting both hands on the home-row keys.
20. Check the illustration to see if you have correctly placed your fingers.

GOAL 3: Learn F and J Finger Keys, Spacebar and Enter

- Your index fingers (the **F** and **J** fingers), which are your strongest, make one reach to the center of the keyboard on each row.
- Notice the keys that your left and right index fingers will strike.
- To space between groups of letters, strike the **Spacebar** with your right thumb.
- When you reach the end of a line, strike the **Enter** key with your right pinky.

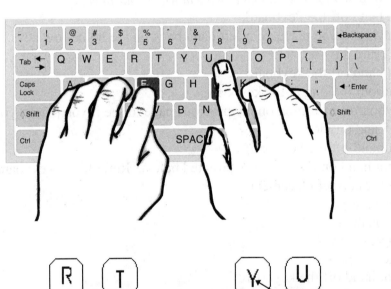

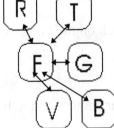

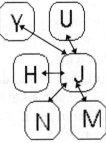

Exercise 3a
Practice F Finger Keys

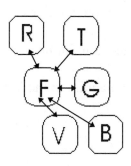

Left-hand finger keys
1. Place your fingers on the home-row keys as shown on page 13.
2. Look at the diagram in the left column. Touch the **F** key.
3. Move your **F** finger up to touch the **R** and back to the **F**.
4. Move your **F** finger up to touch the **T** and back to the **F**.
5. Move your **F** finger right to touch the **G** and back to the **F**.
6. Move your **F** finger down to touch the **B** and back to the **F**.
7. Move your **F** finger down to touch the **V** and back to the **F**.
8. Repeat Steps 3-7 twice.

Exercise 3b
Practice J Finger Keys

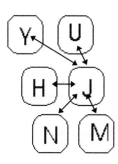

Right-hand finger keys
1. Place your fingers on the home-row keys as shown on page 12.
2. Look at the diagram in the left column. Touch the **J** key.
3. Move your **J** finger up to touch the **U** and back to the **J**.
4. Move your **J** finger up to touch the **Y** and back to the **J**.
5. Move your **J** finger left to touch the **H** and back to the **J**.
6. Move your **J** finger down to touch the **N** and back to the **J**.
7. Move your **F** finger down to touch the **M** and back to the **F**.
8. Touch the **Spacebar** with your right thumb.
9. Move **;** finger to the right to touch the **Enter** key and back to the **;**.
10. Repeat Steps 3-9 twice.

Exercise 3c
F Finger Keys

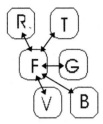

1. Type the following exercise, saying each letter to yourself as you strike the key. You may look at the keys in the diagram to the left or at the illustration below as you strike each key. Try not to look at your fingers.
2. You will see red and/or green wavy lines below the letters.
   - Red wavy lines indicate spelling errors.
   - Green wavy lines indicate grammar errors.
   Since we are not typing actual words in these exercises, we will ignore the lines for now.
3. To space between groups of letters, strike the Spacebar with your right thumb.
4. If you make an error, keep typing.
5. When done, type the same exercise again without looking at the diagram to the left or your fingers.
6. When you are finished, compare your screen with the book.
7. Do not close the document window.

1 frf frf frf ftf ftf ftf fgf fgf fgf fbf fbf fbf fvf fvf fvf ENTER

2 frf frf frf ftf ftf ftf fgf fgf fgf fbf fbf fbf fvf fvf fvf ENTER ENTER

3 frftfgfbfv frftfgfbfv frftfgfbfv frftfgfbfv frftfgfbfv ENTER

4 frftfgfbfv frftfgfbfv frftfgfbfv frftfgfbfv frftfgfbfv ENTER ENTER

Exercise 3d
J Finger Keys

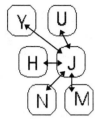

1. Type the following exercise, saying each letter to yourself as you strike the key. You may look at the keys in the diagram to the left or at the illustration below as you strike each key. Try not to look at your fingers. Ignore the red and/or green wavy lines below exercise letters.
2. To space between groups of letters, strike the Spacebar with your right thumb.
3. If you make an error, keep typing.
4. Now type the same exercise again without looking at the diagram at the left or at your fingers.
5. When you are finished, compare your screen with the book.
6. Do not close the document window.

1 juj juj juj jyj jyj jyj jhj jhj jhj jnj jnj jnj jmj jmj jmj ENTER
2 juj juj juj jyj jyj jyj jhj jhj jhj jnj jnj jnj jmj jmj jmj ENTER ENTER

3 jujyjhjnjm jujyjhjnjm jujyjhjnjm jujyjhjnjm jujyjhjnjm ENTER
4 jujyjhjnjm jujyjhjnjm jujyjhjnjm jujyjhjnjm jujyjhjnjm ENTER ENTER

LESSON 2

Exercise 3e
F and J Finger Keys

1. Type the following exercise saying the letters as you strike the keys.
2. If you don't remember the location of a key, you may look at the keyboard illustration.
3. If you have time, type the same exercise again.
4. Try to increase your speed each time you repeat the line.
5. When you are finished, compare your screen with the book.
6. Do not close the document window.

1 frftf frftf frftfgf frftfgf frftfgfbf frftfgfbf frftfgfbfvf ENTER
2 frftf frftf frftfgf frftfgf frftfgfbf frftfgfbf frftfgfbfvf ENTER ENTER

3 jujyj jujyj jujyjhj jujyjhj jujyjhjnj jujyjhjnj jujyjhjnjmj ENTER
4 jujyj jujyj jujyjhj jujyjhj jujyjhjnj jujyjhjnj jujyjhjnjmj ENTER ENTER

5 frfvf frfvf ftfbf ftfbf ftfgfbf ftfgfbf frftfgfbfvf frftfgfbfvf ENTER
6 fbfvfgftfrf fbfvfgftfrf fvfrf fvfrf fbftf fbftf fbfgftf fbfgftf ENTER ENTER

7 jujmj jujmj jyjnj jyjnj jyjhjnj jyjhjnj jujyjhjnjmj jujyjhjnjmj ENTER
8 jmjnjhjyjuj jmjnjhjyjuj jmjuj jmjuj jnjyj jnjyj jnjhjyj jnjhjyj ENTER ENTER

GOAL 4: Move the Insertion Point

- The **insertion point** is a small vertical line that moves to the right as you type.
- To place the insertion point on another line of text, move the mouse until it turns into an I-beam (I). Position the I-beam (I) at the desired location and click the mouse button.

I-beam in a document

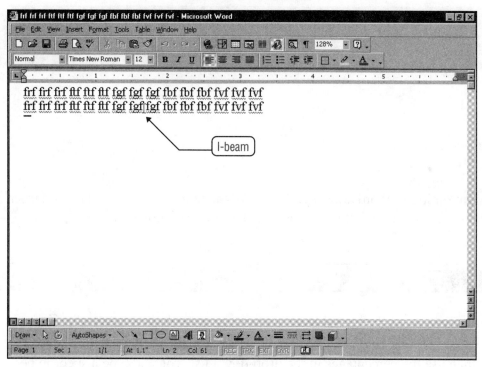

- When you are in Print Layout view or Web Layout view, the I-beam, when moved in blank areas, changes its appearance. Different symbols will appear next to the I-beam, depending on where the I-beam appears on the page. These symbols represent different formatting options, which will be learned in later lessons.

LESSON 2

Exercise 4
Move the Insertion Point

1. Place the insertion point at the beginning of the first line of text from Exercise 3e.
2. Place the insertion point at the end of the third line of text.
3. Place the insertion point at the end of the last line of text.
4. Do not close the document window.

GOAL 5:   Change Zoom Option

- The **Zoom** option in Word allows you to make the text on the screen appear larger or smaller. Note the location of the Zoom button on the Standard toolbar shown below.

Standard toolbar

- To change the size of the viewable area, click the arrow button next to the Zoom box and select a percentage. The higher the percentage, the larger the text will appear.
- Rather than use the percentages in the drop-down list, you can type a specific percentage in the Zoom box. Press the Enter key to activate that percentage.

Exercise 5
Change Zoom Option

1. Click Zoom button arrow.
2. Select 10%.
3. Click Zoom button arrow.
4. Select 50%.
5. Click Zoom button arrow.
6. Select 100%.
7. Click Zoom button arrow.
8. Select 75%.
9. Note the differences in the views.
10. Close the document window.
11. Click No when asked to save the document.
12. Exit Word.

MOUSE/KEYSTROKE PROCEDURES

Turn off AutoCorrect Feature
1. Click **Tools** menu .... `Alt` + `T`
2. Click **AutoCorrect** .... `A`
3. Click **OK** .... `Enter`

Move Insertion Point
1. Move mouse and place I-beam (I) in desired location.
2. Click left mouse button.

Change Zoom Option
1. Click **Zoom** arrow .... `75%` `▼`
2. Click desired percentage .... `%`

GOAL 1:   Touch-Type F and J Finger Keys

- ■ You will practice touch-typing F and J finger key letters and words.

Exercise 1
F and J Finger Reaches

1. Start Word to get a blank document screen.
2. Type the following exercise, saying each letter to yourself as you strike the key. You may look at the keys in the illustration as you strike each key. Try not to look at your fingers. Ignore the red and/or green wavy lines below exercise letters. If you make an error, continue typing.
3. Do not close the document window.

1 frf frf frf ftf ftf ftf fgf fgf fgf fbf fbf fbf fvf fvf fvf ENTER
2 frf frf frf ftf ftf ftf fgf fgf fgf fbf fbf fbf fvf fvf fvf ENTER ENTER

3 frftfgfbfv frftfgfbfv frftfgfbfv frftfgfbfv frftfgfbfv ENTER
4 frftfgfbfv frftfgfbfv frftfgfbfv frftfgfbfv frftfgfbfv ENTER ENTER

5 juj juj juj jyj jyj jyj jhj jhj jhj jnj jnj jnj jmj jmj jmj ENTER
6 juj juj juj jyj jyj jyj jhj jhj jhj jnj jnj jnj jmj jmj jmj ENTER ENTER

7 jujyjhjnjm jujyjhjnjm jujyjhjnjm jujyjhjnjm jujyjhjnjm ENTER
8 jujyjhjnjm jujyjhjnjm jujyjhjnjm jujyjhjnjm jujyjhjnjm ENTER ENTER

9 fur fur fur fur fun fun fun fun gun gun gun gun ENTER
10 fur fur fur fur fun fun fun fun gun gun gun gun ENTER ENTER

11 gum gum gum gum guy guy guy guy buy buy buy buy ENTER
12 gum gum gum gum guy guy guy guy buy buy buy buy ENTER ENTER

13 but but but but hut hut hut hut jut jut jut jut vug vug vug vug ENTER
14 but but but but hut hut hut hut jut jut jut jut vug vug vug vug ENTER ENTER

15 fur fun gun gum guy buy but hut jut vug ENTER
16 fur fun gun gum guy buy but hut jut vug ENTER ENTER

LESSON 3

GOAL 2:   Identify Status Bar Parts

- As you type, notice the **Status bar** at the bottom of the screen. This area gives you information about the location of the insertion point. The following illustration shows the various parts of the Status bar.

Status bar information

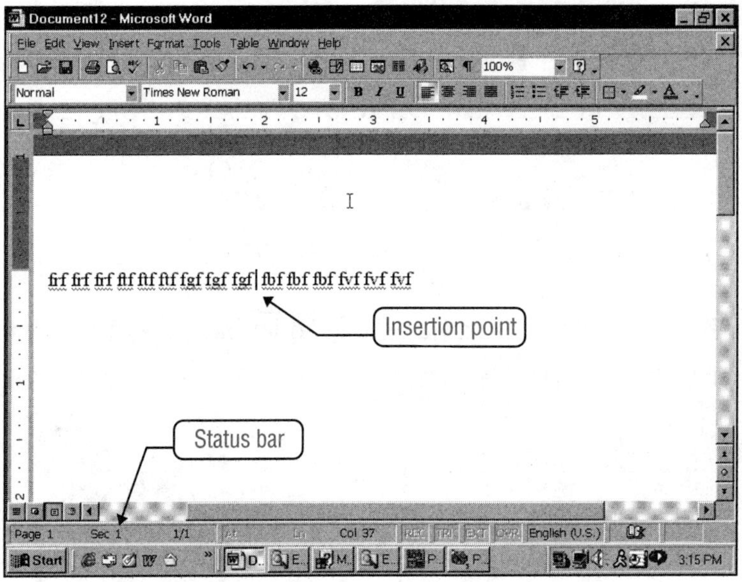

![Screenshot of Microsoft Word window with labels pointing to "Insertion point" and "Status bar"]

- The first section tells you the following:
    - **Page 1** -   Indicates on which page of the document the insertion point is located.
    - **Sec 1** -   Indicates on which section of the document the insertion point is located.
    - **1/1** -   Indicates the number of pages in the document (1) and on which page the insertion point is located (1).
- The second section of the Status bar shows you exactly where the insertion point is on the page.
    - The **At** indicator shows how many inches the insertion point is from the top of the page.
    - The **Ln** indicator shows you what line the insertion point is on.
    - The **Col** indicator shows you how many spaces or characters the insertion point is from the left side of the page.
- The Status bar will also display messages as you are working.
- The last section of the Status bar shows when certain features are active. Word 2000 includes the language selected for the spell check and other proofing tools.

Exercise 2
Status Bar

1. Refer to Exercise 1 and follow the instructions to find the answers to the questions below.
2. Place your insertion point at the beginning of the first line of typing.
   - What page is the insertion point on?
   - How many inches is the insertion point from the top of the page?
   - What line is the insertion point on?
   - What is the horizontal position of the insertion point?
3. Place your insertion point at the end of the last line of typing and find the answers to the same questions.
4. Press the Enter key twice and type the same exercise (Exercise 1) without looking at the keyboard illustration or your fingers.
5. When you are finished, compare your screen with the book.
6. Do not close the document window.

GOAL 3:   Create a New Document

- To start a new document while working in Word, click the **New Blank Document** button 🗋 on the Standard toolbar as shown below.

Standard toolbar

New document button

- Once you have a clear document window, you can begin typing.

LESSON 3

Exercise 3
Create a New Document

1. Click the New Blank Document button on the Standard toolbar.
2. Type the following exercise, saying each letter to yourself as you strike the key. Try to type each repeated word faster than the time before.
3. If you make an error, continue typing.
4. If you have time, type the same exercise again.
5. Try to increase your speed each time you repeat the line.
6. When you are finished, compare your screen with the book.

---

1 frf frftf frftfgf frftfgfvf frftfgfbfvf ENTER

2 frf frftf frftfgf frftfgfvf frftfgfbfvf ENTER ENTER

3 juj jujyj jujyjhj jujyjhjnj jujyjhjnjmj ENTER

4 juj jujyj jujyjhj jujyjhjnj jujyjhjnjmj ENTER ENTER

5 fur fun gun gum guy buy but hut jut vug ENTER

6 fur fun gun gum guy buy but hut jut vug ENTER ENTER

7 vug jut hut but buy guy gum gun fun fur ENTER

8 vug jut hut but buy guy gum gun fun fur ENTER ENTER

GOAL 4:   Save a Document

- If you want to save your document for future use, you must give it a **file name**.
  - A file name may contain up to 255 characters and may include spaces. If you don't give your document a name, Word will assign one for you when you save the document. Word will automatically use the first word or phrase in the document as the file name.
  - The **.doc** extension at the end of the file name identifies the document as a Word file.
    Example: Lucky.doc

- In addition to giving the document a name, you must tell Word where to save the document.
  - You can save a document to a removable disk or to the hard drive.
  - If you save to a disk, you must tell Word the name of the drive you are saving to, such as: A:\ or B:\ or C:\.
  - If you save to the hard drive, you must save your work in a folder. Think of the hard drive as a file cabinet drawer with the document stored inside a folder in the drawer.

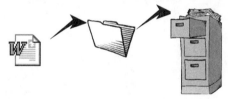

  - Word provides folders for you to save your work in or you can create your own folder.
- When you want to save your work, click the **Save** button 💾 on the Standard toolbar.
- The Save As dialog box appears. A dialog box is an area that asks you for information or instructions.
- Note the different parts of the Save As dialog box shown in the following illustration.

Save As dialog box

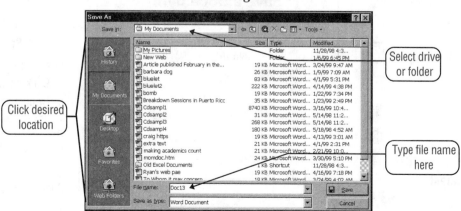

LESSON 3

Exercise 4
Save a Document

1. Save the current document as follows:
   a. Click the Save button on the Standard toolbar.
   b. Select desired folder in the Places Bar or from the Save in drop-down list.
   c. Type **LES3** in the File name text box.
   d. Click the Save button.
2. Close the document window as follows:
   a. Click File menu.
   b. Click Close.
   Note: The first screen now appears, but it will not be saved.
3. Exit Word.
   a. Click File menu.
   b. Click Exit.

MOUSE/KEYSTROKE PROCEDURES

Create a New Document
Ctrl + N

Click **New Blank Document** button  on the Standard toolbar.

OR

1. Click **File** menu............... Alt + F
2. Click **New**.................................. N
3. Click **General** Tab .... Ctrl + Tab
4. Click **Blank Document**.
5. Click **OK** .... Enter

Save a Document
Ctrl + S

1. Click the **Save** button on the Standard toolbar.

OR

   a. Click **File** menu .... Alt + F
   b. Click **Save** .... S
2. Type file name.

3. To change drive and folder:
   a. Click **Save in** down
      arrow........................... Alt + I
   b. Click desired drive............... ↓
   c. Double-click desired folder
      in list box

OR

Click desired folder in
Places Bar........................ ↕

4. Click **Save**....................... Alt + S

28

LESSON 4

- Review F and J Finger Keys • Use Print Preview
- Print a Document • Learn D and K Finger Keys
- Learn Key Words • Resave (Update) a Document

Warm-up
F and J Finger Keys

- Beginning with Lesson 4, each lesson will start with a **warm-up exercise**. The purpose of the warm-up is to practice keys that were previously learned and to get your fingers "warmed-up" the same way you do stretching exercises before running.
  1. Create a new document.
  2. Type the exercise below and on the following page, saying each letter to yourself as you strike the key. You may look at the keyboard illustration as you strike each key. Try not to look at your fingers. Ignore the red and/or green wavy lines below the drill letters.
  3. Remember to strike the Spacebar with your right thumb.
  4. If you make an error, continue typing.
  5. Save the document as **LES4**.
  6. Do not close the document window.

1 frf frf frf ftf ftf ftf fgf fgf fgf fbf fbf fbf fvf fvf fvf ENTER

2 frf frf frf ftf ftf ftf fgf fgf fgf fbf fbf fbf fvf fvf fvf ENTER ENTER

3 frftf frftf frftfgf frftfgf frftfgfvf frftfgfvf frftfgfbfvf ENTER

4 frftf frftf frftfgf frftfgf frftfgfvf frftfgfvf frftfgfbfvf ENTER ENTER

5 juj juj juj jyj jyj jyj jhj jhj jhj jnj jnj jnj jmj jmj jmj ENTER

6 juj juj juj jyj jyj jyj jhj jhj jhj jnj jnj jnj jmj jmj jmj ENTER ENTER

LESSON 4

7 jujyj jujyjhj jujyjhjnj jujyjhjnj jujyjhjnjmj jujyjhjnjmj ENTER

8 jujyj jujyjhj jujyjhjnj jujyjhjnj jujyjhjnjmj jujyjhjnjmj ENTER ENTER

9 fur fur fun fun gun gun gum gum guy guy ENTER

10 fur fur fun fun gun gun gum gum guy guy ENTER ENTER

11 buy buy but but hut hut jut jut vug vug ENTER

12 buy buy but but hut hut jut jut vug vug ENTER ENTER

GOAL 1:   Use Print Preview

- The **Print Preview** feature allows you to see exactly how your document will look when it is printed.
- There are two ways to preview a document:
  - Click the **Print Preview** button ⬚ on the Standard toolbar.

  OR

  1. Click File menu.
  2. Click Print Preview.

- In the Print Preview window the mouse is replaced by a magnifier. Click the left mouse button once to enlarge the document to 100%. Click again to return it to Full Page view.

■ Note the illustration of the Print Preview toolbar below:

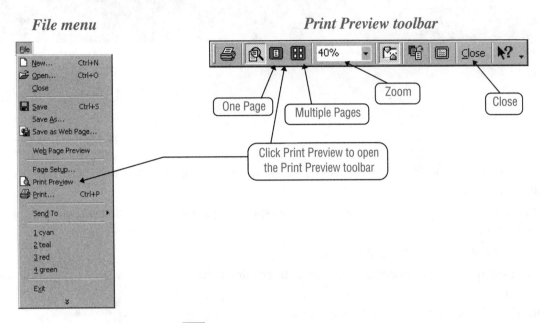

File menu   *Print Preview toolbar*

- Click the **One Page** button to view a single page.
- Click the **Multiple Pages** button to view several pages at a time.
- Click the **Zoom** list box 26% to change the size of the display.
- Click the **Close** button Close to exit the Preview screen and return to the document.

■ Always preview a document before printing it.

Exercise 1
Preview a Document

1. Preview your warm-up document by clicking the Print Preview button on the Standard toolbar.
2. Move the mouse pointer over the document and click the mouse button to enlarge to 100%.
3. Click the mouse again to return it to the Full Page view.
4. Click the Zoom list box and change the zoom factor to 50%.
5. Return the zoom factor to its original setting.
6. Close the Print Preview window.

LESSON 4

GOAL 2:   Print a Document

- After completing and checking the document in the Print Preview window, you may print the document.
- Word allows you to print the entire document, specific pages within a document or a selected part of the document.
- Save a document before printing it.
- Before printing, always check to see that your printer is turned on, the ready light is lit and the paper is loaded.
- There are four ways to print your document.

    - Click the Print button  on the Standard toolbar.

    OR

    1. Click File menu.
    2. Click Print.

    OR

    - Click the Print button on the Print Preview toolbar.

    OR

    - Press Ctrl+P on the keyboard.

Exercise 2
Print a Document

1. Make sure you have **LES4** open as your active document.
2. Turn your printer on.
3. Check the printer to make sure the ready light is lit.
4. Check the printer to make sure it has paper.
5. Print the document by clicking the Print button on the Standard toolbar.
6. Do not close the document window.
7. Write your name in the top-left corner of the printout.

GOAL 3: Learn D and K Finger Keys

- The **D** finger strikes the **E** and **C** keys.
- The **K** finger strikes the **I** and **,** keys.
- Always space one time after a comma. Do not space before the comma.

Exercise 3
D and K Finger Keys

1. Place your insertion point at the end of the document and press the Enter key twice.
2. Place your fingers on the home-row keys.
3. Look at the keyboard illustration below. Touch the **D** key.
4. Move your **D** finger up to touch the **E** and back to the **D**.
5. Move your **D** finger down to touch the **C** and back to the **D**.
6. Place your fingers on the home-row keys.
7. Look at the keyboard illustration below. Touch the **K** key.
8. Move your **K** finger up to touch the **I** and back to the **K**.
9. Move your **K** finger down to touch the **,** and back to the **K**.
10. Type the drill, saying each letter to yourself as you strike the key. You may look at the keys in the illustration on the following page as you strike each key. Try not to look at your fingers. Ignore the red and/or green wavy lines below drill letters.

LESSON 4

11. Remember to space between groups of letters by striking the Spacebar with your right thumb.
12. Use your right pinky to strike the Enter key at the end of a line.
13. If you make an error, continue typing.
14. Now type the same drill again without looking at the illustration or your fingers.
15. When you are finished, compare your screen with the book.

1 ded ded ded dedcd dedcd dedcd dcd dcd dcd ENTER
2 ded ded ded dedcd dedcd dedcd dcd dcd dcd ENTER ENTER

3 kik kik kik kik,k kik,k kik,k kik,k k,k k,k k,k ENTER
4 kik kik kik kik,k kik,k kik,k kik,k k,k k,k k,k ENTER ENTER

GOAL 4: Learn Key Words

- There are 25 **key words** that you will practice over and over as you learn to touch type. Constant practice of these key words will build a strong foundation for keyboarding skills.

Exercise 4a
Key Words

1. Type the following exercise, saying each letter to yourself as you strike the key. You may look at the keys in the illustration on the previous page as you strike each key. Try not to look at your fingers. Ignore the red and/or green wavy lines below drill letters.
2. To space between groups of letters, strike the Spacebar with your right thumb.
3. When you type a comma (,) never leave a space before it but always leave a space after it.
4. If you make an error, continue typing.
5. Now type the same exercise again without looking at the illustration or at your fingers.
6. When you are finished, compare your screen with the book to find your errors.

---

1 jim jim jim jim dim dim dim dim kid kid kid kid ENTER
2 jim jim jim jim dim dim dim dim kid kid kid kid ENTER ENTER

3 red red red red cue cue cue cue my, my, my, my, ENTER
4 red red red red cue cue cue cue my, my, my, my, ENTER ENTER

5 jim dim kid red cue my, jim dim kid red cue my, ENTER
6 jim dim kid red cue my, jim dim kid red cue my, ENTER ENTER

Exercise 4b
Key Words

1. Type the exercise on the following page, saying the letters as you strike the keys.
2. If you don't remember the location of a key, look at the keyboard illustration. Do not look at your hands.
3. If you have time, type the same exercise again.
4. Try to increase your speed each time you repeat the line.
5. When you are finished, compare your screen with the book.
6. Check your document in the Print Preview window.
7. Enlarge the Print Preview screen to 100%.
8. Exit the Print Preview window.
9. Do not close the document window.

LESSON 4

1 fur fur fur fun fun fun gun gun gun gum gum gum ENTER
2 fur fur fur fun fun fun gun gun gun gum gum gum ENTER ENTER

3 guy guy guy buy buy buy but but but hut hut hut ENTER
4 guy guy guy buy buy buy but but but hut hut hut ENTER ENTER

5 jut jut jut vug vug vug jim jim jim dim dim dim ENTER
6 jut jut jut vug vug vug jim jim jim dim dim dim ENTER ENTER

7 kid kid kid red red red cue cue cue my, my, my, ENTER
8 kid kid kid red red red cue cue cue my, my, my, ENTER ENTER

GOAL 5: Resave (Update) a Document

- When a document is open and changes are made, the revised or updated version must be **saved**. When a document is resaved, the old version is replaced with the new one.

- When you resave a document, you are saving it under the same name. The document remains on the screen so you can continue to work.

- It is important to save often. You should develop this habit so that if an accident happens (loss of electricity or computer failure), you will not lose your work.

- There are three ways to resave (update) a file:
  - Click the **Save** button  on the Standard toolbar.

  OR

  1. Click <u>F</u>ile menu.
  2. Click <u>S</u>ave.

  OR

  - Press Ctrl+S on the keyboard.

Exercise 5
Resave a Document

1. Resave the document by clicking the Save button on the Standard toolbar.
2. Print one copy of the document.
3. Close the document window.

MOUSE/KEYSTROKE PROCEDURES

Print Preview	Print a Document	Resave a Document
Click the **Print Preview** button 🔍 on the Standard toolbar.	***Ctrl + P***	***Ctrl + S***
OR	Click the **Print** button 🖨 on the Standard toolbar.	Click the **Save** button 💾 on the Standard toolbar.
1. Click **<u>F</u>ile** menu............... `Alt`+`F`	**OR**	**OR**
2. Click **Print Pre<u>v</u>iew**.................. `V`	1. Click **<u>F</u>ile** menu .... `Alt`+`F`	1. Click **<u>F</u>ile** menu .... `Alt`+`F`
3. Click mouse button to enlarge.	2. Click **<u>P</u>rint**............................. `P`	2. Click **<u>S</u>ave**............................. `S`
4. Click mouse button to return to original size.	3. Click **OK**............................. `Enter`	

LESSON 5

- Open an Existing Document
- Move the Insertion Point within a Document
- Review F/J and D/K Finger Keys, Common Words and Key Words

Warm-up

1. Create a new document.
2. Type each line one time, trying to type faster when the line is repeated.
3. If you make an error, continue typing.
4. Save the document as **LES5**.
5. Close the document window.

---

1 dedcd dedcd dedcd frftfgfbfvf frftfgfbfvf frftfgfbfvf ENTER

2 dedcd dedcd dedcd frftfgfbfvf frftfgfbfvf frftfgfbfvf ENTER ENTER

3 kik,k kik,k kik,k jujyjhjnjmj jujyjhjnjmj jujyjhjnjmj ENTER

4 kik,k kik,k kik,k jujyjhjnjmj jujyjhjnjmj jujyjhjnjmj ENTER ENTER

5 fur fun gun gum guy buy but hut jut vug ENTER

6 fur fun gun gum guy buy but hut jut vug ENTER ENTER

7 jim dim kid red cue my, cue red kid dim jim ENTER

8 jim dim kid red cue my, cue red kid dim jim ENTER ENTER

GOAL 1:   Open an Existing Document

- In order to add text to a closed document, you need to bring the document back to the screen. This is called **opening a document**.

- There are a number of ways to open a document. These are the most common:
  1. Click <u>F</u>ile menu.
  2. At the bottom of the drop-down menu, Word lists the four most recently-saved documents.

File menu

Most recently-saved documents

3. Click on the document you wish to open.
OR

1. Click the Open button  on the Standard toolbar.
   OR
   a. Click <u>F</u>ile menu.
   b. Click <u>O</u>pen.

2. From the Open dialog box shown below, double-click the file you wish to open. If you do not see the file you want, click the **Look in** list box arrow and select the drive and/or folder you need or click on a folder on the **Places Bar**, which is located on the left side of the dialog box. The Places Bar contains shortcuts to the History, My Documents, Desktop, Favorites and Web Folders folders.

Open dialog box

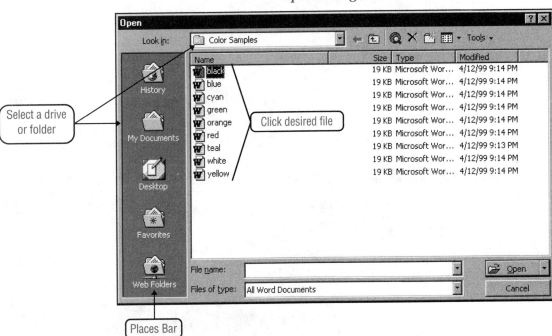

- You can have many documents open at the same time. Each time you press Ctrl+F6 you toggle to a different open document.

Exercise 1
Open a Document

1. Click File menu.
2. Select **LES5** from the drop-down menu.
3. Click the Open button on the Standard toolbar.
4. Select **LES4** and click Open.
5. Click File menu.
6. Click Open.
7. Select **LES3** and click Open.
8. Close all three documents. Do not save any changes.

GOAL 2:   Move the Insertion Point within a Document

- You have learned to use the mouse to locate your insertion point within the document.
- You can also use the **arrow keys** to move the insertion point within the document.
- There are two sets of arrow keys. They are located:

To the **right of the keyboard**

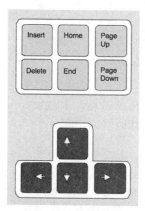

On the **numeric keypad**

Note: If you are using the keypad, make sure that the Num Lock light is off; otherwise you will type numbers.

- The insertion point will only move through existing text. It will not move above the beginning or past the end of a document.
- Use the arrows keys to move the insertion point from one place to another as follows:
  - One character left ⬅
  - One character right ➡
  - One line up ⬆
  - One line down ⬇
- You may combine the arrow keys with other keys to create express arrow keys. These are as follows:
  - Previous word Ctrl + ⬅
  - Next word Ctrl + ➡
  - Top of screen Ctrl + ⬆
  - Bottom of screen Ctrl + ⬇
  - Beginning of document Ctrl + Home
  - End of document Ctrl + End
  - Beginning of line Home
  - End of line End
- You can also move to the top or bottom of a document page by pressing the Page Up or Page Down buttons.

LESSON 5

Exercise 2
Move the Insertion Point within a Document

1. Open **LES5**.
2. Practice the following cursor movements:
   - Press →| 3 times to move the insertion point three characters to the right.
   - Press |Ctrl|+|→| 3 times to move the insertion point three words to the right.
   - Press |Home| to move the insertion point to the beginning of the line.
   - Press |End| to move the insertion point to the end of the line.
   - Press |↓| 3 times to move the insertion point down three lines.
   - Press |Ctrl|+|Home| to move the insertion point to the beginning of the document.
   - Press |Ctrl|+|End| to move the insertion point to the end of the document.
   - Press |Page Up| to move to the top of the current page.
3. With the insertion point at the end of the document, press the Enter key 3 times.
4. Resave the document by clicking the Save button on the Standard toolbar.
5. Close the document window.

GOAL 3:   Review F/J and D/K Finger Keys, Common Words and Key Words

Exercise 3a
F/J and D/K Finger Keys

1. Open **LES5**. Place the insertion point at the end of the document.
2. Type the exercise on the following page, which repeats each word 5 times. Remember, when a comma follows a word, leave one space after the comma but no space before the comma.
3. Use your right pinky to strike the Enter key at the end of a line.
4. If you make an error, continue typing.
5. When you are finished, compare your screen with the book.
6. Resave the document but do not close the document window.

1 he he he he he be be be be be me me me me me ENTER
2 he he he he he be be be be be me me me me me ENTER ENTER

3 re re re re re hi hi hi hi hi in in in in in ENTER
4 re re re re re hi hi hi hi hi in in in in in ENTER ENTER

5 by, by, by, by, by, my, my, my, my, my, it, it, it, it, it, ENTER
6 by, by, by, by, by, my, my, my, my, my, it, it, it, it, it, ENTER ENTER

7 ice ice ice ice ice ire ire ire ire ire tie tie tie tie tie ENTER
8 ice ice ice ice ice ire ire ire ire ire tie tie tie tie tie ENTER ENTER

9 her, her, her, her, her, men, men, men, men, men, ENTER
10 her, her, her, her, her, men, men, men, men, men, ENTER ENTER

11 dug, dug, dug, dug, dug, rug, rug, rug, rug, rug, ENTER
12 dug, dug, dug, dug, dug, rug, rug, rug, rug, rug, ENTER ENTER

Exercise 3b
Common Word Practice

1. This is an exercise on very common words. If you can increase your speed on these common words, you will be able to type faster.
2. If you make an error, continue typing.
3. When you are finished, compare your screen with the book.
4. Resave the document.

1 in in in in in in me me me me me me it it it it it ENTER
2 in in in in in in me me me me me me it it it it it ENTER ENTER

3 be be be be be by by by by by my my my my my ENTER
4 be be be be be by by by by by my my my my my ENTER ENTER

5 did did did did did the the the the the but but but but but ENTER
6 did did did did did the the the the the but but but but but ENTER ENTER

7 buy buy buy buy buy him him him him him her her her her her ENTER
8 buy buy buy buy buy him him him him him her her her her her ENTER ENTER

LESSON 5

Exercise 3c
Key Words

1. Type the following exercise, saying the letters to yourself as you strike the keys.
2. If you make an error, continue typing.
3. If you have time, type the same exercise again.
4. Try to increase your speed each time you repeat a line.
5. When you are finished, compare your screen with the book.
6. Print Preview the document.
7. Resave the document.
8. Print one copy.
9. Close the document window.

```
1  fur fun gun gum guy buy but hut jut vug  ENTER
2  fur fun gun gum guy buy but hut jut vug  ENTER ENTER


3  jim dim kid red cue my,  ENTER
4  jim dim kid red cue my,  ENTER ENTER
```

MOUSE/KEYSTROKE PROCEDURES

Open a Document

Ctrl + O

1. Click the **Open** button 🗁 on the Standard toolbar.

   OR

   a. Click **File** menu .... Alt + F
   b. Click **Open** .... O

2. Click **Look in** .... Alt + I
   text box

3. Click arrow .... ↓
   to move to desired drive and folder.

   OR

1. Click a button on the Places Bar.

2. Double-click desired file name from those listed.

   OR

1. Click **File** menu .... Alt + F

2. Click desired file name from list of recently-opened files.

Move the Insertion Point

Arrow Keys

To Move	Press
One character left.............................	←
One character right	→
One line up..	↑
One line down	↓

Express Arrow Keys

To Move	Press
Previous word..........................	Ctrl + ←
Next word	Ctrl + →
Top of current page	Page Up
Bottom of current page................	Page Down
Beginning of document.......	Ctrl + Home
End of document	Ctrl + End
Beginning of line.........................	Home
End of line....................................	End

44

LESSON 6

- Change View Modes
- Learn S and L Finger Keys

Warm-up

1. Create a new document.
2. Type each line one time, trying to type faster when the line is repeated.
3. If you make an error, continue typing.
4. Save the document as **LES6**.
5. Do not close the document window.

---

1 dedcd dedcd dedcd frftfgfbfvf frftfgfbfvf frftfgfbfvf ENTER
2 dedcd dedcd dedcd frftfgfbfvf frftfgfbfvf frftfgfbfvf ENTER ENTER

3 kik,k kik,k kik,k jujyjhjnjmj jujyjhjnjmj jujyjhjnjmj ENTER
4 kik,k kik,k kik,k jujyjhjnjmj jujyjhjnjmj jujyjhjnjmj ENTER ENTER

5 in in in in in me me me me me it it it it it ENTER
6 in in in in in me me me me me it it it it it ENTER ENTER

7 be be be be be by by by by by my my my my my ENTER
8 be be be be be by by by by by my my my my my ENTER ENTER

GOAL 1: Change View Modes

- Word provides the following ways to view a document on the screen:
  - **Normal view**   This view is the default view, which means that when you start a new document, it will be in the Normal view mode. In this mode, you will not see graphics.

- **Web Layout view**   This view gives an accurate picture of what your document will look like as a Web page.
- **Print Layout view**   This view gives you an accurate picture of what your document will look like when printed. It is useful for editing headers and footers, for adjusting margins and for working with columns and drawing objects.
- **Outline view**   This view is used to see the structure of a document.

- There are two ways to switch view modes:
  - Click one of the following buttons, located to the left of the horizontal scroll bar:
    - * Normal view   ▤   * Print Layout view   ▣
    - * Web Layout view   ▦   * Outline view   ▤

  OR
  1. Click <u>V</u>iew menu.
  2. Click the desired view from the menu.

View menu

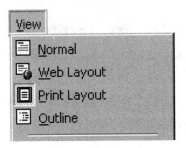

Exercise 1
Change View Modes

1. Change to Print Layout view using the Print Layout button to the left of the horizontal scroll bar.
2. Change the zoom factor to 75%.
3. Return to Normal view using the <u>V</u>iew menu.
4. Close the document.

GOAL 2: Learn S and L Finger Keys

- The **S** finger strikes the **W** and **X** keys.
- The **L** finger strikes the **O** and **.** keys.
- The period is used to end a sentence, to end an abbreviation or as a decimal point in numbers.
- There is one space after a period in an abbreviation.
- There are two spaces after a period at the end of a sentence. With word processor applications, many people now only use one space after a period at the end of the sentence. In this text, we will continue to use two spaces after the period at the end of a sentence.

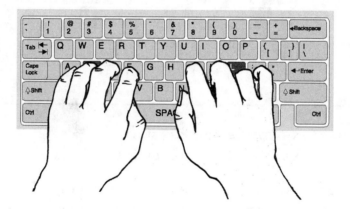

Exercise 2a
S and L Finger Reaches

1. Open **LES6**.
2. Using the express arrow keys, place the insertion point at the end of the document.
3. Press the Enter key twice.
4. Place your fingers on the home-row keys.
5. Look at the keyboard illustration on the following page. Touch the **S** key.

6. Move your **S** finger up to touch the **W** and back to the **S**.
7. Move your **S** finger down to touch the **X** and back to the **S**.
8. Look at the keyboard illustration below. Touch the **L** key.
9. Move your **L** finger up to touch the **O** and back to the **L**.
10. Move your **L** finger down to touch the **.** and back to the **L**.
11. Type the following exercise, saying each letter to yourself as you strike the key. You may look at the keys in the keyboard illustration as you strike the new keys. Try not to look at your fingers. Ignore the red and/or green wavy lines below exercise letters.
12. If you make an error, keep typing.
13. If you have time, type the same exercise again.
14. Press the Enter key 4 times.
15. Resave the file.
16. Do not close the document window.

1 sws sws sws sxs sxs sxs swsxs swsxs swsxs ENTER
2 sws sws sws sxs sxs sxs swsxs swsxs swsxs ENTER ENTER

3 sit sit sit sit wet wet wet wet tex tex tex tex ENTER
4 sit sit sit sit wet wet wet wet tex tex tex tex ENTER ENTER

5 lol lol lol l.l l.l l.l lol.l lol.l lol.l ENTER
6 lol lol lol l.l l.l l.l lol.l lol.l lol.l ENTER ENTER

7 lot lot lot co. co. co. low low low old old old ENTER
8 lot lot lot co. co. co. low low low old old old ENTER ENTER

Exercise 2b
S/L, D/K Finger Reaches

1. Type the following exercise without looking at the keyboard illustration or your fingers.
2. If you make an error, continue typing.
3. When you are finished, compare your screen with the book.
4. Change your view to Print Layout using the View menu.
5. Change back to Normal view using the Normal View button on the horizontal scroll bar.
6. Resave the document, but do not close the document window.

---

1 swsxs swsxs swsxs six six six sew sew sew ENTER
2 swsxs swsxs swsxs six six six sew sew sew ENTER ENTER

3 lol.l lol.l lol.l low low low old old old ill ill ill ENTER
4 lol.l lol.l lol.l low low low old old old ill ill ill ENTER ENTER

5 dedcd dedcd dedcd dew dew dew cod cod cod ENTER
6 dedcd dedcd dedcd dew dew dew cod cod cod ENTER ENTER

7 kik,k kik,k kik,k kit kit kit irk, irk, irk, ENTER
8 kik,k kik,k kik,k kit kit kit irk, irk, irk, ENTER ENTER

Exercise 2c
Drill F/J, S/L, D/K Finger Key Words

1. Type the following exercise, saying the letters to yourself as you strike the keys.
2. Do not correct errors.
3. When you are finished, compare your screen with the book.
4. Resave the document.

---

1 lot lot lot sit sit sit wet wet wet tex tex tex ENTER
2 lot lot lot sit sit sit wet wet wet tex tex tex ENTER ENTER

3 co. co. co. fur fur fur fun fun fun gun gun gun ENTER
4 co. co. co. fur fur fur fun fun fun gun gun gun ENTER ENTER

5 gum gum gum guy guy guy buy buy buy but but but ENTER
6 gum gum gum guy guy guy buy buy buy but but but ENTER ENTER

7 hut hut hut jut jut jut vug vug vug jim jim jim ENTER
8 hut hut hut jut jut jut vug vug vug jim jim jim ENTER ENTER

9 dim dim dim kid kid kid red red red cue cue cue ENTER
10 dim dim dim kid kid kid red red red cue cue cue ENTER ENTER

11 my, my, my, co. co. co. tex tex tex wet wet wet ENTER
12 my, my, my, co. co. co. tex tex tex wet wet wet ENTER ENTER

Exercise 2d
Key Words

1. Type the following exercise, saying the letters to yourself as you strike the keys.
2. If you make a mistake, keep typing.
3. Check your work in the Print Preview window to see that there is a blank line after the first two lines of text.
   - If you need to add a blank line, move the insertion point to the end of the second line and press the Enter key.
4. Resave the document.
5. Close the document window.

1 fur fun gun gum guy buy but hut jut vug ENTER
2 fur fun gun gum guy buy but hut jut vug ENTER ENTER

3 jim dim kid red cue my, ENTER
4 jim dim kid red cue my, ENTER ENTER

Exercise 2e
Express Cursor Keys
Key Words

1. Open **LES6**.
2. Use the express arrow keys to place your insertion point at the end of the document.
3. Press the Enter key twice.
4. Type Exercise 2d again.
5. Try to increase your speed each time you repeat the line.
6. When you are finished, compare your screen with the book.
7. Preview your work.
8. Resave the document.
9. Close the document window.

MOUSE/KEYSTROKE PROCEDURES

Change View Modes

1. Click **View** menu .... Alt + V
2. Click one of the following:

   - **Normal** .... N
   - **Web Layout** .... W
   - **Print Layout** .... P
   - **Outline** .... O

OR

Click one of the following buttons on the horizontal scroll bar:

Normal

Web Layout

Print Layout

Outline

LESSON 7

- Open a Document as a Read-Only File
- Use the Save As Feature
- Review F/J, D/K and S/L Finger Keys

Warm-up

1. Create a new document.
2. Type each line one time, trying to type faster when the line is repeated.
3. If you make an error, keep typing.
4. Save the document as **LES7A**.
5. When finished, compare your screen with the book to find your errors.
6. Close the document window.

---

1 swsxs swsxs swsxs swsxs lol.l lol.l lol.l lol.l ENTER
2 swsxs swsxs swsxs swsxs lol.l lol.l lol.l lol.l ENTER ENTER

3 lot lot lot lot lot sit sit sit sit sit so so so so so ENTER
4 lot lot lot lot lot sit sit sit sit sit so so so so so ENTER ENTER

5 co. co. co. co. co. cod cod cod cod cod do do do do do ENTER
6 co. co. co. co. co. cod cod cod cod cod do do do do do ENTER ENTER

GOAL 1:   Open a Document as a Read-Only File

- If you wish to open a document but not make any changes to it, you can open it as a **read-only** file.
- To open a file as read-only:
  1. Click File menu.
  2. Click Open.

3. Point to the file you want.
4. Click the *right* mouse button.
5. Select Open Read-Only as shown in the illustration below.

Shortcut menu

Read-only →

Open
▶ Open Read-Only
Open as Copy
Print

Quick View
Scan with Norton AntiVirus
Add to Zip
Add to Breakdown Sessions in Puerto Rico.zip

Send To ▶

Cut
Copy

Create Shortcut
Delete
Rename

Properties

■ If you attempt to resave the file, a message appears on the screen informing you that "This file is read-only." Word then automatically displays the Save As dialog box for you to give the file another name. The original document is left unchanged.

Exercise 1
Open a Document as a Read-Only File
Double-Letter Words

1. Open **LES7A** as a read-only file.
2. Place the insertion point at the end of the document.
3. Press the Enter key twice.
4. Type the exercise on the following page, striking the repeated key 2 times quickly.
   Note: Building up speed by typing words that contain double letters will increase your speed in general.
5. If you make an error, continue typing.
6. Now type the same exercise, trying to increase your speed.
7. If you make an error, continue typing.
8. When you are finished, compare your screen with the book.
9. Do not close the document.

LESSON 7

```
1  see see see fee fee fee tee tee tee wee wee wee  ENTER
2  see see see fee fee fee tee tee tee wee wee wee  ENTER ENTER

3  eel eel eel ill ill ill too too too off off off  ENTER
4  eel eel eel ill ill ill too too too off off off  ENTER ENTER
```

GOAL 2: Use the Save As Feature

- If you wish to save a document under a different name or save it in a different location (another folder or drive) select **Save As** from the File menu. The Save As dialog box appears

Save As dialog box

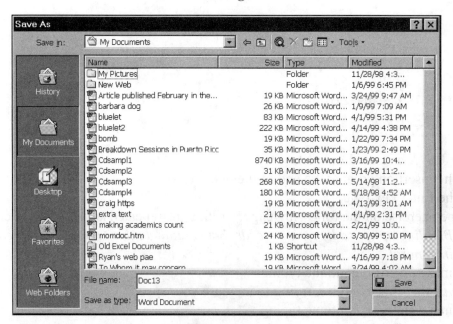

■ Enter a new name for the file in the File name text box. If you wish to save the file to a different location, click the down arrow to the right of the Save in text box and select the location where you wish to save the document.

■ Remember, when you save a document under a new name or to another location, the original document remains unchanged.

Exercise 2
Save As

1. With **LES7A** open as the active document, click File.
2. Click Save As.
3. Save the document under a new name; name it **LES7B**.
4. Click OK.
5. Do not close the document.

GOAL 3: Review F/J, D/K and S/L Finger Keys

■ You will type groups of letters and words using the F/J, D/K and S/L fingers to gain practice and build speed.

■ Avoid looking at your fingers while typing. If necessary, look at the keyboard illustration on the following page.

LESSON 7

Exercise 3a
Review F/J, D/K, S/L Finger Keys

1. Place the insertion point at the end of the document.
2. Press the Enter key 4 times.
3. Type the following exercise without correcting your errors.
4. Ignore the red and/or green wavy lines below the exercise.
5. If you have time, retype the exercise even faster.
6. When you are finished, compare your screen with the book.
7. Resave the document.
8. Do not close the document window.

1 frf ftf fgf fbf fvf juj jyj jhj jnj jmj ENTER
2 frf ftf fgf fbf fvf juj jyj jhj jnj jmj ENTER ENTER

3 frftfgfbfvf frftfgfbfvf jujyjhjnjmj jujyjhjnjmj ENTER
4 frftfgfbfvf frftfgfbfvf jujyjhjnjmj jujyjhjnjmj ENTER ENTER

5 ded dcd kik k,k ded dcd kik k,k ded dcd kik k,k ENTER
6 ded dcd kik k,k ded dcd kik k,k ded dcd kik k,k ENTER ENTER

7 sws sws sws sxs sxs sxs lol lol lol l.l l.l l.l ENTER
8 sws sws sws sxs sxs sxs lol lol lol l.l l.l l.l ENTER ENTER

Exercise 3b
Key Words

1. Type the following exercise.
2. Each word is typed 4 times. Try to type faster each time you repeat the word.
3. When you are finished, compare your screen with the book.
4. If you have time, repeat the exercise.
5. Resave the document.
6. Do not close the document window.

1 fur fur fur fur fun fun fun fun gun gun gun gun ENTER
2 fur fur fur fur fun fun fun fun gun gun gun gun ENTER ENTER

3 gum gum gum gum guy guy guy guy buy buy buy buy ENTER
4 gum gum gum gum guy guy guy guy buy buy buy buy ENTER ENTER

5 but but but but hut hut hut hut jut jut jut jut ENTER
6 but but but but hut hut hut hut jut jut jut jut ENTER ENTER

7 vug vug vug vug jim jim jim jim dim dim dim dim ENTER
8 vug vug vug vug jim jim jim jim dim dim dim dim ENTER ENTER

9 kid kid kid kid red red red red cue cue cue cue ENTER
10 kid kid kid kid red red red red cue cue cue cue ENTER ENTER

11 my, my, my, my, lot lot lot lot sit sit sit sit ENTER
12 my, my, my, my, lot lot lot lot sit sit sit sit ENTER ENTER

13 wet wet wet wet tex tex tex co. co. co. co. ENTER
14 wet wet wet wet tex tex tex co. co. co. co. ENTER ENTER

LESSON 7

Exercise 3c
Common Words

1. Type the following exercise, saying the phrases to yourself as you type. The vertical lines separate each phrase; do not type these lines. Practicing common phrases will build your typing speed.
2. If you make an error, continue typing.
3. If you have time, type the same exercise.
4. If you make an error, continue typing.
5. When you are finished, compare your screen with the book.
6. Resave the document.
7. Print one copy.
8. Close the document window.

```
1 is the | is the | is the | it is | it is | it is |ENTER
2 is the | is the | is the | it is | it is | it is |ENTER ENTER

3 will be | will be | will be | we will | we will | we will |ENTER
  will be | will be | will be | we will | we will | we will |ENTER ENTER

4 did the | did the | did the | but you | but you | but you |ENTER
5 did the | did the | did the | but you | but you | but you |ENTER ENTER

6 to the | to the | to the | be the | be the | be the |ENTER
7 to the | to the | to the | be the | be the | be the |ENTER ENTER
```

MOUSE/KEYSTROKE PROCEDURES

Open a Document
as a Read-Only File

Ctrl + O

1. Click the **Open** button 🖝 on the Standard toolbar.

   OR

   a. Click **File** menu .... Alt + F
   b. Click **Open** .... O

2. Click the **Look in** .... Alt + I
   list box.

3. Click arrow .... ↓
   to locate desired drive and folder.

   OR

   Click a button in the Places Bar.

4. Click the *right* mouse button.

5. Click **Open Read-Only** ...... Alt + O

   OR

   Click the Open drop-down list on the Open dialog box and select Read-Only.

Use Save As

1. Click **File** menu .... Alt + F
2. Click **Save As** .... A
3. Type new file name.
4. Click **Save** .... Enter

   OR

   Press **Ctrl+S** .... Ctrl + S

LESSON 8

• Learn A and ; Finger Keys
• Show and Hide Ruler

Warm-up

1. Create a new document.
2. Type each line one time, trying to type faster when the line is repeated.
3. If you make an error, continue typing.
4. Save the document as **LES8**.
5. When you are finished, compare your screen with the book to find your errors.
6. Do not close the document window.

---

1 swsxs dedcd frftfgfbfvf lol.l kik,k jujyjhjnjmj ENTER
2 swsxs dedcd frftfgfbfvf lol.l kik,k jujyjhjnjmj ENTER ENTER

3 fur fur fun fun gun gun gum gum guy guy ENTER
4 fur fur fun fun gun gun gum gum guy guy ENTER ENTER

5 buy buy but but hut hut jut jut vug vug ENTER
6 buy buy but but hut hut jut jut vug vug ENTER ENTER

7 jim jim dim dim kid kid red red cue cue ENTER
8 jim jim dim dim kid kid red red cue cue ENTER ENTER

9 my, my, lot lot sit sit wet wet tex tex co. co. ENTER
10 my, my, lot lot sit sit wet wet tex tex co. co. ENTER ENTER

LESSON 8

GOAL 1:   Learn A and ; Finger Keys

- The **A** finger strikes the **Q** and the **Z**.
- The **;** finger strikes the **P** and /.

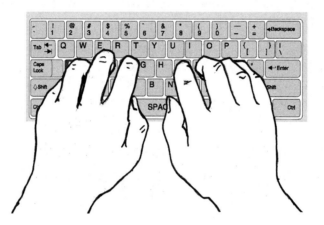

Exercise 1a
A and ; Finger Keys

1. Place your fingers on the home-row keys as shown above.
2. Look at the keyboard illustration on the following page. Touch the **A** key.
3. Move your **A** finger up to touch the **Q** and back to the **A**.
4. Move your **A** finger down to touch the **Z** and back to the **A**.
5. Look at the keyboard illustration on the following page. Touch the **;** key.
6. Move your **;** finger up to touch the **P** and back to the **;**.
7. Move your **;** finger down to touch the / and back to the **;**.
8. Do not close the document window.

Exercise 1b
A and ; Finger Keys

1. Place the insertion point at the end of the document **LES8**. Press the Enter key 4 times.
2. Type the following exercise, saying each letter to yourself as you strike the key. You may look at the keyboard illustration below as you strike each key. Try not to look at your fingers. Ignore the red and/or green wavy lines below the exercise letters.
3. Remember to space between groups of letters by striking the Spacebar with your right thumb.
4. Use your right pinky to strike the Enter key at the end of a line.
5. If you make an error, continue typing.
6. Now type the exercise again, trying to increase your speed.
7. If you make an error, continue typing.
8. When you are finished, compare your screen with the book.
9. Do not close the document window.

1 aqa aqa aqa aqa aqaza aqaza aqaza aqaza aza aza aza aza ENTER
2 aqa aqa aqa aqa aqaza aqaza aqaza aqaza aza aza aza aza ENTER ENTER

3 ;p; ;p; ;p; ;p; ;p;/; ;p;/; ;p;/; ;p;/; ;/; ;/; ;/; ;/; ENTER
4 ;p; ;p; ;p; ;p; ;p;/; ;p;/; ;p;/; ;p;/; ;/; ;/; ;/; ;/; ENTER ENTER

LESSON 8

GOAL 2:   Show and Hide Ruler

- **Rulers** are horizontal and vertical bars that display across the top and left side of the document window. The horizontal ruler is used for viewing and adjusting document margins, tabs and indentation markers. The vertical ruler shows your vertical placement between the top and bottom margins. The grayed areas show the blank margin space. The vertical ruler will display only in the Print Layout view. Click <u>V</u>iew, <u>R</u>uler to display the horizontal ruler.

Horizontal ruler

- You may need to hide the ruler to get a larger document window. Click <u>V</u>iew, <u>R</u>uler to deselect and hide the ruler.

Exercise 2a
Show/Hide Ruler
A/;, S/L, D/K, F/J Finger Keys

1. Show the ruler.
2. Type the exercise on the following page without correcting your errors.
3. Ignore the red and/or green wavy lines below words in the exercise.
4. Hide the ruler.
5. If you have time, retype the exercise even faster.
6. When you are finished, compare your screen with the book.
7. Resave the document.
8. Do not close the document window.

1 fat fat fat fat pat pat pat pat zip zip zip zip qt. qt. qt. qt. ENTER
2 fat fat fat fat pat pat pat pat zip zip zip zip qt. qt. qt. qt. ENTER ENTER

3 aqaza aqaza aqaza quo quo quo quo zoo zoo zoo zoo ENTER
4 aqaza aqaza aqaza quo quo quo quo zoo zoo zoo zoo ENTER ENTER

5 ;p;/; ;p;/; ;p;/; zap; zap; zap; zap; ape; ape; ape; ape; ENTER
6 ;p;/; ;p;/; ;p;/; zap; zap; zap; zap; ape; ape; ape; ape; ENTER ENTER

Exercise 2b
Key Words

1. Type the exercise on the following page containing key words.
2. If you make an error, continue typing.
3. Each word is typed 3 times. Try to type faster each time you repeat a word.
4. When you are finished, compare your screen with the book.
5. If you have time, type the exercise again.
6. If you make an error, continue typing.
7. Resave the document.
8. Print one copy.
9. Close the document window.

1 fat fat fat pat pat pat zip zip zip qt. qt. qt. ENTER
2 fat fat fat pat pat pat zip zip zip qt. qt. qt. ENTER ENTER

3 fur fur fur fun fun fun gun gun gun gum gum gum ENTER
4 fur fur fur fun fun fun gun gun gun gum gum gum ENTER ENTER

5 guy guy guy buy buy buy but but but hut hut hut ENTER
6 guy guy guy buy buy buy but but but hut hut hut ENTER ENTER

7 jut jut jut vug vug vug jim jim jim dim dim dim ENTER
8 jut jut jut vug vug vug jim jim jim dim dim dim ENTER ENTER

9 kid kid kid red red red cue cue cue my, my, my, ENTER
10 kid kid kid red red red cue cue cue my, my, my, ENTER ENTER

11 lot lot lot sit sit sit wet wet wet tex tex tex co. co. co. ENTER
12 lot lot lot sit sit sit wet wet wet tex tex tex co. co. co. ENTER ENTER

13 fat fat fat pat pat pat zip zip zip qt. qt. qt. ENTER
14 fat fat fat pat pat pat zip zip zip qt. qt. qt. ENTER ENTER

- **Congratulations!** You have learned the keys and reaches for the entire alphabet plus two punctuation marks, the comma and the period. You can now type any word, no matter how long or short it is!

- The secret to your keyboarding success is PRACTICE, PRACTICE, PRACTICE. No matter how unsure you are of where a key is, *don't look* at the keys! Continue to touch type and you will gain confidence in your keyboarding skill.

MOUSE/KEYSTROKE PROCEDURES

Show Ruler

1. Click **View** menu.............. Alt + V
2. Click **Ruler**............................. R

Hide Ruler

- Repeat above steps.

LESSON 9

- Set Margins
- Review All Keys Learned
- Learn the Apostrophe Key (')
- Calculate Words a Minute (WAM) Typing Speed

Warm-up

1. Create a new document.
2. The first two lines of the warm-up text are known as the Expert's Rhythm Drill. Use the same fingers on opposite hands (starting with the outside fingers, working in towards the center and then from the center back to the outside). Strike the keys with the same rhythm.
3. Type each line one time, trying to type faster each time you repeat a line.
4. If you make an error, continue typing.
5. When you are finished, compare your screen with the book to find your errors.
6. Save the document as **LES9**.
7. Do not close the document window.

---

1 a;sldkfjghfjdksla; a;sldkfjghfjdksla; a;sldkfjghfjdksla; ENTER

2 a;sldkfjghfjdksla; a;sldkfjghfjdksla; a;sldkfjghfjdksla; ENTER ENTER

3 jujyjhjnjmj jujyjhjnjmj frftfgfbfvf frftfgfbfvf ENTER

4 jujyjhjnjmj jujyjhjnjmj frftfgfbfvf frftfgfbfvf ENTER ENTER

5 aqaza aqaza swsxs swsxs dedcd dedcd frfvf frfvf ENTER

6 aqaza aqaza swsxs swsxs dedcd dedcd frfvf frfvf ENTER ENTER

7 ;p;/; ;p;/; lol.l lol.l kik,k kik,k jujmj jujmj ENTER

8 ;p;/; ;p;/; lol.l lol.l kik,k kik,k jujmj jujmj ENTER ENTER

LESSON 9

GOAL 1: Set Margins

- **Margins** are the empty spaces surrounding your document on the top, bottom, left and right edge of each page.
- Word measures margins in inches.
- The default margins are 1.25" on the left and right and 1" on the top and bottom of the page.
- You can change margins in the Page Setup dialog box as shown below. To do so:
  1. Click File menu.
  2. Click Page Setup from the drop-down list.

Page Setup dialog box

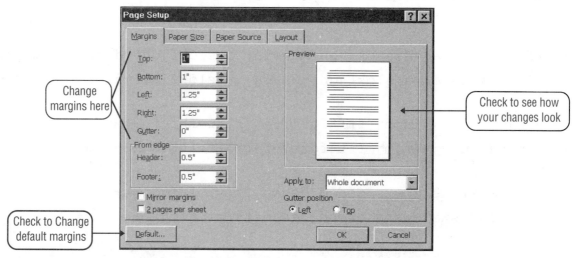

  3. Type the margin measurements you wish to change in the appropriate text boxes or use the arrows to the right of the text box to make the desired change.
  4. You can make margin changes for the entire document (Whole document), to portions of the document (Selected Text) or to the next part of the document (This point forward). The options shown in theApply to text box will vary.

- You can also use the Click and Type method to visually set where you want to begin the first line of text on a page. The Click and Type feature must be turned on. Follow these steps to turn on Click and Type.

  1. Click Tools menu.
  2. Click Options.
  3. Click the Edit tab.
  4. Select Enable click and type checkbox.
  5. Click OK.

- Follow these steps to start the first line using Click and Type.

  1. Select Print Layout view.

     Note: The I beam changes to the following shape 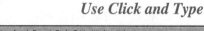.

  2. Position the I beam ($\bar{\text{I}}$) to the right of the desired point on the vertical ruler. Note the illustration below.

Use Click and Type

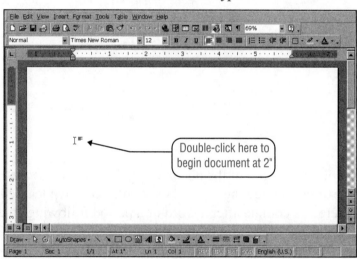

Double-click here to begin document at 2"

> *Note: To begin the document 2" from the top of the page, position the I-beam at the 1" mark on the vertical ruler. Be sure to include the gray area on the ruler in your calculation.*

  3. Double-click the I beam.

Exercise 1
Set Margins

1. Open **LES9**.
2. Set the left and right margins to 1".
3. Change to Print Layout view.
4. Do not close the document window.

LESSON 9

GOAL 2: Review All Keys Learned

- ■ You will type key words as well as groups of letters and characters using all keys learned in order to build speed and accuracy.

Exercise 2a
Review Key Words

1. Place the insertion point at the end of the document **LES9,** and press the Enter key 4 times.
2. Type the following exercise reviewing the 25 key words you have learned.
3. Remember, when there is a comma after a word or a period following an abbreviation, leave one space after but no space before the comma or period.

   Note: This exercise will give you some idea of how many key words you remember.
   If you remember even half of them, you are making progress. Continue to
   memorize these key words in your spare time.

4. Use your right pinky to strike the Enter key at the end of a line.
5. If you make an error, continue typing.
6. When you are finished, compare your screen with the book.
7. Resave the document and close the document window.

```
1 fur fun gun gum guy buy but hut jut vug jim dim kid ENTER
2 fur fun gun gum guy buy but hut jut vug jim dim kid ENTER ENTER

3 red cue my, lot sit wet tex co. fat pat zip qt. ENTER
4 red cue my, lot sit wet tex co. fat pat zip qt. ENTER ENTER
```

Exercise 2b
Review All Keys Learned

1. Create a new document
2. Change the left and right margins to 1.5".
3. Begin the top margin at 2" using the Click and Type method.
4. Type the following exercise while keeping your eyes on the copy. Do not look at the screen.
5. Say each letter as you strike it.
6. If you make an error, continue typing.
7. Now type the exercise again.
8. If you make an error, continue typing.
9. When you are finished, compare your screen with the book.
10. Congratulations! You have just typed the entire alphabet.
11. Save the file; name it **LES9A**.
12. Do not close the document window

1 ab ab ab cde cde cde fg fg fg abcdefg abcdefg abcdefg ENTER
2 ab ab ab cde cde cde fg fg fg abcdefg abcdefg abcdefg ENTER ENTER

3 hi hi hi jkl jkl jkl hijkl hijkl hijkl abcdefghijkl ENTER
4 hi hi hi jkl jkl jkl hijkl hijkl hijkl abcdefghijkl ENTER ENTER

5 mnop mnop mnop abcdefghijklmnop qrs qrs qrs tuv tuv tuv ENTER
6 mnop mnop mnop abcdefghijklmnop qrs qrs qrs tuv tuv tuv ENTER ENTER

7 qrstuv qrstuv qrstuv abcdefghijklmnopqrstuv wxyz wxyz ENTER
8 qrstuv qrstuv qrstuv abcdefghijklmnopqrstuv wxyz wxyz ENTER ENTER

9 abcdefghijklmnopqrstuvwxyz abcdefghijklmnopqrstuvwxyz ENTER
10 abcdefghijklmnopqrstuvwxyz abcdefghijklmnopqrstuvwxyz ENTER ENTER

LESSON 9

- The semi-colon finger moves to the right to strike the apostrophe key.

- The apostrophe is part of the word so there are no spaces before or after it.
- An apostrophe is used to:
  - Show possession
  - Make a contraction out of two words

Exercise 3
Apostrophe Key

1. Place the insertion point at the end of the document **LES9A**.
2. Press the Enter key 4 times.
3. Place your fingers on the home-row keys.
4. Look at the illustration on the following page. Touch the ; key.
5. Move your ; finger to the right and touch the ' key.
6. Practice this 5 times.
7. Now practice it again 5 more times without looking.

8. Type the following exercise, saying each key to yourself as you strike each key. You may look at the keyboard illustration below. Do not look at your fingers. Ignore the red and/or green wavy lines below the exercise letters.
9. If you make an error, continue typing.
10. When you are finished, compare your screen with the book.
11. If you have time, repeat the exercise.
12. If you make an error, continue typing.
13. Resave the document.
14. Print one copy.
15. Close the document window.

1 ;'; ;'; ;'; don't don't don't can't can't can't let's let's ENTER
2 ;'; ;'; ;'; don't don't don't can't can't can't let's let's ENTER ENTER

3 ;'; ;'; ;'; isn't isn't isn't wasn't wasn't wasn't it's it's ENTER
4 ;'; ;'; ;'; isn't isn't isn't wasn't wasn't wasn't it's it's ENTER ENTER

5 the red bug's rug; the red bug's rug; the red bug's rug ENTER
6 the red bug's rug; the red bug's rug; the red bug's rug ENTER ENTER

GOAL 4:   Calculate Words a Minute (WAM) Typing Speed

- A "timed writing" is a timed exercise that lets you know how fast you are typing. Timings can range from ½ minute to five and even ten minutes in length. Always use correct typing techniques to get an idea of how fast you are currently typing.
- The "Words a Minute" average typing speed is also referred to as **WAM**.

LESSON 9

Timed Writing Practice

1. Create a new document
2. Take ten ½-minute timings on the key words shown below.
3. Press the Enter key at the end of each line.
4. If you finish before the ½ minute is up, start again.
5. Do not correct errors. If you make a mistake, continue typing.
6. Press the Enter key 4 times between each timing.
7. A **standard** word in typing is 5 strokes. This includes punctuation marks and spaces.
   - The exercise on the following page contains 25 **actual** words, but only 20 **standard** words.
   - At the end of each line, the number of standard words per line is shown. Below the exercise is a ruler which also shows the number of standard words you typed.
   - For example, if you completed the first line, you typed 10 standard words. If you completed the first line and also typed through the word **sit** on the second line, you typed 14 words—10 on the first line plus 4 standard words on the second line (use the ruler below the exercise for an incomplete line).
   - Since you typed for only ½ a minute, you must multiply the number of words by two to get the WAM 1-minute rate: 14 x 2 = 28.
8. Keep a record of your ½-minute speed on each of the timed writings. See if you can keep increasing your speed.
9. Save the document; name it **L09TIME**.
10. Print one copy.
11. Close the document window.

```
                                                                    WORDS
fur fun gun gum guy buy but hut jut vug jim dim kid        10
red cue my, lot sit wet tex co., fat pat zip qt.          20

....1....2....3....4....5....6....7....8....9...10
```

MOUSE/KEYSTROKE PROCEDURES

Set Margins Using Page Setup

1. Click **File** menu .... Alt + F
2. Click **Page Setup** .... U
3. Click **Margins** tab .... Ctrl + Tab
4. Click increase or decrease arrows to set left margin.

OR

Click **Left** text box .... Alt + F
number and type distance from left edge of paper.

5. Click increase or decrease arrows to set right margin.

OR

Click **Right** text box .... Alt + G
number and type distance from right edge of paper.

6. Click **Apply to** .... Alt + Y
   Whole document,
   This point forward
   or **Selected text** ....
7. Click **OK** .... Enter

LESSON 10

- Learn to Use Shift Keys to Type Capital Letters
- Learn to Type Colon, Less Than, Greater Than, Quotation Mark and Question Mark Keys • Learn to Use Caps Lock Key
- Timed Writing • Review How to Figure Timed Writing Speed

Warm-up

1. Create a new document.
2. Type each line one time, trying to type faster each time you repeat a line.
3. If you make an error, continue typing.
4. Save the document as **LES10**.
5. Close the document window.

---

1 fur fun gun gum guy buy but hut jut vug him dim ENTER
2 fur fun gun gum guy buy but hut jut vug him dim ENTER ENTER

3 kid red cue my, lot sit wet tex co. fat pat zip qt. ENTER
4 kid red cue my, lot sit wet tex co. fat pat zip qt. ENTER ENTER

5 ab cde fg hi jkl mn op qrs tuv wxyz abcdefg hijklmnop ENTER
6 ab cde fg hi jkl mn op qrs tuv wxyz abcdefg hijklmnop ENTER ENTER

7 qrstuv wxyz abcdefghijklmnopqrstuvwxyz ENTER
8 qrstuv wxyz abcdefghijklmnopqrstuvwxyz ENTER ENTER

9 asdf fdsa jkl; ;lkj a;sldkfjghfjdksla; asdf;lkj fdsa jkl; ENTER
10 asdf fdsa jkl; ;lkj a;sldkfjghfjdksla; asdf;lkj fdsa jkl; ENTER ENTER

LESSON 10

GOAL 1:   Learn to Use Shift Keys to Type Capital Letters

■ You have completed all the alphabetic keys and are now able to type all words, with the exception of those that begin with capital letters—proper nouns and the first word in a sentence.

■ The **Shift** keys are the large keys located next to the **Z** key on the left and below the **Enter** key on the right. Holding down either **Shift** key while pressing an alphabetic key will produce a capital letter.

  • If you want to capitalize a letter that is struck with your **left** hand, use the **right Shift** key.
  • If you want to capitalize a letter that is struck with your **right** hand, use the **left Shift** key.

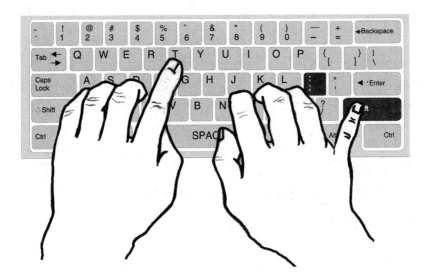

Exercise 1
Shift Keys

1. Open **LES10**.
2. Place the insertion point at the end of the document. Press the Enter key 2 times.
3. Change your left and right margins to 1". Apply to Whole Document.
4. Hold down the right Shift key with the pinky finger on your right hand to strike a capital letter on the left side of the keyboard.
5. Hold down the left shift key with the pinky finger on your left hand to strike a capital letter on the right side of the keyboard.
6. If you make an error, continue typing.
7. Resave the document.
8. Do not close the document window.

1 aaa aAa sss sSs ddd dDd fff fFf aqaza aQaZa ENTER

2 aaa aAa sss sSs ddd dDd fff fFf aqaza aQaZa ENTER ENTER

3 swsxs sWsXs dedcd dEdCd frfvf fRfVf ftfgfbf fTfGfBf ENTER

4 swsxs sWsXs dedcd dEdCd frfvf fRfVf ftfgfbf fTfGfBf ENTER ENTER

5 Ann Ann Sal Sal Derick Derick Fred Fred ENTER

6 Ann Ann Sal Sal Derick Derick Fred Fred ENTER ENTER

7 jjj jJj kkk kKk lll lLl ;;; ;:; jujmj jUjMj jyjhjnj jYjHjNj ENTER

8 jjj jJj kkk kKk lll lLl ;;; ;:; jujmj jUjMj jyjhjnj jYjHjNj ENTER ENTER

LESSON 10

GOAL 2: Learn to Type Colon, Less Than, Greater Than, Quotation Mark and Question Mark Keys

- Remember to hold down the **left Shift** key to strike capital letters, punctuation marks and symbols on the **right** side of the keyboard and the **right Shift** key to strike the same on the **left** side.

- A sentence always begins with a capital letter and ends with a mark of punctuation. You already know how to type a period. When a period ends a sentence, *two spaces* follow it.

- Note the symbols located at the top of the following keys: semicolon [;], comma [,], period [.], forward slash [/] and apostrophe ['].
  - : The colon is generally used for time or before a series of related words. There are *two spaces* after a colon [:] except in a time expression (for example, 9:30) where there are no spaces.
  - < The "less than" symbol is generally used in mathematics. There are *no spaces* before or after the less than [<] symbol.
  - > The "greater than" symbol is generally used in mathematics. There are *no spaces* before or after the greater than [>] symbol.
  - ? The question mark is used at the end of a sentence asking a question. There are *two spaces* after a question mark since it ends a sentence.
  - " The quotation mark is used before and after a quotation, as an inch measurement symbol or on a separate line to show the text above it is to be repeated (ditto).
    When quotation marks are used to surround a quotation, there is *no space* after the opening quotation mark and *no space* before the closing quotation mark. The spacing outside the quotation follows the regular rules—**one space** after a word and **two spaces** after a sentence.

76

Exercise 2a
Punctuation and Special Keys

1. Press the Enter key 4 times.
2. Type each line one time, trying to type faster when the line is repeated.
3. Remember to hold down the left Shift key with the pinky finger on your left hand to strike a capital letter, punctuation mark or symbol on the right side of the keyboard.
4. When you are finished, compare your screen with the book.
5. Resave the document.
6. Do not close the document window.

1 kik,k kIk<k lol.l lOl>l ;p;/; ;P;?; jJj kKk lLl ;:; ENTER
2 kik,k kIk<k lol.l lOl>l ;p;/; ;P;?; jJj kKk lLl ;:; ENTER ENTER

3 ;:; ;:; ;'"; ; ;'"; ;/?; ;/?; ;:; ;:; ;'"; ;'"; ;/?; ;/?; ENTER
4 ;:; ;:; ;'"; ; ;'"; ;/?; ;/?; ;:; ;:; ;'"; ;'"; ;/?; ;/?; ENTER ENTER

5 Jose? Jose? Jose Keisha Keisha Keisha Larry? Larry? Larry? ENTER
6 Jose? Jose? Jose Keisha Keisha Keisha Larry? Larry? Larry? ENTER ENTER

7 Larry yelled, "Jose." Jose yelled, "Larry, did Keisha call?" ENTER
8 Larry yelled, "Jose." Jose yelled, "Larry, did Keisha call?" ENTER ENTER

LESSON 10

Exercise 2b
Left and Right Shift Keys

1. Press the Enter key 4 times.
2. Using the Shift keys to make capital letters for each word, type a copy of this exercise to practice the 25 key words. Say the letters as you strike the keys.
3. When you are finished, compare your screen with the book.
4. If you have time, repeat the exercise.
5. Resave the document but do not close the document window.

1 Fur Fun Gun Gum Guy Buy But Hut Jut Vug Jim Dim Kid ENTER

2 Fur Fun Gun Gum Guy Buy But Hut Jut Vug Jim Dim Kid ENTER ENTER

3 Red Cue My, Lot Sit Wet Tex Co. Fat Pat Zip Qt. ENTER

4 Red Cue My, Lot Sit Wet Tex Co. Fat Pat Zip Qt. ENTER ENTER

GOAL 3: Learn to Use Caps Lock Key

- The **Caps Lock** key is the large key located to the left of the **A** key. Your left pinky finger, the same one that strikes the **A** key, is used to hit the Caps Lock key.

- Move the **A** finger to the left, touch the Caps Lock key and return the **A** finger to the home row.

- The Caps Lock key is an on/off key. Press the Caps Lock key once to type letters in all capitals; press the Caps Lock key again to turn off the capital letters and return to typing lowercase letters.

- Some keyboards have a light that goes on when the Caps Lock key is pressed.

- Use the Caps Lock key if you are typing a series of capital letters such as USA (United States of America) or IBM (International Business Machines). If only one letter is to be capitalized, use the Shift key.

- When only the first letter of each word is capitalized, you are said to be typing in **initial caps**. When all the letters of a word are capitalized, you are said to be typing in **all caps**.

- Sometimes you may forget to turn off the Caps Lock feature. If you press a Shift key while in Caps Lock, you will get a lowercase letter. However, Word has an AutoCorrect feature that changes the word so that the first letter is capitalized. (In Lesson 2, Exercise 1, you were instructed to disable this feature.)

- Caps Lock does not capitalize the number keys at the top of your keyboard.

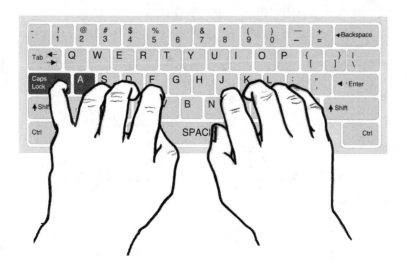

LESSON 10

Exercise 3
Caps Lock Key

1. Type the following exercise while keeping your eyes on the page. Do not look at the screen.
2. Say each letter as you strike it.
3. If you make an error, continue typing.
4. When you are finished, compare your screen with the book. If you have time, press the Enter key 2 times and practice any word you typed incorrectly 5 times.
5. **Congratulations!** You can now type all words and names no matter what letter of the alphabet is used.
6. Resave the document.
7. Print one copy.
8. Close the document window.

1 Is it fun to sit and watch MTV and ESPN with Pat? ENTER
2 Is it fun to sit and watch MTV and ESPN with Pat? ENTER ENTER

3 He said, "Buy a lot of gum for Tex at the RED ZIP HUT." ENTER
4 He said, "Buy a lot of gum for Tex at the RED ZIP HUT." ENTER ENTER

5 Buy these items today: gum, candy, and soda. ENTER
6 Buy these items today: gum, candy, and soda. ENTER ENTER

7 Did Jim, the guy from KNBC, sit with my wet fur? ENTER
8 Did Jim, the guy from KNBC, sit with my wet fur? ENTER ENTER

9 The FAT CO. has a good buy on Zip Lock Bags. ENTER
10 The FAT CO. has a good buy on Zip Lock Bags. ENTER ENTER

Timed Writing

1. Create a new document.
2. Set the left margin to 2" and the right margin to 1½".
3. Take ten ½-minute timings on the key words shown below.
4. Type in wraparound. Do not press the Enter key at the end of the line in the book.
5. If you make an error, continue typing.
6. If you finish before the ½ minute is up, start again.
7. Press the Enter key 4 times between each timing.

```
                                                               WORDS
fur fun gun gum guy buy but hut jut vug jim dim kid             10
red cue my, lot sit wet tex co., fat pat zip qt.               20

....1....2....3....4....5....6....7....8....9...10
```

Review How to Figure
Timed Writing Speed

1. A standard-sized word in typing is 5 strokes. This includes punctuation marks and spaces.
2. The previous timed-writing exercise contained 25 **actual** words but only contains 20 **standard** words.
3. At the end of each line, the number of standard words is shown. Below the drill is a ruler which also shows the number of standard words you typed.
4. For example, if you completed the first line, you typed 10 standard words. If you completed the first line and also typed through the word sit on the second line, you typed 14 words—10 on the first line plus 4 standard words on the second line (use the ruler below the drill for an incomplete line).
5. Since you typed for only ½ a minute, you multiply the number of words by two to get the 1-minute rate: 14 x 2 = 28.
6. Keep a record of your 1-minute speed on each of the timed writings.
7. See if you can keep on increasing your speed.
8. Save the document; name it **L10TIME**.
9. Close the document window.

LESSON 11

• Review All Keys Learned • Review Shift and Caps Lock Keys
• Use Backspace Key to Correct Errors • Select Text
• Change Font, Font Size and Font Color

Warm-up

1. Create a new document.
2. Set the left and right margins to 1".
3. Remember, the first two lines contain the Expert's Rhythm Drill. Try to maintain the same rhythm for the opposite finger on each hand.
4. Type each line twice, trying to increase the speed each time you repeat the line.
5. If you make an error, continue typing.
6. Save the document as **LES11**.
7. Do not close the document.

```
 1  a;sldkfjghfjdksla; a;sldkfjghfjdksla; a;sldkfjghfjdksla; ENTER
 2  a;sldkfjghfjdksla; a;sldkfjghfjdksla; a;sldkfjghfjdksla; ENTER ENTER

 3  fur fun gun gum guy buy but hut jut vug him dim ENTER
 4  fur fun gun gum guy buy but hut jut vug him dim ENTER ENTER

 5  kid red cue my, lot sit wet tex co. fat pat zip qt.  ENTER
 6  kid red cue my, lot sit wet tex co. fat pat zip qt.  ENTER ENTER

 7  ab cde fg hi jkl mn op qrs tuv wxyz abcdefg hijklmnop ENTER
 8  ab cde fg hi jkl mn op qrs tuv wxyz abcdefg hijklmnop ENTER ENTER

 9  qrstuv wxyz abcdefghijklmnopqrstuvwxyz ENTER
10  qrstuv wxyz abcdefghijklmnopqrstuvwxyz ENTER ENTER

11  asdf fdsa jkl; ;lkj a;sldkfjghfjdksla; asdf;lkj fdsa jkl; ENTER
12  asdf fdsa jkl; ;lkj a;sldkfjghfjdksla; asdf;lkj fdsa jkl; ENTER ENTER
```

GOAL 1: Review Shift and Caps Lock Keys

- Using the Shift and Caps Lock keys, you will use all keys learned in order to gain practice and increase speed.

Exercise 1
Review Shift and Caps Lock Keys

1. Place the insertion point at the end of the document **LES11**.
2. Press the Enter key 4 times.
3. Type the lines that appear below and on the next page.
4. If you make an error, continue typing.
5. When you are finished, compare your work with the book.
6. Resave the file.
7. Do not close the document window.

---

1 aAa sSs dDd fFf aQaZa aAa sSs dDd fFf aQaZa ENTER

2 aAa sSs dDd fFf aQaZa aAa sSs dDd fFf aQaZa ENTER ENTER

3 sWsXs dEdCd fRfVf fTfGfBf sWsXs dEdCd fRfVf fTfGfBf ENTER

4 sWsXs dEdCd fRfVf fTfGfBf sWsXs dEdCd fRfVf fTfGfBf ENTER ENTER

5 Allen Allen Samuel Samuel Daniel Daniel Tasha Tasha ENTER

6 Allen Allen Samuel Samuel Daniel Daniel Tasha Tasha ENTER ENTER

7 jJj kKk lLl;:; jUjMj jYjHjNj jJj kKk lLl;:; jUjMj jYjHjNj ENTER

8 jJj kKk lLl;:; jUjMj jYjHjNj jJj kKk lLl;:; jUjMj jYjHjNj ENTER ENTER

9 lOl.l kIk,k jUjMj jYjHjNj lOl.l kIk,k jUjMj jYjHjNj ENTER

10 lOl.l kIk,k jUjMj jYjHjNj lOl.l kIk,k jUjMj jYjHjNj ENTER ENTER

11 Omar Omar Hanoch Hanoch Maria Maria Yonya Yonya ENTER

12 Omar Omar Hanoch Hanoch Maria Maria Yonya Yonya ENTER ENTER

13 Fun: Fun: Fun: Wet? Wet? Wet? Zip? Zip? Zip? ENTER

14 Fun: Fun: Fun: Wet? Wet? Wet? Zip? Zip? Zip? ENTER ENTER

15 Please yell out these names: Yonya, Velda, Omar and Tony. ENTER

16 Please yell out these names: Yonya, Velda, Omar and Tony. ENTER ENTER

17 Did Jim and Tex dim the TV during the movie, THE RED STAR? ENTER

18 Did Jim and Tex dim the TV during the movie, THE RED STAR? ENTER ENTER

19 Mr. Vutgun and Maria had lunch at YONYA'S YOGURT HUT. ENTER

20 Mr. Vutgun and Maria had lunch at YONYA'S YOGURT HUT. ENTER ENTER

21 Yell out these names please: Zonya, Zelda, Omar and Tony. ENTER

22 Yell out these names please: Zonya, Zelda, Omar and Tony. ENTER ENTER

GOAL 2:   Use Backspace Key to Correct Errors

- Use the **Backspace** key to correct errors as you type. The Backspace key deletes the letter to the left of the insertion point.

■ Use the right pinky to reach up to the Backspace key as shown in the following illustration:

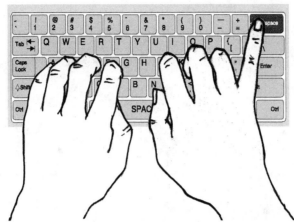

■ After you have used the Backspace key, immediately return the right pinky to the semicolon key.

Exercise 2
Backspace Key

1. Place the insertion point at the end of the document **LES11**.
2. Practice moving your right pinky up to the Backspace key and returning it to the semicolon key.
3. Practice this step 5 times.
4. Now practice Step 2 again 5 more times without looking at the keys.
5. After the fifth try, check that your right pinky is on the semicolon.
6. Press Enter 4 times and then type the exercise that appears on the following page.
7. Immediately correct your errors using the Backspace key.
8. Remember:
   - There are no spaces before any punctuation mark.
   - There are two spaces after the period or question mark at the end of sentence.
   - There is one space after the period in an abbreviation.
   - If a sentence ends with an abbreviation, only one period is used, followed by two spaces.
   - There is one space after a comma or semicolon.
   - There are two spaces after a colon (unless it is used to indicate time; for example, 2:30 p.m.).
9. When you are finished, compare your screen with the book.
10. If you have time, repeat this exercise.
11. Resave the document.
12. Close the document window.

LESSON 11

1 Fur Fun Gun Gum Guy Buy But Hut Jut Vug Jim Dim Kid ENTER
2 Fur Fun Gun Gum Guy Buy But Hut Jut Vug Jim Dim Kid ENTER ENTER

3 Red Cue My, Lot Sit Wet Tex Co. Fat Pat Zip Qt. ENTER
4 Red Cue My, Lot Sit Wet Tex Co. Fat Pat Zip Qt. ENTER ENTER

5 kik,k kIk<k lol.l lOl>l ;p;/; ;P;?; ;';"; jJj kKk lLl ;:; ENTER
6 kik,k kIk<k lol.l lOl>l ;p;/; ;P;?; ;';"; jJj kKk lLl ;:; ENTER ENTER

7 Why have fun? Buy red gum. Jim is wet. Is Jim wet? ENTER
8 Why have fun? Buy red gum. Jim is wet. Is Jim wet? ENTER ENTER

9 Pat's fur is very wet. Buy a qt. Keisha and Tex have fun. ENTER
10 Pat's fur is very wet. Buy a qt. Keisha and Tex have fun. ENTER ENTER

11 Did Ed's dog shed his fur? Did the kid sit in his wet suit? ENTER
12 Did Ed's dog shed his fur? Did the kid sit in his wet suit? ENTER ENTER

13 My four sons are: Jim, Tex, Pat and Vug, Jr. ENTER
14 My four sons are: Jim, Tex, Pat and Vug, Jr. ENTER ENTER

GOAL 3: Select Text

- In order to make changes to a word or a block of text, you need to select the text.
- When you select text, the selected word or words appear in white letters on a dark background. This is called **reverse video**.

> This text has been selected. You may use the mouse, keyboard or a combination of the two to select text. Once the text is selected, it appears in reverse video, which means the letters are now in white on a black background.

- Text may be selected several ways:

  - **Mouse**   Drag the mouse over the text you wish to select. To select a single word, double-click the word.

  - **Keyboard**   Hold down the Shift key while pressing the insertion point movement keys (End, Home, Page Up, Page Down and arrow keys).

  - **Keyboard and Mouse**   Click where the selection should begin, hold down the Shift key and click where the selection should end.

  - **F8 Key**   Press F8 to place Word in Extend mode (notice the letters EXT on the Status bar at the bottom of the screen). Use the arrow keys to extend the selection or continue to press F8 until the desired text is selected.

- You can deselect the text three ways:

  - Click the left mouse button anywhere in the document window.

  OR

  - Press any arrow key.

  OR

  - Press ESC and the up arrow key.

LESSON 11

Exercise 3
Select Text

1. Create a new document.
2. Use the default margins.
3. Type the following exercise, which contains many key words.
4. Immediately correct your errors using the Backspace key.
5. After typing the exercise, select the following word(s) using the methods indicated below:
   a. Double-click the word "snug" in Sentence 1. Deselect it by clicking anywhere in the text.
   b. Using the mouse, select "star of the school play" in Sentence 3. Deselect it by pressing ESC and the up arrow key.
   c. Using the Shift and arrow keys, select "J. F. K. High School" in Sentence 5. Use any method to deselect it.
   d. Using the keyboard and mouse, select the entire line in Sentence 6. Use any method to deselect it.
   e. Using the F8 key, select Sentences 7-10. Deselect it by pressing ESC and the up arrow key.
6. Save the file; name it **LES11A**.
7. Do not close the document window.

---

1 Did Mr. Vug say he was as snug as a bug in a rug? ENTER

2 Did Mr. Vug say he was as snug as a bug in a rug? ENTER ENTER

3 Vug Gun, star of the school play, missed his cue in Act I. ENTER

4 Vug Gun, star of the school play, missed his cue in Act I. ENTER ENTER

5 Are Tex, Pat and Jim joining FBLA at J. F. K. High School? ENTER

6 Are Tex, Pat and Jim joining FBLA at J. F. K. High School? ENTER ENTER

7 Tell Jim to zip his coat, go to the store, and buy a qt. of milk. ENTER

8 Tell Jim to zip his coat, go to the store, and buy a qt. of milk. ENTER

ENTER

9 After filling Ed's cavity, Dr. Gunvug told him not to chew gum. ENTER

10 After filling Ed's cavity, Dr. Gunvug told him not to chew gum. ENTER ENTER

GOAL 4: Change Font, Font Size and Font Color

- A **font** (also known as a typeface) is a family of characters in a specific design, size and font style. Most fonts includes upper- and lowercase letters, numbers, symbols and punctuation marks. A typical font available in Word is Times New Roman.

- There are three basic types of fonts:
  - **Serif font**   A serif font contains small strokes or curves at the ends of each letter. In general, serif fonts are used for document text because they are easier to read. An example of a serif font is **Times New Roman**.
  - **Sans Serif**   A sans serif font does not contain curves at the ends of each letter. "Sans" is a French word meaning without; therefore, a sans serif font is without serifs. In general, sans serif fonts are used for headlines or technical material. An example of a sans serif font is **Arial**.
  - **Script**   Script fonts resemble handwriting. In general, they are used for formal writing such as wedding invitations or announcements. An example of a script font is *Shelly Allegro BT*.

- In addition to the standard fonts such as Times New Roman and Arial, Word offers many additional, decorative fonts that help convey a mood or feeling. Be careful to choose your fonts wisely so that they enhance the message you are trying to send. As a general rule, use no more than two or three fonts in any document.

- **Font size** refers to the height of the font. It is measured in points.

- There are 72 points to one inch. Therefore, if you need a ½ inch font, you would choose 36; a ¼ inch font, you would choose 18; etc.

- Use an 11 or 12 point serif font for document text and larger sizes in a sans serif font for headings and headlines.

- You can change a font and font size in the Font dialog box and see the result of your selections in the Preview window. Follow these steps to access the Font dialog box shown below:
  1. Click Format menu.
  2. Click Font.
  3. Click Font tab.

Font dialog box

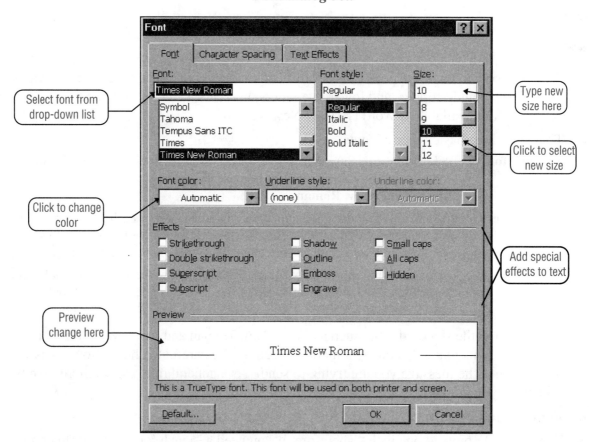

- You can make any of the following changes to the font using the font dialog box shown above:
  - **Font**   Changes the font face. You can type the name of the desired font or use the arrow keys to locate your choice.
  - **Size**   Changes the size of the font. You can type the desired size in the Size box or use the arrow keys to locate your choice.
  - **Color**   Changes the color of the selected font.

  Note: If you do not have a color printer, the document will print in black, white and shades of gray.
- You may also change the font and font size by using the Font and Font Size buttons on the Formatting toolbar shown on the next page.

Formatting toolbar

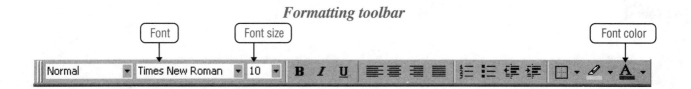

Font — Font size — Font color

- You can make changes to the font, font size and font color before or after typing the text.

Exercise 4
Change Font, Font Size and Font Color

1. Place the insertion point at the beginning of the first line in **LES11A**.
2. Press the Enter key twice and the up arrow twice.
3. Type your name in all caps using a sans serif font (Arial) in 16 point. Use the Formatting toolbar to make your changes.
4. In Sentence 1, select the entire line and change it to 14 point. Use the Formatting toolbar to make your changes.
5. In Sentence 3, select *star of the school play* and change to a sans serif font (Arial) in 14 point. Use the Font dialog box to make your changes.
6. In Sentence 5, select *FBLA* and change it to a script font in 16 point, Blue. Use the Font dialog box to make your changes.
7. In Sentences 7 and 8, select all key words and change them to a decorative font in 14 point.
   Note: Choose a font other than Times New Roman or Arial. Try one that conveys a cheerful message. Use both the Font dialog box and the Formatting toolbar to make your changes.
8. In Sentences 9 and 10, select *Dr. Gunvug* and change to a different serif font in 16 point, Red and Emboss. Use the Font dialog box to make your changes.
9. Resave the document.
10. Print one copy.
11. Close the document window.

LESSON 11

Timed Writing

1. Create a new document.
2. Change the left margin to 1.75" and the right margin to 1.5".
3. Change the font to Courier New, 12 point.
4. Take five ½-minute timings on the key words.
5. Type in wraparound. (Do not press the Enter key at the end of the line.)
6. If you finish before the ½ minute is up, start again.
7. Press the Enter key 4 times between each timing.
8. Do not correct errors.
   - A standard word in typing is 5 strokes. This includes punctuation marks and spaces.
   - The following timed writing contains 25 actual words. It contains 20 standard words.
   - At the end of each line, the number of standard words is shown. Below the timed writing is a ruler which also shows the number of standard words you typed.
   - For example, if you completed the first line, you typed 10 standard words. If you completed the first line and also typed through the word sit on the second line, you typed 14 words—10 on the first line plus 4 standard words on the second line (use the ruler below the drill for an incomplete line).
   - Since you typed for only ½ a minute, you multiply the number of words by two to get the 1-minute rate: 14 x 2 = 28.
   - Keep a record of your 1-minute speed on each of the timed writings.
9. Save the document as **L11TIME**.
10. Print one copy.

```
                                                       WORDS

fur fun gun gum guy buy but hut jut vug jim dim kid      10
red cue my, lot sit wet tex co., fat pat zip qt.         20

....1....2....3....4....5....6....7....8....9...10
```

MOUSE/KEYSTROKE PROCEDURES

Select Text

USING THE MOUSE

To select text:

1. Place insertion point at beginning of text to select.
2. Hold down left mouse button and drag to end of desired text.

To select a word:

1. Place insertion point anywhere in word.
2. Double-click mouse button.

To select a sentence:

1. Place insertion point anywhere in sentence.
2. Hold down Ctrl and click mouse button.

To select a paragraph:

1. Place insertion point anywhere in paragraph.
2. Triple-click mouse button.

USING THE KEYBOARD

Place insertion point where the selection is to begin.

To select:

One character to the left......... `Shift`+`←`

One character to the right ...... `Shift`+`→`

One line up............................ `Shift`+`↑`

One line down .... `Shift`+`↓`

To end of line .... `Shift`+`End`

To beginning of line .... `Shift`+`Home`

Beginning of document................. `Shift`+`Ctrl`+`Home`

End of document.......... `Shift`+`Ctrl`+`End`

Entire document......................`Ctrl`+`A`

USING F8 KEY

1. Place insertion point where selection is to begin.
2. Press **F8** .... `F8`

   EXT appears on the Status bar.

3. Press any character, punctuation mark or symbol to extend the selection to the next occurrence of that key.

   OR

   Press any arrow key or express arrow key to extend the selection.

   OR

   Continue to press **F8** until all desired text is selected.

Deselect Text

Press **Esc+up arrow** .... `Esc`+`↑`

OR

Click mouse button anywhere in the document window.

Change Font

1. Select text for which font is to be changed.

   OR

   Place insertion point where new font is to begin.

2. Click **Format** menu ....`Alt`+`O`
3. Click **Font** .... `F`
4. Click **Font** text box...........`Alt`+`F`
5. Click desired font..................`↕`
6. Click **OK** ....`Enter`

   OR

   Click the **Font** list arrow `▼` on the Formatting toolbar and select desired font.

Change Font Size

1. Select text for which font is to be changed.

   OR

   Place insertion point where new font is to begin.

2. Click **Format** menu ....`Alt`+`O`
3. Click **Font** .... `F`
4. Select **Font** tab.................`Alt`+`N`
5. Select **Size**...................`Alt`+`S`
6. Click or type desired point size.
7. Click **OK** ....`Enter`

   OR

   Click the **Font Size** list arrow `▼` on the Formatting toolbar and select desired font size.

Change Font Color

1. Select text for which font is to be changed.

   OR

   Place insertion point where new font is to begin.

2. Click **Format** menu ....`Alt`+`O`
3. Click **Font** .... `F`
4. Select **Font** tab.................`Alt`+`N`
5. Click **Font color** ....`Alt`+`C`
6. Select desired color from drop-down palette.
7. Click **OK** ....`Enter`

   OR

   Click the **Font Color** button `A▾` on the Formatting toolbar to select desired color.

Warm-up

1. Create a new document.
2. Set the left and right margin to 1".
3. The first two lines of the warm-up text are known as the Expert's Rhythm Drill. This drill uses all the home-row fingers starting with the outside fingers, working in toward the center and then from the center back to the outside. Strike all keys with the same rhythm.
4. Type each line one time, trying to type faster when a line is repeated.
5. If you make an error, continue typing.
6. Save the document as **LES12**.
7. Do not close the document window.

---

1 a;sldkfjghfjdksla; a;sldkfjghfjdksla; a;sldkfjghfjdksla; ENTER
2 a;sldkfjghfjdksla; a;sldkfjghfjdksla; a;sldkfjghfjdksla; ENTER ENTER

3 ab cde fg hi jkl mn op qrs tuv wxyz abcdefg hijklmnop ENTER
4 ab cde fg hi jkl mn op qrs tuv wxyz abcdefg hijklmnop ENTER ENTER

5 fur fun gun gum guy buy but hut jut vug him dim ENTER
6 fur fun gun gum guy buy but hut jut vug him dim ENTER ENTER

7 Fur Fun Gun Gum Guy Buy But Hut Jut Vug Him Dim ENTER
8 Fur Fun Gun Gum Guy Buy But Hut Jut Vug Him Dim ENTER ENTER

9 kid red cue my, lot sit wet tex co. fat pat zip qt. ENTER
10 kid red cue my, lot sit wet tex co. fat pat zip qt. ENTER ENTER

11 Kid Red Cue My, Lot Sit Wet Tex Co. Fat Pat Zip Qt. ENTER
12 Kid Red Cue My, Lot Sit Wet Tex Co. Fat Pat Zip Qt. ENTER ENTER

13 For fun, Mr. Gum watched the NFL on the TV. ENTER
14 For fun, Mr. Gum watched the NFL on the TV. ENTER ENTER

GOAL 1:   Review All Keys

- In order to type some of the text in this and future exercises, you need to deselect the "Internet and network paths with hyperlinks" feature.

- Follow these steps to deselect this feature:
  1. Click Tools menu.
  2. Click AutoCorrect.
  3. Click the AutoFormat As You Type tab.
  4. Click the "Internet and network paths with hyperlinks" option so there is no checkmark in the checkbox.
  5. Click OK.

Exercise 1
Review All Keys

1. Type the exercise on the following page giving particular attention to the spacing before and after all punctuation.
2. Immediately correct errors using the Backspace key.
3. Press the Enter key 4 times.
4. When you are finished compare your work with the book.
5. Resave the file.
6. Close the document window.

1 kik,k kIk<k lol.l lOl>l ;p;/; ;P;?; ;';"; jJj kKk lLl ;:; ENTER

2 kik,k kIk<k lol.l lOl>l ;p;/; ;P;?; ;';"; jJj kKk lLl ;:; ENTER ENTER

3 Fun: Fun: Fun: Wet? Wet? Wet? Zip? Zip? Zip? ENTER

4 Fun: Fun: Fun: Wet? Wet? Wet? Zip? Zip? Zip? ENTER ENTER

5 the kids sit; Pat has fun; he has a fat cat; she has a lot of gum; ENTER

6 the kids sit; Pat has fun; he has a fat cat; she has a lot of gum; ENTER
ENTER

7 Were the kids able to sit still during Mrs. Vug's lesson? ENTER

8 Were the kids able to sit still during Mrs. Vug's lesson? ENTER ENTER

9 Please look at this new web site: http://www.ddcpub.com ENTER

10 Please look at this new web site: http://www.ddcpub.com ENTER ENTER

11 Did Allen say, "Buy a qt. of WET RED GUM for the kids."? ENTER

12 Did Allen say, "Buy a qt. of WET RED GUM for the kids."? ENTER ENTER

13 When Pat missed her cue, Jim told Ed to dim the stage lights. ENTER

14 When Pat missed her cue, Jim told Ed to dim the stage lights. ENTER ENTER

15 Send the letter c/o Ms. Pat Vughut and include the zip code. ENTER

16 Send the letter c/o Ms. Pat Vughut and include the zip code. ENTER ENTER

GOAL 2:   Apply Font Styles

Formatting toolbar

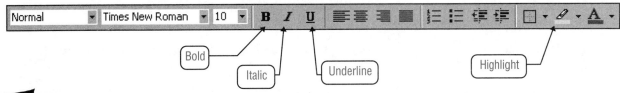

- You can use the **bold**, **italic, underline** or **highlight** features to emphasize certain words in a document.

- Click the desired font style button on the Formatting toolbar before typing the word or words. Once you have typed the words, click the button again to turn off the feature.

- You can also change the font style using the Font dialog box. To access the Font dialog box shown below:
  1. Click F**o**rmat menu.
  2. Click **F**ont.

Font dialog box

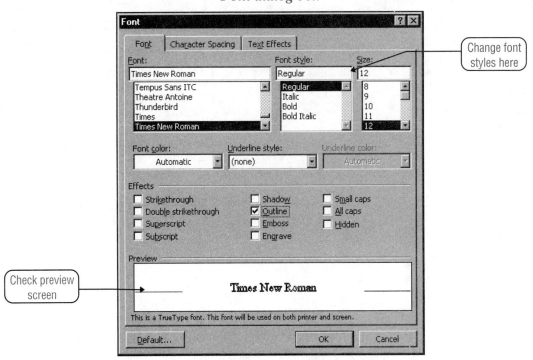

3. Click the desired font style. If you do not wish to use a font style, click Regular. If you want both bold and italic text, click the Bold Italic option.
4. Check your changes in the Preview window.
5. Use the Font dialog box if you are making more than one change to the text. For example, if you are changing the font, size, color and font style for a block of text, make the changes in the Font dialog box.

- You can apply font styles before or after typing text. If you want to apply a font style after the text is typed, first select the text as described in Lesson 11. Once the text is selected, press the desired font style button on the Formatting toolbar.

- The Highlight font style can be selected only from the Formatting toolbar. It is not available from the Font dialog box.

- The default highlight color is yellow. If you wish to use another color, click the list arrow next to the Highlight button and choose a different color from the drop-down color palette shown below.

Highlight drop-down color palette

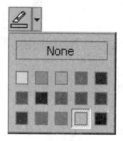

- Highlighted text will appear in color on the screen, but will print in shades of gray unless you have a color printer.

- To remove a font style from text, select the text and then click the related Formatting toolbar button. This will undo the font style.

- You can delete all font formatting, except highlighting, in one operation. First, select the text; then press Ctrl+Spacebar. All font styles applied to the text will be removed.

- To remove highlighting, select the highlighted text and choose None from the Highlight drop-down color list.

Exercise 2
Apply Font Styles

1. Create a new document.
2. Type the sentences below, applying the font styles shown.
3. Immediately correct errors using the Backspace key.
4. Remove all font styles and make the following changes:
   - Bold each occurrence of the word **buy**.
   - In sentences 1 and 2, underline <u>NBA</u>.
   - Highlight all sentences in yellow.
   - Place all company names in italics.
5. Bold and italicize all words that contain errors.
6. If you have time, press the Enter key 2 times and practice typing any word you typed incorrectly 5 times.
7. Save the document; name it **LES12A**.
8. Print one copy.
9. Close the document window.

---

1 It is fun to sit and watch *NBA* games on TV with Tex. ENTER
2 It is fun to sit and watch *NBA* games on TV with Tex. ENTER ENTER

3 Pat and Jim had a lot of fun at the **WET VUG CO.** ENTER
4 Pat and Jim had a lot of fun at the **WET VUG CO.** ENTER ENTER

5 Did you buy the red toy gun at <u>MY KID AND CO.</u>? ENTER
6 Did you buy the red toy gun at <u>MY KID AND CO.</u>? ENTER ENTER

Note: Do not underline the punctuation marks following underlined text.

7 Did Pat buy more <u>RAM and a zip drive</u> for his kid? ENTER
8 Did Pat buy more <u>RAM and a zip drive</u> for his kid? ENTER ENTER

LESSON 12

Timed Writing

1. Create a new document.
2. Change the left margin to 1.75" and the right margin to 1.5".
3. Change the font to Courier New, 12 point.
4. Take five ½-minute timings on the lines below.
5. Type in wraparound. (Do not press the Enter key at the end of the line.)
6. Immediately correct your errors as you type.
7. If you finish before the ½ minute is up, start again.
8. Press the Enter key 4 times between each timing.
9. Keep a record of your 1-minute speed on each of the timed writings.
10. Highlight all errors.
11. Save the document as **L12TIME**.
12. Print one copy.

	WORDS
fur fun gun gum guy buy but hut jut vug jim dim kid	10
red cue my, lot sit wet tex co., fat pat zip qt.	20

```
....1....2....3....4....5....6....7....8....9...10
```

MOUSE/KEYSTROKE PROCEDURES

Bold

Ctrl + B

BEFORE TYPING

1. Place insertion point where bolding is to begin.
2. Click **Bold** button **B**.
3. Type text.
4. Click **Bold** button **B** to discontinue bolding.

EXISTING TEXT

1. Select text to bold.
2. Click **Bold** button **B**.

Underline

Ctrl + U

BEFORE TYPING

1. Place insertion point where underlining is to begin.
2. Click **Underline** button **U**.
3. Type text.
4. Click **Underline** button **U** to discontinue underlining.

EXISTING TEXT

1. Select text to underline.
2. Click **Underline** button **U**.

Italics

Ctrl + I

BEFORE TYPING

1. Place insertion point where italicizing is to begin.
2. Click **Italic** button **I**.
3. Type text.
4. Click **Italic** button **I** to discontinue italicizing.

EXISTING TEXT

1. Select text to italicize.
2. Click **Italic** button **I**.

Highlight

1. Select text to highlight.
2. Click **Highlight** button.

Remove Font Styles

1. Select text containing Font Styles.
2. Click one of the following to deselect:

   Bold **B**

   Italic **I**

   Underline **U**

   Highlight

OR

1. Select text containing Font Styles.
2. Press
   Ctrl + Spacebar.......... Ctrl + Space

Deselect Hyperlink Formatting

1. Click **Tools** menu .... Alt + T
2. Click **AutoCorrect** .... A
3. Click the **AutoFormat As You Type** tab.
4. Click **Internet and network paths with hyperlinks** checkbox I
   Note: The checkbox should be empty.
5. Click **OK** .... Enter

LESSON 13

• Review Font Styles   • Add Font Effects to Text
• Change Horizontal Alignment   • Change Vertical Alignment

Warm-up

1. Create a new document.
2. Set the left and right margins to 1".
3. Type your name at the top of the page.
4. Press the Enter key 3 times after your name.
5. Type each line, trying to type faster when a line is repeated.
6. If you make an error, continue typing.
7. Save the document as **LES13**.
8. Do not close the document.

1   a;sldkfjghfjdksla; a;sldkfjghfjdksla; a;sldkfjghfjdksla; ENTER

2   a;sldkfjghfjdksla; a;sldkfjghfjdksla; a;sldkfjghfjdksla; ENTER ENTER

3   a; sl dk fj gh gh fj dk sl a; sl dk fj gh gh fj dk sl a; ENTER

4   a; sl dk fj gh gh fj dk sl a; sl dk fj gh gh fj dk sl a; ENTER ENTER

5   ab cdef ghijkl mnop qrst uvw xyz abcdefg hijklmnop qrstuvwxyz ENTER

6   ab cdef ghijkl mnop qrst uvw xyz abcdefg hijklmnop qrstuvwxyz ENTER ENTER

7   fur fun gun gum guy buy but hut jut vug jim dim ENTER

8   fur fun gun gum guy buy but hut jut vug jim dim ENTER ENTER

9   Fur Fun Gun Gum Guy Buy But Hut Jut Vug Him Dim ENTER

10 Fur Fun Gun Gum Guy Buy But Hut Jut Vug Him Dim ENTER ENTER

11 kid red cue my, lot sit wet tex co. fat pat zip qt. ENTER

12 kid red cue my, lot sit wet tex co. fat pat zip qt. ENTER ENTER

13 Kid Red Cue My, Lot Sit Wet Tex Co. Fat Pat Zip Qt. ENTER

14 Kid Red Cue My, Lot Sit Wet Tex Co. Fat Pat Zip Qt. ENTER ENTER

15 For fun, Mr. Gum watched the NFL on the TV. ENTER

16 For fun, Mr. Gum watched the NFL on the TV. ENTER ENTER

102

GOAL 1: Review Font Styles

- Font styles are used to enhance the appearance of your text.
- You can change the font style by clicking the Bold, Italic, Underline or Highlight buttons on the Formatting toolbar, or by selecting Font from the Format menu, clicking the Font tab and selecting the desired styles from the Font dialog box. You can apply one or more of the available styles.
- Font styles can be applied before or after typing the text.

Exercise 1
Font Styles

1. In order to type some of the text in this exercise, you must deselect the "Internet and network paths with hyperlinks" feature. See Lesson 12, Mouse/Keystroke Procedures section, for instructions on deselecting this feature.
2. Position the insertion point at the end of your open document.
3. Press the Enter key 4 times.
4. Type the exercise on the following page.
5. Immediately correct errors using the Backspace key.
6. When you are finished, compare your work with the book.
7. Bold **B** the first 10 words that begin with the letter "s".
8. Highlight in blue all text between quotation marks.
9. Underline **U** every word that begins with the letter "c".
10. Italicize *I* all words in the last two lines you typed.
11. Resave the file.
12. Do not close the document window.

LESSON 13

1 aqaza aqaza swsxs swsxs dedcd dedcd frfvftfgfbf frfvftfgfbf ENTER
2 aqaza aqaza swsxs swsxs dedcd dedcd frfvftfgfbf frfvftfgfbf ENTER ENTER

3 ;'; ;'; ;p;/; ;p;/; lol.l lol.l kik,k kik,k jujmjyjhjnj jujmjyjhjnj ENTER
4 ;'; ;'; ;p;/; ;p;/; lol.l lol.l kik,k kik,k jujmjyjhjnj jujmjyjhjnj ENTER
ENTER

5 ;:; ;:; ;:; ;"; ;"; ;"; ;?; ;?; ;?; k<k k<k k<k l>l l>l l>l ENTER
6 ;:; ;:; ;:; ;"; ;"; ;"; ;?; ;?; ;?; k<k k<k k<k l>l l>l l>l ENTER ENTER

7 sum rum gum bum hum rut cut but jut nut put ENTER
8 sum rum gum bum hum rut cut but jut nut put ENTER ENTER

9 sue due rue cue hue sat cat rat fat bat hat mat pat ENTER
10 sue due rue cue hue sat cat rat fat bat hat mat pat ENTER ENTER

11 gum gum mug mug but but tub tub pat pat tap tap ENTER
12 gum gum mug mug but but tub tub pat pat tap tap ENTER ENTER

13 fun funny funny gum gummy gummy fur furry furry ENTER
14 fun funny funny gum gummy gummy fur furry furry ENTER ENTER

15 Is the gum from the Tex Co.? No, but it is good gum. ENTER
16 Is the gum from the Tex Co.? No, but it is good gum. ENTER ENTER

17 Type these words: fur, fun, gun, gum, guy, buy, but and hut ENTER
18 Type these words: fur, fun, gun, gum, guy, buy, but and hut ENTER ENTER

19 Go to this web site: http://www.fatpattex.com ENTER
20 Go to this web site: http://www.fatpattex.com ENTER ENTER

21 Buy gum at the hut. The fat cat has red fur. Do you sit a lot? ENTER
22 Buy gum at the hut. The fat cat has red fur. Do you sit a lot? ENTER
ENTER
23 Did the guy's red car zip past the hut? The cat had wet fur. ENTER
24 Did the guy's red car zip past the hut? The cat had wet fur. ENTER ENTER

25 Did Jim Gun say, "Why buy the guy gum at the hut?" ENTER
26 Did Jim Gun say, "Why buy the guy gum at the hut?" ENTER ENTER

27 The sign for greater than is >. The sign for less than is <. ENTER
28 The sign for greater than is >. The sign for less than is <. ENTER ENTER

GOAL 2:   Add Font Effects to Text

- In addition to changing the font and font style, you can also add **font effects** to your text.
- You can add font effects from the Font dialog box. Click Format, Font to access the Font dialog box as shown below.

Font dialog box

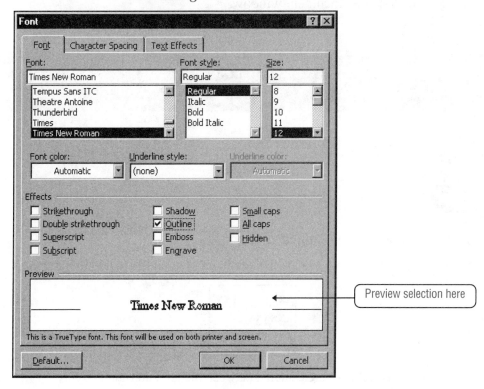

- Check the Preview screen to see the results of your selections.
- Use the Font dialog box to make changes to your text if your changes involve more than one or two options (font, font size, font color, font styles and effects). In this way, you can preview the changes before applying them.
- Some printers may not print certain font effects.

LESSON 13

Exercise 2
Add Font Effects

1. Use the Font dialog box to make changes to **LES13**.
2. Change the Internet address in lines 19 and 20 to 14 point, bold and shadow.
3. Change the quotation in lines 25 and 26 to 11 point, italic and emboss.
4. Resave the file.
5. Print one copy.
6. Do not close the document window.

GOAL 3: Change Horizontal Alignment

■ Word allows you to **align** text in four ways:

- **Left** - all lines are even at the left margin but ragged at the right margin.

```
XXXXXXXXXX
XXXXXXX
XXXXXXXXX
```

- **Center** - all lines are centered between the left and right margins.

```
   XXXX
XXXXXXXX
XXXXXXXXX
```

- **Right** - all lines are even at the right margin but ragged at the left margin.

```
  XXXXXX
XXXXXXXX
XXXXXXXXX
```

- **Justify** - all lines are even at both the left and right margins.

```
xxxxxxxxxx
xxxxxxxxxx
xxxxxxxxxx
```

- The horizontal alignment option applies to entire paragraphs. Pressing the Enter key ends a paragraph. Therefore, a paragraph can be a single line or many lines.

- Alignments can be changed before or after typing text.

- Follow these steps to align text before typing:

  1. Press the Enter key to begin a new paragraph.
  2. Click the Center button  on the Formatting toolbar as shown below.

Formatting toolbar

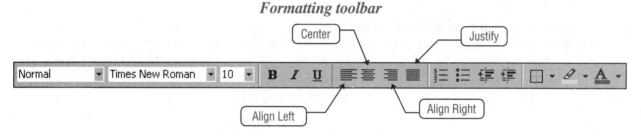

  3. Type the text to be centered and press the Enter key.
  4. Click the Align left button [image] to return to the default left alignment.

- To align existing text:

  1. Place the insertion point within the line or paragraph you want to align.
  2. Click the desired alignment button (Left, Center, Right, Justify) on the Formatting toolbar.

- You can use the following keyboard shortcuts to change alignment:

  - `Ctrl` + `E` to center text.
  - `Ctrl` + `L` to left-align text.
  - `Ctrl` + `R` to right-align text.
  - `Ctrl` + `J` to justify text.

- When you change the alignment of the paragraph, no matter what size the paragraph is, the alignment is applied to the entire paragraph.

- You may need to switch alignments within a document. For example, titles are usually centered and body text is usually left aligned. To accomplish this, you need to press the Enter key after the title, then click the Align Left button on the Formatting toolbar to return text to left alignment.

- If your document contains a title, press the Enter key twice after typing the title.

- If your document contains a title and subtitle, press the Enter key once after the title and twice after the subtitle.

LESSON 13

Exercise 3a
Change Horizontal Alignment

Part I

1. Place the insertion point at the end of the open document, **LES 13**.
2. Press the Enter key 4 times.
3. Click the Center button on the Formatting toolbar.
4. Type your first name. (Do not press the Enter key.)
5. Click Align Right button on the Formatting toolbar to move your name to the right margin.
6. Click Align Left button on the Formatting toolbar to move your name back to the left margin.
7. Press the Enter key one time.

Part II

1. Press the Enter key 2 times.
2. Type the word CENTER in all caps.
3. Click the Center button on the Formatting toolbar to center the text.
4. Press the Enter key 1 time.
5. Type the word RIGHT in all caps.
6. Click the Align Right button on the Formatting toolbar to right align the text.
7. Press the Enter key 1 time.
8. Type the word LEFT in all caps.
9. Click the Align Left button on the Formatting toolbar to left align the text.
10. Press the Enter key 3 times.
11. Close the document.
12. Do not save the changes.

Exercise 3b
Change Horizontal Alignment

1. Create a new document.
2. Center the title in Arial, 16 point and bold.
3. Press the Enter key twice after the title.
4. Change the font to Times New Roman in 12 point, regular (no bold).
5. Change the font color of each line to the color of the word or a color close to it.
6. Center each line in the exercise.
7. Press the Enter key once between each color.
8. Save the document; name it **RAINBOW**.
9. Print one copy.
10. Close the document window.

COLORS OF A RAINBOW

Red
Orange
Yellow
Green
Blue
Violet

GOAL 4: Change Vertical Alignment

- Text can be aligned **vertically** on a page. For example, you can have your text align at the top of a page or you can have it centered vertically between the top and bottom margins.
- The default setting is Top.
- To center the text vertically:
  1. Click File menu.
  2. Click Page Setup.
  3. Click Layout tab to display the following Page Setup dialog box:

Page Setup dialog box

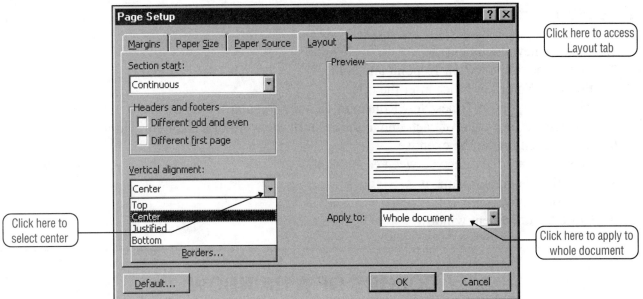

4. Click <u>V</u>ertical alignment list arrow.
5. Click Center from the list.
6. Click OK.

■ Check the Print Preview window to see if your page is vertically centered.

Exercise 4
Change Vertical Alignment

1. Create a new document.
2. Center the following exercise vertically and horizontally.
3. Type the title in a script font, 18 point, with underline and shadow. Press the Enter key once after the title.
4. Type the subtitle. Use the same font as you did in Step 3, changing to 14 point, no underline or shadow. Press the Enter key twice after the subtitle.
5. Change the font to Times New Roman, 12 point, regular, no shadow.
6. Press the Enter key once between each line.
7. Save the document; name it **ASTRONAUT**.
8. Print one copy.
9. Close the document window.

The First American Astronauts

Mercury Space Missions

Walter Schirra, Jr.
Donald K. Slayton
John H. Glenn, Jr.
M. Scott Carpenter, Jr.
Alan B. Shepard, Jr.
Virgil I. Grissom
L. Gordon Cooper, Jr.

Timed Writing

1. Create a new document.
2. Change the left margin to 1.75" and the right margin to 1.5".
3. Change font to Courier New, 12 point.
4. Take five 1-minute timings on the paragraph on the following page.
5. Type in wraparound. (Do not press the Enter key at the end of each line.)
6. Immediately correct your errors as you type.
7. If you finish before one minute is up, press the Enter key twice and start again.
8. Since you typed for one minute, the number of words you typed is your actual speed. For example, if you completed the first line only, you typed 10 words a minute. If you finished the entire paragraph, you typed 45 words a minute.
9. Save the document as **L13TIME**.
10. Print one copy.
11. Close the document window.

LESSON 13

You have come a long way in a very short time. You   10
have learned all the keys and can strike these keys   20
without looking down at your fingers, at a chart or   30
at your screen. You will get better and better and   40
make fewer and fewer errors.   50
....1.....2.....3....4....5....6....7....8....9...10

MOUSE/KEYSTROKE PROCEDURES

Font Effects

1. Click **Format** menu .... `Alt` + `O`
2. Click **Font**................................ `F`
3. Click **Font** tab.................. `Alt` + `N`
4. Click one or more of the following Effects:

   Strikethrough .... `Alt` + `K`
   Double strikethrough .... `Alt` + `L`
   Superscript..................... `Alt` + `P`
   Subscript....................... `Alt` + `B`
   Shadow .... `Alt` + `W`
   Outline .... `Alt` + `O`
   Emboss.......................... `Alt` + `E`
   Engrave .... `Alt` + `G`
   Small Caps..................... `Alt` + `M`
   All caps .... `Alt` + `A`
   Hidden.......................... `Alt` + `H`

Center Align Text
Ctrl + E

   BEFORE TYPING TEXT

1. Click **Center** button ▤ .
2. Type text.

   WITH EXISTING TEXT
1. Select text to be centered.
2. Click **Center** button ▤ .

Right Align Text
Ctrl + R

   BEFORE TYPING TEXT

1. Click **Align Right** button ▤ .
2. Type text.

   WITH EXISTING TEXT
1. Select text to right-align.
2. Click **Align Right** button ▤ .

Justify Text
Ctr+J

   BEFORE TYPING TEXT

1. Click **Justify** button ▤ .
2. Type text.

   WITH EXISTING TEXT
1. Select text to justify.
2. Click **Justify** button ▤ .

Left Align Text
Ctrl + L

   BEFORE TYPING TEXT

1. Click **Align Left** button ▤ .
2. Type text.

   WITH EXISTING TEXT
1. Select text to left-align.
2. Click **Align Left** button ▤ .

Vertically Center Text

1. Click **File** menu .... `Alt` + `F`
2. Click **Page Setup**.................... `U`
3. Click **Layout** tab .... `Alt` + `L`
4. Click **Vertical Alignment**.. `Alt` + `V`
5. Select **Center** .... `↓`
6. Click **OK** .... `Enter`

- Review Horizontal and Vertical Alignment Options
- Display Show/Hide Codes • Review All Keys

Warm-up

1. Create a new document.
2. Set the left and right margins to 1".
3. Type each line, trying to type faster when you repeat the line. When you see the vertical lines between phrases, say the phrase to yourself as you type. Do not type the vertical lines.
4. If you make an error, keep typing.
5. Save the document as **LES14**.
6. Close the document window.

---

1 a;sldkfjghfjdksla; a;sldkfjghfjdksla; a;sldkfjghfjdksla; ENTER
2 a;sldkfjghfjdksla; a;sldkfjghfjdksla; a;sldkfjghfjdksla; ENTER ENTER

3 ab cdef ghijkl mnop qrst uvw xyz abcdefg hijklmnop qrstuvwxyz ENTER
4 ab cdef ghijkl mnop qrst uvw xyz abcdefg hijklmnop qrstuvwxyz ENTER ENTER

5 fur fun gun gum guy buy but hut jut vug jim dim ENTER
6 fur fun gun gum guy buy but hut jut vug jim dim ENTER ENTER

7 kid red cue my, lot sit wet tex co. fat pat zip qt. ENTER
8 kid red cue my, lot sit wet tex co. fat pat zip qt. ENTER ENTER

9 ask ask ask can can can you you you with with with ENTER
10 ask ask ask can can can you you you with with with ENTER ENTER

11 in the|in the|in the|in the|can you|can you|can you|can you ENTER
12 in the|in the|in the|in the|can you|can you|can you|can you ENTER ENTER

13 Guy asked, "Can you chew gum in the hut with Red?" ENTER
14 Guy asked, "Can you chew gum in the hut with Red?" ENTER ENTER

LESSON 14

GOAL 1:   Review Horizontal and Vertical Alignment Options

- As you learned in the previous lesson, text can be aligned at the left margin, centered, aligned at the right margin or justified.
- You can change the alignment before or after typing the text.
- To change the alignment of existing text, you must first select the text, then give the desired alignment command.
- You can use the Formatting toolbar buttons or keyboard shortcut commands to change the alignment.
  - To left align text, click the Align Left button ▤ on the Formatting toolbar or press Ctrl+L.
  - To center text, click the Center button ▤ on the Formatting toolbar or press Ctrl+E.
  - To right align text, click the Align Right button ▤ on the Formatting toolbar or press Ctrl+R.
  - To justify text, click the Justify button ▤ on the Formatting toolbar or press Ctrl+J.
- Text can be centered vertically between the top and bottom margins. This is done in the Page Setup dialog box.
- Text can be vertically centered before or after it is typed.
- To center text vertically, click File, Page Setup, and click the Layout tab. Click the down arrow to the right of the Vertical Alignment textbox and choose Center.

Exercise 1
Horizontal and Vertical Alignments

1. Create a new document
2. Center the page vertically.
3. Center the title. Use a decorative font, 24 point, bold (Mead Bold font is used in the example below).
4. Press the Enter key twice after the title.
5. Type the body text in a sans serif font, 14 point, bold.
6. Center each line horizontally.
7. Immediately backspace to correct errors.
8. When done, change to the Whole Page view. Check to see that the text is centered both horizontally and vertically.
9. Change back to the 100% View.
10. Compare your work with the book.
11. Save the document; name it **INPUT**.
12. Print one copy.
13. Close the document window.

INPUT DEVICES

keyboard
mouse
touch pad
digitizing pen
joystick
scanner
digital camera
microphone

LESSON 14

GOAL 2:   Display Show/Hide ¶ Codes

- Sometimes it is difficult to see how many spaces there are between words or between lines of text. The **Show All** (Show/Hide ¶) feature displays codes so that you can see exactly how many spaces exist between words or lines of text.

- To display the codes, click the Show/Hide ¶ button ¶ on the Standard toolbar.

- When the codes are displayed, your text will look like this:

RULES·FOR·A·DEBATE¶
by···Your·Name¶
¶
An·equal·number·of·questions¶
Equal·time·limits·to·answer·questions¶
An·equal·number·of·turns¶
No·interruptions¶

Exercise 2
Show/Hide ¶ Codes

1. Create a new document.
2. Center the page vertically.
3. Center the title in a sans serif font, 20 point, bold.
4. Press the Enter key once after the title.
5. Type the subtitle in the same sans serif font, 14 point, bold.
6. Press the Enter key twice after the subtitle.
7. Type the body text in a serif font, 12 point.
8. Center align each line of the exercise.
9. Immediately backspace to correct errors.
10. When done, change to the Whole Page View. Check to see that the text is centered both horizontally and vertically.
11. Change back to the 100% View.
12. Display the Show/Hide ¶ Codes.
13. How many times did you press the Enter key after the subtitle?
14. Hide the codes.
15. Compare your work with the book.
16. Save the document as **DEBATE**.
17. Print one copy.
18. Close the document window.

RULES FOR A DEBATE
by: Your Name

An equal number of questions
Equal time limits to answer questions
An equal number of turns
No interruptions

LESSON 14

GOAL 3: Review All Keys

Exercise 3
Review All Keys

1. Open **LES14**.
2. Place your insertion point at the end of the document. Press the Enter key twice.
3. To type some of the lines contained in this exercise, you must deselect the "Internet and network paths with hyperlinks" feature (see Lesson 12, Mouse/Keystroke Procedures section for instructions).
4. Type the lines on the following page.
5. Type each line twice, trying to type faster when you repeat the line. When you see the vertical lines between phrases, say the phrase to yourself as you type. Do not type the vertical lines.
6. Immediately correct errors using the Backspace key.
7. When done, compare your work with the book.
8. Highlight all text between quotation marks.
9. Italicize all words in the last two lines you typed.
10. Resave the document.
11. Print one copy.
12. Close the document window.

1 aqaza aqaza swsxs swsxs dedcd dedcd frfvftfgfbf frfvftfgfbf ENTER
2 aqaza aqaza swsxs swsxs dedcd dedcd frfvftfgfbf frfvftfgfbf ENTER ENTER

3 ;'; ;'; ;p;/; ;p;/; lol.l lol.l kik,k kik,k jujmjyjhjnj jujmjyjhjnj ENTER
4 ;'; ;'; ;p;/; ;p;/; lol.l lol.l kik,k kik,k jujmjyjhjnj jujmjyjhjnj ENTER ENTER

5 ;:; ;:; ;:; ;"; ;"; ;"; ;?; ;?; ;?; k<k k<k k<k l>l l>l l>l ENTER
6 ;:; ;:; ;:; ;"; ;"; ;"; ;?; ;?; ;?; k<k k<k k<k l>l l>l l>l ENTER ENTER

7 fur fun gun gum guy buy but hut jut vug jim dim kid ENTER
8 fur fun gun gum guy buy but hut jut vug jim dim kid ENTER ENTER

9 red cue my, lot sit wet tex co. fat pat zip qt. ENTER
10 red cue my, lot sit wet tex co. fat pat zip qt. ENTER ENTER

11 qt. zip pat fat co. tex wet sit lot my, cue red kid ENTER
12 qt. zip pat fat co. tex wet sit lot my, cue red kid ENTER ENTER

13 dim jim vug jut hut but buy guy gum gun fun fur ENTER
14 dim jim vug jut hut but buy guy gum gun fun fur ENTER ENTER

15 eat seat feat heat wheat neat meat peat pleat treat ENTER
16 eat seat feat heat wheat neat meat peat pleat treat ENTER ENTER

17 ear sear dear rear fear tear gear bear hear near lear pear ENTER
18 ear sear dear rear fear tear gear bear hear near lear pear ENTER ENTER

19 having having having going going going doing doing doing ENTER
20 having having having going going going doing doing doing ENTER ENTER

21 in the|in the|in it|in it|in our|in our| in as|in as ENTER
22 in the|in the|in it|in it|in our|in our| in as|in as ENTER ENTER

23 you are|you are|you will|you will|I will|I will|we will|we will| ENTER
24 you are|you are|you will|you will|I will|I will|we will|we will| ENTER ENTER

25 On cue, the red cat passed the kid on the way out of the hut. ENTER
26 On cue, the red cat passed the kid on the way out of the hut. ENTER ENTER

27 Look for this new web site: http://dimjim.tex.com ENTER
28 Look for this new web site: http://dimjim.tex.com ENTER ENTER

29 Jan said, "The WET TEX CO. is having a sale on red vugs." ENTER
30 Jan said, "The WET TEX CO. is having a sale on red vugs." ENTER ENTER

31 Go to this web site: http://www.fatpattex.com ENTER
32 Go to this web site: http://www.fatpattex.com ENTER ENTER

LESSON 14

Timed Writing

1. Create a new document.
2. Change the left margin to 1.75" and the right margin to 1.5".
3. Change the font to Courier New, 12 point.
4. Take five 1-minute timings on the sentences below.
5. Type in wraparound. (Do not press the Enter key at the end of the line.)
6. Immediately correct your errors as you type.
7. If you finish before the 1-minute is up, start again.
8. Press the Enter key 4 times between each timing.
9. Since you typed for one minute, the number of words you typed is your actual speed. For example, if you completed the first line only, you typed 10 words a minute. If you finished all the sentences, you typed 40 words a minute.
10. Save the document as **L14TIME**.
11. Print one copy.
12. Close the document window.

```
                                                              WORDS
Now that you have had a lot of practice on the key             10
words, you will be able to gain speed by practicing            20
the common words and phrases.  By building on these            30
words and phrases, your overall speed will go up.              40
....1....2....3....4....5....6....7....8....9...10
```

MOUSE/KEYSTROKE PROCEDURES

Show/Hide

*   Click **Show/Hide ¶** button ¶ on the Standard toolbar to display the codes.

*   Click **Show/Hide ¶** button ¶ on the Standard toolbar to turn off the codes.

• Use the Tab Key • Create Headers and Footers
• Insert a Date Field • Insert a Filename Field
• Review of Horizontal and Vertical Centering

Warm-up

1. Create a new document.
2. Set the left and right margins to 1".
3. Check to see that the "Internet and network paths with hyperlinks" option has been disabled (see Lesson 12, Mouse/Keystroke Procedures for instructions).
4. Type each line, trying to type faster when you repeat a line. When you see the vertical lines between phrases, say the phrase to yourself as you type.
5. If you make an error, keep typing.
6. If you have time, repeat the exercise.
7. Save the document as **LES15**.
8. Do not close the document window.

---

1 a;sldkfjghfjdksla; a;sldkfjghfjdksla; a;sldkfjghfjdksla; ENTER

2 a;sldkfjghfjdksla; a;sldkfjghfjdksla; a;sldkfjghfjdksla; ENTER ENTER

3 fur fun gun gum guy buy but hut jut vug jim dim ENTER

4 fur fun gun gum guy buy but hut jut vug jim dim ENTER ENTER

5 kid red cue my, lot sit wet tex co. fat pat zip qt. ENTER

6 kid red cue my, lot sit wet tex co. fat pat zip qt. ENTER ENTER

7 did you|did you|did you|and my|and my|and my ENTER

8 did you|did you|did you|and my|and my|and my ENTER ENTER

9 Pat asked, "Did you visit the http://www.jutcuezip.vug web site?" ENTER

10 Pat asked, "Did you visit the http://www.jutcuezip.vug web site?" ENTER

ENTER

LESSON 15

- The **Tab** key indents a single line of text. Word contains preset tabs every .5". When you press the Tab key once, the insertion point advances half an inch; pressing it twice will move the insertion point one inch, etc.

- Use the **A** finger to strike the Tab key. The **A** finger moves up to the left, strikes the Tab key and returns to the home-row position.

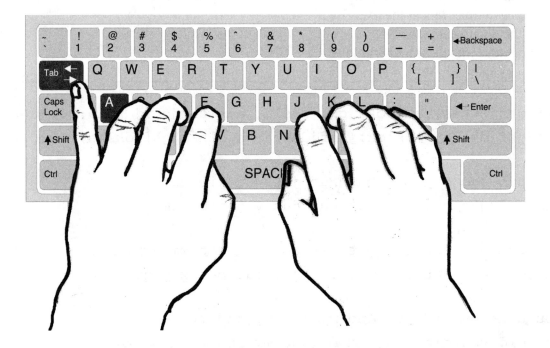

Exercise 1a
Use the Tab Key

1. Place the insertion point at the end of the last line in the document **LES15**.
2. Press the Enter key 4 times.
3. Place your hands on the home-row keys.
4. Look down at the keyboard and watch as you move your **A** finger (left pinky) up to the left to the Tab key.
5. Do not strike the Tab key.
6. Watch as you move your finger back to the home-row position.
7. Practice moving your **A** finger to the Tab key and back to the **A** key five times.
8. Type an *a*, then press the Tab key. (You may look at your fingers.) Type the line as follows:

    a   a   a   a   a   a   a **ENTER**

9. Repeat the line without looking at your fingers. You may look at the keyboard illustration below.
10. Type the following exercise, pressing the Tab key after each word.
11. When you are finished, compare your work with the book.
12. Resave the file.
13. Close the document window.

1	fur	fun	gun	gum	guy	buy	jim	dim	lot	sit	fat ENTER
2	fur	fun	gun	gum	guy	buy	jim	dim	lot	sit	fat ENTER ENTER
3	but	hut	jut	vug	kid	red	cue	my,	tex	co.	zip ENTER
4	but	hut	jut	vug	kid	red	cue	my,	tex	co.	zip ENTER ENTER

LESSON 15

Exercise 1b
Review All Keys
Use the Tab Key

1. Create a new document.
2. Type the paragraphs below and be sure to:
   a. Indent one tab stop at the beginning of each paragraph.
   b. Press the Enter key 2 times after each paragraph.
3. Immediately correct errors using the Backspace key.
4. Bold **B** the word **Internet** every time it appears.
5. Underline **U** the word <u>site</u> every time it appears.
6. Italicize *I* the word *information* every time it appears.
7. When you are finished, compare your work with the book. (Your line endings may differ.)
8. If you have time, retype the paragraphs.
9. Save the document; name it SITES.
10. Print one copy.
11. Remove all bold, italics and underlining wherever it was applied.
12. When finished, resave the document.
13. Print one copy.
14. Close the document window.

The **Internet** contains incredible amounts of *information* on almost every topic. However, some of it is not reliable. Anyone can publish a Web <u>site</u>, and the **Internet** does not check the accuracy of the contents. It is up to you to judge the quality of the *information*.

First, know your source. Make sure that a recognized expert or organization in the field created the <u>site</u>. Then verify the accuracy of the *information* by checking with other reliable sites. By doing this, you will be able to search the **Internet** more wisely and obtain accurate data.

GOAL 2: Create Headers and Footers

- A **header** is text that, by default, appears .5" from the top of the page. A **footer** is text that, by default, appears .5" from the bottom of the page. These areas usually contain text that identifies the document. Typical identifying information would be a chapter title or a page number.

- For identification purposes, many exercises from this lesson forward will have a header that contains your name and date, and a footer that contains the document's file name.

- Headers and footers can be added before, during or after the document is typed.

- To view a header or footer in the document window, you must be in the Print Layout view or the Print Preview window.

- Follow these steps to create a header or footer:
  1. Click View menu.
  2. Click Header and Footer.

View menu

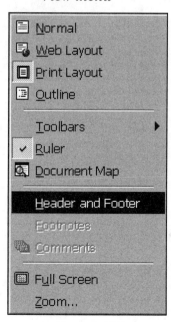

3. You will see the header and footer areas, and the Header and Footer toolbar will display.
   Note: Only the buttons used in this lesson are labeled.

LESSON 15

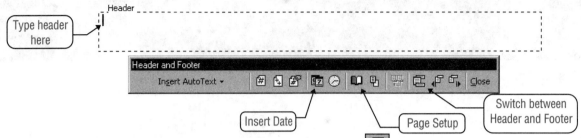

4. Click the Switch Between Header and Footer button ⬚ to toggle between the header and footer. Note the illustration of the footer area below.

5. Click the Insert Date button ⬚ to insert a date field.

6. Format the text (align, bold, underline, italicize, etc.) in the header and/or footer just as you would format text in the actual document.

7. Type text in the header and footer area. Text is automatically left-aligned. There are also two preset tabs. Press the Tab key once and type text to be centered. Press the Tab key again and type text to be right-aligned.

8. Click the Close button ⬚Close to return to the document.

■ Starting with this lesson, use the following header for all exercises in this book.

    Header
    Your Name   4/28/99

    Click Insert Date button to insert date

Exercise 2
Insert a Date Field into a Header

1. Create a new document.
2. Create a header as follows:
   a. Click View menu.
   b. Click Header and Footer.
   c. Type your name at the left in the header area.
   d. Press the Tab key twice.
   e. Click the Insert Date button.
3. Click Close to close the Header window.
4. Save the document; name it **PRESENT**. Close the document window.

GOAL 3:   Insert a Filename Field

- As previously discussed, many exercises that you will create for this book will contain your name and the date in a header. For further identification, you will insert a **Filename field** into a footer. In this way, you will be able to easily identify the exercise from your printout and locate it on your disk or hard drive.

- Click the Switch Between Header and Footer button [icon] to access the footer area. Follow these steps to insert the Filename field:

  1. Click Insert AutoText button | Insert AutoText ▾ | on the Header and Footer toolbar.
  2. Click Filename from the drop-down list.

Header and Footer toolbar

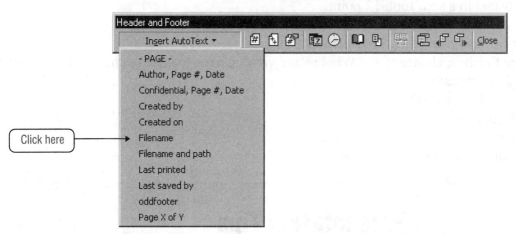

- When you insert the Filename field using this method, you are inserting a field code for the file name, not the actual name. If you change the file name by saving it under a different name, the field code automatically shows the new file name.

- This method can be used to insert the Filename field in either a header or footer.

Exercise 3
Insert a Filename Field Into a Footer

1. Open **PRESENT**.
2. Follow these steps to access the Footer window.
   a. Click View menu.
   b. Click Header and Footer.
   c. Click Switch Between Header and Footer button.
3. Insert the Filename field into the footer as follows:
   a. Click Insert AutoText on the Header and Footer toolbar.
   b. Click Filename.
4. Center the page vertically.
5. Center the title in a sans serif font, 20 point, bold.
6. Press the Enter key twice after the title.
7. Type the body text in a serif font, 12 point.
8. Center align each line.
9. Immediately correct errors using the Backspace key.
10. When you are finished, change to the Whole Page view. Check to see that the text is centered both horizontally and vertically.
11. Change the view back to 100%.
12. Resave the document.
13. Print one copy.
14. Close the document window.

Presentation Tips

Make eye contact
Involve your audience by asking questions
Show enthusiasm
Use gestures when you want to make a point
Speak very clearly, stand up straight and have fun

Timed Writing

1. Create a new document.
2. Change the left margin to 1.75" and the right margin to 1.5".
3. Change the font to Courier New, 12 point.
4. Take five 1-minute timings on the paragraph below.
5. Type in wraparound. (Do not press the Enter key at the end of the line.)
6. Immediately correct your errors as you type.
7. If you finish before the 1 minute is up, start again.
8. Press the Enter key 4 times between each timing.
9. Since you typed for 1 minute, the number of words you typed is your actual speed. For example, if you completed the first line only, you typed 10 words a minute. If you finished all sentences, you typed 44 words a minute.
10. Save the document as **L15TIME**.
11. Print one copy.
12. Close the document window.

	WORDS
Do you know what a vug really is? A vug is a	10
small indent in a rock. This indentation is often	20
lined with crystals. The spelling of the word vug	30
varies. Sometimes it is spelled vugg and sometimes	40
it is spelled vugh.	44

```
....1....2....3....4....5....6....7....8....9...10
```

MOUSE/KEYSTROKE PROCEDURES

Create a Header

1. Click **View** menu............. `Alt`+`V`
2. Click **Header and Footer** .... `H`
   to display the Header and Footer toolbar.
3. Type and format header or footer text as desired.
   AND/OR
   Choose from one or more of the following options:
   - Click **Date** button `Ez` if desired.
   - Click **Time** button `⊙` if desired.
4. Click **Close** button `Close` . `Alt`+`C`

Create a Footer

1. Click **View** menu............. `Alt`+`V`
2. Click **Header and Footer** .... `H`
   to display the Header and Footer toolbar.
3. Click **Switch Between Header and Footer** button `🖳`, if necessary, to switch to footer.
4. Type and format footer text as desired.
   AND/OR
   Choose from one or more of the following options:
   - Click **Date** button `Ez` if desired.
   - Click **Time** button `⊙` if desired.
5. Click **Close** button `Close` . `Alt`+`C`

Insert a Filename

1. Click **View** menu .... `Alt`+`V`
2. Click **Header and Footer**........... `H`
   to display the Header and Footer toolbar.
3. Click **Switch Between Header and Footer** button `🖳` to switch to footer
4. Click **Insert AutoText**........ `Alt`+`S`
   button list box.
5. Click Filename ....`↓`
   from drop-down list

Warm-up

1. Create a new document.
2. Set the left and right margins to 1".
3. Use the Click and Type method to begin the document 2" from the top of the page.
4. Type the exercise, trying to type faster each time you repeat a line. (Do not type the vertical lines that separate the phrases.) When you see the vertical lines between phrases, say the phrase to yourself as you type.
5. If you make an error, continue typing.
6. If you have time, repeat the exercise.
7. Save the document as **LES16**.
8. Close the document window.

---

1 a;sldkfjghfjdksla; a;sldkfjghfjdksla; a;sldkfjghfjdksla; ENTER

2 a;sldkfjghfjdksla; a;sldkfjghfjdksla; a;sldkfjghfjdksla; ENTER ENTER

3 kid red cue my, lot sit wet tex co. fat pat zip qt. ENTER

4 kid red cue my, lot sit wet tex co. fat pat zip qt. ENTER ENTER

5 fur fun gun gum guy buy but hut jut vug jim dim ENTER

6 fur fun gun gum guy buy but hut jut vug jim dim ENTER ENTER

7 the the the they they they they're they're these these these ENTER

8 the the the they they they they're they're these these these ENTER ENTER

9 thee thee then then there there their their them them ENTER

10 thee thee then then there there their their them them ENTER ENTER

11 and the| and the| and they|and they|and these|and these ENTER

12 and the| and the| and they|and they|and these|and these ENTER ENTER

13 Pat and Guy thought these were theirs and they were right. ENTER

14 Pat and Guy thought these were theirs and they were right. ENTER ENTER

LESSON 16

GOAL 1:   Review Headers and Footers

- Headers and footers are areas that, by default, appear .5" from the top and/or bottom margins of a page. They usually contain identifying elements, such as page numbers and chapter titles.

- To access the Header and Footer feature:
  1. Click View menu.
  2. Click Header and Footer.

- Type your information and/or click the appropriate Header and Footer toolbar button. Before typing, press the Tab key once to center align your text or codes; press the Tab key twice to right align text or codes.

- Click the Switch Between Header and Footer button to access the footer area.

- You will use the Header and Footer feature to create a heading for each document. Type your name in the left corner of the header window, then press the Tab key twice. Click the Insert Date button to insert the date in the right corner.

- You will use the footer to insert a file name for each document. Insert the Filename field in the left corner of the footer area.

- You can switch from the document text to the header or footer text. Make sure you are in Print Layout view and double-click the header or footer. To return to the document, double-click in the dimmed document area.

Exercise 1
Review Headers and Footers

1. Create a new document.
2. Create a header to include your name and the date field. Type your name in the left corner of the header window. Press the Tab key twice and click the Insert Date button.
3. Create a footer to include the Filename field. Insert the Filename field in the left corner of the footer window.
4. Close the footer window.
5. Save the document; name it **SAND1**.
6. Close the document window.

GOAL 2:   Review Tab Key

- As you learned in the previous lesson, the Tab key is used to indent the first line of a new paragraph.
- Use the **A** finger to strike the Tab key.
- Remember to press the Enter key twice between paragraphs.

Exercise 2a
Review Tab Key

1. Open **SAND1**.
2. Type the exercise below and complete the following steps:
   a. Center the title in a serif font, 18 point and underline.
      Note: Use the Font dialog box to make these changes.
   b. Press the Enter key twice after the title.
   c. Switch the document to left alignment.
   d. Type the body text in the same serif font, 12 point.
   e. Using the Tab key, indent one tab stop at the beginning of each paragraph.
   f. Press the Enter key twice after each paragraph.
3. Immediately correct errors using the Backspace key.
4. When you are finished, compare your work with the book.
5. Bold **B** the word **sand** every time it appears in the body text.
6. Italicize *I* the word *particles* every time it appears.
7. If you have time, retype the paragraphs.
8. Resave the file.
9. Print one copy.
10. Close the document window.

HOW SAND IS FORMED

When solid rock, with or without vugs, is exposed to the wind, rain and frost, it gets broken up into small particles. If the particles are small enough, they are considered sand.

The main place where sand is formed is at the beach. The tide hitting the rocks and the wind rubbing the rock particles together form the sand. The desert is another place where sand is found. The sand may have been formed by the decay of rocks or by the wind blowing it there. In some cases, the sea dried up and the sand was left in what is now a desert.

Exercise 2b
Review Tab Key

1. Create a new document.
2. Create a header to include your name and Date field.
3. Create a footer to include the Filename field.
4. Center the page vertically.
5. Press the Enter key twice after the title.
6. Type the exercise below and complete the following steps:
   a. Center the title in a sans serif font, 20 point, bold and italic.
      Note: Use the Font dialog box to make these changes.
   b. Press the Enter key twice after the title.
   c. Switch the document to left alignment.
   d. Type the body text in a serif font, 12 point.
   e. Using the Tab key, indent one tab stop at the beginning of each paragraph.
   f. Press the Enter key twice after each paragraph.
7. Immediately correct errors using the Backspace key.
8. When done, change the Zoom setting to Whole Page. Check to see that the text is centered vertically.
9. Change the zoom settings back to 100%.
10. When you are finished, compare your work with the book.
11. Save the document; name it **INTERVIEW**.
12. Print one copy.
13. Close the document window.

INTERVIEWING

Interviewing properly is an art and something that is learned through experience. There are certain rules of behavior that should be followed to have a successful interview. These include, among others, dressing professionally, making eye contact, having knowledge about the company and asking appropriate questions.

However, there are also guidelines to follow to avoid notorious *interview bloopers*. Some of the more common mistakes are: speaking too loudly, talking too much, slouching, fidgeting and complaining about a former employer or job.

Remember that an interview is a business meeting where you are marketing a product, and that product is YOU. Always conduct yourself in a professional way and most likely that job will be yours.

GOAL 3: Check Document for Spelling and Grammar Errors

- Word can check for errors in spelling and grammar, repeated words, spacing and capitalization. Word starts the spell check at the beginning of the document. If you want only a section of the document checked, select the section you want, then run the spell check feature.

- The spell check feature is a great tool that helps to improve the accuracy of the document. However, it cannot tell you if you have used the wrong word. For example, many people confuse *there* and *their*, and since both are spelled correctly, the spell check will not pick up the incorrect usage. You must **proofread** your work very carefully.

- Word automatically checks your document for both spelling and grammar errors. This process places a red wavy line under any word that is not in Word's dictionary and a green wavy line under a possible grammatical error. Click the *right* mouse button on a wavy line to receive suggestions for correcting the spelling or grammar error.

- If you find the red and green lines confusing, you can turn off the automatic spell and grammar check features. Follow these steps to turn off the automatic spell or grammar check:
  1. Click Tools menu.
  2. Click Options.
  3. Select the Spelling & Grammar tab.
  4. Deselect the Check spelling as you type checkbox.
  5. Deselect the Check grammar as you type checkbox.
  6. Click OK.

- Word comes with an **AutoCorrect** feature that corrects common spelling, typing and grammar errors as you type. AutoCorrect makes corrections based on the spell checker's dictionary as well as from a list of predefined entries. You can add other words to this list to include words you commonly misspell. Follow these steps to customize the AutoCorrect feature:
  1. Click Tools menu.
  2. Click AutoCorrect.
  3. Select AutoCorrect tab.
  4. Click to select the Replace text as you type checkbox
  4. Type the misspelled word in the Replace text box.
  5. Type the correctly spelled word in the With text box.
  6. Click Add.
  7. Click OK.

- You can turn off options in AutoCorrect to prevent it from making certain corrections. For example, you might not want to capitalize the first letter of a sentence. Follow these steps to turn off options:

1. Click Tools menu.
2. Click AutoCorrect.
3. Select AutoCorrect tab.
4. Click checked items to deselect them.
5. Click OK.

■ Follow these steps to spell check a document:

1. Select the section you want to check or don't select anything to check the entire document.
2. Click the Spelling and Grammar button ☑ on the Standard toolbar.

   OR

   a. Click Tools menu.
   b. Click Spelling and Grammar.

3. When Word finds a word it does not recognize, the following Spelling and Grammar dialog box appears:

Spelling and Grammar dialog box

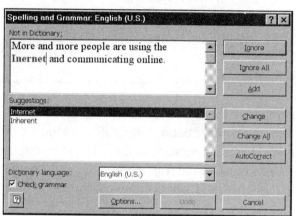

4. You can do one of the following:

   • Click the Ignore button ⸢Ignore⸥ to leave the word as is.
   • Click the Ignore All button ⸢Ignore All⸥ to ignore all occurrences of the word.
   • Click a suggested spelling and click the Change button ⸢Change⸥.
   • Click the Change All button ⸢Change All⸥ to change all occurrences of the word.
   • If there are no suggestions, you can correct the word in the Not in Dictionary box, then click Change.
     OR
     Click the Add button ⸢Add⸥ to add the word to the dictionary.
   • Click the Delete button ⸢Delete⸥ to remove the second occurrence of a repeated word.
   • Click the AutoCorrect button ⸢AutoCorrect⸥ to add the misspelled word and its correct spelling to the AutoCorrect list.

5. Click Close to discontinue spell check.
6. When spell check is finished, you will get either a message telling you the check is completed, or a message asking if you want to check the remainder of the document.

■ Word checks the grammar by default. If you want to omit a grammar check, click the **Check grammar** checkbox on the Spelling and Grammar dialog box, as shown above, to turn off the grammar checker.

137

LESSON 16

Exercise 3
Spell and Grammar Check Document

1. Create a new document.
2. Use the default margins.
3. Type the paragraphs below. Include the errors (they are circled to help you find them).
4. Use the spell check feature to make the necessary corrections.
   Note: In line 3, change "not without its dangers" to "a potentially dangerous situation."
5. Save the document; name it **CRIME**.
6. Print one copy.
7. Close the document window.

More and more people are using the Internet and communicating online. We are now able to obtain information and contact people from all over the world. However, this is is not without its dangers. There are people out there in cyberspace who would pray on innocent Web travelers. You must be careful. Cyberspace is a new frontier, and like the Wild West of years ago, it is greatly in need of law and order.

The laws governing cyberspace are just being developed, and the legal experts are first making dicisions as to to what constitutes a crime. At present, there are a number of crimes that are recognized and prosecuted. However, until laws are clearly wriTten, the basic rule to follow when you are online is: Whatever is illegal in our societys is illegal in cyberspace.

GOAL 4:   Insert Text

Insert Text

- In order to add new text to an existing document, place the **insertion point** to the left of the character (letter, number, punctuation mark) that will follow the newly inserted text.

- Look at the example below. To insert the missing word *apple* after the first word, place your insertion point as indicated.

> Place insertion point here

An|a day keeps the doctor away.

- When you type the new text, the existing text moves to the right. When inserting a word, make sure there is one space after the newly inserted word.

- Use the insertion point movement keys to place the insertion point at the desired location. These keys may include: Home, End, Page Up, Page Down, the arrow keys or the arrow keys in combination with the Control key. Once the I-beam (I) is positioned at the correct location, double-click the left mouse button to place the insertion point.

- You may also use the mouse to relocate the insertion point.

- After inserting text, make sure that the spacing between words is correct. You may display the Show/Hide ¶ codes. A small dot between the words indicates one space.

Split a Paragraph

- You may wish to split an existing paragraph into two paragraphs. To do this, place the insertion point where you want the new paragraph to begin and press the Enter key twice.

- Remember to press the Tab key if your document contains indented paragraphs.

- Make sure that you have the correct spacing between paragraphs. If you are using single spacing, you should have two paragraph codes between each paragraph. Again, display the Show/Hide ¶ codes to view the paragraph symbols.

LESSON 16

Use Proofreaders' Marks

- **Proofreaders' marks** are symbols on a document that indicate changes to be made. In this lesson, you will learn the following proofreaders' marks:
  - The proofreaders' mark for **insertion** is: ∧
  - The proofreaders' mark for a **new paragraph** is: ¶

Exercise 4
Insert Text

1. Open **SAND1**.
2. Make the indicated insertions.
3. Save the file as **SAND2**.
4. Print one copy.
5. Close the document window.

HOW SAND IS FORMED

When solid rock, with or without vugs, is exposed to the wind, rain and frost, it gets broken up into small *particles*. If the *particles* are small enough, they are considered **sand**.

The main place where **sand** is formed is at the beach. The tide hitting the rocks and the wind rubbing the rock *particles* together form the **sand**. The desert is another place where **sand** is found. The **sand** may have been formed by the decay of rocks or by the wind blowing it there. In some cases, the sea dried up and the **sand** was left in what is now a desert.

(handwritten insertions: a; se; then; very; most; by the seashore; se; commonly; small; over the years; action of the; known as)

140

Timed Writing

1. Create a new document.
2. Change the left margin to 1.75" and the right margin to 1.5".
3. Change the font to Courier New, 12 point.
4. Create a header to include your name and the Date field.
5. Create a footer and insert the Filename field in the left corner of the footer.
6. Take five 1-minute timings on the following paragraph.
7. Type in wraparound. (Do not press the Enter key at the end of each line.)
8. Immediately correct your errors as you type.
9. If you finish before the 1 minute is up, start again.
10. Press the Enter key 4 times between each timing.
11. Since you typed for one minute, the number of words you typed is your actual speed. For example, if you completed the first line only, you typed 10 words a minute. If you finished all of the sentences, you typed 51 words a minute.
12. Save the document as **L16TIME**.
13. Print one copy.
14. Close the document window.

	WORDS
When you plan to go away on a trip, what do you	10
do with your dog or cat? You can send the dog or cat	20
to a hotel. You can have a friend go to your house	30
to feed and play with your dog or cat. Or, you may	46
leave your dog or cat alone.	51

```
....1....2....3....4....5....6....7....8....9...10
```

141

LESSON 16

Insert Text

1. Place insertion point to **left** of character that will immediately follow inserted text.
2. Type text.

Insert New Paragraph

1. Place insertion point where new paragraph is to begin.
2. Press the **Enter** key.... `Enter`, `Enter` twice.

   Note: Press the Tab key if all paragraphs are indented.

AutoCorrect

1. Click **Tools** menu .... `Alt`+`T`
2. Click **AutoCorrect**..................... `A`
3. Click **AutoCorrect** tab.
4. Click **Replace text as you type** checkbox........... `Alt`+`T`
5. Click **Replace** text box..... `Alt`+`R`
6. Type misspelled word.
7. Click **With** text box........... `Alt`+`W`
8. Type correct spelling.
9. Click **OK**.............................. `Enter`

Spell Check

1. Place the insertion point where spell check is to begin.

   OR

   Select the text to be spell checked.

2. Click the **Spelling** button 🔤 on the Standard toolbar.

   OR

   a. Click **Tools** menu .... `Alt`+`T`
   b. Click **Spelling and Grammar** .... `S`

   Note: When the program finds a word that is not in the dictionary, the word displays in the Not in Dictionary box.

3. You can make one of the following choices:
   - Click **Ignore**.................. `Alt`+`I` to continue without changing the word.

   OR

   - Click **Ignore All** .... `Alt`+`G` to continue without changing any occurrence of the word.

   OR

   a. Edit the word in the **Not in Dictionary** box.
   b. Click **Change**................ `Alt`+`C`

   OR

   a. Click suggested spelling...... 📝
   b. Click **Change**................ `Alt`+`C`

OR

- Click **Change All** .... `Alt`+`L` to change all occurrences of the word.

OR

- Click **Add**...................... `Alt`+`A` to add the word to the dictionary.

OR

- Click **AutoCorrect**......... `Alt`+`R` to add misspelled word and correction to AutoCorrect list.

OR

- Click **Delete** .... `Alt`+`D` to delete a repeated word.

OR

- Click **Close** to discontinue the spell check.

Automatic Spell/ Grammar Check

1. Place mouse on red or green wavy lines.
2. Click *right* mouse button.
3. Select option to correct error.

   OR

   - Click **Spelling** .... `Alt`+`S`

   OR

   - Click **Grammar** .... `Alt`+`G`

LESSON 17

- Review Insert
- First-Line Indent
- Change Line Spacing

Warm-up

1. Create a new document.
2. Set the left and right margins to 1".
3. Type your name and insert the date field in the header. Insert the Filename field in the footer.
4. Type each line, trying to type faster each time you repeat a line.
5. When you see the vertical lines between phrases, say the phrase to yourself as you type. Try to think of the phrase as one unit. Do not type the vertical lines.
6. If you make an error, continue typing.
7. If you have time, repeat the exercise.
8. Save the document as **LES17**.
9. Close the document window.

---

1 a;sldkfjghfjdksla; a;sldkfjghfjdksla; a;sldkfjghfjdksla; ENTER

2 a;sldkfjghfjdksla; a;sldkfjghfjdksla; a;sldkfjghfjdksla; ENTER ENTER

3 kid red cue my, lot sit wet tex co., fat pat zip qt. ENTER

4 kid red cue my, lot sit wet tex co., fat pat zip qt. ENTER ENTER

5 fur fun gun gum guy buy but hut jut vug jim dim ENTER

6 fur fun gun gum guy buy but hut jut vug jim dim ENTER ENTER

7 would would would should should should could could could ENTER

8 would would would should should should could could could ENTER ENTER

9 he he he she she she her her her here here here were were were ENTER

10 he he he she she she her her her here here here were were were ENTER ENTER

11 could he|could he|could he| would she| would she|would she ENTER

12 could he|could he|could he| would she| would she|would she ENTER ENTER

13 Did Jim rescue my furry wet red cat from the lake by the hut? ENTER

14 Did Jim rescue my furry wet red cat from the lake by the hut? ENTER ENTER

LESSON 17

- To insert text, place the insertion point to the left of the character that will follow the inserted text.
- Use the insertion point movement keys (Page Up, Page Down, etc.) or mouse to move the insertion point.
- Be careful to leave the correct number of spaces between words and paragraphs.

Exercise 1
Review Insert

1. Open **INPUT**.
2. Insert the indicated text.
3. Resave the document.
4. Print one copy.
5. Close the document window.

COMPUTER **INPUT DEVICES**

keyboard
mouse
trackball ⟶ **touch pad**
touch screen ⟶ **digitizing pen**
drawing tablet ⟶ **joystick**
bar code reader ⟶ **scanner**
digital camera
video camera ⟶ **microphone**

GOAL 2: First-Line Indent

- In the previous exercises, you used the Tab key to indent the first line of a new paragraph. However, you can also accomplish a **first-line indent** without having to press the Tab key by using Word's first-line indentation feature.
- When you are using the first-line paragraph indentation option, Word automatically indents the first line every time you begin a new paragraph.
- Follow these steps to create an automatic first-line indentation:
  1. Click Format menu.
  2. Click Paragraph.

Format menu

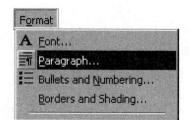

  3. Click Indents and Spacing tab.
  4. Click the Special drop-down list arrow and select **First line**.

Paragraph dialog box

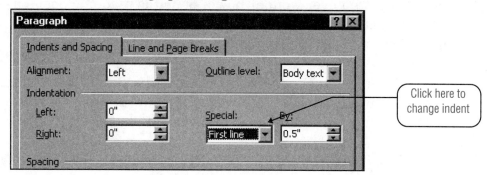

  5. Click OK.

- Word indents all paragraphs .5" by default. You can specify a different amount to indent the paragraph in the By text box.
- To stop using the First-line indentation, select **(none)** from the Special drop-down list, or press Ctrl+Q.

LESSON 17

Exercise 2
First-line indent

1. Create a new document.
2. Create a header to include your name and date.
3. Create a footer to include the file name.
4. Type the title 1" from the top of the page.
   Note: Check the Status bar to make sure the insertion point is at 1".
5. Center the title in a sans serif font, 18 point, bold. Press the Enter key twice after the title.
6. Change the paragraphs to have an automatic first-line indent.
7. Type the body text in a serif font, 12 point.
8. Immediately correct errors using the Backspace key.
9. When you are finished, compare your work with the book. Your line endings will differ.
10. Bold **B** the word **pencil** every time it appears in the paragraph text.
11. Italicize *I* the word *graphite* every time it appears in the paragraph text.
12. Save the file; name it **PENCIL**.
13. Print one copy.
14. Close the document window.

THE TRUTH ABOUT PENCILS

Did you ever wonder how a pencil is made? Pencils used to be called "lead pencils" but there is no lead in the pencils made today. Instead, a pencil contains graphite.

To make a pencil, graphite is mixed together with water and clay. This mixture is put into a forming press and it comes out as a thin rope. The rope is cut into pieces and put into ovens to bake.

The outside of the pencil is made from pine or red cedar. The wood is shaped in halves with a groove to hold the graphite rope.

After the graphite is inserted into the groove, two halves are glued together. The wooden case is painted, a metal band and an eraser are added, and then you have a pencil.

GOAL 3: Change Line Spacing

- **Line spacing** refers to the spacing between lines of text within a paragraph.
- Word offers a number of line spacing options. The most commonly used line spacing options are single and double spacing. Word offers additional options so you can customize your line spacing.
- You can change line spacing before or after typing the text. If you want to change line spacing after typing text, you must first place the insertion point within the paragraph you wish to change.
- There are two methods for changing line spacing.
  - **Shortcut keys**. This is the fastest method.
    * Press Ctrl+1 for single spacing.
    * Press Ctrl+2 for double spacing.
    * Press Ctrl+5 for 1.5 spacing.
  - **Paragraph dialog box**. This method provides the most options for changing and customizing the line spacing. Follow these steps to use the Paragraph dialog box:
    1. Click F_ormat menu.
    2. Click P_aragraph to access the Paragraph dialog box below.

Paragraph dialog box

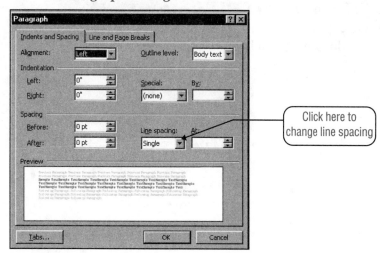

Click here to change line spacing

3. Click I_ndents and Spacing tab.
4. Click the Li_ne Spacing drop-down list arrow.
5. Select desired line spacing.
6. Click OK.

- When typing a **single-spaced** document, press the Enter key **twice** between paragraphs; when typing a **double-spaced** document, press the Enter key once.

LESSON 17

Exercise 3
Change Line Spacing

1. Create a new document.
2. Create a header and insert your name and the Date field.
3. Create a footer and include the Filename field.
4. Change the paragraph line spacing to double using the Paragraph dialog box.
5. Change the paragraphs to have an automatic first-line indent.
6. Begin the title at 1".
7. Type the title text provided in the illustration on the next page. Use a sans serif font, 18 point, bold.
8. Center the title.
9. Type the subtitle text provided in the illustration on the next page. Use the same sans serif font, 14 point, italic.
10. Center the subtitle.
11. Type the body text in a serif font, 12 point.
    Note: Remember to press the Enter key only once between paragraphs when creating a double-spaced document.
12. Bold the last sentence.
13. When you are finished, compare your work with the book.
14. Save the file; name it **REPTILES**.
15. Print one copy.
16. Close the document window.

ALLIGATORS VS. CROCODILES

What's the Difference?

Do you have trouble telling crocodiles and alligators apart? Well, you are not alone. Both are reptiles, but they are very different animals. Here are some facts to help you identify which one is which.

Alligators have broader snouts and the teeth in the upper jaw overlap the bottom teeth and hide them from view. They eat a wide variety of animals ranging from insects to dogs and pigs. There are different species of alligator, but the longest on record is nineteen feet. Do they attack humans? Rarely, according to the experts.

Crocodiles are more aggressive than alligators and can be identified by the narrower snout and protruding teeth. These protruding teeth give them their distinctive *smile*. They eat birds, fish or larger prey such as deer. Do crocodiles attack humans? Here's the bad news: The larger species are known to attack humans.

Now that you can identify these animals, you can find them in the southern part of the United States. **Just make sure you don't get too close**.

LESSON 17

Timed Writing

1. Create a new document.
2. Change the left margin to 1.75" and the right margin to 1.5".
3. Change the font to Courier New, 12 point.
4. Create a header to include your name and the Date field.
5. Create a footer to include the Filename field.
6. Take five ½-minute timings on the key words.
7. Type in wraparound. (Do not press the Enter key at the end of each line.)
8. If you finish before the ½ minute is up, start again.
9. If you make an error, continue typing.
10. Press the Enter key 4 times between each timing.
11. Since you typed for ½ a minute, the number of words you typed must be multiplied by 2 to get your actual speed. For example, if you completed the first line only, you typed 10 x 2 = 20 words a minute.
12. Save the document as **L17TIME**.
13. Print one copy.
14. Close the document window.

```
                                                        WORDS
fur fun gun gum guy buy but hut jut vug jim dim kid       10
red cue my, lot sit wet tex co., fat pat zip qt.          20

....1....2....3....4....5....6....7....8....9...10
```

MOUSE/KEYSTROKE PROCEDURES

First-line Indent

1. Place insertion point in desired paragraph.
2. Click **Format** menu .... `Alt`+`O`
3. Click **Paragraph** .... `P`
4. Click .... `Alt`+`I`
   Indents and Spacing tab.
5. Click **Special** .... `↓`,`Alt`+`S`
6. Select **First Line** .... `↓`
7. Select **By** .... `Alt`+`Y`
8. Type desired amount.
9. Click **OK** .... `Enter`

Change Line Spacing
USING SHORTCUT KEYS

1. Place insertion point where new line spacing is to begin.

   OR

   Select the paragraphs in which line spacing is to be changed.
2. Select desired line spacing options:
   • Press **Ctrl+2** to change to double-space.
   • Press **Ctrl+1** to change to single-space.
   • Press **Ctrl+5** to change to 1.5-spacing.

USING PARAGRAPH DIALOG BOX

1. Place insertion point where new line spacing is to begin.

   OR

   Select the paragraphs in which line spacing is to be changed.
2. Click **Format** menu .... `Alt`+`O`
3. Click **Paragraphs** .... `P`
4. Click .... `Alt`+`I`
   Indents and Spacing tab.
5. Click **Line Spacing** .... `Alt`+`N`
6. Click desired option .... `↕`
7. Click **OK** .... `Enter`

<table>
<tr><td>

LESSON
18

</td><td>

• Review Line Spacing • Learn to Delete
• Change Typing Mode: Insert, Typing Replaces Selection
and Overtype • Undo and Redo Functions

</td></tr>
</table>

Warm-up

1. Create a new document.
2. Set the left and right margins to 1".
3. Type each line, trying to type faster each time you repeat the line.
4. When you see the vertical lines between phrases, say the phrase to yourself as you type. Do not type the vertical lines that separate the phrases.
5. If you make an error, continue typing.
6. If you have time, repeat the exercise.
7. Save the document as **LES18**.
8. Close the document window.

---

1 a;sldkfjghfjdksla; a;sldkfjghfjdksla; a;sldkfjghfjdksla; ENTER

2 a;sldkfjghfjdksla; a;sldkfjghfjdksla; a;sldkfjghfjdksla; ENTER ENTER

3 kid red cue my, lot sit wet tex co. fat pat zip qt. ENTER

4 kid red cue my, lot sit wet tex co. fat pat zip qt. ENTER ENTER

5 fur fun gun gum guy buy but hut jut vug jim dim ENTER

6 fur fun gun gum guy buy but hut jut vug jim dim ENTER ENTER

7 you you you your your your four four four for for for or or or ENTER

8 you you you your your your four four four for for for or or or ENTER ENTER

9 more more more am am am an an an any any any one one one ENTER

10 more more more am am am an an an any any any one one one ENTER ENTER

11 for you|for you|for you|four or more|four or more|four or more ENTER

12 for you|for you|for you|four or more|four or more|four or more ENTER ENTER

13 Gum is on sale at Red's Hut. Buy some for Guy's and Jim's kids. ENTER

14 Gum is on sale at Red's Hut. Buy some for Guy's and Jim's kids. ENTER ENTER

GOAL 1:   Review Line Spacing

- Line spacing changes can be made before or after typing the text.
- You can make changes to the line spacing by using the following shortcut keys:
  - Ctrl+1 for single spacing.
  - Ctrl+2 for double spacing.
  - Ctrl+5 for 1.5 spacing.
- You can also make changes to the line spacing option in the Paragraph dialog box. Access the dialog box as follows:
  1. Click Format menu.
  2. Click Paragraph.
  3. Click Indents and Spacing tab.
  4. Click Line spacing drop-down list arrow.
  5. Select desired spacing.
  6. Click OK.

Paragraph dialog box

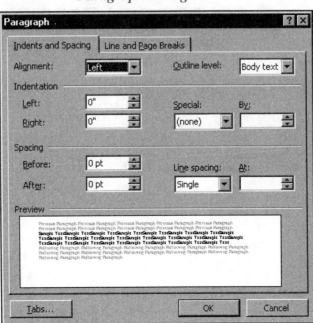

LESSON 18

Exercise 1
Review Line Spacing

1. Open **RAINBOW**.
2. Create a header containing your name and the Date field.
3. Create a footer to include the Filename field.
4. Center the document vertically.
5. Select the list of text beneath the heading.
6. Change the line spacing to double using the shortcut keys (Ctrl+2).
7. When you are finished, change to Whole Page view. Check to see that the text is centered both horizontally and vertically.
8. Change back to 100% Zoom.
9. Compare your work with the book.
10. Resave the document.
11. Print one copy.
12. Close the document window.

COLORS OF A RAINBOW

Red

Orange

Yellow

Green

Blue

Violet

GOAL 2: Learn to Delete

- Deleting is the process of removing text, spaces, graphics or blank lines.
- You can use different procedures to delete text depending on what is being deleted.
- To delete a single character at a time:
  - Press the **Backspace** key to delete a character to the **left** of the insertion point.

  OR
  - Press the **Delete** key to delete a character to the **right** of the insertion point.
- To delete a block of text:
  1. Select the text to be deleted.
  2. Press the Delete key.

     OR

     a. Click Edit menu.

     b. Click Cut.

     OR

     Click Clear.

     OR

     Click Cut button ✂ on the Standard toolbar.
- You can delete one word at a time by using the following keyboard shortcuts:
  - Press Ctrl+Delete to delete one word to the **right** of the insertion point.

  OR
  - Press Ctrl+Backspace to delete one word to the **left** of the insertion point.
- The following proofreaders' marks will be used in this lesson:
  - **Delete:** ℘
  - **Uppercase:** ≡

LESSON 18

Exercise 2
Learn to Delete

1. Open **SAND2**.
2. Make the indicated deletions using the most efficient method for each type of deletion.
3. Compare your work with the book.
4. Resave the document.
5. Print one copy.
6. Close the document window.

HOW SAND IS FORMED

When ~~a solid~~ rock, ~~with or without vugs,~~ is exposed to the wind, rain and frost, it gets broken up into very small *particles*. If these *particles* are small enough, they are then considered **sand**.

~~The main place where~~ most **sand** is formed ~~is~~ at the beach by the seashore. The tide hitting ~~these~~ rocks and the wind rubbing the small rock *particles* ~~together~~ form the **sand**.

The desert is another place where **sand** is commonly found. The **sand** may have been formed ~~over the years~~ by the decay of rocks or by the action of the wind ~~blowing it there.~~ In some cases, the sea dried up and the **sand** was left in what is now known as a desert.

156

GOAL 3: Change Typing Mode: Insert, Typing Replaces Selection and Overtype

Insert Mode

- The default typing mode for all documents is **Insert mode**. As you type new text in Insert mode, the existing text moves to the right and the line endings automatically readjust.

Typing Replaces Selection

- The **Typing Replaces Selection** feature allows you to delete the text and type the new text, simultaneously.
- To use the Typing Replaces Selection feature:
  - Select the text to be deleted.
  - Type the new text.

  The old text is automatically replaced with the new text.

Overtype Mode

- **Overtype mode** is a correction method that is used for an exact letter-for-letter replacement. The new letters are typed <u>over</u> the existing letters. Use this method only when the replacement text has the same number of characters as the original text; otherwise, you will lose additional characters.
  - For example, the names Edward and George both contain six characters. Therefore, to replace one name with the other, you would switch to the Overtype mode, type the new name, then switch back to the Insert mode.
- You can switch to the Overtype mode by double-clicking the **OVR** indicator OVR on the Status bar.
- After making your replacement, be sure to double-click the **OVR** indicator OVR on the Status bar to return to the Insert mode.

LESSON 18

Exercise 3
Typing Replaces Selection

1. Open **INPUT**.
2. Create a header containing your name and the Date field.
3. Create a footer and insert the Filename field.
4. Change the list to double space.
5. Make the following changes:
    a. Using the Typing Replaces Selection feature, change the title to TOOLS FOR CREATING A DOCUMENT.
    b. Make all other indicated deletions using any desired method.
6. Resave the file.
7. Do not close the document window.

~~COMPUTER INPUT DEVICES~~

Double space list

keyboard
mouse
trackball
~~touch pad~~
~~touch screen~~
digitizing pen
drawing tablet
joystick
scanner
~~bar code reader~~
digital camera
video ~~camera~~
microphone

GOAL. 4:   Undo and Redo Functions

- Text may be **restored** after it has been changed and/or resaved. However, once the document has been closed, you will not be able to restore the changes.

- In order to undo a change, select **Undo** from the Edit menu or click the Undo button 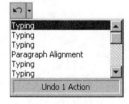 on the Standard toolbar. The keyboard shortcut for Undo is Ctrl+Z.

- Word remembers up to 300 actions and allows you to undo starting from the last action.

- If you choose Undo from the **Edit** menu or use the keyboard shortcut, Ctrl+Z, you undo only one action. Each time you repeat the procedure, you undo a previous action.

- To see a list of the most recent actions, click the arrow next to the Undo button . Click the action you wish to undo. When you undo an action in the list, you also undo all the actions above it.

- If you decide you want to keep the change, select Redo from the Edit menu or click the Redo button on the Standard toolbar. The keyboard shortcut for Redo is Ctrl+Y.

Undo an action

| Typing |
| Typing |
| Typing |
| Paragraph Alignment |
| Typing |
| Typing |
| Undo 1 Action |

Exercise 4
Undo and Redo

1. Place insertion point at the top of the open document.
2. Click the Undo drop-down list on the Standard toolbar and choose the second to last deletion.
   Note: The last two changes will be undone.
3. Redo the last deletion.
4. Resave the file.
5. Print one copy.
6. Close the document window.

LESSON 18

Timed Writing

1. Create a new document.
2. Use the default margins.
3. Change the font to Courier New, 12 point.
4. Create a header containing your name and the date.
5. Create a footer and insert the file name.
6. Take three timings on the following paragraph:
   - ½ minute
   - 1 minute
   - ½ minute
7. Type in wraparound. (Do not press the Enter key at the end of each line.)
8. If you finish before the time is up, start again.
9. Press the Enter key 4 times between each timing.
10. If you make an error, continue typing.
11. See if your final ½ minute timing is faster than your first ½-minute timing.
12. Save the document as **L18TIME**.
13. Print one copy.
14. Close the document window.

	WORDS
There are times when your teacher will return an assignment	12
you handed in and ask you to make changes. If you wrote the	24
assignment, to make the changes you must rewrite the entire	36
assignment. If the computer was used to do your assignment,	48
changing it will only require recalling the file, inserting	60
and deleting some text, and then printing it again.	70

....1....2....3....4....5....6....7....8....9...10...11...12

MOUSE/KEYSTROKE PROCEDURES

Delete a Character

1. Place insertion point to the left of the character to be deleted.
2. Press **Delete** key .... `Del`

Delete a Word

1. Place insertion point to the left of the word to be deleted.
2. Press **Ctrl+Delete** .... `Ctrl` + `Del`

OR

1. Double-click desired word.
2. Press **Delete** key .... `Del`

OR

1. Place insertion point to the right of the word to be deleted.
2. Press **Ctrl+Backspace** ..... `Ctrl` + `Backspace`

Delete a Block of Text

Ctrl+X

1. Select text to delete using highlighting procedures learned in Lesson 11.
2. Click **Cut** button `✂`.

   OR

   Press **Delete** key .... `Del`

Overtype Mode

1. Place insertion point where text is to be overwritten.
2. Double-click **OVR** button `OVR` to enter OVR mode.
3. Type text.
4. Double-click **OVR** button `OVR` to return to Insert mode.

Typing Replaces Selection Option

To turn the Typing Replaces Selection option on:

1. Click **Tools** menu .... `Alt` + `T`
2. Click **Options** .... `O`
3. Click **Edit** tab.
4. Click **Typing replaces selection** to place check in check box .... `T`

Typing Replaces Selection

1. Select text to be replaced.
2. Type new text.

Undo

Ctrl + Z

This procedure is to be used immediately after performing the command you wish to undo.

Click **Undo** button `↺▾`.

OR

1. Click **Edit** .... `Alt` + `E`
2. Click **Undo** .... `U`

Redo

Ctrl+Y

This procedure is to be used immediately after undoing a command.

Click **Redo** button `↻▾`.

OR

1. Click **Edit** menu .... `Alt` + `E`
2. Click **Redo** .... `R`

- Review Delete • Combine Paragraphs
- Type Bulleted Text

Warm-up

1. Create a new document.
2. Set the left and right margins to 1".
3. Type your name and insert the Date field in the header. Insert a Filename field in the footer.
4. Type each line, trying to type faster each time you repeat a line. When you see the vertical lines between phrases, say the phrase to yourself as you type.
5. If you make an error, continue typing.
6. If you have time, repeat the exercise.
7. Save the document as **LES19**.
8. Close the document window.

```
1 a;sldkfjghfjdksla; a;sldkfjghfjdksla; a;sldkfjghfjdksla; ENTER

2 a;sldkfjghfjdksla; a;sldkfjghfjdksla; a;sldkfjghfjdksla; ENTER ENTER


3 fur fun gun gum guy buy but hut jut vug jim dim ENTER

4 fur fun gun gum guy buy but hut jut vug jim dim ENTER ENTER


5 kid red cue my, lot sit wet tex co. fat pat zip qt. ENTER

6 kid red cue my, lot sit wet tex co. fat pat zip qt. ENTER ENTER


7 no no no now now now know know know known known known ENTER

8 no no no now now now know know know known known known ENTER ENTER


9 old sold sold cold cold fold fold gold gold bold bold hold hold ENTER

10 old sold sold cold cold fold fold gold gold bold bold hold hold ENTER ENTER


11 you know|you know|you know|hold no| hold no| hold no ENTER

12 you know|you know|you know|hold no| hold no| hold no ENTER ENTER


13 Zip Jim's wet red coat for him.  Pat, my cat, is in the hut. ENTER

14 Zip Jim's wet red coat for him.  Pat, my cat, is in the hut. ENTER ENTER
```

GOAL 1:   Review Delete

- The delete feature allows you to remove text, graphics, spaces and codes.
- Use any of the following deletion methods:
    - Press the **Delete** key to remove text to the **right** of the insertion point.
    - Press the **Backspace** key to remove text to the **left** of the insertion point.
    - Press **Ctrl+Delete** to remove a word to the **right** of the insertion point.
    - Press **Ctrl+Backspace** to remove a word to the **left** of the insertion point.
    - Select blocks of text to be deleted, then press the **Delete** key or select Cut from the Edit menu.
- Use the **Overtype** mode to replace a word with another word containing the same number of characters. Double-click OVR on the Status bar to activate Overtype mode. Once your change is made, make sure you double-click OVR to return to Insert mode; otherwise, you will lose additional text.
- The **Typing Replaces Selection** mode allows you to select text you want removed and type new text to take its place in one operation.
- The **Undo** feature allows you to undo a change you made to the document. Word keeps a history of the last 300 actions so you can restore a change. Remember, if you restore a change from the Undo list, all of the changes before it (on the list) will also be restored. Use the **Redo** command if you decide you didn't want to undo an action.

Exercise 1
Review Delete

1. Open **PRESENT**.
2. In line 1, use the Typing Replaces Selection feature to change the word "Tips" to "Guidelines."
3. In line 3, change to Overtype mode and replace the word "Involve" with the word "Include." Delete the text "by asking questions" by selecting it and pressing the Delete key.
4. In line 6, use Ctrl+Delete to delete the word "very." Press the Delete key to delete the word "up."
5. Use the Undo feature to restore the last deletion.

LESSON 19

6. Resave the file.
7. Print one copy.
8. Close the document window.

Presentation Tips ~~Tips~~ *Guidelines*

Include Make eye contact
~~Involve~~ your audience ~~by asking questions~~
Show enthusiasm
Use gestures when you want to make a point
Speak ~~very~~ clearly, stand ~~up~~ straight and have fun

GOAL 2:   Combine Paragraphs

- When you want to **combine paragraphs** or **eliminate blank lines**, it is necessary to delete the paragraph marks. You can see the paragraph marks if you click the Show/Hide ¶ button ¶ on the Standard toolbar.

- To delete a paragraph mark, place the insertion point immediately to the left of the paragraph mark and press the **Delete** key.

- Once the paragraphs are combined, you may have to add a space or spaces between the last word of the former first paragraph and the first word of the former second paragraph.

- The proofreaders' mark for combining paragraphs is: *no ¶* (or) *delete ¶*

Exercise 2
Combine Paragraphs

1. Open **PENCIL**.
2. Change line spacing to double.
3. Delete the extra space between the paragraphs.
4. Make the indicated revisions using the most efficient method.
5. Resave the document.
6. Print one copy.
7. Close the document window.

~~THE TRUTH~~ *ALL* ABOUT PENCILS

~~Did you ever wonder how a **pencil** is made?~~ Pencils used to be called "lead pencils" but there is no lead in the pencils ~~made~~ *sold* today. Instead, a **pencil** contains *graphite*.

To make a **pencil**, *graphite* is mixed ~~together~~ with water and clay. This mixture is put into a forming press and ~~it~~ comes out as a thin rope. The rope is cut into pieces and put into ovens to bake. *Delete ¶*

The outside of the **pencil** is made from pine or red cedar. The wood is shaped in halves with a groove ~~to hold~~ *for* the *graphite* rope.

After the *graphite* is inserted into the groove, two halves are glued together. The wooden case is painted, a metal band and ~~an~~ eraser are added, and then you have a **pencil**.

LESSON 19

- A **bullet** is a dot, symbol or graphic image used to emphasize a point of information. It can also be used to list items that do not need to be in a numbered order.

- Select the **Bullets** button on the Formatting toolbar to begin your bulleted list. Type the text to be bulleted and press the Enter key. Word automatically inserts a new bullet when you press the Enter key.

- The default bullet shape is a small circle. You can change the bullet shape by using the Bullets and Numbering dialog box shown below.

Bullets and Numbering dialog box

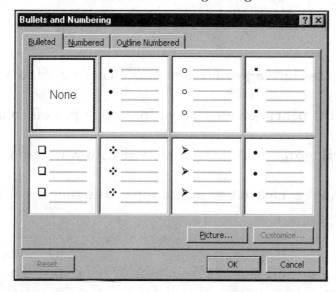

- Follow these steps to access the Bullets and Numbering dialog box:
  1. Click Format menu.
  2. Click Bullets and Numbering.
  3. Click the Bulleted tab.
  4. Click the desired bullet shape.
  5. Click OK.

- You can bullet a list before or after typing the text. Remember to select existing text before bulleting it.

- To end the bulleted list, click the **Bullets** button on the Formatting toolbar or press the Enter key twice.

- You may remove bullets from a bulleted list by selecting the list and clicking the **Bullets** button  on the Formatting toolbar.

- The **Increase Indent** button allows you to indent your bulleted item ½" each time you click the button. Click the **Decrease Indent** button to bring the bulleted item back ½".

    Note: The indentation buttons on the Formatting toolbar may also be used to indent standard paragraph text.

Exercise 3a
Type Bulleted Text

1. Create a new document.
2. Type your name and insert the Date field in the header.
3. Insert the Filename field in the footer.
4. Change the paragraph line spacing to double.
    Note: Use the paragraphs dialog box.
5. Type the exercise on the next page and complete the following steps:
    a. Center the title in a serif font, 14 point, bold.
    b. Type the body text using a serif font, 12 point.
    c. Use the Tab key to indent one Tab stop at the beginning of each paragraph.
    d. Use bullets as indicated.
        Note: Use the Bullets button to bullet the list.
    e. Click the Increase Indent button to indent the bulleted items.
6. Immediately correct errors using the Backspace key.
7. Save the document; name it **MARSUP**.
8. Print one copy.
9. Close the document window.

MARSUPIALS

Marsupials are a classification of animals. Marsupial comes from the Greek word "marsypion," which means pouch. What makes these animals different is that their young, after they are born, live and feed in a pouch on their mother's body. Some of the marsupials that you may see in the zoo are:

- kangaroos

- opossums

- koala bears

- bandicoots

- wombats

Though marsupials once inhabited all parts of the world, today they are found mostly in Australia. The only common marsupial found in North America is the opossum.

Exercise 3b
Type Bulleted Text

1. Create a new document.
2. Type your name and insert the Date field in the header.
3. Insert the Filename field in the footer.
   Note: From this point on, unless otherwise instructed, you will automatically provide the header and footer for each document you save.
4. Change the paragraph line spacing to double.
5. Type the exercise below and do the following:
   a. Center the title in bold.
   b. Indent one tab stop at the beginning of each paragraph using the Tab key.
   c. Use arrow bullets as indicated.
      Note: Use the Bullets and Numbering dialog box to select the new bullet shape.
   d. Press the Increase Indent button two times to indent the bulleted items.
6. Immediately correct errors using the Backspace key.
7. When you are finished, save the document; name it **MODEM**.
8. Compare your work with the book.
9. Print one copy.
10. Close the document window.

WHAT IS A MODEM?

A modem is a piece of equipment that allows your computer to communicate over telephone or cable lines. By using a modem, you can:

➤ access the Internet, bulletin boards, and online services

➤ send and receive electronic mail and faxes

➤ transfer files from one computer to another

➤ gain remote access to other computers

Different modems communicate at different speeds. The fastest type of modem is a cable modem that allows Internet access at very high speeds by using the fiber optic network of the local cable television company. A cable modem is at least one hundred times faster than a modem that uses the telephone lines.

LESSON 19

Timed Writing

1. Create a new document.
2. Type your name and insert the Date field in the header. Insert the Filename field in the footer.
3. Take three timings on the paragraph below: ½ minute, 1 minute and then ½ minute.
4. Type in wraparound. (Do not press the Enter key at the end of each line.)
5. If you finish before the time is up, start again.
6. Press the Enter key 4 times between each timing.
7. Immediately correct errors as you type.
8. See if your final ½-minute timing is faster than your first timing.
9. Save the document as **L19TIME**.
10. Print one copy.
11. Close the document window.

	WORDS
To be sure that you are being fair to yourself, do everything	12
you can to make sure that you are really trying to learn to	24
type by touch. This means that you do not depend on seeing	36
letters on the keyboard or on the keyboarding chart. Also,	48
do not check the computer screen as you are typing. Every	60
step you take to insure against looking will be beneficial.	72

....1....2....3....4....5....6....7....8....9...10...11...12

MOUSE/KEYSTROKE PROCEDURES

Delete Paragraph Marks

1. Click **Show/Hide Paragraphs** button ¶ to show symbols.
2. Place insertion point to the left of the paragraph mark.
3. Press the **Delete** key .... Del

Bullets

1. Place the insertion point where text will be typed.
   OR
   Select text to convert to a bulleted list.

2. Click **Bullets** button .
   OR
   - Click **Format** menu....... Alt +O
   - Click **Bullets and Numbering**.......................... N
   - Click **Bulleted**.............. Alt +B
   - Click desired bullet style......
   - Click **OK** .... Enter

Remove Bullets

1. Select the part of the list from which bullets are to be removed.

2. Click the **Bullets** button .

Increase/Decrease Indent

1. Place insertion point on line to be indented.

2. Click **Increase Indent** button to indent text.
   OR
   Click **Decrease Indent** button to move text back to the left.

LESSON
20

• Learn to Type Number Keys • Review of Insert and Delete
• Review Bulleted List • Create a Customized Bullet

Warm-up

1. Create a new document.
2. Set the left and right margins to 1".
3. Use Click and Type to begin the document 1.5" from the top of the page.
4. Type each line twice. Try to type faster each time you repeat a line. When you see the vertical lines between phrases, say the phrase to yourself as you type. Try to say and type the phrase as one word rather than a group of words.
5. If you make an error, continue typing.
6. If you have time, repeat the exercise.
7. Save the document as **LES20**.
8. Do not close the document window.

---

1 `a;sldkfjghfjdksla; a;sldkfjghfjdksla; a;sldkfjghfjdksla;` ENTER

2 `a;sldkfjghfjdksla; a;sldkfjghfjdksla; a;sldkfjghfjdksla;` ENTER ENTER

3 `fur fun gun gum guy buy but hut jut vug jim dim` ENTER

4 `fur fun gun gum guy buy but hut jut vug jim dim` ENTER ENTER

5 `kid red cue my, lot sit wet tex co. fat pat zip qt.` ENTER

6 `kid red cue my, lot sit wet tex co. fat pat zip qt.` ENTER ENTER

7 `are are are ware ware ware dare dare dare care care care` ENTER

8 `are are are ware ware ware dare dare dare care care care` ENTER ENTER

9 `hare hare hare mare mare mare pare pare pare area area area` ENTER

10 `hare hare hare mare mare mare pare pare pare area area area` ENTER ENTER

11 `are you|are you|are you|are you|are we|are we|are we|are we|` ENTER

12 `are you|are you|are you|are you|are we|are we|are we|are we|` ENTER ENTER

13 `Are Jim's cats sitting by the hut?  Mr. and Mrs. Tex Red are here.` ENTER

14 `Are Jim's cats sitting by the hut?  Mr. and Mrs. Tex Red are here.` ENTER

ENTER

LESSON 20

GOAL 1:   Learn to Type Number Keys

- **Number keys** can be typed using two different sets of keys on the computer keyboard.
  - The row of keys below the function keys contain numbers **1** through **0**. To strike these keys, the home-row fingers move up and slightly to the left. In addition, the **F** and **J** fingers make one reach to the center on the number row keys. When numbers are combined with text, the number row keys are used.

  - The number keypad is located on the right side of the computer keyboard. The number keypad will be covered in Lesson 22. When typing only numbers, the number keypad is used.

Exercise 1a
Practice Number Keys

1. Place your fingers on the home-row keys.
2. Look at the keyboard illustration below.
3. Reach the **A** finger up and to the left to the **Q** and then up again to the **1** and back down to the **A**.
4. Reach the **S** finger up and to the left to the **W** and then up again to the **2** and back down to the **S**.
5. Reach the **D** finger up and to the left to the **E** and then up again to the **3** and back down to the **D**.
6. Reach the **F** finger up and to the left to the **R** and then up again to the **4** and back down to the **F**.
7. Reach the **F** finger up and to the left to the **R** and then up again to the **5** and back down to the **F**.
8. Reach the **J** finger up and to the left to the **Y** and then up again to the **6** and back down to the **J**.
9. Reach the **J** finger up and to the left to the **U** and then up again to the **7** and back down to the **J**.
10. Reach the **K** finger up and to the left to the **I** and then up again to the **8** and back down to the **K**.
11. Reach the **L** finger up and to the left to the **O** and then up again to the **9** and back down to the **L**.
12. Reach the **;** finger up and to the left to the **P** and then up again to the **0** and back down to the **;**.
13. Now try reaching up to the number keys, directly from the home row to the number row.
14. Repeat Steps 3 through 13 without looking at the illustration.

Exercise 1b
Drill Number Keys

1. Press the Enter key 4 times after the warm-up exercise.
2. Type the exercise on the next page, saying each letter and number to yourself as you strike the keys. You may look at the keyboard illustration as you strike each key. Try not to look at your fingers.
3. If you make an error, continue typing.
4. If you have time, repeat the exercise.
5. Resave the document
6. Close the document window.

LESSON 20

1 aq1a aq1a aq1a sw2s sw2s sw2s de3d de3d de3d fr45f fr45f fr45f ENTER
2 aq1a aq1a aq1a sw2s sw2s sw2s de3d de3d de3d fr45f fr45f fr45f ENTER ENTER

3 ju76j ju76j ju76j ki8k ki8k ki8k lo91 lo91 lo91 ;p0; ;p0; ;p0; ENTER
4 ju76j ju76j ju76j ki8k ki8k ki8k lo91 lo91 lo91 ;p0; ;p0; ;p0; ENTER ENTER

5 a1a a1a a1a s2s s2s s2s d3d d3d d3d f4f f4f f4f f5f f5f f5f ENTER
6 a1a a1a a1a s2s s2s s2s d3d d3d d3d f4f f4f f4f f5f f5f f5f ENTER ENTER

7 j6j j6j j6j j7j j7j j7j k8k k8k k8k l9l l9l l9l ;0; ;0; ;0; ENTER
8 j6j j6j j6j j7j j7j j7j k8k k8k k8k l9l l9l l9l ;0; ;0; ;0; ENTER ENTER

9 as 12 as 12 as 12 sad 312 sad 312 sad 312 fad 413 fad 413 fad 413 ENTER
10 as 12 as 12 as 12 sad 312 sad 312 sad 312 fad 413 fad 413 fad 413 ENTER
ENTER

11 dart 3145 dart 3145 dart 3145 free 4433 free 4433 free 4433 ENTER
12 dart 3145 dart 3145 dart 3145 free 4433 free 4433 free 4433 ENTER ENTER

13 joy 796 joy 796 joy 796 kill 8899 kill 8899 kill 8899 up 70 up 70 ENTER
14 joy 796 joy 796 joy 796 kill 8899 kill 8899 kill 8899 up 70 up 70 ENTER
ENTER

GOAL 2:   Review of Insert and Delete

- When inserting text, place the insertion point where you want to type the new text. As you type, the existing text will move to the right. Make sure OVR is **not** selected.

- Press Ctrl+Delete to delete a word to the right of the insertion point. Use Ctrl+Backspace to delete a word to the left of the insertion point.

- After you have inserted or deleted text, check to see that the spacing between words and paragraphs is correct.

- If you need to remove the last change made to the document, click <u>E</u>dit, <u>U</u>ndo, press the **Undo** button ⟲▾ on the Standard toolbar or press Ctrl+Z. Try to undo an action before making any further changes to the document.

- Remember, when you select an action from the Undo list, you undo all actions listed above it. If you want to reverse an undo, click the **Redo** button ⟳▾.

- You will use the following proofreaders' marks in this lesson:
  - Change to uppercase Do you want to live on the <u><u>west</u></u> <u><u>coast</u></u>?
  - Change to lowercase Do you want to go ̶West?

Exercise 2
Insert and Delete

1. Open **REPTILES**.
2. Make the indicated revisions on the following page.
3. Use the most efficient methods to make your changes.
4. Change the line spacing to single.
5. Insert a blank line between the subtitle and the first paragraph.
6. Insert a blank line between each of the remaining paragraphs.
7. Undo the last change.
8. Restore the last change.
9. Resave the file.
10. Print one copy.
11. Close the document window.

ALLIGATORS VS. CROCODILES

What's the Difference?

Do you have ~~trouble~~ *difficulty* telling crocodiles and alligators apart? ~~Well, you are not alone. Both are reptiles,~~ *Many people confuse them* but they are very different animals. Here are some facts to help you identify which one is which.

Alligators have broader snouts and the teeth in the upper jaw overlap the ~~bottom~~ *lower* teeth and hide them from view. They ~~eat a wide variety of animals~~ *have a varied diet* ranging from insects to dogs and pigs. There are different species of alligator, but the longest on record is ~~nineteen~~ *over 19* feet. Do they attack humans? ~~Rarely,~~ according to the experts *, they rarely do.*

Crocodiles are more aggressive than alligators and ~~can be~~ *are easily* identified by the narrower snout and protruding teeth. These protruding teeth give them their distinctive *smile*. They eat birds, fish or larger prey such as deer. *Sizes can vary, with lengths of 30 feet reported for the larger species.* Do crocodiles attack humans?

Here's the bad news: The larger species are known to attack humans.

Now that you ~~can~~ *are able to* identify these animals, you can find them in the southern part of the United States. **Just make sure you don't get too close**.

GOAL 3:   **Review Bulleted List**

- Use the bullet feature to emphasize points of information.

- Bullets can be added before or after typing text.

- You can add a bullet by clicking the **Bullets** button ▦ on the Formatting toolbar or by selecting the Bullets and Numbering option from the Format menu.

- You can also create a bulleted list automatically as you type. Type an asterisk (*), press the Spacebar or Tab key, type the text and press the Enter key. Word automatically starts the next line with a bullet.

- To end the bulleted list, press the Enter key twice after the last bullet.

- You can choose a different bullet character from the Bullets and Numbering dialog box. Once you select a new bullet, the bullet button on the toolbar will apply the most recently selected bullet style.

- To remove bullets, select the bulleted item and click the **Bullets** button ▦ on the Formatting toolbar.

Bullets and Numbering dialog box

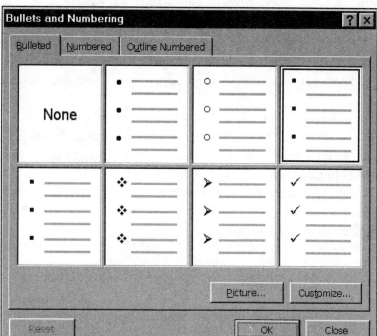

LESSON 20

Exercise 3
Type a Bulleted List

1. Create a new document.
2. Type the exercise below and complete the following steps:
   a. Center the title in a sans serif font, 24 point, bold, blue and outline.
   b. Type the body text in a serif font, 12 point.
   c. Indent one tab stop at the beginning of each paragraph.
   d. Use a square bullet and indent as indicated.
3. Immediately correct errors using the Backspace key.
4. Save the document; name it **EVEREST1**.
5. Compare your work with the book.
6. Print one copy.
7. Close the document window.

Mt. Everest Facts

The Himalayas is the world's tallest mountain range that has 10 of the world's highest peaks. Among them is Mt. Everest, tempting adventurers time and again to reach its summit at 29,028 feet. The conditions are brutal. Freezing temperatures, raging winds and little oxygen have caused many accomplished climbers to meet their deaths on its icy slopes. Here are some facts about Mt. Everest:

- Summit winds can reach over 130 mph.
- Temperatures can be as low as 45 degrees below zero Celsius.
- At 26,000 feet, human beings must use supplemental oxygen to survive.
- The best months to climb are May and October.
- In 1953, Sir Edmund Hillary was the first to officially reach the summit.
- There have been 4,000 attempts to reach the summit.
- Only 669 climbers have succeeded.

Each year there are many expeditions that set out to reach the top; only a few succeed. The lure of the mountain remains for future generations.

GOAL 4: Create a Customized Bullet

- You can add more emphasis or drama to your text by using a **customized bullet.**
- To customize a bullet, you need to select Bullets and <u>N</u>umbering from the F<u>o</u>rmat menu. Click the <u>B</u>ulleted tab, select a bullet type and click Cus<u>t</u>omize. The following Customize Bulleted List dialog box appears.

Customize Bulleted List dialog box

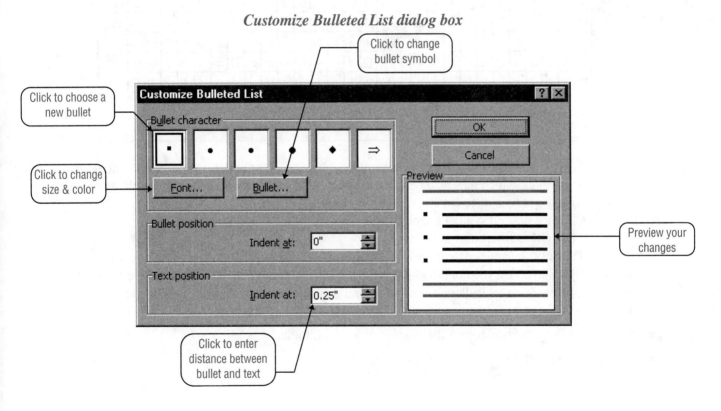

- From the Customize Bulleted List dialog box you may choose one or more of the following options:
  - Click one of the six available bullet options.
  - Click <u>B</u>ullet if you want a different bullet symbol. The following Symbol dialog box displays:

Symbol dialog box

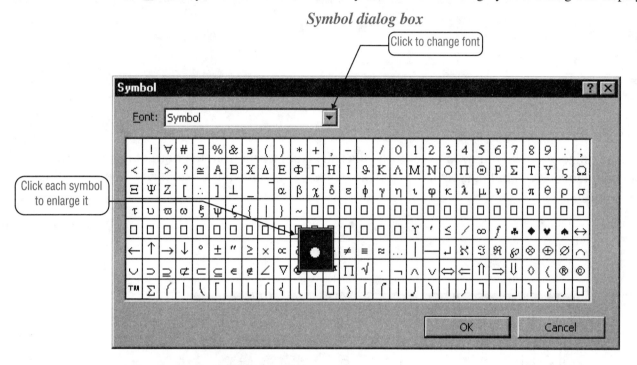

- * The Wingdings or Webdings fonts provide a wide range of bullets. Most fonts contain their own set of symbols, which may also be used as bullets. Click the arrow to the right of the <u>F</u>ont list if you wish to access a different set of symbols.
  - * Click the desired symbol to enlarge the view.
  - * Click OK to insert it as a bullet.
  - * The bullet becomes one of the six options in the Customize Bulleted List dialog box.
- Click <u>F</u>ont to access the Font dialog box where you can change the size, color, and effects.
- Click Indent <u>a</u>t under Bullet position to enter a distance between the bullet and the text.
- Click <u>I</u>ndent at under Text position to change the position of the text.

- Check the Preview box to see the results of your changes.

- Once you are satisfied with the changes, click OK.

Exercise 4
Customize a Bullet

1. Open **EVEREST1** as a Read-only file.
2. Change the document to double-space.
3. Make the revisions indicated on the next page.
4. Click the Bullet option.
5. Select the mountain bullet in the Webdings font box.
6. Click the Font option.
7. Change bullet to 14 point, bold.
8. Click Indent at under Bullet position.
9. Change to .5".
10. Click Indent at under Text position.
11. Change to .75".
12. Undo the second from the last change.
13. Restore the changes.
14. Save the file; name it **EVEREST2**.
15. Print one copy.
16. Close the document window.

Mt. Everest Facts

The Himalayas ~~is~~ *has* the world's tallest mountain ~~range that has 10 of the world's highest peaks.~~ *10 s.* Among them is Mt. Everest, tempting adventurers time and again to reach its summit at 29,028 feet. The conditions are *very* brutal. Freezing temperatures, raging winds and little oxygen have caused many accomplished climbers to meet their deaths on its icy slopes. Here are some *interesting* facts about Mt. Everest:

Change to mountain shape bullet

- Summit winds can reach over 130 mph.

- Temperatures can be as low as 45 degrees below zero Celsius.

- At 26,000 feet, ~~human beings~~ *climbers* must use supplemental oxygen to survive.

- The best months to climb are May and October.

- In 1953, Sir Edmund Hillary was the first to ~~officially~~ reach the summit.

- There have been 4,000 attempts to reach the summit.

- ~~Only 669 climbers have succeeded.~~

Each year there are many expeditions that set out to reach the top *, but* only a few succeed. The ~~lure of the~~ mountain remains for future generations *to conquer*.

Timed Writing

1. Create a new document.
2. Use the default margins.
3. Change the font to Courier New, 12 point.
4. Take three timings on the paragraph below ½ minute, 1 minute and then ½ minute
5. Type in wraparound. (Do not press the Enter key at the end of each line.)
6. If you finish before the time is up, start again.
7. Press the Enter key 4 times between each timing.
8. Do not correct errors. If you make a mistake, continue typing.
9. Highlight all errors.
10. Save the document as **L20TIME**.
11. Print one copy.

	WORDS
If you are not afraid of any animal, there is one animal you	12
would most likely run away from. Can you guess which animal	24
it is? It is the skunk. A skunk is a very friendly animal,	36
and it could make a very good pet. What does make people run	48
away from a skunk is, of course, its odor. A skunk has two	60
scent glands under its tail. The skunk aims and shoots the	72
liquid out in a spray. The scent glands of the skunk can be	84
removed.	85

....1....2....3....4....5....6....7....8....9...10...11...12

MOUSE/KEYSTROKE PROCEDURES

Customize a Bullet

1. Place insertion point where text is to be typed.

   OR

   Select text to be bulleted.
2. Click **Format** menu .... `Alt`+`O`
3. Click **Bullets and Numbering** .... `Alt`+`N`

4. Click **Bulleted** .... `Alt`+`B`
5. Click **Customize** .... `Alt`+`T`
6. Choose from one or more of the following options:
   - Click **Font** .... `Alt`+`F` to change size and color.
   - Click **Bullet** .... `Alt`+`B` to change bullet symbol.

- Click **Indent at** .... `Alt`+`A` to set the bullet position ..... `↕`
- Click **Indent at** .... `Alt`+`I` to set the text position .... `↕`
7. Click **OK** .... `Enter`

<table>
<tr><td>

LESSON
21

</td><td>

- Review Number Keys
- Type Fractions, Mixed Numbers and Ordinal Numbers
- Use Time and Date Expressions • Review Bulleted Lists

</td></tr>
</table>

Warm-up

1. Create a new document.
2. Set the left and right margins to 1".
3. Type each line, trying to type faster when you repeat a line. Press the Enter key twice after you repeat a line. From this exercise forward, the "Enter" symbol will NOT be present in each exercise. Remember to continue to press Enter twice after every second line.
4. When you see the vertical lines between phrases, say the phrase to yourself as you type. Do not type the vertical lines.
5. If you make an error, continue typing.
6. If you have time, repeat the exercise.
7. Save the document as **LES21**.
8. Do not close the document window.

```
1  a;sldkfjghfjdksla; a;sldkfjghfjdksla; a;sldkfjghfjdksla;

2  a;sldkfjghfjdksla; a;sldkfjghfjdksla; a;sldkfjghfjdksla;


3  fur fun gun gum guy buy but hut jut vug jim dim kid red cue

4  fur fun gun gum guy buy but hut jut vug jim dim kid red cue


5  my, lot sit wet tex co. fat pat zip qt. s2l9 d3k8 f4j7 f5j6 ;0

6  my, lot sit wet tex co. fat pat zip qt. s2l9 d3k8 f4j7 f5j6 ;0


7  are are are fare fare fare rare rare rare bare bare bare

8  are are are fare fare fare rare rare rare bare bare bare


9  sear sear sear wear wear wear dear dear dear fear fear fear

10 sear sear sear wear wear wear dear dear dear fear fear fear


11 we are| we are| we are| they are| they are| they are|

12 we are| we are| we are| they are| they are| they are|


13 I fear a fat pat of butter will fall on my cute brown cat.

14 I fear a fat pat of butter will fall on my cute brown cat.
```

GOAL 1: Review Number Keys

- When you type numbers contained within text, you should use the number keys (located in the row below the function keys).

- Place your fingers on the home-row keys.
    1. Reach the **A** finger up to the **1** and back down to the **A**.
    2. Reach the **S** finger up to the **2** and back down to the **S**.
    3. Reach the **D** finger up to the **3** and back down to the **D**.
    4. Reach the **F** finger up to the **4** and back down to the **F**.
    5. Reach the **F** finger up to the **5** and back down to the **F**.
    6. Reach the **J** finger up to the **6** and back down to the **J**.
    7. Reach the **J** finger up to the **7** and back down to the **J**.
    8. Reach the **K** finger up to the **8** and back down to the **K**.
    9. Reach the **L** finger up to the **9** and back down to the **L**.
    10. Reach the **;** finger up to the **0** and back down to the **;**.

LESSON 21

Exercise 1
Practice Number Keys

1. Place the insertion point at the end of the document **LES21**.
2. Press the Enter key 4 times.
3. Type the exercise on the following page, saying each letter and number to yourself as you strike the keys. You may look at the keys in the keyboard illustration as you strike each key. Try not to look at your fingers.
4. For lines 11-14, calculate the total and type the answer at the end of the sentence.
5. If you make an error, continue typing.
6. If you have time, repeat the exercise.
7. Resave the document.
8. Do not close the document window.

1 aq1a aq1a aq1a sw2s sw2s sw2s de3d de3d de3d fr45f fr45f fr45f

2 aq1a aq1a aq1a sw2s sw2s sw2s de3d de3d de3d fr45f fr45f fr45f

3 ju76j ju76j ju76j ki8k ki8k ki8k lo9l lo9l lo9l ;p0; ;p0; ;p0;

4 ju76j ju76j ju76j ki8k ki8k ki8k lo9l lo9l lo9l ;p0; ;p0; ;p0;

5 a1a a1a a1a s2s s2s s2s d3d d3d d3d f4f f4f f4f f5f f5f f5f

6 a1a a1a a1a s2s s2s s2s d3d d3d d3d f4f f4f f4f f5f f5f f5f

7 j6j j6j j6j j7j j7j j7j k8k k8k k8k l9l l9l l9l ;0; ;0; ;0;

8 j6j j6j j6j j7j j7j j7j k8k k8k k8k l9l l9l l9l ;0; ;0; ;0;

9 1 and 2 and 3 and 4 and 5 and 6 and 7 and 8 and 9 and 10

10 1 and 2 and 3 and 4 and 5 and 6 and 7 and 8 and 9 and 10

11 1 plus 11 plus 2 plus 22 plus 3 plus 33 plus 4 plus 44 equals
(type in the total).

12 5 plus 6 plus 7 plus 8 plus 9 plus 10 plus 100 equals
(type in the total).

13 1 plus 10 plus 100 plus 1,000 plus 10,000 minus 50 equals
(type in the total).

14 5 plus 10 plus 15 plus 20 plus 25 plus 30 minus 35 equals
(type in the total).

LESSON 21

GOAL 2:   Type Fractions, Mixed Numbers and Ordinal Numbers

Fractions and Mixed Numbers

- When you type **fractions**, use the slash key  to separate the numerator from the denominator.

- There are no spaces before or after the slash.

- To type a fraction:
    1. Type the numerator.
    2. Type the slash.
    3. Type the denominator.

- **Mixed numbers** are numbers that contain a whole number and a fraction. When typing mixed numbers, type the whole number, a space and then the fraction (as described above). For example, to type 1 5/8, type the 1, a space and then 5/8. If you don't put a space between the whole number and the fraction, it will look like 15/8 (fifteen eighths).

- Word has a special feature that condenses 1/2, 1/4 and 3/4 fractions. When you strike the spacebar (or a punctuation mark) after the denominator, Word automatically condenses the fraction as follows: ½, ¼ or ¾. The numerator is placed above the denominator. This is a default setting.

- If you are typing text containing many fractions or mixed numbers, use the same format for all fractions. Word condenses only the ½, ¼ and ¾ fractions; therefore, you will need to turn off the condensed fraction feature so that all fractions will appear uniform.

- Follow these steps to turn off this feature:
    1. Click Tools menu.
    2. Click AutoCorrect.
    3. Click AutoFormat As You Type tab.
    4. Click Fractions (1/2) with fraction character (½) checkbox to deselect.
    5. Click OK.

AutoCorrect dialog box

Click here to turn off condensed fractions

Ordinal Numbers

- **Ordinal numbers** are numbers of order, such as *first*, *second*, *third*, etc.

- Ordinal numbers can also be written as 1st, 2nd, 3rd, etc.

- When ordinal numbers are expressed as numbers, Word automatically changes the *st, nd* or *rd* to a superscript (smaller, raised text) which takes up the space of one typed character. This is a default setting.

- As you did with fractions, you can change the default to eliminate the superscript. To do this:
  1. Click Tools menu.
  2. Click AutoCorrect.
  3. Click the AutoFormat As You Type tab.
  4. Click the Ordinals (1st) with superscript checkbox to deselect.
  5. Click OK.

LESSON 21

Exercise 2
Fractions, Mixed Numbers and Ordinal Numbers

1. Place the insertion point at the end of the document **LES21**.
2. Press the Enter key 4 times.
3. The AutoFormat As You Type fraction feature should be turned off to type lines 3-6.
4. Type the following exercise saying each letter and number to yourself as you strike the keys. If you make an error, continue typing.
5. If you have time, repeat the exercise.
6. Resave the document.
7. Do not close the document window.

---

1 To add 1/2 plus 1/4 plus 3/4, change all the denominators to 4.

2 When Jim added 3/4 plus 1/4 he calculated the total as 1.

3 The 1st and 2nd place winners received cash and games.

4 The 3rd place recipe uses 2 1/3 lbs. butter and 1/4 cup sugar.

5 To add 4/5 plus 2/25, change all the denominators to 25.

6 Vug 'n Jug stock was selling at 2 7/8, up 1/4 since yesterday.

GOAL 3:   Use Time and Date Expressions

- **Time** can be expressed several different ways. For example:
  - 10 p.m.
  - 10 PM
  - ten o'clock
  - 10:45 a.m.

190

- Note that:
  - There are no spaces between the letters in a.m. or p.m.
  - There are no spaces before or after the colon separating the hour and minutes when expressing the time as 10:45.
  - The number is spelled out when the hour is written with *o'clock* as in ten o'clock.

- You can automatically enter the time in a header or footer using the **Time** button  on the Header and Footer toolbar or by using the <u>I</u>nsert menu to insert the field for Time. The time will automatically be updated whenever the document is reopened or printed.

- **Dates** can also be expressed several different ways. For example:
  - January 27, 1998
  - January 27th
  - January 27
  - 1/27/98

- You can automatically enter the date in a header or footer using the **Date** button on the Header and Footer toolbar or by using the <u>I</u>nsert menu to insert the field for Date. The date will automatically be updated whenever the document is reopened or printed.

Exercise 3
Use Time and Date Expressions

1. Locate the insertion point at the end of the document **LES21**.
2. Press the Enter key 4 times.
3. Type the following exercise, saying each letter and number to yourself as you strike the keys.
4. Immediately correct errors using the Backspace key.
5. If you have time, repeat the exercise.
6. Resave the document.
7. Close the document window.

---

1 Subtract 3/10 from 99/100; tell Guy the answer by one o'clock.

2 Please arrive before 8:30 a.m. on May 10 to claim your prize.

3 I heard 1/8 of the people voted in the election held on 1/21/98.

4 Jim said for the first time 3/4 of the tickets were sold by 12:45 p.m.

5 It is now 2 p.m.; did you vote for the 1st, 2nd and 3rd place winners?

6 Please call Red at 12:45 p.m. on October 25, 1998, to remind him.

LESSON 21

Review Bulleted Lists

- Select the **Bullets** button  on the Formatting toolbar to begin a bulleted list.

- To indent a bulleted list, select the **Increase Indent** button on the Formatting toolbar.

Exercise 4
Paragraphs Containing Numbers and Bullets

1. Create a new document.
2. Use the default margins.
3. Change the paragraph line spacing to double.
4. Type the paragraphs shown on the next page and complete the following steps:
   a. Center the title in a sans serif font, 18 point, bold. Press the Enter key once after the title.
   b. Type the document text in a serif font, 12 point.
   c. Indent one tab stop at the beginning of each paragraph.
   d. Use bullets as indicated, pressing the Indent button once.
5. Immediately correct errors using the Backspace key.
6. When you are finished, save the document; name it **DINO1**.
7. Compare your work with the book.
8. Unbold **B** the title.
9. Italicize **I** all numbers.
10. Resave the document.
11. Print one copy.

DINOSAURS

Did you ever wonder how big a dinosaur was? Dinosaurs came in many different sizes. Some were as small as a chicken while others were larger than a house. For example:

- The Stegosaurus was about *20* feet long and weighed about *2* tons.

- The Brachiosaurus was *60* to *80* feet long and weighed *50* to *80* tons.

- The Diplodocus was *87* feet long and weighed about *11* tons.

These are just a few examples of the many dinosaurs that roamed the earth in prehistoric times.

Timed Writing

1. Create a new document.
2. Use the default margins.
3. Change font to Courier New, 12 point.
4. Take two ½-minute timings from Line 1 on the following page.
   a. If you finish before the time is up, press the Enter key and start again.
   b. Press the Enter key 4 times between each timing.
   c. Do not correct errors. If you make an error, continue typing.
   d. To calculate your WAM (word a minute) speed, double the number of words you typed.
5. Take two more ½-minute timings from Line 2 following the same instructions in Step 4 above.
6. Take two more ½-minute timings from Line 3 following the same instructions in Step 4 above.
7. Take two 1-minute timings on the entire paragraph. Calculate your WAM speed.
8. Compare your speeds.
9. Save the document as **L21TIME**.
10. Print one copy.
11. Close the document window.

LESSON 21

You know that you can run faster for a short period of time   12
than you can for a longer period of time. The same is true   24
in keyboarding. You can type faster for shorter periods of   36
time than you can for longer periods of time. You type for   48
short periods to develop faster speeds and for long periods   60
to develop more and more endurance. Keep this idea in mind   72
at all times and you will get much more out of your effort.   84

....1....2....3....4....5....6....7....8....9...10...11...12

MOUSE/KEYSTROKE PROCEDURES

Change the Default Fraction Format

1. Click **Tools** menu .... Alt + T
2. Click **AutoCorrect** .... A
3. Click **AutoFormat As You Type** tab .... Ctrl + Tab
4. Click **Fractions (1/2) with fraction character (½)** check box .... Alt + F
5. Click **OK** .... Enter

Change the Default Ordinal Format

1. Click **Tools** menu.............. Alt + T
2. Click **AutoCorrect** .... A
3. Click **AutoFormat As You Type** tab .... Ctrl + Tab
4. Clear the check mark from **Ordinals (1st) with superscript** check box...... Alt + O
5. Click **OK** .... Enter

194

• Review Number Keys • Learn the Number Keypad
• Create Numbered Lists • Customize Numbered Lists

Warm-up

1. Create a new document.
2. Set the left and right margins to 1".
3. Type each line, trying to type faster when you repeat a line. Press the Enter key twice after you repeat a line.
4. When you see the vertical lines between phrases, say the phrase to yourself as you type. Do not type the vertical lines.
5. If you make an error, continue typing.
6. If you have time, repeat the exercise.
7. Save the document as **LES22**.
8. Do not close the document window.

```
1 a;sldkfjghfjdksla; a;sldkfjghfjdksla; a;sldkfjghfjdksla;
2 a;sldkfjghfjdksla; a;sldkfjghfjdksla; a;sldkfjghfjdksla;

3 fur fun gun gum guy buy but hut jut vug jim dim kid red cue
4 fur fun gun gum guy buy but hut jut vug jim dim kid red cue

5 my, lot sit wet tex co. fat pat zip qt. s2l9 d3k8 f4j7 f5j6 ;0
6 my, lot sit wet tex co. fat pat zip qt. s2l9 d3k8 f4j7 f5j6 ;0

7 kid did kid rid kid bid kid hid kid lid kid mid kid
8 kid did kid rid kid bid kid hid kid lid kid mid kid

9 red wed red fed red Ted red bed red led red ped red
10 red wed red fed red Ted red bed red led red ped red

11 who are| what are| where are| why are| when are|
12 who are| what are| where are| why are| when are|

13 Jim and Pat will buy a qt. of red cherries for Tex Vug.
14 Jim and Pat will buy a qt. of red cherries for Tex Vug.
```

LESSON 22

- When striking the number keys located in the row below the function keys, your home-row fingers move up and slightly to the left. The only exception is the **F** finger reaches up to the right to strike the **5** key.

Exercise 1
Review Number Keys

1. Place the insertion point at the end of the document **LES22** and press the Enter key 4 times.
2. Type the exercise shown on the following page, saying each letter and number to yourself as you strike the keys. You may look at the keyboard illustration as you strike each key. Try not to look at your fingers.
3. Press the Enter key twice after each set of two lines.
4. If you make an error, continue typing.
5. If you have time, repeat the exercise.
6. Resave the document.
7. Do not close the document window

1 fur 474 fun 476 gun 576 gum 577 guy 576 buy 576 hut 665
2 fur 474 fun 476 gun 576 gum 577 guy 576 buy 576 hut 665

3 jut 775 vug 575 jim 787 dim 387 kid 883 red 433 cue 373
4 jut 775 vug 575 jim 787 dim 387 kid 883 red 433 cue 373

5 lot 995 sit 285 wet 235 tex 532 fat 415 pat 015 zip 180
6 lot 995 sit 285 wet 235 tex 532 fat 415 pat 015 zip 180

7 Less than 1/2 of the group left the hut on time on 3/30/97.
8 The 1ˢᵗ, 2ⁿᵈ, and 5ᵗʰ place winners will arrive by 8:30 a.m.

9 The class of 2000 will hold its graduation on May 6 at 10 a.m.
10 To subtract 1/8 from 5/16, change the denominators to 16.

GOAL 2:   Learn the Number Keypad

- When typing text that contains only numbers, it is usually easier to use the **number keypad**. The number keypad is the group of keys located on the right side of the keyboard.

- In order to use the number keypad to type numbers, **NumLock** must be turned on. The NumLock (number lock) key is in the top-left corner of the number keypad. You will be able to tell if NumLock is turned on by looking above the NumLock key. There is usually an indicator light that turns on when the number lock is activated.

Number keypad

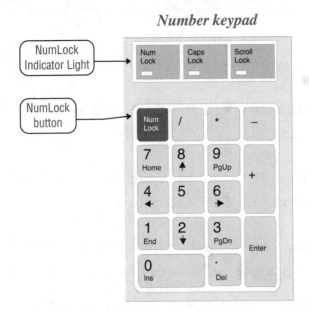

- Just as you position your fingers on the home row of the alphabetic keyboard, you also position your fingers on the home row of the number keypad. Four fingers of your right hand are kept on the number keypad home row:
  - The right index finger (**J** finger) on the **4**.
  - The right middle finger (**K** finger) on the **5**.
  - The right ring finger (**L** finger) on the **6**.
  - The right thumb on the **0**, which is located on the bottom row.
  - Note the finger placement on the illustration below.

- Your right pinky (**;** finger) is used for the Enter key on the number keypad.

- There is usually a raised dot or dash on the **5** so that when you touch type you will be able to feel your fingers in the right place on the home row of the number keypad.

- There are special character keys on the number keypad. They are the / (diagonal or division sign), * (asterisk or multiplication sign), - (hyphen or minus sign) and + (plus or addition sign).

Exercise 2a
Number Keypad Home Row Placement

1. Place the right hand on the number keypad keys as instructed below. Refer to the keypad illustration on the previous page for correct placement.
   - Right index finger on the **4**.
   - Right middle finger on the **5**.
   - Right ring finger on the **6**.
   - Right thumb on the **0**.
2. Feel the dot or dash on the **5** key.
3. Take your right hand off the keypad.
4. Look at the number keypad and place your right hand back on the home-row keys.
5. Feel the dot on the **5** key.
6. Repeat Steps 3-5 twice.
7. Take your right hand off the keypad.
8. Put it back without looking at the number keypad. Feel the dot or dash on the **5** key.
9. Look down at the number keypad to see if you placed your fingers correctly.
10. Repeat Steps 7 and 9 twice.
11. Check to see that NumLock is turned on.
12. Place your fingers on the number keypad home-row keys as shown on the previous page.
13. Look at the keypad illustrated on the previous page. Touch the **4** key.
14. Move your **4** finger up to touch the **7** and back to the **4**.
15. Move your **4** finger down to touch the **1** and back to the **4**.
16. Move your **5** finger up to touch the **8** and back to the **5**.
17. Move your **5** finger down to touch the **2** and back to the **5**.
18. Move your **6** finger up to touch the **9** and back to the **6**.
19. Move your **6** finger down to touch the **3** and back to the **6**.
20. Move your **6** finger down to the bottom row to touch the **.** and back to the **6**.
21. Move your **4** finger up to touch the **7** and back to the **4**.
22. Touch the **0** with your thumb.
23. Touch the Enter key with your right pinky.
24. Practice the following reaches:
    - Move your **5** finger up to touch the **/** and back to the **5**.
    - Move your **6** finger up to touch the ***** and back to the **6**.
    - Move your **6** finger up to touch the **–** and back to the **6**.
    - Move your **6** finger to the left to touch the **+** and back to the **6**.

LESSON 22

Exercise 2b
Use the Number Keypad

1. Place the insertion point at the end of the document **LES22** and press the Enter key 4 times.
2. Type the following exercise, saying each number to yourself as you strike the key. You may look at the keypad illustration as you strike each key. Try not to look at your fingers.
3. The numbers have been grouped together to make them easier to read. Do not type the vertical line between number groups.
4. Press the Enter key twice after each set of two lines.
5. If you make an error, continue typing.
6. Now type the same exercise without looking at the diagram or your fingers.
7. When you are finished, compare your screen with the book.
8. Resave the document.
9. Close the document window.

1 444555666|456|456|456|474|474|474|414|414|414|
2 444555666|456|456|456|474|474|474|414|414|414|

3 444555666|456|456|456|585|585|585|525|525|525|
4 444555666|456|456|456|585|585|585|525|525|525|

5 666555444|696|696|696|636|636|636|63.6|63.6|63.6|
6 666555444|696|696|696|636|636|636|63.6|63.6|63.6|

7 456|789|456|123|410|410|410|6.36|6.36|6.36|
8 456|789|456|123|410|410|410|6.36|6.36|6.36|

9 5/5/5|6*6*6|6-6-6|6+6+6|5/5/5|6*6*6|6-6-6|6+6+6
10 5/5/5|6*6*6|6-6-6|6+6+6|5/5/5|6*6*6|6-6-6|6+6+6

GOAL 3:   Create Numbered Lists

- You can number items in a list in the same way you added bullets to a list. Use the **numbered list** feature to number items that need to be in a particular order. Numbers can be added to new or existing text.

- Place the insertion point where you want to begin your list and click the **Numbering** button on the Formatting toolbar to begin the numbered list. If you wish to add numbers to a previously typed list, select the text to be numbered then click the **Numbering** button.

- You can also number a list by using the Bullets and Numbering dialog box shown below. Click Format, Bullets and <u>N</u>umbering, and select the <u>N</u>umbered tab in the Bullets and Numbering dialog box.

Bullets and Numbering dialog box

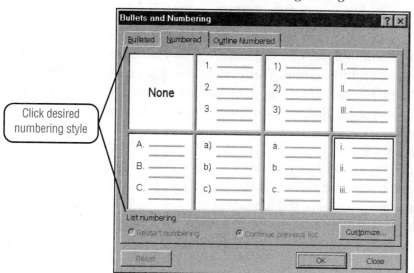

- You can create a numbered list as you type. Type a number followed by a period, press either the Spacebar or the Tab key and then type the text. When you press the Enter key, Word automatically inserts the next number in the sequence.

- To stop numbering, press the Enter key twice, or click the **Numbering** button on the Formatting toolbar.

- You can convert a bulleted list to a numbered list by selecting the list and then clicking the Numbering button or by using the Bullets and Numbering dialog box.

Exercise 3
Type a Numbered List

1. Create a new document.
2. Type the title in a sans serif font, 14 point, bold.
3. Press the Enter key twice.
4. Type the remaining text in a serif font, 12 point.
5. Press the Tab key to indent the paragraph.
6. Press the Enter key twice after the paragraph and begin the numbered list using any desired method.
7. Immediately correct errors using the Backspace key.
8. When you are finished, save the document; name it **JOBS**.
9. Compare your work with the book.
10. Print one copy.

TOP JOBS

An additional 18.6 million jobs are expected by the year 2006. The greatest areas of growth are for jobs that require additional education past high school. Within the next 5 to 7 years, most of these top jobs are likely to be in the computer and health fields. Here's a sampling of occupations that are estimated to have better than average growth.

1. Computer support specialists will increase by 118 percent.
2. Computer engineers will increase by 109 percent.
3. Personal and home care aides will increase by 85 percent.
4. Physical therapy assistants and aides will increase by 79 percent.
5. Home health aides will increase by 76 percent.
6. Medical assistants will increase by 74 percent.
7. Desktop publishing specialists will increase by 74 percent.
8. Occupational therapists will increase by 69 percent.
9. Paralegals will increase by 68 percent.
10. Special education teachers will increase by 66 percent.

GOAL 4: Customize Numbered Lists

■ You can customize numbers as you did bullets. Follow these instructions to customize number style:
1. Click Format menu.
2. Click Bullets and Numbering.
3. Click the Numbered tab.
4. Click one of the styles.
5. Click Customize.
6. Choose one or more of the following options from the dialog box, as shown below:
   - **Number format**   Adds text before or after the number.
   - **Number style**   Provides various numbering styles.
   - **Font**   Allows changes to Font via the Font dialog box.
   - **Start at:**   Sets the starting number for the list.
   - **Number position**   Sets where the number will start (left, centered, right).
   - **Aligned at:**   Sets the distance of numbers from the left margin.
   - **Indent at:**   Sets the distance between the number and the text.
7. Check the Preview window to see the results of your selections.

Customize Numbered List dialog box

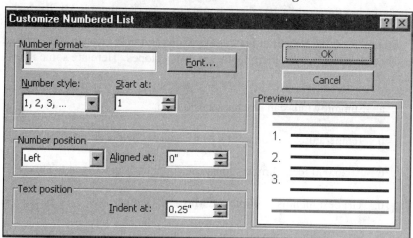

LESSON 22

Exercise 4
Customize Numbered List

1. Open **EVEREST2**.
2. Using the Font dialog box, change the title to a different sans serif font, 20 point, italic and shadow.
3. Change the line spacing to single.
4. Press the Enter key between each paragraph, including the bulleted list paragraphs.
5. Start the first and last paragraphs at the left margin by deleting the first-line indents.
6. Select the bulleted list and convert to lowercase letters. Use the Bullets and Numbering dialog box and select the third numbering style in the bottom row.
7. Click the Customize button and change the Aligned at: option to .75". Change the Indent at: feature to 1".
8. When you are finished, compare your results with the book.
9. Resave the document.
10. Print one copy.
11. Close the document window.

Mt. Everest Facts

The Himalayas has the world's 10 tallest mountains. Among them is Mt. Everest, tempting adventurers time and again to reach its summit at 29,028 feet. The conditions are very brutal. Freezing temperatures, raging winds and little oxygen have caused many accomplished climbers to meet their deaths on its icy slopes. Here are some interesting facts about Mt. Everest:

a. Summit winds can reach over 130 mph.

b. Temperatures can be as low as 45 degrees below zero Celsius.

c. At 26,000 feet, climbers must use supplemental oxygen to survive.

d. The best months to climb are May and October.

e. In 1953, Sir Edmund Hillary was the first to reach the summit.

f. There have been 4,000 attempts to reach the summit.

Each year there are many expeditions that set out to reach the top, but only a few succeed. The mountain remains for future generations to conquer.

Timed Writing

1. Create a new document.
2. Use the default margins.
3. Change font to Courier New, 12 point.
4. Take two ½-minute timings from Line 1.
   a. If you finish before the time is up, press the Enter key and start again.
   b. Press the Enter key 4 times between each timing.
   c. Do not correct errors. If you make an error, continue typing.
   d. To calculate your WAM speed, double the number of words you typed.
5. Take two more ½-minute timings from Line 2 following the same instructions in Step 4 above.
6. Take two more ½-minute timings from Line 3 following the same instructions in Step 4 above.
7. Take two 1-minute timings on the entire paragraph. Calculate your WAM speed.
8. Compare your speeds.
9. Save the document as **L22TIME**.
10. Print one copy.
11. Close the document window.

	WORDS
Since the only way to measure your typing speed is by taking	12
timings, you should learn all the little tricks of relaxing	24
before getting the signal to start the timing. When you are	36
getting ready for a series of timings, make a real effort to	48
relax your fingers, arms, and shoulders. Do not hold down	60
the shift key while waiting for the signal to begin typing.	72
You will just build up tension in the hand being used. Wait	84
for the signal and start off smoothly.	91

```
....1....2....3....4....5....6....7....8....9...10...11...12
```

MOUSE/KEYSTROKE PROCEDURES

Create a Numbered List

1. Place the insertion point where text will be typed or select block of text to convert to a numbered list.
2. Click **Format** menu .... `Alt`+`O`
3. Click **Bullets and Numbering** ... `N`
4. Click **Numbered** tab.......... `Alt`+`N`
5. Choose the desired number style.
6. Click **OK** .... `Enter`

Customize a Numbered List

1. Click **Format**.................... `Alt`+`O`
2. Click **Bullets and Numbering**.... `N`
3. Click **Numbered tab** .... `Alt`+`N`
4. Choose a number style.
5. Click **Customize** .... `Alt`+`T`
6. Choose customization options.
   a. **Number format**............ `Alt`+`O`
   b. **Number style**............... `Alt`+`N`
   c. **Font** .... `Alt`+`F`
   d. **Start at:** .... `Alt`+`S`
   e. **Number position** .... `↓`
   f. **Aligned at:**.................. `Alt`+`A`
   g. **Indent at:** .... `Alt`+`I`
7. Click **OK** .... `Enter`

LESSON 23

- Review Number Keys and Keypad
- Learn Special Character Keys
- Review Numbered Lists

Warm-up

1. Create a new document.
2. Set the left and right margins to 1".
3. Type each line, trying to type faster when you repeat the line. Press the Enter key twice after you repeat the line.
4. When you see the vertical lines between phrases, say the phrase to yourself as you type. Do not type the vertical lines.
5. If you make an error, keep typing.
6. If you have time, repeat the exercise.
7. Save the document as **LES23**.
8. Do not close the document window.

```
1 a;sldkfjghfjdksla; a;sldkfjghfjdksla; a;sldkfjghfjdksla;
2 a;sldkfjghfjdksla; a;sldkfjghfjdksla; a;sldkfjghfjdksla;

3 fur fun gun gum guy buy but hut jut vug jim dim kid red cue my, lot sit
4 fur fun gun gum guy buy but hut jut vug jim dim kid red cue my, lot sit

5 wet tex co. fat pat zip qt. s2l9 d3k8 f4j7 f5j6 ;0
6 wet tex co. fat pat zip qt. s2l9 d3k8 f4j7 f5j6 ;0

7 cue Sue cue due cue rue cue hue cue blue cue true cue
8 cue Sue cue due cue rue cue hue cue blue cue true cue

9 lot dot lot cot lot rot lot tot lot got lot hot lot not lot
10 lot dot lot cot lot rot lot tot lot got lot hot lot not lot

11 and my|are my|will my|for my|still my|can my|
12 and my|are my|will my|for my|still my|can my|

13 Pat's wet red and blue dress was made by the Tex Co.
14 Pat's wet red and blue dress was made by the Tex Co.
```

LESSON 23

GOAL 1:   Review Number Keys and Keypad

- When you are typing numbers along with alphabetic text, use the number keys on the regular keyboard.
- When you type text that contains only numbers, use the number keypad.

Exercise 1a
Review Number Keys

1. Press the Enter key twice.
2. Check to make sure that the "Internet and Network paths with hyperlinks" feature has been deselected (see Lesson 12, Mouse/Keystroke Procedures section, for instructions).
3. Type the following exercise, saying each letter and number to yourself as you strike the keys. Use the regular keyboard number keys to type the numbers. Refer to the keyboard illustration on the previous page for the proper reaches. Try not to look at the keys.
4. If you make an error, keep typing.
5. If you have time, repeat the exercise.
6. Resave the document.

1 More than ¼ of the guys who work for the Zip Co. chew gum.
2 The phone in the hut rang at 12:45, 2:30, 6:39, and 9:18.

3 Look for the 16 fat wet ducks; they should arrive by 7/23/98.
4 Pat said you can seat 15 on the 1st step and 20 on the 2nd step.

5 By 5:15 p.m. the 1st and 2nd place winners should be decided.
6 My web site, www.utype2.com, had 4,675 visitors as of 12/30/98.

Exercise 1b
Review Number Keypad

1. Press the Enter key twice.
2. Type the exercise using the number keypad.
3. Refer to the number keypad illustration for proper reaches.
4. The numbers have been grouped together to make it easier to read. Do not space between the groups of numbers. Do not type the vertical lines.
5. If you make an error, keep typing.
6. If you have time, repeat the entire exercise.
7. Resave the document.

1 445566|456|654|644|655|666|455|466|444|000|0456|

2 4174|5825|6936|40|50|60|123|456|789|7410|8520|9630|

3 4.4|5.5|6.6|.369|.258|.147|.0147|.963|.852|.741|.7410|

4 456|456|456|789|789|789|123|123|123|000|011|022|3.3

GOAL 2:   Learn Special Character Keys

- **Special character** keys are also called **symbol keys**.

- You have already learned some of the special character keys: < (less than), > (greater than) and / (diagonal).

- The following special character keys may be located in different places on different keyboards or may not be present on certain keyboards: ~ `

- Most of the special character keys can be found on the top row of the keyboard and on the top half of the number keys. To type these special characters, the Shift key must be used.

- To learn the reaches refer to the table provided on the next two pages.
  - The first column contains the **symbol** to be learned.
  - The second column states which **finger** is used to type the symbol.
  - The third column gives the **reach** to the symbol.
  - The fourth column gives the **spacing** before and after the symbol.

LESSON 23

Symbol	Finger	Reach	Spacing
!	**A** finger	Reach to **1**, press **right Shift** key, strike **1** to get **!**. Return to home row.	No space before; two spaces after. Ex: Help me! Help me!
@ (at sign)	**S** finger	Reach to **2**, press **right Shift** key, strike **2** to get @. Return to home row.	One space before and after. Ex: 3 lbs. @ .50 per lb.
# (number sign if before a number pound sign if after a number)	**D** finger	Reach to **3**, press **right Shift** key, strike **3** to get #. Return to home row.	When used as a number sign, one space before; no space after. Ex: #45 When used as a pound sign, no space before; one space after. Ex: 45#
$ (dollar sign)	**F** finger	Reach to **4**, press **right Shift** key, strike **4** to get $. Return to home row.	One space before; no space after. Ex: $25
% (percent sign)	**F** finger	Reach to **5**, press **right Shift** key, strike **5** to get %. Return to home row.	No space before; one space after. Ex: 100%
^ (caret)	**J** finger	Reach to **6**, press **left Shift** key, strike **6** to get the ^. Return to home row.	One space before and after. Ex: The ^ means to insert text.
& (ampersand)	**J** finger	Reach to **7**, press **left Shift** key, strike **7** to get **&**. Return to home row.	One space before and after. Ex: Henry & Sons
* (asterisk)	**K** finger	Reach to **8**, press **left Shift** key, strike **8** to get *. Return to home row.	When following a word, no space before; one space after. Ex: Use the MLA* style. When used at the end of a sentence, no space before; two spaces after. Ex: Help!* Call 911. When used for footnotes, no space after. Ex: *Dembel, p. 3.

Symbol	Finger	Reach	Spacing
((left parenthesis)	**L** finger	Reach to **9**, press **left Shift** key, strike **9** to get (. Return to home row.	One space before; no space after. Ex: (see below).
) (right parenthesis)	; finger	Reach to **0**, press **left Shift** key, strike **0** to get). Return to home row.	No space before; one space after. Ex: Say yes (or no) now.
- (hyphen)	; finger	Reach to -. Return to home row.	No space before or after. Ex: self-esteem Use two hyphens to make a dash. *Note: Word will automatically convert the dash into a solid line.* No spaces before or after. Ex: Get it—now!
_ (underline)	; finger	Reach to -, press **left Shift** key, strike - to get _. Return to home row.	Spacing varies depending on use. Ex: Use for signature line. Ex: By: _____
= (equal sign)	; finger	Reach to =. Return to home row.	One space before and after. Ex: 2 - 1 = 1
+ (plus sign)	; finger	Reach to =, press the **left Shift** key, strike = to get +. Return to home row.	One space before and after. Ex: 2 + 2 = 4
[(left bracket)	; finger	Reach up and right, strike the [bracket. Return to the ;.	One space before; no space after.
] (right bracket)	; finger	Reach up and over more] bracket. Return to the ;.	No space before; one space after. Ex: Ten [10] hats
{ (left French bracket)	; finger	Reach to the ;, press the **left Shift** key, strike ; to get {. Return to the ;.	One space before; no space after.
} (right French bracket)	; finger	Reach up and over more to right, press the **left Shift** key strike the }. Return to the ;.	No space before; one space after. Ex: He {she} cooks eggs.

LESSON 23

Exercise 2a
Special Character Keys

1. Place your fingers on the home-row keys.
2. Look at the keyboard illustration.
3. Practice the reaches in the 3 column of the table 5 times each.
4. Repeat Step 3 again without looking at the chart.

Exercise 2b
Practice Number and Special Character Keys

1. Press the Enter key twice.
2. Type the exercise on the next page, saying each letter, number or special character to yourself as you strike the keys. You may look at the keys on the keyboard illustration as you strike each key. Try not to look at your fingers.
3. If you make an error, keep typing.

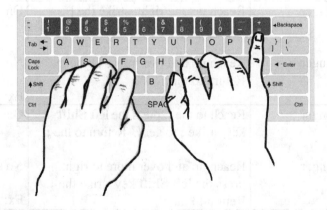

1 s2@s s2@s s2@s d3#d d3#d d3#d f4$f f4$f f4$f f5%f f5%f f5%f
2 j6^j j6^j j6^j j7&j j7&j j7&j k8*k k8*k k8*k l9(l l9(l l9(l

3 ;0); and ;0); and ;-_; and ;-_; and ;=+; and ;=+;
4 Please calculate the formula if x = 5:   3x + (x-2) - x.

5 The caret, ^, is used to indicate something is being inserted.
6 The left and right parentheses, ( ), are used around optional text.

7 The at symbol, @, is used in e-mail addresses or for prices.
8 If 72% bring #2 pencils to the test, what will the other 18% use?

9 Please read my home page—find it at http://www.type_2.com.
10 An asterisk, *, is used at the end of a page to add an explanation.

LESSON 23

Exercise 2c
Type Special Character Keys

1. Press the Enter key twice.
2. Type the following exercise. Try not to look at your fingers.
3. If you make an error, keep typing.
4. If you have time, repeat the exercise.
5. Resave the file.
6. Do not close the document.

---

1 Please ask [or tell] Pat that Jim will not go to the hut.

2 I saw Jim {James} Zip going to the Zip Co. store yesterday.

3 Zip & Co. headquarters are located at 32 Bunker Hill, Apt. #17.

4 Send me a message at vugfungum@cue.com if you are going.

5 One dozen #2 red pencils will cost you $12 (12 @ $1 each).

6 Don't forget to use the ^ to insert the missing words!

7 If Joe worked 20 hours @ $6.50 per hour, his gross pay is
   (calculate the total)

8 If Al earned $125 with $75 deducted in taxes, his take-home pay is
   (calculate the total)

9 Henry sold 125 CDs, 45 videos and 65 tapes for a total of
   (calculate the total) items.

10 If Zack's grades are 90, 85, 75, 95 and 70, his average is
   (calculate the total)

GOAL 3:   Review Numbered Lists

- Use the numbered list feature to number items that need to be placed in a particular order.

- You can create a numbered list before or after typing the text.

- To begin numbering:
  - Click the **Numbering** button [icon] on the Formatting toolbar.

  OR
  1. Click Format menu.
  2. Bullets and Numbering.
  3. Click the Numbered tab.
  4. Click desired numbering style
  5. Click OK.

- You can create a numbered list as you type. Type the number and a period, press the Tab key or spacebar and type the text. When you press the Enter key the next number in the sequence displays.

- To make changes to the number format, click the Customize button in the Bullets and Numbering dialog box. You can make one or more of the following changes:
  - Font, font size and style
  - Number format
  - Starting number
  - Numbering style
  - Number position and alignment
  - Amount the number is indented from the left margin

- To end numbering, click the **Numbering** button [icon] on the Formatting toolbar, or press the Enter key twice.

Exercise 3
Numbered Lists

1. Create a new document.
2. Set the left and right margins to 1".
3. Center the document vertically.
4. Type the title provided in the illustration on the next page. Use a sans serif font, 16 point, bold.
5. Center the title.
6. Press the Enter key once after the title.
7. Type remaining text in a serif font, 12 point.
8. Do not do any calculations until directed to do so in the last paragraph.
9. Use the numbered list feature as follows:
   a. Select the first numbering option.
   b. Make the following changes in the Customize dialog box:
      - Change the number to a 9 point font size.
      - Change Aligned at: to .5".
      - Change Indent at: to .75".
10. Double space the document (including the numbered list).
    Note: Select text to be spaced. Press Ctrl+2 for double spacing.
11. Calculate and type the answer in the last sentence.
12. Type your answer two spaces after the colon in the last sentence. Add a period to complete the sentence.
13. Save the file; name it **BUDGETS**.
14. Print one copy.
15. Close the document window.

BUDGETS

How are you meeting your expenses? Do you work (babysit or mow lawns), or do your parents give you an allowance? Are you old enough to work at a fast-food place and earn a weekly salary? Do you get bonus money if you get 100% on a test? No matter how you "earn" money, you should budget wisely so you can meet your expenses.

Here are some typical* expenses you may incur now or in the near future:

1. Car expenses—5 gallons of gas per week @ $1.20 per gallon (multiply 5 * $1.20).

2. Entertainment—movies and/or bowling at least once per week @ $8.00 per event.

3. Food—eating out @ approximately $6.00 per meal (probably costs more).

Calculate the total expenses in lines 1-3. Assume that you go to one movie and eat one meal out a week. How much would you have to earn each week to save $40.00 each month, assuming there are four weeks to a month? The answer is: (*type your answer here*).

*Expenses may vary.

LESSON 23

Timed Writing

1. Create a new document.
2. Use the default margins.
3. Change font to Courier New, 12 point.
4. Take two ½-minute timings from Line 1.
    a. If you finish before the time is up, press the Enter key and start again.
    b. Press the Enter key 4 times between each timing.
    c. Do not correct errors. If you make a mistake, continue typing.
    d. To calculate your WAM speed, double the number of words you typed.
5. Take two more ½-minute timings from Line 2 following the same instructions in Step 4 above.
6. Take two more ½-minute timings from Line 3 following the same instructions in Step 4 above.
7. Take two 1-minute timings on the entire paragraph. Calculate your WAM speed.
8. Compare your speeds.
9. Save the document as **L23TIME**.
10. Print one copy.
11. Close the document window.

WORDS

Now that you are learning to touch type, you will want to	12
use the computer to do more and more typing. The exercises	24
you are typing help you to build up your speed and accuracy.	36
Soon you will be using Microsoft Word to put your own words	48
on to the computer screen. You will be able to use Word to	60
type up your own homework or reports. You may even want to	72
type letters to your friends. You are beginning to see that	84
all the time you have put into learning to type will assist	96
you for the rest of your life. No matter what you do, you	108
will always have the touch typing skill you are developing	120
to use a computer efficiently.	126

....1....2....3....4....5....6....7....8....9...10...11...12

LESSON 24

- Review Special Character Keys
- Move or Copy Text

Warm-up

1. Create a new document.
2. Set the left and right margins to 1".
3. Type each line, trying to type faster when you repeat a line. Press the Enter key twice after you repeat the line.
4. When you see the vertical lines between phrases, say the phrase to yourself as you type. Do not type the vertical lines.
5. If you make an error, continue typing.
6. If you have time, repeat the exercise.
7. Save the document as **LES24**. Do not close the document window.

```
 1 a;sldkfjghghfjdksla; a;sldkfjghfjdksla; a;sldkfjghfjdksla;
 2 a;sldkfjghghfjdksla; a;sldkfjghfjdksla; a;sldkfjghfjdksla;

 3 fur fun gun gum guy buy but hut jut vug jim dim kid red cue
 4 fur fun gun gum guy buy but hut jut vug jim dim kid red cue

 5 my, lot sit wet tex co. fat pat zip qt. s219 d3k8 f4j7 f5j6 ;0
 6 my, lot sit wet tex co. fat pat zip qt. s219 d3k8 f4j7 f5j6 ;0

 7 sit wit sit fit sit bit sit hit sit mit sit lit sit pit sit
 8 sit wit sit fit sit bit sit hit sit mit sit lit sit pit sit

 9 wet set wet get wet bet wet yet wet met wet let wet pet wet
10 wet set wet get wet bet wet yet wet met wet let wet pet wet

11 let me|let my|let our|let you|let her|let his|
12 let me|let my|let our|let you|let her|let his|

13 Will Pat let Jim buy gum for the guy in the red hat?
14 Will Pat let Jim buy gum for the guy in the red hat?
```

221

LESSON 24

- Some special character keys, such as ~ (tilde) and ` (accent), are located in different places or in different combinations on different keyboards, or may not be present on certain keyboards. Locate these keys and find the correct reaches for them.

- The following special characters are repeated on the number keypad: **/ * - +**. Turn the NumLock key on to access them. Practice the reaches for those keys.

Exercise 1a
Review Special Character Keys

1. Review special character reaches by referring to the Special Characters table on pages 212 and 213.
2. Place your fingers on the home-row keys.
3. Practice the reaches in column 3 of the Special Characters table 3 times.

Exercise 1b
Special Character Keys

1. Press the Enter key twice after the warm-up exercise.
2. Change font to Courier New, 12 point.
3. Check to make sure that "Internet and network paths with hyperlinks" feature has been deselected. (See Lesson 12, Mouse/Keystroke Procedures section, for instructions.)
4. Type the following exercise twice, saying each letter and number to yourself as you strike the keys. You may look at the keys on the keyboard illustration as you strike each key. Try not to look at your fingers.
5. If you make an error, continue typing.
6. If you have time, repeat the exercise.
7. Resave and close the document.

1 a1!a a1!a a1!a s2@s s2@s s2@s d3#d d3#d d3#d f4$f f4$f f4$f f5%f f5%f

2 j6^j j6^j j6^j j7&j j7&j j7&j k8*k k8*k k8*k l9(l l9(l l9(l

3 ;0); and ;0); and ;-_; and ;-_; and ;=+; and ;=+;

4 If x = 7, find the answer to this formula: 5x + (2x * 4) - x.

5 Please use the ^ to insert the following numbers: 14, 36, 890.

6 I will bring 4 copies of the $50 book to you next week (May 14).

7 You can reach me at **klist@prhs.com** or **red@emhs.com**.

8 The #13 bus is late 25% of the time during the weekends!

9 Visit our new home page—find it at http://www.learn_2_type.com.

10 You can look in the **progra~1** folder for the file named **ON & ON**.

LESSON 24

GOAL 2: Move or Copy Text

- Word allows you to easily **move text** or **copy text** from one part of a document to another.

- There are two methods used to move or copy text:
  - **Cut and Paste** Use the Cut and Paste or Copy and Paste options from the Edit menu, the **Cut** ✂ or **Copy** 📋 and **Paste** 📋 buttons on the Formatting toolbar or the keyboard shortcut procedures (Ctrl+X to cut, Ctrl+C to copy and Ctrl+V to paste) to move or copy small or large units of text.
  - **Drag and Drop** Use the mouse for drag-and-drop editing to move or copy text. This procedure works better on small units of text.

- The cut and paste procedure **cuts** text from its original location and **pastes/moves** it to a new location. The copy and paste procedure **copies** text from its original location and **pastes** it to a new location, leaving it in the original location as well.

- When you cut or copy text from a document, it is sent to the Windows Clipboard and held there until a different item is cut or copied. If you cut or copy more than one block of text without pasting it, the text is sent to the Office Clipboard. A floating Office Clipboard toolbar sometimes appears:
  Note: If the Office Clipboard does not automatically appear, choose View, Toolbars, Clipboard to display it.

Clipboard toolbar

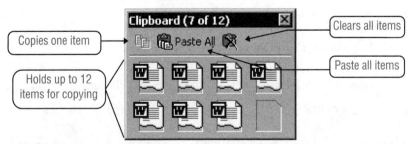

  You can then paste one item, selected items, or all items.

- The proofreaders' marks for **moving** text are: *move* ⌒ or *transpose* ⌢

- The proofreaders' mark for **copying** text is: ⌒

- When moving or copying a word or paragraph, be sure you move or copy the space following the word or paragraph as well. When moving or copying a paragraph, make sure that the paragraph and tab symbols are moved or copied with the text. Click the **Show/Hide ¶** button ¶ to display the hidden codes.

- Follow these steps to perform cut or copy and paste operations:
    1. Select the text to be moved or copied.
    2. Click the **Cut** button ✂ or the **Copy** button 📋 on the Standard toolbar.

       OR

       Click Edit menu; click Cut or Copy.

       OR

       Press Ctrl+X to cut or Ctrl+C to copy.
    3. Relocate the insertion point where you want the text to be placed.
    4. Click the **Paste** button 📋 on the Standard toolbar.

       OR

       Click Edit menu; click Paste.

       OR

       Press Ctrl+V.

- When you use the mouse to cut or copy text, you **drag** text from one location and **drop** it in another location.

- Follow these steps to use the mouse to move text:
    1. Select the text to be moved or copied.
    2. Move the mouse until the I-beam (I) turns into an arrow (↖).
    3. To move the text, hold down the left mouse button and drag the arrow shape to where you want the text moved.

       Note: As you drag you see the following arrow shape: ↖. *This indicates that you are in the process of moving selected text.*

       OR

       To copy the text, hold down the Ctrl key and the left mouse button and drag the arrow shape to where you want the text copied.

       Note: As you drag you see the following arrow shape: ↖. *This indicates that you are in the process of copying selected text.*
    4. Release the mouse button at the desired location.

- Remember, it is best to use the drag and drop procedure to move or copy smaller units of text and the cut and paste procedure to move or copy larger units of text or units that are more separated.

LESSON 24

Exercise 2a
Move Text

1. Open **DINO1**.
2. Move the text as indicated.
3. Use the mouse to drag and drop smaller units of text.
4. Use Cut and Paste to move the lines.
5. Save the document; name it **DINO2**.
6. Print one copy.
7. Close the document window.

DINOSAURS

Did you ever wonder how big a dinosaur was? Dinosaurs came in

many different sizes. Some were as small as a chicken while others were

larger than a house. For example:

> Move bulleted items into alphabetical order by dinosaur name

- The Stegosaurus was about *20* feet long and weighed about *2* tons.
- The Brachiosaurus was *60* to *80* feet long and weighed *50* to *80* tons.
- The Diplodocus was *87* feet long and weighed about *11* tons.

These are just a few examples of the many dinosaurs that roamed the

earth in prehistoric times.

226

Exercise 2b
Copy Text

1. Create a new document.
2. Type the following text: If I said it once, I'll say it again.
3. Press the Enter key one time.
4. Select the text you just typed.
5. Using the Copy and Paste procedure, copy and paste the text five times.
6. Select the first line of text.
7. Press the Ctrl key and drag a copy of the first line of text down past the last line of text.
8. Release the mouse and insert the text as your sixth line of text.
9. If you completed the copy and paste procedures successfully, the sentence will now be repeated six times within the current document.
10. Close the document; do not save the file.

Timed Writing

1. Create a new document.
2. Use the default margins.
3. Change font to Courier New, 12 point.
4. Take two ½-minute timings from Line 1.
   a. If you finish before the time is up, press the Enter key and start Line 1 again.
   b. Press the Enter key 4 times between each timing.
   c. Do not correct errors. If you make an error, continue typing.
   d. To calculate your WAM speed, double the number of words you typed.
5. Take two more ½-minute timings from Line 2 following the same instructions in Step 4 above.
6. Take two more ½-minute timings from Line 3 following the same instructions in Step 4 above.
7. Take two 1-minute timings on the entire paragraph. Calculate your WAM speed.
8. Compare your speeds.
9. Save the document as **L24TIME**.
10. Print one copy.
11. Close the document window.

LESSON 24

	WORDS
To be really good at a skill, you must keep practicing the	12
same thing over and over again. This is true of learning to	24
touch type. Do you remember when you first began learning	36
to type; it was very difficult. You wanted to keep looking	48
at your keys. Now, what was very hard in the beginning is	60
probably very easy for you. Why? You have been practicing	72
your skill over and over again. Every word you touch type	84
is practice and will help increase your skill. The more you	96
type, the more your speed and accuracy will increase.	107

....1....2....3....4....5....6....7....8....9...10...11...12

MOUSE/KEYSTROKE PROCEDURES

Cut and Paste Text
Ctrl+X, Ctrl+V

1. Select text to move.
2. Click **Cut** button ✂ on the Standard toolbar.
   a. Click **Edit** menu .... `Alt`+`E`
   b. Click **Cut** .... `T`
3. Position insertion point where text is to be reinserted.
4. Click **Paste** button 📋 on the Standard toolbar.
   OR
   a. Click **Edit** menu .... `Alt`+`E`
   b. Click **Paste** .... `P`

Drag and Drop/Move Text
1. Select text to be moved.
2. Position mouse pointer on selected text.
3. Click and hold left mouse button.
   Note: Mouse shape changes to ⬚.
4. Drag text to new location.
5. Release mouse button.

Copy and Paste Text
Ctrl+C, Ctrl+V

1. Select text to copy.
2. Click the **Copy** button 📋 on the Standard toolbar.
   OR
   a. Click **Edit** .... `Alt`+`E`
   b. Click **Copy** .... `C`
3. Relocate the insertion point where you want the text to be placed.
4. Click **Paste** button 📋 on the Standard toolbar.
   OR
   a. Click **Edit** menu .... `Alt`+`E`
   b. Click **Paste** .... `P`

Drag and Drop/Copy Text
1. Select text to be copied.
2. Position mouse pointer on selected text.
3. Click and hold **Ctrl** button .... `Ctrl`
4. Click and hold left mouse button.
   Note: Arrow shape changes to ⬚.
5. Drag to copy text to new location.

6. Release mouse button and **Ctrl** button .... `Ctrl`

Collect and Paste Text
1. Select text to copy.
2. Click **Copy** button 📋 on the Standard toolbar.
   OR
   a. Click **Edit** menu............ `Alt`+`E`
   b. Click **Copy** .... `C`
   OR
   Click **Copy** button 📋 on Clipboard toolbar.
3. Repeat Step 2 until you copy all text units (up to 12) you want.
4. Position insertion point where text is to be reinserted.
5. Click **Paste All** button 📋 on Clipboard toolbar.
   OR
   Click icon to paste 📄 on the Clipboard toolbar.
6. Repeat for each text unit to paste.

228

LESSON 25

- Type Paragraphs Containing Numbers and Special Characters
- Review Proofreaders' Marks (Delete, Insert, Uppercase, Lowercase, Etc.) • Review Moving and Copying Text

Warm-up

1. Create a new document.
2. Set the left and right margins to 1".
3. Type each line, trying to type faster when you repeat a line. Press the Enter key twice after you repeat the line.
4. When you see the vertical lines between phrases, say the phrase to yourself as you type. Do not type the vertical lines.
5. If you make an error, continue typing.
6. If you have time, repeat the exercise.
7. Save the document as **LES25**.
8. Close the document window.

```
1 a;sldkfjghghfjdksla; a;sldkfjghfjdksla; a;sldkfjghfjdksla;
2 a;sldkfjghghfjdksla; a;sldkfjghfjdksla; a;sldkfjghfjdksla;

3 fur fun gun gum guy buy but hut jut vug jim dim kid red cue
4 fur fun gun gum guy buy but hut jut vug jim dim kid red cue

5 my, lot sit wet tex co. fat pat zip qt. s219 d3k8 f4j7 f5j6 ;0
6 my, lot sit wet tex co. fat pat zip qt. s219 d3k8 f4j7 f5j6 ;0

7 fat sat fat cat fat rat fat vat fat bat fat hat fat mat fat pat
8 fat sat fat cat fat rat fat vat fat bat fat hat fat mat fat pat

9 zip sip zip rip zip tip zip hip zip nip zip lip zip pip
0 zip sip zip rip zip tip zip hip zip nip zip lip zip pip

1 I am|I will|I have|I want|I was|I hope|I may|I know|
2 I am|I will|I have|I want|I was|I hope|I may|I know|

3 Tex Zip and Jim Guy say it is fun to chew a fat wad of gum.
4 Tex Zip and Jim Guy say it is fun to chew a fat wad of gum.
```

229

LESSON 25

- When typing text containing numbers, use the number keys on the standard keyboard.
- Touch-typing the number and special character keys will increase your typing speed.

Exercise 1
Numbers and Special Characters

1. Create a new document.
2. Type the following paragraphs using a sans serif font, 12 point.
3. Press the Enter key twice between paragraphs.
4. If you make an error, correct it using the Backspace key.
5. If you have time, repeat the exercise.
6. Save the document as **J&W1**.
7. Close the file.

I have found that about 25% of the time, JONES & WILSON does not have the sale items that are advertised.

When there was a sale on #2 pencils (buy 2 cases @ $7.50 a case), the store was sold out by 10:30 a.m. When there was a sale on specialty pens (buy one, get one free), they were sold out by 10:15 a.m.

I spoke to 14 different employees and they all agreed that there is a problem!

GOAL 2: Review Proofreaders' Marks (Delete, Insert, Uppercase, Lowercase, Etc.)

- **Proofreaders' marks** are symbols that show the changes that need to be made to the document.
- Up to this point, you have learned the following proofreaders' marks:

PURPOSE	MARK
Delete	℘
Insert	∧
Move	⟲
Uppercase	≡
Lowercase	l.c. /
New paragraph	¶
No paragraph	no¶
Transpose	∿

- In this lesson, you will use the following new proofreaders' marks:

Insert a period	⊙
Insert a space	#

xercise 2
se Proofreaders' Marks

1. Open **MODEM**.
2. Make the changes indicated with proofreaders' marks.
3. Save the document.
4. Print one copy.
5. Close the document window.

WHAT IS A MODEM?

A modem is a piece of equipment that allows your computer to communicate over

telephone or cable lines. #By using a modem, you can:

> ➤ access the Internet, bulletin boards, and online services

> ➤ send and receive electronic e-mail and faxes

> ➤ transfer files from one computer to another computer

> ➤ gain remote access to other computers

Different modems communicate at different speeds. The fastest type of modem is

a cable modem. #A cable modem that allows Internet access at very high speeds by using the fiber

optic network of the local cable television company. A cable modem is at least

one hundred 100 times faster than a modem that uses the telephone lines.

GOAL 3:   Review Moving and Copying Text

- You can move text using the Cut and Paste features. Once you select the text to be moved, click Cut from the Edit menu. Reposition your insertion point where you want the text reinserted, and click Paste from the Edit menu.

- You can also use the Cut and Paste buttons on the Standard toolbar to accomplish the move.

- In addition to cut and paste, you can use the mouse to drag and drop small units of text to another location.

- Make sure the spacing before and after the moved text is correct. If you move a paragraph and the space between the paragraphs did not move, place your insertion point where the new paragraph is to begin and press the Enter key to restore the space.

- You can copy text using the Copy and Paste features. Once you select the text to be copied, click Copy from the Edit menu. Reposition your insertion point where you want the text copied, and click Paste from the Edit menu.

- You can also use the Copy and Paste buttons on the Standard toolbar or the drag and drop procedure to copy text to another location.

- If you cut or copy more than one block of text without pasting it, the text is sent to the Office Clipboard. You can then paste one item, selected items or all items using the floating Office Clipboard.

  Note: If the Office Clipboard does not automatically appear, choose View, Toolbars, Clipboard to display it.

Exercise 3a
Move Text

1. Open **BUDGETS**.
2. Move the numbered list in the order indicated on the following page.
3. Make all indicated revisions.
4. When done, resave the document.
5. Print one copy.
6. Close the document window.

LESSON 25

BUDGETS

How are you meeting your expenses? Do you work (babysit or mow lawns), or do your parents give you an allowance? Are you old enough to work at a fast-food place and earn a weekly salary? Do you get bonus money if you get 100% on a test? No matter how you "earn" money, you should budget wisely so you can meet your expenses.

Here are some typical* expenses you may incur now or in the near future:

Move into the indicated order

3 1. Car expenses—5 gallons of gas per week @ $1.20 per gallon (multiply 5 * $1.20).

1 2. Entertainment—movies and/or bowling at least once per week @ $8.00 per event.

2 3. Food—eating out @ approximately $6.00 per meal (probably costs more).

Calculate the total expenses in lines 1-3. Assume that you go to one movie and eat one meal out a week. How much would you have to earn each week to save $40.00 each month, assuming there are four weeks to a month? The answer is: $30.00.

*Expenses may vary.

Exercise 3b
Move Text

1. Open **J&W1**, which you created earlier in this lesson.
2. Reverse the two sentences in the second paragraph by moving the first sentence after the second sentence.
3. Save the document as **J&W2**.
4. Print one copy.
5. Close the document window.

234

Timed Writing

1. Create a new document.
2. Use the default margins.
3. Change font to Courier New, 12 point.
4. Take two 3-minute timings.
   a. If you finish before the time is up, press the Enter key and start again.
   b. Press the Enter key 4 times between each timing.
   c. If you make an error, correct it using the Backspace key.
5. To calculate your WAM speed, find the total number of words you typed and divide that number by 3.
6. Compare your speeds.
7. Save the document as **L25TIME**.
8. Print one copy.
9. Close the document window.

	WORDS
There is a wrong way and a right way to chop an onion. To	12
chop an onion the correct way, place it on a cutting board	24
and use a paring knife. First, peel off the thin dry outer	36
and inner covering. Then cut the onion in half. Place the	48
halves, cut side down, on the cutting board. Cut each half	60
into seven or eight thin slices. Then cut each one of the	72
slices the opposite way into three or four pieces. At this	84
point, you will probably be crying.	91

```
....1....2....3....4....5....6....7....8....9...10...11...12
```

LESSON 26

- Use Additional Proofreaders' Marks (Move Left, Move Right, Stet)
- Format and Type a One-Page Report

Warm-up

1. Create a new document.
2. Set the left and right margins to 1".
3. Type each line twice, trying to type faster when you repeat the line. Press the Enter key twice after you repeat the line.
4. When you see the vertical lines between phrases, say the phrase to yourself as you type. Do not type the vertical lines.
5. Correct any errors you make using the Backspace key.
6. If you have time, repeat the exercise.
7. Save the document as **LES26**.
8. Close the document window.

   Note: From Lesson 26 forward, each warm-up line of text will only be displayed once. However, as stated in the exercise steps, you should continue to type each line twice.

---

1 a;sldkfjghghfjdksla; a;sldkfjghfjdksla; a;sldkfjghfjdksla;

2 aqaza swsxs dedcd frftfgfbfvf jujyjhjnjmj kik,k lol.l ;p;/;

3 fur fun gun gum guy buy but hut jut vug jim dim kid red cue

4 my, lot sit wet tex co. fat pat zip qt. s219 d3k8 f4j7 f5j6 ;0

5 new knew no now know knows known knowing knowingly

6 any anyone anything anywhere anyhow anybody anymore

7 I can|you can|we can|who can|how can|what can|why can|

8 Zippy, the fat cat, came home to Jim Dim with wet fur.

236

GOAL 1: Use Additional Proofreaders' Marks
(Move Left, Move Right, Stet)

- The following proofreaders' marks will be used in this lesson:

PURPOSE	MARK
move left	⊏
move right	⊐
let it stand; ignore the change	..... *or stet*

Exercise 1
Proofreaders' Marks

1. Open **SITES**.
2. Make the changes indicated with proofreaders' marks on the next page.
3. Change the exercise to double spacing.
   Note: You must delete the blank line between the paragraphs. Show the paragraph codes and make sure there is one paragraph code between each paragraph.
4. Use the first-line indent feature to indent each paragraph.
5. When finished, resave the document.
6. Print one copy.
7. Close the document window.

World Wide Web

stet

The ~~Internet~~ contains incredible amounts of information on ~~almost~~ every topic. However, some of it is not reliable. Anyone can publish a Web site, and the Internet does not check the accuracy of the contents. It is up to you to judge the quality of the information.

First, know your source. Make sure that a recognized expert or organization in the field created the site. Then verify the accuracy of the information by checking with other reliable sites. ~~By doing this,~~ you will be able to search the Internet more wisely and obtain accurate data.

Become an experienced and educated user and

GOAL 2: Format and Type a One-Page Report

- A **one-page report** or essay begins 2" from the top of the page. The report is double spaced. All paragraphs are indented .5" from the left margin. You may use the first-line indent feature covered in Lesson 17 to indent the first line of each paragraph or you may press the Tab key once at the beginning of each new paragraph.
- Set the left and right margins to 1".
- The title of the report is centered in all caps. Press the Enter key once after the title.

Exercise 2
One-Page Report

1. Create a new document.
2. Set the top margin to 2".
3. Set the left and right margins to 1".
4. Set the line spacing to double.
5. Type the title provided in the illustration on the next page.
6. Use a sans serif font, 18 point, bold.
7. Center the title.
8. Press the Enter key once after the title.
9. Press the Tab key once to begin each paragraph.
10. Type the body of the report shown on the next page in a serif font, 12 point.
11. Create a bulleted list using the diamond shape bullet. Press the Increase Indent button on the toolbar to indent the list.
12. Save the document; name it **KILOBYTE**.
13. Print one copy.
14. Close the document window.

KILOBYTES, MEGABYTES AND GIGABYTES

Do you know how many KB in a MB or how many MB in a GB? Many people find these terms confusing and difficult to understand. However, it is necessary to have an understanding of these concepts in order to determine file sizes and the availability of storage space. In addition, this information is important for e-mailing and setting up web pages.

Technically speaking, there are 1024 (2 to the 10th power) bytes in a kilobyte, 1024 kilobytes in a megabyte, and 1024 megabytes in a gigabyte.

The real numbers look like this:

- Kilobyte = 1024 bytes

- Megabyte = 1,048,576 bytes

- Gigabyte = 1,073,741,824 bytes

Since we are dealing with such large numbers, most of the time people round down the numbers to make it easier to remember. If this is the case, there are 1000 bytes in a kilobyte, 1000 kilobytes in a megabyte, and 1000 megabytes in a gigabyte.

- Kilobyte = a thousand (1000) bytes

- Megabyte = a million (1,000,000) bytes

- Gigabyte = a billion (1,000,000,000) bytes

You decide how you want to express these numbers!

Timed Writing

1. Create a new document.
2. Use the default margins.
3. Change font to Courier New, in 12 point.
4. Take a three-minute timing on the entire paragraph.
   a. If you finish before the time is up, press the Enter key twice and start again.
   b. Do not correct errors. If you make a mistake, continue typing.
   c. To calculate your WAM speed, find the total number of words you typed and divide that number by 3.
5. Press the Enter key 4 times.
6. Take two 1-minute timings from the same paragraph.
   a. Type as fast as you can for the first 1-minute timing.
   b. Type as accurately as you can for the second 1-minute timing.
   c. Do not correct your errors. If you make a mistake, keep typing.
   d. Press the Enter key 4 times between the timings.
   e. Calculate your WAM speed.
7. Take another 3-minute timing on the entire paragraph, following the same instructions as in Step 4 above. Calculate your WAM speed.
8. Compare your speeds.
9. Save the document as **L26TIME**.
10. Print one copy.
11. Close the document window.

	WORDS
A few years ago, people would go to the library to look up	12
information in books. Now, there are many new choices. We	24
can go to the library to look for information in electronic	36
databases, on the internet, or on a library network. We can	48
even stay home and do library research through the internet.	60
We can look for information in encyclopedias using the CDs	72
on our computers. Does this mean that we do not need books?	84
I do not think so.	87

```
....1....2....3....4....5....6....7....8....9...10...11...12
```

LESSON 27

- Create Footnotes in a Report
- Use Additional Proofreaders' Marks (Bold, Italic, Insert Punctuation Mark, etc.)

Warm-up

1. Create a new document.
2. Set the left and right margins to 1".
3. Type each line twice, trying to type faster when you repeat the line. Press the Enter key twice after you repeat the line.
4. When you see the vertical lines between phrases, say the phrase to yourself as you type. Do not type the vertical lines.
5. Correct any errors you make using the Backspace key.
6. If you have time, repeat the exercise.
7. Save the document as **LES27**.
8. Close the document window.
   Note: To familiarize you with typing from handwritten text, some exercise text will be displayed in a script font.

---

1 `a;sldkfjghghfjdksla; a;sldkfjghfjdksla; a;sldkfjghfjdksla;`

2 `aqaza swsxs dedcd frftfgfbfvf jujyjhjnjmj kik,k lol.l ;p;/;`

3 `fur fun gun gum guy buy but hut jut vug jim dim kid red cue`

4 `my, lot sit wet tex co. fat pat zip qt. s2l9 d3k8 f4j7 f5j6 ;0`

5 `like like likely likely likes likes liked liked liking liking`

6 `do do does does doesn't doesn't did did didn't didn't`

7 `I did|you did|why did|who does|how does|what does|`

8 *The baby kid and the fat cat played a lot in the wet field.*

242

GOAL 1:   Create Footnotes in a Report

- **Footnotes** or **endnotes** are used to give sources for quoted material or to clarify information given in the body of a report. Footnotes give the information at the bottom of the page; endnotes place it at the end of the report. For the purposes of this book, we will use the footnote feature.

- There are three parts to a footnote entry:
    1. A **reference mark** (raised number or symbol) that follows the text in the body of the report.
    2. The reference mark and the footnote text at the bottom of the page.
    3. A **separator** line to divide the body from the footnote area. The program automatically inserts this line.

- It is best to use Print Layout View when creating footnotes.

- To create a footnote:
    1. Place the insertion point where you want the reference mark to appear. Make sure there is no space between the last character and the insertion point.
    2. Click Insert menu.
    3. Click Footnote to access the following dialog box:

Footnote and Endnote dialog box

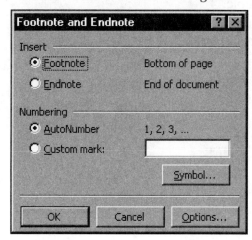

    4. Select the Footnote option.

5. Select <u>A</u>utoNumber to have Word number the footnotes for you.

   OR

   Select <u>C</u>ustom mark and type the symbol to use as the footnote mark.

   OR

   Click the <u>S</u>ymbol button [<u>S</u>ymbol...] and choose a desired symbol. Select a different font from the Font box to view different symbols. Each font contains a different set of symbols.

   Note: The Wingdings or Webdings fonts provide the widest variety of symbols.

6. Click OK.
7. Word inserts the footnote number or symbol.
8. Type the footnote text.
9. Click in the document to continue typing the body of the report.

Exercise 1
Type a Report with Footnotes

1. Create a new document.
2. Set the top margin to 2".
3. Set the left and right margins to 1".
4. Set the line spacing to double.
5. Type the title shown in the illustration on the next page.
6. Use a sans serif font, 18 point, bold.
7. Center the title.
8. Press the Enter key once after the title.
9. Type the report on the next page.
10. Use a serif font, 12 point.
11. Insert footnotes as shown.
12. Save the file; name it **CLIQUES**.
13. Print one copy.
14. Close the document window.

TO CLIQUE OR NOT TO CLIQUE

We're not talking about mouse clicking here. We're discussing why young people join cliques. Everyone feels the need to belong, but no one feels this more than young people. That's why they may join clubs or form cliques.[1]

Cliques provide young people with a sense of support. Studies show that youngsters start joining cliques around the age of 11 or 12.[2] This is when young people become more independent from their families and can feel a little insecure. The clique can provide a sense of security and substitute for the family as they venture from the "nest."

Although cliques serve a purpose, they also have disadvantages. Usually these become obvious after someone becomes a member. Cliques generally look more attractive from the outside. Cliques can suppress individualism and prevent members from following their own interests. For example, members may feel pressure to act or dress in a certain way. In time, members may begin to feel that being in a clique is not much fun.

Cliques are *not* for everyone. Some people prefer to have one or two close friends, while others like to be friendly with a wide variety of people. As an alternative to cliques, young people may join clubs, sports teams, or participate in after-school activities where they can meet to share similar interests.

---

[1] A small group of people who share common interests and beliefs.
[2] The Harsteph Research Institute conducted the most recent study in 1997.

GOAL 2: Use Additional Proofreaders' Marks (Bold, Italic, Insert Punctuation Mark, etc.)

- The following proofreaders' marks will be used in this lesson:

PURPOSE	MARK
Bold	Text
Italics	
Insert punctuation mark	∧ ∧ ∧ ∨ ∨
Center text	⊐text⊏
Close up space	
Spell it out	

Exercise 2
Proofreaders' Marks

1. Open **INTERVIEW**.
2. Change left and right margins to 1".
3. Change to double spacing.
4. Make the changes indicated with proofreaders' marks on the following page.
5. Create a footnote as shown using the asterisk for the footnote symbol.
6. Resave the file.
7. Print one copy.
8. Close the document window.

INTERVIEWING *Tips*

practice and

Interviewing properly is ~~an art and something that is~~ learned through experience.

guidelines   *in order*

There are certain ~~rules of behavior~~ that should be followed to have a successful

interview. These include, among others, dressing professionally, making eye contact,

having knowledge about the company and asking appropriate questions.

no #

However, there are also guidelines to follow to avoid notorious _interview_

↙ Insert footnote

bloopers. Some of the more common mistakes are: ~~speaking too loudly, talking too~~

~~much, slouching, fidgeting, and complaining about a former employer or job.~~

Remember that an interview is a business meeting where you are marketing a

ital

product, and that product is (YOU). Always conduct yourself in a professional way and

most likely that job will be yours.

Failing to Make Eye Contact

#

Talking Too Much

Talking Too Little

Fidgeting   *Add this list where*
                             indicated

Using Improper (Lang.)

Displaying Poor Body Language

Dressing Inappropriately

*Taken from the Dembel Interview Survey, 2000.

LESSON 27

Timed Writing

1. Create a new document.
2. Use the default margins.
3. Change font to Courier New, 12 point.
4. Take a 3-minute timing on the entire document.
   a. If you finish before the time is up, press the Enter key twice and start again.
   b. Do not correct errors. If you make a mistake, continue typing.
   c. To calculate your WAM speed, find the total number of words you typed and divide that number by 3.
5. Press the Enter key 4 times.
6. Take two 1-minute timings.
   a. Type as fast as you can for the first 1-minute timing.
   b. Type as accurately as you can for the second 1-minute timing.
   c. Do not correct your errors. If you make a mistake, keep typing.
   d. Press the Enter key four times between the timings.
   e. Calculate your WAM speed.
7. Take another 3-minute timing on the entire document, following the same instructions in Step 4 above. Calculate your WAM speed.
8. Compare your speeds.
9. Save the document as **L27TIME**.
10. Print one copy.
11. Close the document window.

WORDS

Every four years athletes from twenty-four countries meet   12
to compete. What are they competing for? They are there to   24
fight for the World Cup. The fight is really not a fight   36
but a soccer tournament instead.   43

Soccer looks like a very simple sport. The object of the   55
game is to kick a soccer ball into the goal that belongs to   67
the other team. To get the ball to the other side, players   79
must get the ball past the other team. This is not an easy   91
task, especially when you realize that it is illegal to use   103
your hands. You can use your entire body, except for your   115
hands.   116

....1....2....3....4....5....6....7....8....9...10...11...12

MOUSE/KEYSTROKE PROCEDURES

Footnotes

Alt+Ctrl+F

1. Click **View** menu .... `Alt`+`V`
2. Click **Page Layout** .... `P`
3. Place the insertion point where you want the reference mark.
4. Click **Insert** .... `Alt`+`I`
5. Click **Foot*n*ote** .... `N`

6. Click **AutoNumber** .... `Alt`+`A`
   OR
   a. Click **Custom mark** .... `Alt`+`C`
   b. Type new mark in Custom mark textbox.
      OR
   a. Click the **Symbol** button
      `Symbol...` .... `Alt`+`S`
   b. In the **Font** .... `Alt`+`F`
      drop-down list, click
      desired font .... `↕`

   c. Click desired
      symbol .... `Tab` , `↕`
   d. Click **OK** .... `Enter`
7. Click **OK** .... `Enter`
8. Type footnote text.
9. Click document to continue typing body text.

249

LESSON 28

- Insert and Size Graphics • Text Wrapping Options
- Move Graphic Object • Copy Graphic Objects
- Resize Graphic Objects Using Exact Measurements

Warm-up

1. Create a new document.
2. Set the left and right margins to 1".
3. Type each line twice, trying to type faster when you repeat a line. Press the Enter key twice after you repeat a line.
4. When you see vertical lines between phrases, say the phrase to yourself as you type. Do not type the vertical lines.
5. Correct errors using the Backspace key.
6. If you have time, repeat the exercise.
7. Save the document as **LES28**.
8. Close the document window.

---

1 a;sldkfjghghfjdksla; a;sldkfjghfjdksla; a;sldkfjghfjdksla;

2 aqaza swsxs dedcd frftfgfbfvf jujyjhjnjmj kik,k lol.l ;p;/;

3 fur fun gun gum guy buy but hut jut vug jim dim kid red cue

4 my, lot sit wet tex co. fat pat zip qt. s219 d3k8 f4j7 f5j6 ;0

5 for for for get get get forget forget forget forgotten forgotten

6 wing wing sing sing ring ring king king thing thing bring bring

7 bring it|bring it|bring it|for it|for it|for it|it is|it is|it is|

8 *Sit with Jim and Guy in the dimly lit hut and wait for my cue*

GOAL 1: Insert and Size Graphics

- **Graphic** images can add to the attractiveness of your document and help to convey the message contained in your document.

- You can obtain graphics from many sources. **Clip art** and **pictures** are the most common types of graphics. You can also scan in pictures and photographs or obtain them from a digital camera.

- Clip art consists of ready-made graphics that come with the Word program. They are contained in the **Clip Gallery**. The Clip Gallery also includes sound clips, video clips and photographs.

- The Clip Gallery is arranged by categories. Click a category to view its graphics. To return to the main list of categories, click the **All Categories** button ▦.

- Clip art may also be acquired through other sources and added to the program. If you have access to the Internet, you can download more clip art images. In addition, the Clip Gallery can organize clip art images from other Microsoft programs installed on your computer. In this way, you can easily access and preview all clip art that is on your hard drive.

- Follow these instructions to insert a clip art graphic:
  1. Click Insert menu.
  2. Click Picture.
  3. Click Clip Art.
  4. Click Pictures tab to access the following dialog box.

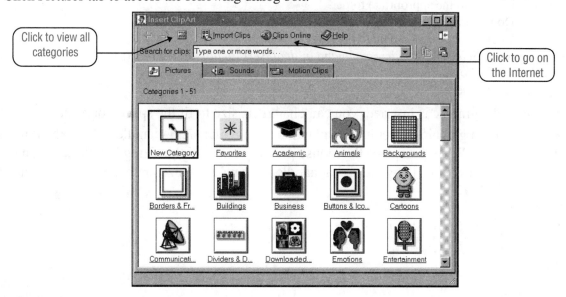

5. Click desired category.
   Note: Use the scroll bar on the right to view additional categories
6. Right-click the graphic.
7. Click Insert.

   OR

   Click the desired graphic to access a pop-up menu. Choose from the options shown in the illustration below:

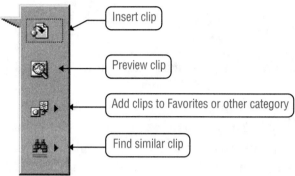

a. Insert clip
b. Preview clip
c. Add clips to Favorites or other category
d. Find similar clip

8. Click the Close button to exit the Clip Gallery.

   OR

   Click All Categories button to continue selecting clip art.

- To insert a graphic other than clip art:
  1. Click Insert menu.
  2. Click Picture.
  3. Click From File.
  4. Browse to the appropriate folder.
  5. Double-click the folder.
  6. Click the desired graphic to preview.
     Note: Select the Preview command in the Insert Picture dialog box (fourth option in the Views drop-down list).
  7. Click Insert.

- Once the graphic is inserted, you can change its size to fit the space you want.
- To resize a graphic, select it to display the rectangular sizing handles. Note the illustration on the next page. When you place the mouse pointer on one of the sizing handles, it changes to a double-headed arrow ↔. Drag the sizing handle to change the size or shape of the graphic.

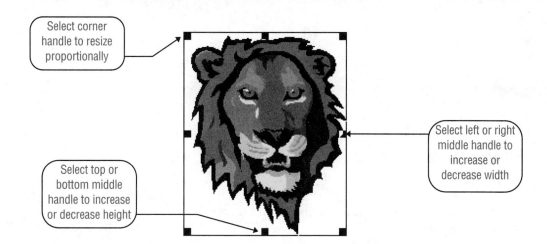

Select corner handle to resize proportionally

Select left or right middle handle to increase or decrease width

Select top or bottom middle handle to increase or decrease height

- Drag any of the four corner handles to change the image's size while still retaining its proportions. If you drag any of the four middle handles, only the height or the width will change, and the image may become distorted.

- Note the changes to the image below. The first two images were changed by dragging a corner handle; the last two were changed by dragging the middle handles (height and width are distorted).

Note: Image maintains proportions when sized with corner handles.

Note: Image becomes distorted when sized with top or middle handles.

LESSON 28

Exercise 1
Insert and Resize a Graphic

1. Create a new document.
2. Position the insertion point at the top of the screen.
3. Click Insert, Picture.
4. Click Clip Art.
5. Click Pictures tab.
6. Click Animals category.
7. Insert the *lion* graphic (first graphic in the first row).
8. Change the zoom factor to Whole Page.
9. Click the graphic to display the handles.
10. Resize the graphic as follows:
    a. Use a corner handle to make the graphic smaller.
    b. Use a corner handle to make the graphic bigger.
    c. Use the bottom middle handle to make the graphic taller.
    d. Use the right middle handle to make the graphic wider.
11. Close the document window.
12. Do not save the changes.

GOAL 2: Text Wrapping Options

- The **text wrapping** options control how a graphic is integrated with text. By default, clip art and pictures are inserted with the **In line with text** text wrapping style. Word allows you to format your text and graphics in a number of other ways.

- Below are samples of Word's text wrapping options:

    - In line with text option: This is the default text-wrap option. It places the graphic at the insertion point in a line of text. See sample below:

        XXXXXXXXX   XXXX XXXXXXX XXXXXXX
        XX X XXXX X XXX XX X XXXX XXX XXX XXXXX

    - Square option: Surrounds the all sides of the graphic. See sample below:

        XX XXX XXX XXXXXXXX XXXX XXXXXX XXXX XXX XX
        X XX X XXX XXX   XXXXXXX XXX XXXX XX

    - Tight option: Wraps text closer to the image. See sample below:

        XX XXXXXXX XXXX XXXX XXXX XXXX XXXXXXXXX XXX
            XX X XX X XXX XXX   XXXXXX XXX XXXX XX

    - Behind text: Places the graphic behind the text in the document. See sample below:

        XX XXXXXXX XXXX XXXX XXXX XX XX X XXXXXXXXXX XXX
            XX X XX X XXX XXX XXXXXX XXX XXXXX XX

    - In front of text: Places the graphic in front of the text in the document. See sample below:

        XX XXXXXXX XXXX XXXX XX   XXXXXXXXX XXX XX X XX X
            XXX XXX XXXXXX XXX X

255

- You can change the wrapping options as well as the horizontal alignment (left, right, center) of the graphic in the Format Picture dialog box. Follow these instructions to change the text wrapping and alignment options:

  1. Double-click the graphic to access the Format Picture dialog box shown below.

Format Picture dialog box

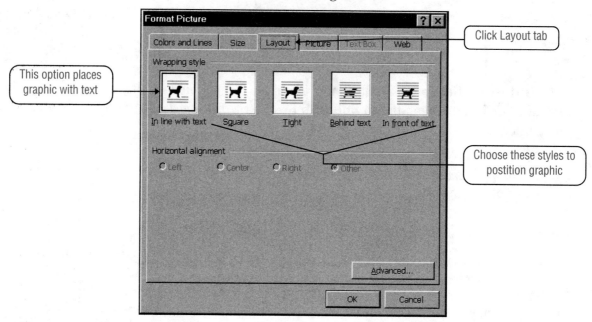

  2. Click the Layout tab.
  3. Choose desired wrapping style.
  4. Click the desired horizontal alignment.
  5. Click OK.

Exercise 2
Text Wrapping Options

1. Create a new document.
2. Change the left and right margins to 2.5".
3. Type the paragraphs in Illustration A.
4. Press the Enter key 3 times after each paragraph.
5. Save the file; name it **WRAP**.
6. Do not close the document.
7. Place your insertion point at the very beginning of the first paragraph.
8. From the Clip Gallery, Buildings category, insert the *schools* graphic (third graphic in the second row).
9. Use the corner handles to resize the graphic to duplicate the illustration in the book.
10. Place your insertion point in the second paragraph after the word *surrounds*.
11. From the Clip Gallery, Dividers & Decorations category, insert the *drop cap letters* graphic (fourth graphic in the first row).
12. Resize the graphic to match Illustration B in the book.
13. Double-click the graphic and choose the Layout tab.
14. Click the **Square** option in the Format Picture dialog box.
15. Place your insertion point in the third paragraph before the word *However*.
16. From the Clip Gallery, Healthcare & Medicine category, insert the *medical* graphic (first graphic in the first row).
17. Resize the graphic to match Illustration B in the book.
18. Double-click the graphic and choose the Layout tab.
19. Click the **Tight** option in the Format Picture dialog box.
20. Place your insertion point in the fourth paragraph after the word *example*.
21. From the Clip Gallery, Maps category, insert the *unity* graphic (2nd graphic in the 1st row).
22. Resize the graphic to match Illustration B in the book.
23. Double-click the graphic and choose the Layout tab.
24. Click the **Behind text** option in the Format Picture dialog box.
25. Place your insertion point in the fifth paragraph after the word *example*.
26. From the Clip Gallery, Communications category, insert the *debates* graphic, (third graphic in the first row).
27. Resize the graphic to match Illustration B in the book.
28. Double-click the graphic and choose the Layout tab.
29. Click the **In front of text** option in the Format Picture dialog box.
30. Compare your work to Illustration B in the book.

31. Make any necessary adjustments to duplicate the illustration.
32. Resave the file.
33. Print one copy.
34. Close the document window.

Illustration A

This is an example of the In line with text option. It places the graphic at the insertion point. Note that the handles are black.

This is an example of the Square option. This option surrounds the graphic with text on all sides. Note that the handles have changed to white.

This is an example of the Tight option. This option is similar to the Square option. However, the text is closer to the graphic. Note that the handles have changed to white.

This is an example of the Behind text option. This option allows you to place the graphic behind the text. Note that the handles have changed to white.

This is an example of the In front of text option. This option allows you to place the graphic in front of the text. Note that the handles have changed to white.

Illustration B

This is an example of the Inline with text option. It places the graphic at the insertion point. Note that the handles are black.

This is an example of the Square option. This option surrounds the graphic with text on all sides. Note that the handles have changed to white.

This is an example of the Tight option. This option is similar to the Square option. However, the text is closer to the graphic. Note that the handles have changed to white.

This is an example of the Behind text option. This option allows you to place the graphic behind the text. Note that the handles have changed to white.

This is an example of the In front of text option. This option allows you to place the graphic in front of the text. Note that the handles have changed to white.

LESSON 28

GOAL 3:   Move Graphic Objects

- You can move a clip art graphic or picture as you do text. You can use the cut and paste or the drag and drop method.

- However, if you want to move a graphic freely on a blank page, you will need to change the text wrap option. When you insert a picture onto a blank page, it displays in the top-left corner of the document. To move the graphic elsewhere on the page, change the text wrap option from the **In line with text** option to any of the other four options. These other options allow you to move the graphic anywhere on a blank page.

- Follow these steps to change the text wrapping option:
  1. Click Insert.
  2. Click Picture.
  3. Click Clip Art.
  4. Click Pictures tab.
  5. Select a category and click the desired graphic.
  6. Once inserted, double-click the graphic.
  7. Click the Layout tab.
  8. Change to a different text wrapping option.
  9. Click OK.

- Once the text wrap option is changed, you can freely move the graphic.

- It is easiest to move a graphic by using the mouse.

- Follow these steps to move a graphic:
  1. Place the insertion point in the center of the picture. The mouse pointer turns to a four-sided arrow, as shown below:

Four-sided arrow

  2. Click and drag the picture to its new location and release the mouse button.

Exercise 3
Move a Graphic

1. Create a new document.
2. From the Clip Gallery, insert the first graphic in the first row of the Foods & Dining category.
3. Place the insertion point on the graphic.
4. Move the graphic to the top left, top right, bottom left and bottom right of the screen.
5. Move the graphic so it is centered both horizontally and vertically on the screen.
6. Close the document window.
7. Do not save the changes.

GOAL 4:   Copy Graphic Objects

- You can **copy** a graphic in the same way you copy text.

- Copying a graphic is similar to moving it. The only difference is that copying retains the original and places a duplicate in a new location.

- You can use the mouse, menu commands or keyboard shortcuts to copy graphics.

- As with text, you must select the graphic before you can move or copy it. Click the graphic to display handles.

- Once the handles are displayed, use one of the following methods to copy and paste the graphic:
  Menu commands
  1. Click Edit menu.
  2. Click Copy.
  3. Click Edit menu.

4. Click Paste.
5. While the handles are still displayed, click and drag the copied graphic to the new location using the left mouse button.

Note: Remember, if you are trying to move a graphic to a blank portion of a page, you will need to change the text wrap option first.

OR

Mouse method

1. Hold down the Ctrl key and drag the graphic to an additional location.

Note: The arrow changes to an arrow with a plus sign ⬚.

2. Release the left mouse button to place graphic in the new location.

OR

Keyboard shortcuts

1. Press Ctrl+C to copy the graphic.
2. Press Ctrl+V to paste the graphic.
3. While the handles are still displayed, click and drag the copied graphic to the new location using the left mouse button.

Exercise 4
Copy a Graphic

1. Create a new document.
2. From the Clip Gallery Entertainment category, insert the *motion pictures* graphic in the first row.
3. Change the zoom factor to Whole Page.
4. Double-click the graphic and change from the In line text wrap option.
   Note: The handles should be white.
5. Use the mouse to drag a corner handle to resize the graphic proportionally to approximately one-half its original size.
6. Use the menu commands (Copy and Paste) to copy the graphic.
7. Drag the copy to the top-right corner of the page.
8. Use the mouse method (Ctrl+drag) to copy the graphic.
9. Drag the copy to the bottom-left corner of the page.
10. Use the keyboard shortcuts (Ctrl+C, Ctrl+V) to copy and paste the graphic.
11. Drag the copy to the bottom-right corner of the page.
12. Compare your result with the book.
13. Save the file; name it **MOVIE**.
14. Print one copy.
15. Close the document window.

Desired Result

LESSON 28

- In addition to resizing a graphic by estimating the size using the mouse, you can resize a graphic using an **exact measurement**. For example, you may want to reduce a graphic to 50% of its original size, or you may want to change its proportions to an exact height and width.

- Follow these steps to get an exact size measurement for a graphic:
  1. Select the graphic.
  2. Click Format menu.
  3. Click Picture to access the Format Picture dialog box shown below.

     OR

     Double-click the graphic.

Format Picture dialog box

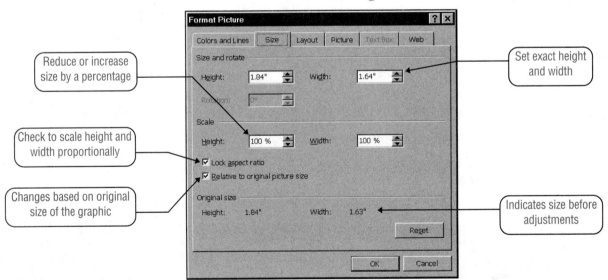

  4. Click Size tab.
  5. Specify an exact Height and Width under Size and rotate.

     OR

     Specify a percentage change under Scale.

     Notes: To change the size while the graphic keeps its original proportions, select the Lock aspect ratio check box. To change the graphic based on its original size, select the Relative to original pictur size check box.
  6. Click OK.

Exercise 5
Insert, Copy, Size and Move a Graphic

1. Create a new document.
2. Change all margins to .5".
3. Change the zoom factor to Whole Page.
4. From the Clip Gallery, Plants category, insert the *trees* graphic (third graphic in the first row).
5. Select the graphic.
6. Resize it to approximately 50% of its original size using the mouse.
7. Move it to the top-left corner.
8. Copy the graphic.
9. Move the copied graphic to the top-right corner.
10. Resize it to 75% of its original size using exact measurements.
    Note: Make sure the Lock aspect ratio and the Relative to original picture size check boxes are selected.
11. Copy the graphic.
12. Move the copied graphic to the bottom-left corner.
13. Resize it as follows: height: 4.0", width: 2.0".
    Note: Deselect the Lock aspect ratio check box.
14. Copy the graphic.
15. Move the copied graphic to the bottom-right corner.
16. Resize it as follows: height: 1.5", width: 3.0".
17. Compare your results to the illustration on the next page.
18. Save the file; name it **TREE**.
19. Print one copy.
20. Close the document window.

Desired Result

Timed Writing

1. Create a new document.
2. Use the default margins. Change the font to Courier New, 12 point.
3. Take a 3-minute timing on the entire document.
   a. If you finish before the time is up, press the Enter key twice and start again.
   b. Do not correct errors. If you make an error, continue typing.
   c. To calculate your WAM speed, find the total number of words you typed and divide that number by 3.
4. Press the Enter key 4 times.
5. Take another 3-minute timing on the entire document, following the same instructions as in Step 3 above. Calculate your WAM speed.
6. Compare your speeds.
7. Save the document as **L28TIME**.
8. Print one copy.
9. Close the document window.

	WORDS
If you have heard a parrot or other bird talk, you are not	12
really hearing the bird talk. Instead what you are hearing	24
is the bird imitating the sounds people make when talking.	36
Many kinds of birds mimic the sounds they hear around them.	48
They can copy the songs other birds sing and they can even	60
imitate the sounds other types of animals make.	70
Not every type of bird can talk. There are three families	82
of birds that talk. These are the parrot, starling, and	94
crow families. Birds in these families can mimic the human	106
voice if they begin their training when they are very young.	118
To train a bird to talk, words must be repeated slowly and	130
clearly, over and over. Once a word or phrase is learned,	142
the bird will never forget it.	148

....1....2....3....4....5....6....7....8....9...10...11...12

LESSON 28

Insert a Graphic

1. Click **Insert** menu .... `Alt`+`I`
2. Click **Picture** .... `P`
3. Choose one of the following options:

   Clip Art
   a. Click **Clip Art** .... `C`
   b. Click **Pictures** tab .... `Ctrl`+`Tab`
   c. Click desired category .... `↕`
   d. Right-click desired graphic.
   e. Click **Insert** .... `I`

   OR
   a. Click clip art to insert.
   b. Click the **Insert** button `🗐`.

   f. Click **All Categories**
      button `🔳` .... `Alt`+`Home`
      to select other graphics.

   OR

   Click the **Close** button `X` to exit
   the Gallery.

   From File:
   a. Click **From File** .... `F`
   b. Browse to folder containing
      graphic.
   c. Double-click folder.
   d. Click **Preview** button `🔳`.
      (fourth option on View drop-down
      list in Insert Picture dialog box)
   e. Click desired graphic.
   f. Preview graphic.
   g. Click **Insert** .... `Alt`+`S`

Resize a Graphic

1. Click graphic to display sizing handles.
2. Drag a corner handle to resize
   proportionately.

   OR

   Drag a middle handle to change the
   height or width.

Resize a Graphic Using Exact Measurements

1. Select the graphic.
2. Click **Format** menu .... `Alt`+`O`
3. Click **Picture** .... `I`
4. Click **Size** tab.
5. Click **Lock aspect ratio** ..... `Alt`+`A`
   to keep proportions.
6. Click **Relative to**
   picture size .... `Alt`+`R`
7. Choose one of the following:

   Size and Rotate:
   a. Click **Height** .... `Alt`+`E`
   b. Type measurement.
   c. Click **Width** .... `Alt`+`D`
   d. Type measurement.
   Note: Deselect Lock aspect ratio to
   give exact height and width.

   OR

   Scale:
   a. Click **Height** .... `Alt`+`H`
   b. Type percentage.
   c. Click **Width** .... `Alt`+`W`
   d. Type percentage.

Move a Graphic

Ctrl+X, Ctrl+V

1. Select the graphic.
2. Click **Edit** menu .... `Alt`+`E`
3. Click **Cut** .... `T`
4. Relocate insertion point.
5. Click **Edit** .... `Alt`+`E`
6. Click **Paste** .... `P`

OR

1. Select the graphic.
2. Drag to new location.

Copy a Graphic

Ctrl+C, Ctrl+V

1. Select the graphic.
2. Click **Edit** menu .... `Alt`+`E`
3. Click **Copy** .... `C`
4. Relocate insertion point.
5. Click **Edit** menu .... `Alt`+`E`
6. Click **Paste** .... `P`

OR

1. Select the graphic.
2. Place mouse pointer over graphic.
3. Four-sided arrow appears `✥`.
4. Hold down **Ctrl** key and drag graphic
   to desired location.

   Note: The arrow shape turns into
   and an outline of the graphic
   follows the mouse movement.

LESSON 29

- Review Graphics • Create Text Boxes
- Create Flyers and Letterheads

Warm-up

1. Create a new document.
2. Set the left and right margins to 1".
3. Type each line twice, trying to type faster each time you repeat a line.
4. When you see the vertical lines between phrases, say the phrase to yourself as you type. Do not type the vertical lines.
5. If you make an error, continue typing.
6. If you have time, repeat the exercise.
7. Save the document as **LES29**.

---

1 `a;sldkfjghfjdksla; a;sldkfjghfjdksla; a;sldkfjghfjdksla;`

2 `aqaza swsxs dedcd frftfgfbfvf jujyjhjnjmj kik,k lol.l ;p;/;`

3 `fur fun gun gum guy buy but hut jut vug jim dim kid red cue`

4 `my, lot sit wet tex co. fat pat zip qt. s2l9 d3k8 f4j7 f5j6 ;0`

5 `zoo zoo zoo zoom zoom zoom zero zero zero quiz quiz quiz`

6 `your your your yell yell yell yellow yellow yellow yes yes yes`

7 `yell yes| yell yes|yell yes|your quiz|your quiz|your quiz|`

8 *It's fun to go with Jim and Pat to Red's Hut at 219 Guncue Road.*

LESSON 29

- Graphics are used to increase the attractiveness of a document. They should be used to help convey the message you are trying to send. Make sure your graphic is related to the content of the document.

- You can use clip art, drawn or scanned photos and artwork in a Word document.

- To place a graphic image in a document, click Insert, Picture, then choose either Clip Art or From File.
  - The Clip Art option gives you access to ready-made graphics that come with Word. In addition, it allows you to download additional graphics from the Internet. The Clip Gallery organizes your clip art collection.
  - The From File option gives you access to images from other sources. These may include scanned images, pictures taken with a digital camera, original graphics or downloaded images. Make sure the Preview button is selected so you can view the graphic before inserting it. Sound clips and video clips can be inserted using this process as well.

- Once the graphic is inserted into the document, you may size or move it. Remember that the graphic must be selected before it can be sized or moved.

- When resizing a graphic, use the corner handles to keep the same proportions. Using the middle handles will change the shape by lengthening or widening the image. Use the mouse to resize it approximately. You can also change the size of the picture to an exact height or width or to a percentage of its original size.

- Graphics are inserted automatically with the **In line with text** option. This option places the graphic on the same line as the text. If you wish to move a graphic freely to place it precisely on a page, you will need to change the wrap option. Changing the wrap option turns the graphic into a **floating object** so it can be moved independently of the text. Wrap options include Square, Tight, Behind text and In front of text.

- Changes can be made to the graphic's size, alignment and color in the Format Picture dialog box. Double-click the graphic to access the dialog box, or select the object and then click Format, Picture.

Exercise 1
Review Graphics

1. Create a new document.
2. Use the default margins.
3. Center the title as shown in the illustration on the next page. Use a decorative sans serif font, 36 point, bold (Comic Sans MS is used in the illustration).
4. From the Clip Gallery Maps category, select the *world* graphic (third graphic in first row).
5. Change to the Square wrap option.
6. Use the Exact Measurements feature to resize the graphic to 1" in height and width. Deselect the Lock aspect ratio.
7. Move the graphic to the left of the title.
8. Copy the graphic and place the copy to the right of the title.
9. Click elsewhere to deselect the graphic.
10. Place the insertion point at the end of the title and press the Enter key twice.
11. Change to left alignment and type the paragraphs in a serif font, 24 point.
12. Press the Enter key 4 times between each paragraph.
13. Insert the graphic for the first paragraph as follows:
    a. From the Clip Gallery Maps category, select the *unity* graphic (second graphic in the first row).
    b. Keep the In line with text wrap option.
    c. Use the Exact Measurements feature to resize it to 35% of its original size.
14. Insert the graphic for the second paragraph as follows:
    a. From the Clip Gallery Communications category, select the *conversation* graphic (first graphic in the second row).
    b. Change to the Square wrap option.
    c. Resize using the mouse to match the graphic in the illustration on the next page.
    d. Use the drag-and-drop method to move the graphic into the middle of the paragraph.
15. Insert the graphic for the third paragraph as follows:
    a. From the Clip Gallery People at Work category, select the *handshakes* graphic (second graphic in the first row).
    b. Change to the Tight wrap option.
    c. Resize the graphic using any desired method.
    d. Use the cut and paste method to move the graphic to the right of the paragraph.
16. Compare your results with the book.
17. Move and resize the graphics to duplicate the illustration on the next page as closely as possible.
18. Save the document; name it **EFFECTS**.
19. Print one copy.
20. Close the document window.

Major Effects of the Internet

Made the world a smaller place because people from all over the globe can communicate easily and quickly.

Provided methods of and access information. people with new communication to vast amounts of

Created a new way of doing business and created new jobs such as Webmaster and Web page designer.

GOAL 2: Create Text Boxes

- You can combine text and graphics on a page. However, if you want to place text in a specific location, you should use a text box.

- Text boxes allow you to create professional-looking documents. Putting text in a text box allows you to move the text freely about the page without interfering with the placement of other text or graphics. You can even place the text box in the margins.

- Follow these steps to create a text box:
  1. Click Insert menu.
  2. Click Text Box.
  3. The mouse pointer changes to a crosshair +.
  4. Place the crosshair where you want to position the text box.
  5. Drag the crosshair until the text box is the desired size.
  6. Start typing at the flashing insertion point inside the text box.
  7. When you are finished, click outside the text box.

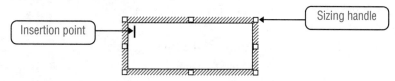

  8. Resize the text box the same way you resize graphic objects.
- You must be in Print Layout view to see a text box.

- If you cannot see all the text contained in your text box, drag one of the sizing handles until the text box reaches the desired size.

- You can make changes to the text box in the same way you changed graphics. In order to edit a text box, double-click the text box frame to access the Format Text Box dialog box shown on the next page. Use the dialog box to change the color, size, and layout of a text box.

- To add colors and borders to your text box, follow these steps:
  1. Double-click the text box frame.
  2. Click the Colors and Lines tab to see the dialog box shown on the next page.

LESSON 29

Format Text Box dialog box

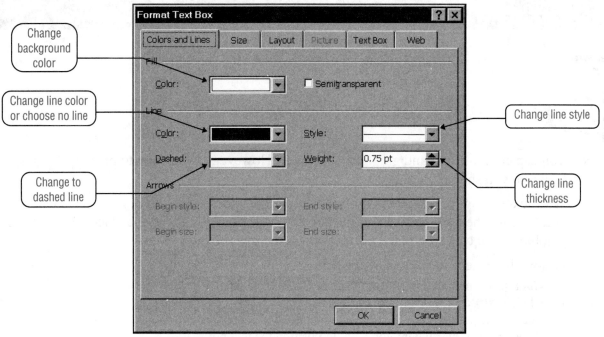

5. You can make one or more of the following changes to the text box:
   - Fill <u>C</u>olor   Specify a background color for the box.
   - Line C<u>o</u>lor   Specify the border color or no line.
   - <u>D</u>ashed Line   Specify a dashed style or solid style.
   - Line <u>S</u>tyle   Specify a line style.
   - Line <u>W</u>eight   Specify the thickness of the line.
6. Click OK.

- To align a text box on a page, double-click the text box frame and select the Layout tab of the dialog box shown above. Select the desired horizontal alignment.

- To remove a text box, select it, click the text box frame (mouse pointer will change to a four-sided arrow), then press the Delete key. Both the box and its contents will be removed from the page.

Exercise 2
Text Boxes

1. Create a new document.
2. Change all margins to .5".
3. Center the title in a decorative sans serif font, 36 point, bold. (See following page.)
4. Press the Enter key 3 times.
5. From the Clip Gallery Business category, insert the *finance* graphic (last graphic in the fourth row).
6. Copy the graphic twice. Resize and move the graphics to match the illustration on the next page. Use any method to achieve the results.
7. Create a text box and format as follows:
   a. Type the word YOUR.
   b. Center the word in a decorative, sans serif font, 24 point, bold. (Use the same font as the title.)
   c. Specify green as the background color for the box.
   d. Move the text box to the right of the first graphic, as shown in the illustration on the next page.
   e. Resize the text box to match the illustration.

8. Create a second text box and format as follows:
   a. Type the word MONEY.
   b. Center the word in a decorative, sans serif font, 30 point, bold. (Use the same font as the title.)
   c. Specify green as the background color for the box.
   d. Move the text box to the right of the second graphic, as shown in the illustration on the next page.
   e. Resize the text box to match the illustration.

9. Create a third text box and format as follows:
   a. Type the word GROW.
   b. Center the word in a decorative, sans serif font, 36 point, bold. (Use the same font as the title.)
   c. Specify green as the background color for the box.
   d. Move the text box to the right of the third graphic, as shown in the illustration on the next page.
   e. Resize the text box to match the illustration.

10. Delete the last text box.
11. Undo the deletion.
12. Compare your result with the book.
13. Make any adjustments necessary to duplicate the illustration on the next page.
    Note: You may need to move and/or resize graphics and text boxes to achieve the desired result.
        Remember, the document must fit on one page.
14. Save the document; name it **MONEY**.
15. Print one copy.
16. Close the document window.

Desired Result

Invest Wisely and Watch

YOUR

MONEY

GROW

GOAL 3   Create Flyers and Letterheads

Flyers

- A **flyer** is a document that presents information. It can be an advertisement or an announcement of an event. Many different types of organizations use flyers.

- Here are some guidelines to follow when creating a flyer:
  - Flyers should attract the reader's attention. Use interesting text and graphics.
  - Decide on the main point and make it the outstanding part of the flyer.
  - Don't clutter the page with too many graphics and fonts. It causes confusion.
  - It is preferable to use a sans serif font for the headline (a straight-edged font—no curves at the ends of the strokes).
  - Use a serif font for body text (this is the text that gives the information or description). It is easier to read.
  - Use an interesting but relevant graphic.
  - Change the default margins as needed to accommodate the text and graphics.

Letterheads

- A **letterhead** appears on the top (or side) of a letter and identifies who is sending the letter. It may contain the name, address, phone number, fax number and e-mail address of the sender. It may also contain a company **logo** (a symbol representing a company) or a related graphic. Other identifying information may also be included.

- A letterhead can be created using a variety of fonts, font sizes, font styles, colors and graphics.

- Guidelines for creating a letterhead are:
  - The letterhead should be sized so that there is enough blank room for the letter.
  - Reduce the top margin to .5" for more room for the letterhead.
  - The most important part of the letterhead should be given the greatest emphasis.
  - Use the company logo or include an interesting but related graphic.
  - Don't clutter the letterhead.

- You can save the letterhead and use it again with each new letter. However, you must be sure to save each new letter under a different file name; otherwise, you will overwrite the letterhead file.

Exercise 3a
Create a Flyer

1. Create a new document.
2. Change all margins to .5".
3. Begin the exercise at the top of the screen.
4. Create a text box and type the following text: Has Your E-Mail Been
5. Format the text as follows:
   a. Use a decorative font (Mead Bold is used here), 36 point, bold and yellow.
   b. Center the text in the box.
6. Format the text box as follows:
   a. Center the text box horizontally between the left and right margins.
   b. Specify black as the background color for the box.
7. From the Clip Gallery Business category, insert the *decisions* graphic (second graphic in the first row).
8. Size the graphic to exactly 122% of its original size.
9. Change the wrap option and move the graphic to match the illustration.
10. From the Clip Gallery Communications category, insert the *correspondence* graphic (first graphic in the first row).
11. Resize the graphic and place it on the top-left corner of the larger graphic, as shown in the illustration on the next page.
12. Copy the graphic and move it to the right corner of the larger graphic.
13. Create a text box and type the following text: Lost in Cyberspace?
14. Format the text as follows:
    a. Use the same decorative font, 48 point, bold and red.
    b. Center the text in the box.
    c. Move the box under the large graphic, as illustrated.
    d. Remove the borders of the text box.
       Note: Select the text box, then click F̲ormat, Text B̲ox, and then click the Colors and Lines tab. In the Line C̲olor drop-down list, click No Line.
15. Create a third text box and type the following text: Tired of lost e-mail, busy signals and too much traffic?
16. Center the text in the text box, press the Enter key and type the following: Call 1-800-555-LOST.
17. Format the text as follows:
    a. Center the text in the same decorative font, 22 point, bold and red.
    b. Change the border of the text box to a dashed line in red.
18. Make any adjustments to duplicate the illustration as closely as possible.
19. Save the file; name it **MAIL**.
20. Print one copy.
21. Close the document window.

Desired Result

Has Your E-Mail Been

Lost in Cyberspace?

Tired of lost e-mail, busy signals and too much traffic?

Call 1-800-555-LOST

Exercise 3b
Create a Letterhead Document

1. Create a new document.
2. Set the top margin to .5".
3. Set all other margins to 1".
4. Insert a text box and format the text as follows using a decorative font:
   - Party Magic—48 point, red.
   - *by Peter Rabitz*—20 point, blue and italic.
   - address and city, state and zip—14 point, red.
5. Center all text in the text box.
6. Create a double-lined border in red around the text box.
7. Move and resize the text box to match the illustration on the next page.
8. Create a footer.
9. Center the following footer text: Visit Our Home Page at: http://www.partytime.com
10. Format footer text in the same font as the letterhead, in 12 point.
11. Use the Clip Gallery Entertainment category to insert the *magic* graphic (second graphic in second row) into the footer.
12. Resize the graphic to 12%.
13. Copy the graphic and place one copy on each side of the Web page address, as shown in the illustration.
14. Make necessary adjustments to duplicate the illustration.
15. Save the document; name it **MAGICIAN**.
16. Print one copy.
17. Close the document window.

Desired Result

Party Magic

by Peter Rabitz

234 Bunnyhop Road
Cottontail, NY 15544
1-800-555-Magi

 Visit Our Home Page at: http://www.partytime.com

LESSON 29

Timed Writing

1. Create a new document.
2. Use the default margins.
3. Change the font to Courier New, 12 point.
4. Take a 5-minute timing on the entire document.
   a. If you finish before the time is up, press the Enter key 2 times and start again.
   b. Do not correct errors. If you make an error, continue typing.
   c. To calculate your WAM speed, find the total number of words you typed and divide that number by 5.
5. Press the Enter key 4 times.
6. Take two 1-minute timings.
   a. Type as fast as you can for the first 1-minute timing.
   b. Type as accurately as you can for the second 1-minute timing.
   c. Do not correct your errors. If you make an error, continue typing.
   d. Press the Enter key four times between the timings.
   e. Calculate your WAM speed.
7. Take another 5-minute timing on the entire document, following the same instructions as in Step 4 above. Calculate your WAM speed.
8. Compare your speeds.
9. Save the document as **L29TIME**.
10. Print one copy.
11. Close the document window.

WORDS

Has this ever happened to you? Your teacher assigned a report 12
over a month ago and now it is due today and you have not even 24
started. What happened is that you probably didn't know where 36
to begin, so you didn't begin at all!   43

The solution so this does not happen again is to think of the 55
project as a group of small tasks. This way you can work on   67
the project one step at a time. Once you have broken up the   79
project into small tasks, make up a schedule of all the things 91
you have to accomplish. Prepare a to-do list. As you finish 103
each small task, check it off on your list. This will help   115
you feel a sense of accomplishment. Before you know it, you   127
will have completed the entire project. Your success will be 139
a boost to your self image.   145

....1....2....3....4....5....6....7....8....9...10...11...12

MOUSE/KEYSTROKE PROCEDURES

Text Box

1. Click **Insert** menu .... `Alt`+`I`
2. Click **Text Box** .... `X`
3. Drag crosshair ✛ until box reaches desired size.
4. Type text at insertion point.

Resize a Text Box

1. Select the text box.
2. Drag handle to resize as desired.

Move a Text Box

1. Select the text box.
2. Place four-sided arrow on text box border.
3. Drag to desired location.

Center a Text Box

1. Double-click the text box frame.
2. Click the **Layout** tab. .... `↰`
3. Click **Center** .... `Alt`+`C`
4. Click **OK** .... `Enter`

Add Border and Shading to Text Box

1. Select text box.
2. Click **Format** menu .... `Alt`+`O`
3. Click **Text Box** .... `O`

   OR

   Double-click the text box frame.
4. Click **Colors and Lines** tab .... `Ctrl`+`Tab`
5. Select one or more of the following:
   - **Fill Color**
     a. Click **Color** .... `Alt`+`C`
     b. Select desired color for background.
   - **Line Color**
     a. Click **Color** .... `Alt`+`O`
     b. Select desired color.
   - **Line Dash**
     a. Click **Dashed** .... `Alt`+`D`
     b. Click desired dashed line style.
   - **Line Style**
     a. Click **Style** .... `Alt`+`S`
     b. Select desired line style.
   - **Line Weight**
     a. Click **Weight** .... `Alt`+`W`
     b. Select desired line width.
6. Click **OK** .... `Enter`

Remove Text Box Border or Shading

1. Select text box.
2. Click **Format** menu .... `Alt`+`O`
3. Click **Text Box** .... `O`
4. Click **Colors and Lines** tab .... `Ctrl`+`Tab`
5. Click **Color** .... `Alt`+`C`
6. Select **No Fill** .... `↓`
7. Click **Color** .... `Alt`+`O`
8. Select **No line** .... `↓`
9. Click **OK** .... `Enter`

Remove a Text Box

1. Select the text box.
2. Click the frame.
3. Press the **Delete** key .... `Del`

LESSON 30

- Apply Borders
- Apply Shading
- Add Picture Bullet

Warm-up

1. Create a new document.
2. Set the left and right margins to 1".
3. Type each line twice, trying to type faster each time you repeat a line. When you see the vertical lines between phrases, say the phrase to yourself as you type. Do not type the vertical lines.
4. If you make an error, continue typing.
5. If you have time, repeat the exercise.
6. Save the document as **LES30**.

---

1 a;sldkfjghfjdksla; a;sldkfjghfjdksla; a;sldkfjghfjdksla;

2 aqaza swsxs dedcd frftfgfbfvf jujyjhjnjmj kik,k lol.l ;p;/;

3 fur fun gun gum guy buy but hut jut vug jim dim kid red cue

4 my, lot sit wet tex co. fat pat zip qt. s2l9 d3k8 f4j7 f5j6 ;0

5 seen seen queen queen teen teen between between

6 ear ear wear wear tear tear swear swear bear bear

7 hear hear heart heart near near pear pear learn learn

8 *The fat cat sat in the hut on the lot of the Texzip Co.*

GOAL 1:   Apply Borders

- The **Borders and Shading** feature adds a finishing touch to the appearance of your text and graphics. You can add lines or a box around selected text, paragraphs or graphics.

- The Borders and Shading feature allows you to make changes to the width, color and style of the lines and boxes.

- Follow these steps to create a border:
  1. Select the text, paragraph(s) or picture you want bordered.
  2. Click Format menu.
  3. Click Borders and Shading.
  4. Click the Borders tab to access the following dialog box:

Borders and Shading dialog box

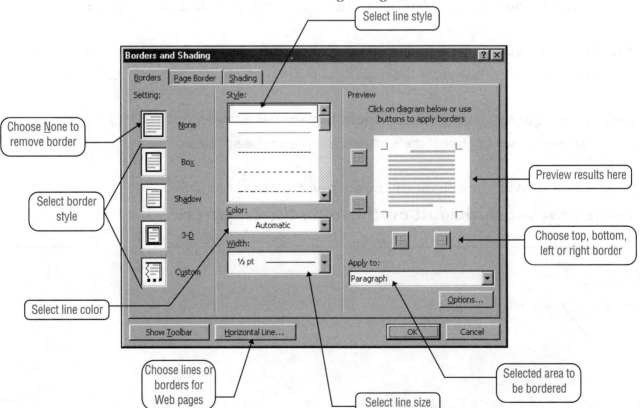

5. Choose from one or more of the following options:
   - **Setting**   Allows you to select the type of border you want.
     Note: A Custom border allows you to add a border to one or more sides of the text or graphic.
   - **Style**   Allows you to select the line style you want.
   - **Color**   Provides a drop-down list of border color options.
   - **Width**   Allows you to select the thickness of the line.
     Note: To remove a border, click the None setting in the Borders and Shading dialog box.
6. Click OK.

- In addition to adding borders to text and graphics, you can add borders to a full page.

- You can view the results of your selections in the Preview box.

- Follow these steps to add a border to your page:
  1. Position the insertion point anywhere on the page.
  2. Click Format menu.
  3. Click Borders and Shading.
  4. Click the Page Border tab to access the following dialog box:

Borders and Shading dialog box

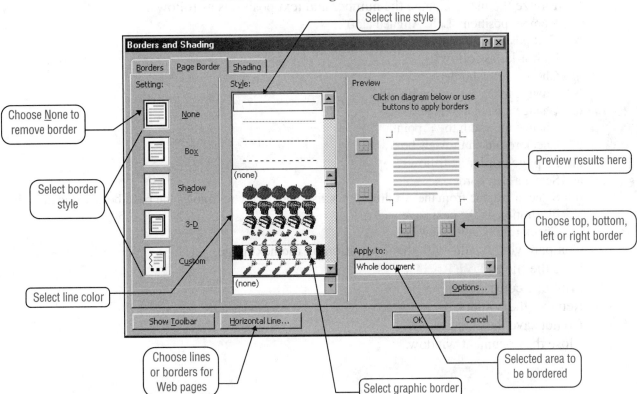

5. The Page Border options work the same as those on the Borders tab. The only difference is that the Page Border tab also offers an Art drop-down list. This list allows you to add a graphic border to your page. Make your selections and check the results in the Preview window.
   Note: To remove the graphic border from a page, click the None setting on the Page Border tab of the Borders and Shading dialog box.
6. Click OK.

LESSON 30

Exercise 1
Apply a Border

1. Open **EVEREST2**.
2. Center the document vertically on the page.
3. Change the entire document to double space.
4. Indent the first line of each paragraph.
5. Delete the extra spaces between paragraphs and after the heading.

   Note: Press the ¶ *button to display paragraph codes and delete extra codes between paragraphs. You should have one paragraph symbol between paragraphs.*

6. Select the numbered items (lowercase letters).
7. Customize the list to change the number and text positions as follows:
   a. Number position: Left, Aligned at: 0".
   b. Text position: Indent at: .25".
8. Add a border as follows:
   a. Choose a Box border.
   b. Change the style to a double line.
   c. Change the color to blue.
   d. Change the width to ¾" point.
   e. Check results in Preview box.
9. Add a page border as follows:
   a. Select a Box border.
   b. Select a graphic from the Art drop-down list that closely resembles the page border shown in the illustration on the next page.
   c. Check results in Preview box.
10. Compare your results with the illustration on the next page.
11. Save the file as **EVEREST3**.
12. Print one copy.
13. Remove the borders.
14. Do not save the changes.
15. Close the document window.

Mt. Everest Facts

The Himalayas has the world's 10 tallest mountains. Among them is Mt. Everest, tempting adventurers time and again to reach its summit at 29,028 feet. The conditions are very brutal. Freezing temperatures, raging winds and little oxygen have caused many accomplished climbers to meet their deaths on its icy slopes. Here are some interesting facts about Mt. Everest:

a. Summit winds can reach over 130 mph.

b. Temperatures can be as low as 45 degrees below zero Celsius.

c. At 26,000 feet, climbers must use supplemental oxygen to survive.

d. The best months to climb are May and October.

e. In 1953, Sir Edmund Hillary was the first to reach the summit.

f. There have been 4,000 attempts to reach the summit.

Each year there are many expeditions that set out to reach the top, but only a few succeed. The mountain remains for future generations to conquer.

GOAL 2: Apply Shading

- The **Shading** option fills the background space in the selected text, paragraph or graphic. You can shade an area in either a solid color or a pattern. A pattern contains two colors—a foreground color and a background color. You can experiment with different combinations of these colors to achieve the effect you want.

- Follow these steps to add shading to your work:
  1. Select the text, paragraph(s) or picture you want to shade.
  2. Click Format menu.
  3. Click Borders and Shading.
  4. Click the Shading tab to access the dialog box below.

Borders and Shading dialog box

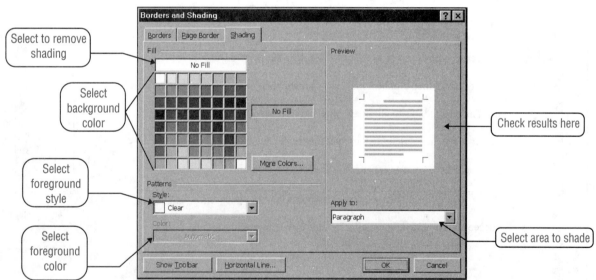

  5. Choose from one or more of the following options:
     - **Fill**   Allows you to select a background color.
     - **Style**   Allows you to select a percentage for a pattern, or select a ready-made pattern. A higher percentage gives more pattern to the shading. Select the clear option for no pattern.
     - **Color**   Allows you to select a foreground color for the pattern. This feature is not available if the selected Style option is Clear.
       Note: To remove shading, click No Fill in the Fill area on the Shading tab of the Borders and Shading dialog box.
  6. Check the results of your selections in the Preview box.
  7. Click OK.

Exercise 2a
Apply Shading

1. Open **PENCIL**.
2. Center the document vertically.
3. Select the title and change it to reverse video (white on black).
   Hint: Click F̲ormat, B̲orders and Shading, click the Shading tab, and choose 100% solid from the
   Style drop-down list.
4. Select the second paragraph and apply a 25% gray pattern from the St̲yle drop-down list.
5. Remove the shading you just applied in both the title and the second paragraph.
6. Select the title again and apply the following changes:
   a. Select a Shadow box border.
   b. Select a pink shading for the fill.
   c. Select 35% pattern in the St̲yle drop-down list.
   d. Select Teal from the C̲olor drop-down list.
7. Select the second paragraph and apply a yellow fill.
8. Select a pencil page border.
9. Compare your results to the illustration on the next page.
10. Save the document as **COLOR PENCILS**.
11. Print one copy.

Desired Result

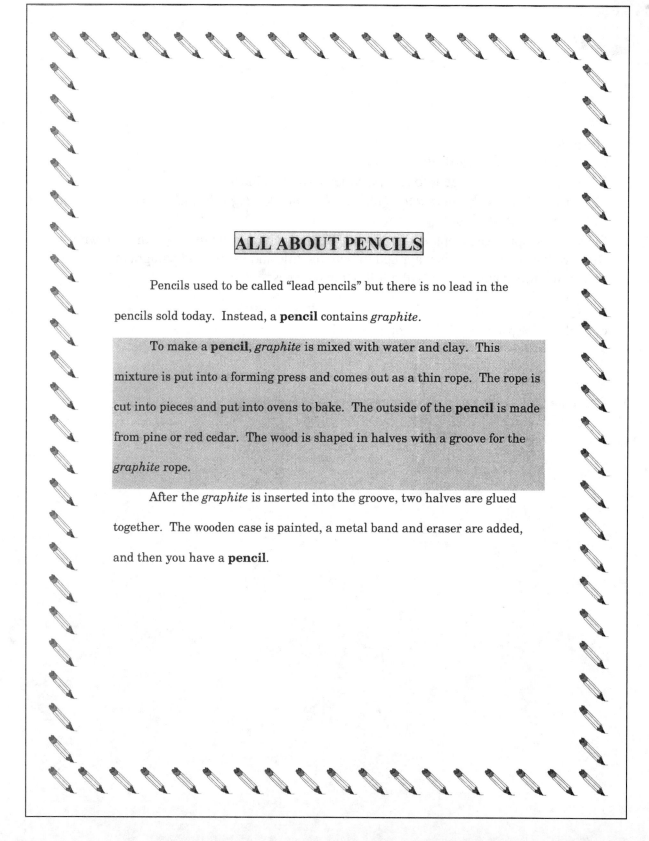

ALL ABOUT PENCILS

Pencils used to be called "lead pencils" but there is no lead in the pencils sold today. Instead, a **pencil** contains *graphite*.

To make a **pencil**, *graphite* is mixed with water and clay. This mixture is put into a forming press and comes out as a thin rope. The rope is cut into pieces and put into ovens to bake. The outside of the **pencil** is made from pine or red cedar. The wood is shaped in halves with a groove for the *graphite* rope.

After the *graphite* is inserted into the groove, two halves are glued together. The wooden case is painted, a metal band and eraser are added, and then you have a **pencil**.

Exercise 2b
Apply Border and Shading to a Flyer

1. Create a new document.
2. Set left and right margins to 1".
3. Type the title EARTH DAY in all caps:
    a. Use a decorative font, 72 point.
    b. Center the title.
    c. Add a single line black box border around the text.
        Note: Be careful to select only the words. The Apply to box should display "Text."
    e. Shade the area in a bright green color.
4. Type the subtitle Art Contest:
    a. Use a sans serif font, 36 point.
    b. Center the text.
    c. Press the Enter key once after Art Contest.
5. From the Clip Gallery Plants category, insert the *sunshine* graphic (second graphic in first row).
6. Size the graphic to resemble the illustration.
7. Center the graphic horizontally on the page.
8. Create a text box and type the remaining text in it as follows:
    a. Use the same sans serif font, 30 point.
    b. Center each line of text using initial caps.
9. Add a bright green border to the text box.
10. Enclose the entire flyer in a globe border. Set the point size to 20.
11. Preview your document.
12. Compare your results to the illustration on the next page.
13. Make any necessary adjustments to duplicate the illustration.
14. Save the document; name it **ART**.
15. Print one copy.
16. Close the document window.

Desired Result

EARTH DAY

Art Contest

Submit Your Design
by April 2
to the
Student Government Office

GOAL 3:   Add Picture Bullets

- In addition to using the standard bullets or symbols for bulleted lists, you can turn clip art, scanned images or downloaded images into picture bullets.

- Follow these steps to use a picture bullet:
    1. Select the items to which you want to add picture bullets.
    2. Click Format.
    3. Click Bullets and Numbering.
    4. Click the Bulleted tab.
    5. Click the Picture button to open the Clip Gallery.
    6. Click the desired picture bullet.
    7. Click the Insert clip icon.

- You can also create a picture bulleted list as you type by choosing an image as the bullet. Follow these steps to automatically insert an image as a bullet:
    1. Click Insert.
    2. Click Picture.
    3. Select Clip Art or From File.
    4. From the Clip Gallery, click the picture you want to use as a bullet.
    5. Click the Insert clip icon.
       OR
       From file, browse to the folder containing the picture you want to use as a bullet. Select the file.
    6. Resize the bullet as needed.
    7. Press the Tab key or Spacebar after the picture bullet.
    8. Type your text.
    9. Press Enter key to automatically insert the next bullet.
    10. Repeat Steps 8-9 as needed.
    11. Press Enter twice to finish the list.

- If you wish to create picture bullets and add them to an existing list, follow these steps:
    1. Place your insertion point where you want the first bullet to appear.
    2. Follow the above steps to automatically insert an image as a picture bullet.
    3. Select the remaining text to be bulleted and click the Bullets button on the Formatting toolbar.
    4. Adjust the indents and spacing so all the bulleted items are formatted the same way.

LESSON 30

Exercise 3
Add a Picture Bullet

1. Open **EVEREST3**.
2. Remove the border around the list.
3. Select the list.
4. Remove the letters.
5. Deselect the list and place the insertion point where you want the first bullet to appear.
6. Open Clip Gallery and choose a picture that contains a mountain.
7. Insert the picture and resize it as necessary.
8. Press the Tab key to separate the picture bullet from the text.
9. Select the remaining list and click the Bullets button on the Formatting toolbar.
10. Adjust the indents and spacing so all the bulleted items are formatted the same way.
11. Save the file as **EVEREST4**.
12. Print one copy.
13. Close the document window.

Desired Result

Mt. Everest Facts

The Himalayas has the world's 10 tallest mountains. Among them is Mt. Everest, tempting adventurers time and again to reach its summit at 29,028 feet. The conditions are very brutal. Freezing temperatures, raging winds and little oxygen have caused many accomplished climbers to meet their deaths on its icy slopes. Here are some interesting facts about Mt. Everest:

- Summit winds can reach over 130 mph.

- Temperatures can be as low as 45 degrees below zero Celsius.

- At 26,000 feet, climbers must use supplemental oxygen to survive.

- The best months to climb are May and October.

- In 1953, Sir Edmund Hillary was the first to reach the summit.

- There have been 4,000 attempts to reach the summit.

Each year there are many expeditions that set out to reach the top, but only a few succeed. The mountain remains for future generations to conquer.

LESSON 30

Timed Writing

1. Create a new document.
2. Use the default margins.
3. Change the font to Courier New, 12 point.
4. Take a 5-minute timing on the entire document.
   a. If you finish before the time is up, press the Enter key 2 times and start again.
   b. Do not correct errors. If you make an error, continue typing.
   c. To calculate your WAM speed, find the total number of words you typed and divide that number by 5.
5. Press the Enter key 4 times.
6. Practice each word that contained an error or each word or phrase that slowed you down. Practice them 5 times each.
7. Take another 5-minute timing. Follow the same instructions as in Step 4 above. Calculate your WAM speed.
8. Compare your speeds.
9. Save the document as L30TIME.
10. Print one copy.
11. Close the document window.

WORDS

We have all heard of snow and ice sports such as skating and   12
skiing, but there are other ice and snow sports that are not   24
as common. One such competitive Olympic sport is the luge.   36

Luge is a French word meaning sled. The luger rides on the   48
sled on his or her back, with feet in front. The luger does   60
not see where he or she is going but through practice has   72
memorized every turn in the luge track. The sled has no brakes 84
or way of steering. The luger steers the sled by pressing to   96
the left or right with his or her legs or shoulders.   106

The sleds race one at a time through the twists and turns of   118
the luge course. The course is about three-quarters of a mile 130
long. The fastest races were won in just under 3 minutes.   142

This is a sport only for trained competitors.   151

....1....2....3....4....5....6....7....8....9...10...11...12

MOUSE/KEYSTROKE PROCEDURES

Add Border

1. Select text or graphic to be bordered.
   OR
   Place the insertion point in the paragraph to be bordered.
2. Click **Format** menu .... Alt + O
3. Click **Borders and Shading** .... B
4. Click **Borders tab** .... Alt + B

5. Select one of the following setting options:
   - **None** .... Alt + N
   - **Box** .... Alt + X
   - **Shadow** .... Alt + A
   - **3D** .... Alt + D
   - **Custom** .... Alt + U
6. Click **Style** .... Alt + Y
7. Select desired line style .... ⤢

8. Click **Color** .... Alt + C
9. Select desired color .... ⤢
10. Click **Width** .... Alt + W
11. Select desired width .... ⤢
12. Click **Apply to** .... Alt + L
13. Select desired area .... ⤢
14. Check preview for results.
15. Click **OK** .... Enter

299

LESSON 30

Page Borders

1. Click **F̲ormat** menu .... `Alt`+`O`
2. Click **B̲orders and Shading**....... `B`
3. Click **P̲age Border** tab...... `Alt`+`P`
4. Select one of the following setting options:
   - **N̲one** ....`Alt`+`N`
   - **Bo̲x**............................`Alt`+`X`
   - **Sha̲dow**......................`Alt`+`A`
   - **3D̲** ....`Alt`+`D`
   - **Cu̲stom**......................`Alt`+`U`
5. Click **St̲yle** ....`Alt`+`Y`
6. Select desired line style ....`↑↓`
7. Click **C̲olor** ....`Alt`+`C`
8. Select desired color ....`↑↓`
9. Click **W̲idth** ....`Alt`+`W`
10. Select desired width ....`↑↓`
11. Click **A̲rt** ....`Alt`+`R`
12. Select desired graphic ....`↑↓`
13. Click **Ap̲ply to** ....`Alt`+`L`
14. Select desired area ....`↑↓`
15. Check preview for results.
16. Click **OK**..............................`Enter`

Shading

1. Select text or graphic to be shaded.
   OR
   Place insertion point in paragraph to be shaded.
2. Click **F̲ormat** menu .... `Alt`+`O`
3. Click **B̲orders and Shading**....................`B`
4. Click **S̲hading** tab ....`Alt`+`S`
5. Select one or more of the following options:
   - Select a fill color for background.
   AND/OR
   - Click **St̲yle** ....`Alt`+`Y`
   - Select a percentage for a pattern.......................`↑↓`
   AND/OR

- Click **C̲olor**...................`Alt`+`C`
- Select a color from the palette...........................`↓`
6. Click **App̲ly to** ....`Alt`+`L`
7. Select desired area ....`↑↓`
8. Check preview for results.
9. Click **OK**...............................`Enter`

Remove Borders/Shading/ Page Borders

1. Click **F̲ormat** menu ....`Alt`+`O`
2. Click **B̲orders and Shading**.......`B`
3. Click **B̲orders** tab ....`Alt`+`B`
4. Click **N̲one** ....`Alt`+`N`

Insert Picture Bullet

1. Select text to format as numbered/lettered list.
2. Click **F̲ormat** ....`Alt`+`O`
3. Click **Bullets and N̲umbering** ... `N`
4. Click **B̲ulleted** tab ....`Alt`+`B`
5. Click **Picture** button
   | Picture... | ....`Alt`+`P`
6. Click desired bullet.
7. Click **Insert clip** button .

Insert Image as Picture Bullet

1. Click **I̲nsert** ....`Alt`+`I`
2. Click **P̲icture** ....`P`
3. Click **C̲lip Art** ....`C`
   a. Click desired bullet picture.
   b. Click **Insert clip** button .
   OR
   Click **F̲rom File**........................`F`
   a. Browse to the desired folder.
   b. Select the desired file.
   c. Click **I̲nsert**..................`Alt`+`I`
4. Resize picture bullet.

---

5. Press **Tab** key or **Spacebar** after bullet... `Tab`/`Space`
6. Type text and press **Enter** to continue list....................`Enter`

Insert Image as Picture Bullet to Existing List

1. Place insertion point
2. Click **I̲nsert** ....`Alt`+`I`
3. Click **P̲icture** ....`P`
4. Click **C̲lip Art** ....`C`
   a. Click desired bullet picture.
   b. Click **Insert clip** button .
   OR
   Click **F̲rom File**........................`F`
   a. Browse to the desired folder.
   b. Select the desired file.
   c. Click **I̲nsert**..................`Alt`+`I`
5. Resize picture bullet.
6. Press **Tab** key or **Spacebar** after bullet ....`Tab`/`Space`
7. Select remaining text to be bulleted.
8. Click **Bullets** button on Formatting toolbar.
9. Adjust indents and spacing for all bulleted items.

- Draw Basic Shapes Using the AutoShapes Toolbar
- Draw Lines • Size a Drawing Shape or Line
- Move or Copy a Drawing Shape or Line
- Add or Change Color of a Drawing Shape or Line

Warm-up

1. Create a new document.
2. Set the left and right margins to 1".
3. Type each line twice, trying to type faster each time you repeat the line. When you see the vertical lines between phrases, say the phrase to yourself as you type. Do not type the vertical lines.
4. If you make an error, continue typing.
5. If you have time, repeat the exercise.
6. Save the document as **LES31**.

---

1 a;sldkfjghfjdksla; a;sldkfjghfjdksla; a;sldkfjghfjdksla;

2 aq1qaza sw2wsxs de3edcd fr4rfvf ft5tfgfbf fr45rftfgfbfvf

3 fur fun gun gum guy buy but hut jut vug jim dim kid red cue

4 my, lot sit wet tex co. fat pat zip qt. s219 d3k8 f4j7 f5j6 ;0

5 ax ax axe axe exit exit wax wax taxi taxi Max Max ox ox

6 we we were were was was saw saw will will well well ow ow

7 if you| if you| if we| if we| if she| if she| if they| if they|

8 Jim Vug saw 38 wet ducks run from 15 guys with red hair.

LESSON 31

GOAL 1: Draw Basic Shapes Using the Autoshapes Toolbar

- The **Draw** feature allows you to create your own pictures and shapes. The Drawing toolbar provides the necessary tools.

- To display the Drawing toolbar, click the **Drawing** button ⊞ on the Standard toolbar. The Drawing toolbar, which is displayed below the document window, contains the following drawing tools:

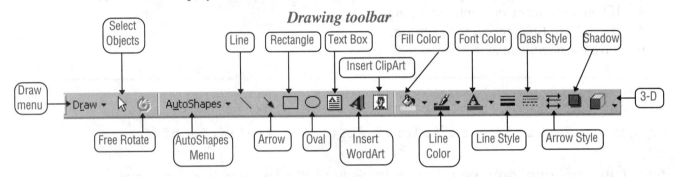

Drawing toolbar

- In this book, we will only use some of the features of the Drawing toolbar. The first button we will learn is the **AutoShapes** button AutoShapes ▾. When you click the AutoShapes button, you will see a new menu of AutoShape choices. If you choose Basic Shapes, you will be able to choose one of the shapes shown below.

AutoShapes menu

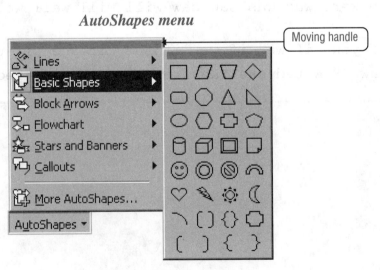

- If you are going to use AutoShapes often, follow these steps to add the AutoShapes toolbar to your document window:
  1. Click AutoShapes button `AutoShapes ▾` on the Drawing toolbar.
  2. Click the moving handle ▓▓▓▓▓▓▓▓▓▓▓ at the top of the AutoShapes toolbar and drag the toolbar into the document window.

- The **AutoShapes toolbar**, which floats in the document window, will be available at all times until you close it. The Drawing toolbar will also be available below the document window. When you are ready to close the AutoShapes toolbar, click the Close button ☒ in the upper right-hand corner of the toolbar.

AutoShapes toolbar

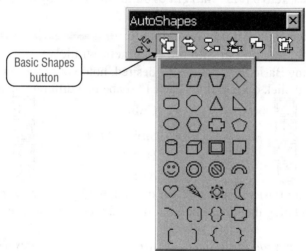

- To draw a shape from the Basic Shapes menu:
  1. Click on desired shape.
  2. Position the pointer ╋ in the document window where you want to begin drawing the shape.
  3. Click where you want the shape to appear and it will appear perfectly proportioned (square, round, etc.) at 1" in size.

     OR

     a. Drag the pointer in the direction you want the shape to appear.
        - Hold down the Ctrl key while you drag to draw the shape from the center.
        - Hold down the Shift key while you drag to draw a perfectly proportioned shape.
        - Hold down the Shift and Ctrl keys while you drag to draw a perfectly proportioned shape from the center.
     b. Release the mouse button when you reach the shape's desired size.

- The Drawing toolbar also contains a Rectangle button ▢ and an Oval button ⬭. You can also create a rectangle or oval by selecting these objects from the Basic Shapes pull-down box.

- Move an AutoShape the same way you would move a graphic.

LESSON 31

Exercise 1
Draw Shapes

1. Create a new document.
2. Set all margins to .5".
   Note: When drawing shapes, leave a .5" margin around the edges of the page, since most printers will not print in the 5" area around the page.
3. Open the AutoShapes toolbar (Click the moving handle ▭▭▭▭▭▭ at the top of the AutoShapes toolbar and drag the toolbar into the document window).
   a. Select each of the following Basic Shapes tools (if desired, hold your mouse pointer over the shape to see the name of the shape) and click once to draw each 1" shape in a different area of the document window.

   - **Rectangle**   ▢
   - **Diamond**   ◈
   - **Oval**   ◎
   - **Isosceles Triangle** △

   - **Cube**   ▣
   - **Smiley Face**   ☺
   - **Heart**   ♡
   - **Arc**   ◝

   b. Select each of the following Basic Shapes tools (if desired, hold your mouse pointer over the shape to see the name of the shape) and drag the mouse pointer in any direction to draw each shape in a different area of the document window.
   Note: Do not make the shapes too large since you will have over 30 shapes when the exercise is complete.

   - **Rectangle**   ▭
   - **Oval**   ◯
   - **Sun**   ☼

   - **Lightning Bolt**   ⚡
   - **Block Arc**   ◠

   c. Select each of the following Basic Shapes tools (if desired, hold your mouse pointer over the shape to see the name of the shape) and hold down the Ctrl key as you drag the mouse pointer in any direction to draw each shape in a different area of the document window:

   - **Oval**   ◯
   - **Can**   ⬙

   - **Bevel**   ▣
   - **Folded Corner**   ◳

   d. Select each of the following Basic Shapes tools (if desired, hold your mouse pointer over the shape to see the name of the shape) and hold down the Shift key as you drag the mouse pointer in any direction to draw each shape in a different area of the document window:

   - **Octagon** ⬡   - **"No" Symbol** ⊘   - **Moon** ☾

   e. Select each of the following Basic Shapes tools (if desired, hold your mouse pointer over the shape to see the name of the shape) and hold down the Shift and Ctrl keys as you drag the mouse pointer in any direction to draw each shape in a different area of the document window:

   - **Rectangle** ▭   - **Oval** ◯   - **Cross** ✚

   f. Use any method you wish to draw any shapes that have not been used.

4. Save the file as **SHAPE1**.
5. Print one copy.
6. Close the document window.
7. On your printout, label each shape with its name.
8. Save the printout for reference.

GOAL 2: Draw Lines

■ Click the **Lines** button 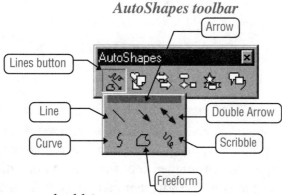 on the AutoShapes toolbar to view the different types of lines available in Word 2000.

AutoShapes toolbar

Arrow

Lines button — AutoShapes

Line

Curve

Double Arrow

Scribble

Freeform

■ To draw a line, arrow or double arrow:
   1. Click desired line.
   2. Drag the pointer in the direction you want the line to appear.
   3. Release the mouse button when you reach the line's desired length.

■ When drawing a line, arrow or double arrow, you can:

   • Hold down the Ctrl key while you drag to draw the line from the center out.

   OR

   • Hold down the Shift key while you drag to draw a straight line that is horizontal, vertical or diagonal.

   OR

   • Hold down the Shift and Ctrl keys while you drag to draw a perfectly straight line from the center out.

■ To draw a scribble line:
   1. Drag the mouse pointer (which turns into a pen as you drag) as though you were moving a pen or pencil.
   2. Release mouse button to end line.

- To draw a curve:

    1. Drag the pointer in the direction you want the free form shape to run.
    2. Click at the point where you want the curve to turn and drag the mouse pointer in the new direction. Repeat this step for each curve.
    3. Double-click to stop drawing the curve.

- To draw a freeform shape:

    1. Drag the pointer in the direction you want the line or curve to run.
    2. For a freeform shape with straight lines, click and release at the point where you want the line to turn and drag the mouse pointer in the new direction. Repeat this step for each turn. Double-click to stop drawing the free formshape.
    3. For a freeform shape with curves, drag your mouse pointer as though you were drawing with a pen or pencil. Double-click to stop drawing the freeform shape.
    4. If you want a closed freeform shape, double-click at the same point where your line began.

Exercise 2
Draw Lines

1. Create a new document.
2. Set all margins to .5".
   Note: When drawing lines, leave a .5" margin around the edges of the page.
3. Click AutoShapes. Click the moving handle ▬▬▬▬▬▬▬ at the top of the AutoShapes toolbar and drag the toolbar into the document window if it is not already open.
4. Select each of the following line tools from the Lines pull-down box and drag the mouse pointer in the indicated direction to draw each line as indicated in a different area of the document window:
   Note: If desired, hold your mouse pointer over the line to see the name of the line.

   - **Line** ⬜—downward from left to right
   - **Arrow** ⬜—downward from right to left
   - **Double Arrow** ⬜—horizontal from left to right
   - **Curve** ⬜—two upward and downward curves from left to right (remember to click at each curve to change the direction)
   - **Freeform** ⬜—any closed shape
   - **Scribble** ⬜—any shape

5. Select each of the following line tools and hold down the Ctrl key as you drag the mouse pointer in any direction to draw each line in a different area of the document window:

   - **Line** ⬜—horizontal
   - **Arrow** ⬜—vertical
   - **Double Arrow** ⬜—vertical

306

6. Select each of the following line tools and hold down the Shift key as you drag the mouse pointer in any direction to draw each line in a different area of the document window:

- **Line** —horizontal
- **Arrow** —upward from left to right

7. Select each of the following Lines tools (if desired, hold your mouse pointer over the shape to see the name of the shape) and hold down the Shift and Ctrl keys as you drag the mouse pointer in any direction to draw each shape in a different area of the document window:

- **Arrow** —downward from left to right
- **Double Arrow** —upward from left to right

8. Save the file as **LINE1**.
9. Print one copy.
10. Close the document window.

GOAL 3:   Size a Drawing Shape or Line

- The size and proportions of any basic shape can be changed after it is drawn. To change the shape:
  1. Click on the shape to select it. Sizing handles appear around the shape.
  2. Drag any of the sizing handles in the desired direction to change the shape.

- On some drawing shapes you will also see an **adjustment handle**—a yellow diamond. This handle allows you to adjust the appearance of the shape—not the size. For example, you can adjust a moon shape so it is thinner or thicker.

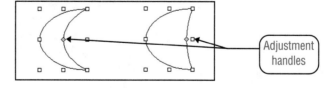

Adjustment handles

- To delete a drawing object, click on it to select it and press the Delete key.

- Once a line is drawn, the style of the line can be changed by selecting the **Line Style** button ≡ on the Drawing toolbar.
  1. Click on the line to select it. Sizing handles will appear.
  2. Click the Line Style button ≡ on the Drawing toolbar.
  3. Select a line style.

Exercise 3a
Size a Line

1. Create a new document.
2. Set all margins to .5".
   Note: When drawing shapes and/or lines, leave a .5" margin around the edges of the page.
3. Set the Zoom Control to Whole Page.
4. Click AutoShapes. Click the moving handle ▭▭▭▭▭▭ at the top of the AutoShapes toolbar and drag the toolbar into the document window if it is not already open.
5. Use the Lines pull-down box and select the Scribble shape.
6. Draw any scribble near the center of the page.
7. The scribble should be selected (it will have sizing handles). If not, click on any part of the scribble to select it.
8. Drag the top middle handle upward.
9. Drag the lower right handle downward.
10. Drag the left-side middle handle to the left.
11. Drag any of the handles so the scribble fills the page (within .5" of the edges).
12. Save the file as **SCRIBBLE**.
13. Print one copy.
14. Close the document window.

Exercise 3b
Size a Shape

1. Create a new document.
2. Set all margins to .5".
   Note: When drawing shapes and/or lines, leave a .5" margin around the edges of the page.
3. Set the Zoom Control to Whole Page.
4. Click AutoShapes. Click the moving handle [▬▬▬▬▬▬▬] at the top of the AutoShapes toolbar and drag the toolbar into the document window if it is not already open.
5. Use the Basic Shapes pull-down box and select the Sun shape.
6. Use the Shift+Ctrl keys and drag the mouse pointer to draw a small sun in the middle of the page.
7. Click on the sun. Drag one of the corner handles of the sun while holding down the Shift+Ctrl keys to enlarge the sun to within .5" of the horizontal edges of the page.
8. Use the Basic Shapes pull-down box and select the Smiley Face shape.
9. Use the Shift+Ctrl keys and drag the mouse pointer to draw a smiley face in the middle of the sun, making it almost as large as the sun's circle.
10. Drag the adjustment handle of the smiley face to change the smile to a frown.
11. Use the Basic Shapes pull-down box and select the Regular Pentagon shape.
12. Click in the middle of the frowning face to add the Regular Pentagon shape.
13. Click on the regular pentagon shape. Drag one of the corner handles to size the shape so it looks like a nose.
14. Save the file as **FROWN1**.
15. Print one copy.
16. Close the AutoShapes toolbar.
17. Close the document window.

LESSON 31

- Once you have drawn a shape or line, you may want to change its location on the page.
- To **move** a shape or line to another location:
    1. Click on the shape or line to select it.
    2. When mouse pointer turns to a 4-sided arrow ✥, drag it to the new location.
- To move a shape or line in a straight line, press the Shift key while you are dragging it to the new location.
- To **nudge** (slightly move) a shape or line, hold down the Alt key while you are dragging the shape or line to the new location. This will allow you to fine-tune your shape or line movement.
- To **copy** a shape or line:
    1. Hold down the Ctrl key and click on the shape or line to select it.
    2. Pointer will have a small + next to it.
    3. As you drag, a copy of the shape or line will move to the new location.
- To copy a shape or line and keep it in a straight line with the original shape or line, press the Shift key along with the Ctrl key while you are dragging it to the new location.

Exercise 4
Move, Copy and Size Shapes and Lines

1. Create a new document.
2. Set all margins to .5".
   Note: When drawing shapes and/or lines, leave a .5" margin around the edges of the page.
3. Click AutoShapes. Click the moving handle [▬▬▬▬▬▬▬] at the top of the AutoShapes toolbar and drag the toolbar into the document window if it is not already open.
4. Use the Basic Shapes and Lines pull-down boxes to select shapes to create a robot. Follow the example shown below or create your own.
5. Move and size the shapes and lines as needed.
6. Save the file as **ROBOT1**.
7. Print one copy.
8. Close the document window.

GOAL 5: Add or Change Color of a Drawing Shape or Line

- You can add **color** to a drawing shape by choosing the **Fill Color** button on the Drawing toolbar. You can also change the color of the drawing shape outline by choosing the **Line Color** button on the Drawing toolbar. To add or change color:
  1. Click on the shape to select it.
  2. Click on the arrow next to the **Fill Color** button or **Line Color** button.
  3. Select a fill color from the Fill Color box or a line color from the Line Color box. In addition to choosing a fill or line color, you can also choose Fill Effects or Patterned Lines (this will be explained in more detail below).

- Once a fill or line color is chosen, the color will be displayed below the paint can or paintbrush. Each time you select an object and click on the paint can or paintbrush, that color will fill or outline the object.

- In addition to selecting a color from the Fill Color menu, you can also select a **pattern** or **texture** by clicking Fill Effects. Select the Pattern or Texture tab on the Fill Effects dialog box and then choose the desired pattern or texture. If you choose a fill color, the pattern will take on that color. A texture will only reflect the color shown on the Texture tab menu.

Fill Effects dialog box

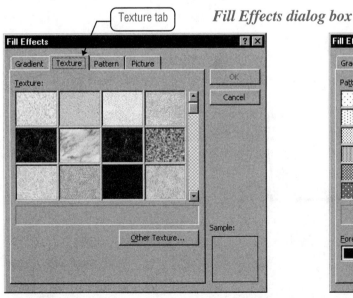

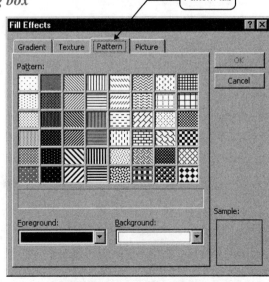

- A colored pattern can be added to a line by first selecting a line color and then selecting a pattern.
- If desired, you can select No Fill or No Line from the Fill Color or Line Color drop-down boxes.

Exercise 5a
Add Color to Shapes and Lines

1. Open **ROBOT1**.
2. Save the file as **ROBOT2**.
3. Click on each shape and select a color using the Fill Color button.
4. Click on each line and select a color using the Line Color button.
5. Resave the file.
6. Print one copy.
7. Close the document window.

Exercise 5b
Add Color to Shapes and Lines

1. Open **FROWN1**.
2. Save the file as **FROWN2**.
3. Click on the face and add yellow using the Fill Collor button.
4. Click on the sun and add light yellow using the Fill Color button.
5. Color the pentagon-shaped nose red.
   *Note: If you click on a shape and select the wrong one, just click again outside of the Basic Shape to
   deselect it.*
6. Resave the file.
7. Print one copy.
8. Close the document window.

Exercise 5c
Add Color to Shapes and Lines

1. Open **SHAPE1**.
2. Save the file as **SHAPE2**.
3. Click on different shapes and add color, texture or patterns using the Fill Color button.
   Note: To add a pattern with a color, you must first select a color and then select a pattern.
4. Resave the file.
5. Print one copy.
6. Close the document window.

Exercise 5d
Add Color to Shapes and Lines

1. Open **LINE1**.
2. Save the file as **LINE2**.
3. Click on different lines and add color, patterns or change the line style using the Line Color and Line Style buttons.
4. Resave the file.
5. Print one copy.
6. Close the document window.

Timed Writing

1. Create a new document.
2. Use the default margins.
3. Change font to Courier New, 12 point.
4. Take a 5-minute timing on the entire document.
   a. If you finish before the time is up, press the Enter key twice and start again.
   b. Do not correct errors. If you make a mistake, continue typing.
   c. To calculate your WAM speed, find the total number of words you typed and divide that number by 5.
5. Press the Enter key 4 times.
6. Practice each word that contained an error or each word or phrase that slowed you down. Practice them 5 times each.
7. Take another 5-minute timing. Follow the same instructions in Step 4 above. Calculate your WAM speed.
8. Compare your speeds.
9. Save the document as **L31TIME**.
10. Print one copy.
11. Close the document window.

	WORDS
Water is one of the things that is needed by both plants and	12
animals to survive. Some varieties of animals, such as fish	24
or frogs, need water to live in. People need water but not	36
to live in. They use water for drinking, cooking, cleaning,	38
and also for recreation. About two thirds of the surface of	50
the earth is water. Most of this water is seawater. Some	62
of it is frozen and forms ice and glaciers. We have a large	74
problem facing us both now and for the future. The problem	86
is pollution. When our fresh water supply becomes polluted,	98
it cannot readily be used for drinking, swimming, cooking,	110
or cleaning. The plants and animals that live in the water	119
become poisoned by the pollution.	126

It is important to our future that we clean up the polluted   138
water and prevent future pollution. It is our duty to make   150
sure future generations will have a clean water supply.   161

....1....2....3....4....5....6....7....8....9...10...11...12

LESSON 31

Display Drawing Toolbar

Click **Drawing** button 🦋 on the Standard toolbar.

Access AutoShapes

Click **A̲utoShapes** button AutoShapes ▾ on Drawing toolbar.

OR

a. Click **A̲utoShapes** button AutoShapes ▾ on Drawing toolbar.

b. Click moving handle ▬▬▬ on AutoShapes toolbar.

c. Drag AutoShapes toolbar into the document window.

Draw Basic Shapes

1. Click **Basic Shapes** button 🖐 on floating AutoShapes toolbar.

   OR

   a. Click **A̲utoShapes** button AutoShapes ▾.

   b. Click **B̲asic Shapes** .... Ⓑ

2. Select a basic shape.

3. Position pointer .... ┼ to begin drawing.

4. Drag pointer to create shape.
   - Hold **Ctrl** key when dragging to draw from center.
   - Hold **Shift** key when dragging for perfect proportioned shape.
   - Hold **Shift** and **Ctrl** keys when dragging for perfectly proportioned shape drawn from center.

5. Release mouse button when shape is complete.

Draw Lines

1. Click **Lines** button 🔷 on the Floating AutoShapes toolbar.

   OR

a. Click **A̲utoShapes** button AutoShapes ▾ on the Drawing toolbar.

b. Click **L̲ines** button 🔷.

2. Select a line.

3. Position pointer ┼ to begin drawing.

4. Drag pointer to create line.
   - Hold **Ctrl** key when dragging to draw from center out.
   - Hold **Shift** key when dragging for perfect straight line.
   - Hold **Shift** and **Ctrl** keys when dragging for perfectly straight line drawn from center out.

5. Release mouse button when line is complete.

Draw Freeform Shape or Curve

If using the:

1. Click **Lines** button 🔷 on floating AutoShapes toolbar.

2. Select :
   - **Freeform** button 🖵.
     OR
   - **Curve** button 𝄓.

3. For freeform shape with straight lines:
   a. Click where you want shape to begin.
   b. Click at each corner.
   c. Double-click to end shape

4. For freeform shape with curved line:
   a. Click where you want shape to begin.
   b. Drag and double click to end shape.

Draw Scribble Line

1. Click **Lines** button 🔷 on floating AutoShapes toolbar.

2. Click **Scribble** button 🖉.

3. Drag mouse pointer as though you were moving a pen or pencil.

4. Release mouse button to end line.

Size A Shape or Line

1. Select the shape.

2. Drag sizing handles.

Change Line Style

1. Select the line.

2. Click **Line Style** button ▤ on the Drawing toolbar.

3. Select style .... ▣.

Move Shape or Line

1. Click on shape or line to select it.

2. Mouse pointer turns into a 4-way arrow.................. ✥

3. Drag to a new location.
   - Hold **Shift** key when dragging to move in a straight line.
   - Hold **Alt** key to nudge to a new location.

Copy Shape or Line

1. Hold down **Ctrl** key and click on shape or line to select it.

2. A "+" appears next to the mouse pointer

3. Drag copy to a new location.

   Note: Hold Shift and Ctrl keys to drag copy in a straight line.

Add/Change Color of Shape or Line

1. Select shape or line.

2. Click **Fill Color** 🪣 or **Line Color** 🖌 button arrow.

3. Click on fill or line color ....

LESSON 32

- Group Drawing Shapes to Form an Object
- Order, Nudge, Flip and Rotate Drawing Shapes or Objects
- Add Text to Shapes

Warm-up

1. Create a new document.
2. Set the left and right margins to 1".
3. Type each line twice, trying to type faster when you repeat the line. Press the Enter key twice after the second line.
4. When you see the vertical lines between phrases, say the phrase to yourself as you type. Do not type the vertical lines.
5. If you make an error, continue typing.
6. If you have time, repeat the exercise.
7. Save the document as **LES32**.

---

1 a;sldkfjghfjdksla; a;sldkfjghfjdksla; a;sldkfjghfjdksla;
2 aq1qaza sw2wsxs de3edcd fr4rfvf ft5tfgfbf fr45rftfgfbfvf

3 fur fun gun gum guy buy but hut jut vug jim dim kid red cue
4 my, lot sit wet tex co. fat pat zip qt. s2l9 d3k8 f4j7 f5j6 ;0

5 on use out get also up down want should could would
6 self itself yourself myself herself himself oneself

7 go yourself|go yourself|up and down|up and down|on up|on up|
8 At the Zip Co., Jim Vug paid $37.25 but Pat Gun paid $35.75.

LESSON 32

GOAL 1: Group Drawing Shapes to Form an Object

- By combining different shapes, you can form an object. For example, if you want to move, size, or fill an object or several connected lines or shapes, Word's **Group** feature allows you to join the lines and shapes so that they form one object.

- To group shapes into an object, it is best to use the **Select Objects** button ![cursor] which is located on the Drawing toolbar. To group the objects:

  1. Click the Select Objects button ![cursor].
  2. Hold the Shift key and click on each Shape or Line you want included in the object.

     OR

     Drag the mouse pointer around all the lines and shapes you wish to group. As you drag the mouse pointer a dotted line will be dragged around the objects.

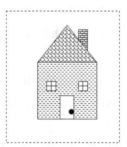

  3. When you release the mouse button, all the objects will be selected.
  4. Click the Draw button ![Draw] on the Drawing toolbar.
  5. On the Draw button menu, select Group. You will see by the sizing handles that all the objects are now grouped together as one object.

- To ungroup objects:
  1. Click on the object to select it.
  2. Click the Draw button ![Draw] on the Drawing toolbar.
  3. On the Draw button menu, select Ungroup.

- Grouped objects can be inserted into any document the same way a picture is inserted.

Exercise 1a
Group Shapes Into an Object

1. Open **ROBOT2**.
2. Save the file as **ROBOT3**.
3. Use the Select Objects tool and drag a box to surround the robot.
4. Click the D̲raw button on the Drawing toolbar.
5. On the D̲raw button menu, select G̲roup.
6. Resize the robot so you can copy it and place the copied object next to the original.
7. Arrange the two robots so that they are holding hands.
8. Resave the file.
9. Print one copy.
10. Close the document window.

Exercise 1b
Group Shapes Into an Object

1. Create a new document.
2. Use the default margins.
3. Click A̲utoShapes. Click the move handle [▭▭▭▭▭▭] at the top of the AutoShapes toolbar and drag the toolbar into the document window.
4. Use the Rectangle, Oval, Lines, and Fill Color buttons to create a desk. Follow the example shown below or create your own.

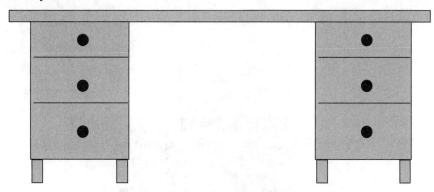

   a. Use the rectangle tool to draw the top of the desk and add brown fill.
   b. Use the rectangle tool to draw the left side of the desk and add brown fill.
      Hint: Use the Alt key to nudge the objects into position.

    c. Use the line tool to draw a line 1/3 of the way down to create a drawer and add brown fill.

    d. Copy (hold down the Ctrl and Shift keys) the line to create two more drawers.

    e. Use the oval tool to create a drawer knob and add black fill.

    f. Copy (hold down the Ctrl and Shift keys) the drawer knob to the other two drawers.

    g. Use the rectangle tool to add a leg to the left side of the desk and add brown fill.

    h. Copy (hold down the Ctrl and Shift keys) the leg and add it to the other side of the bottom drawer.

    i. Group objects on the left side of the desk.

    j. Copy (hold down the Ctrl and Shift keys) the left side of the desk and drag it to the right side.

5. Use the Select Object tool to select all parts of the desk.
6. Group the selected objects.
7. Save the file; name it **DESK**.
8. Print one copy.
9. Close the document window.

GOAL 2: Order, Nudge, Flip and Rotate Drawing Shapes or Objects

- When combining shapes into an object, you may want part of one shape hidden under part of another. An example might be a circle and a triangle combined to form an ice cream cone 🍦. The bottom portion of the circle must be hidden by the cone (the triangle). This is done by layering the shapes.

- To layer shapes, select the shape you wish to hide or bring forward.

    1. Click the Draw button ⎡ Draw ▾ ⎤ on the Drawing toolbar.

    2. Click Order.

    3. Select the layering order for the selected shape.

Draw menu

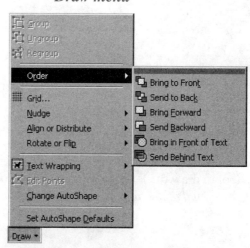

- To layer the ice cream behind the cone , select the circle and then choose Send to Ba<u>c</u>k from the O<u>r</u>der submenu.

- There will be times when many layers are required. You will have to Bring <u>F</u>orward or Send <u>B</u>ackward each shape as many times as necessary to get the layering effect needed for the completed object.

- There will be times you will need to move a shape into a specific position. You have already learned to nudge a shape by holding down the Alt key as you move the shape. You can also use the <u>N</u>udge feature to move the shape a little farther up, down, left or right. To nudge the shape, select the shape and:

1. Click the D<u>r</u>aw button <u>Draw</u> ▾ on the Drawing toolbar.
2. On the D<u>r</u>aw button menu, select <u>N</u>udge.

Draw menu

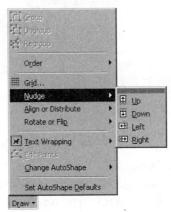

3. Select <u>U</u>p, <u>D</u>own, <u>L</u>eft, or <u>R</u>ight.

- For even finer nudge control, select the shape and hold down the Ctrl key as you press an arrow key. Every time you press the arrow key (with the Ctrl key pressed), you will nudge the object left, right, up or down in very small increments.

- When working with a drawing that contains small details, you will have more control over the shapes if you click the Zoom button on the Standard toolbar and change to a high percentage. You can go as high as 500%.

- If a shape is in the wrong position, you can change the position by rotating or flipping it. For example, the ice cream cone drawn with the triangle shape was upside down and had to be flipped vertically. To ro<u>t</u>ate or flip a shape:

1. Click the D<u>r</u>aw button <u>Draw</u> ▾ on the Drawing toolbar.
2. On the D<u>r</u>aw button menu, select Rotate or Fli<u>p</u>.

Draw menu

Note: You can also select the Free Rotate button 🔄 *on the Drawing toolbar.*

3. To flip an object or shape, select either Flip <u>H</u>orizontal or Flip <u>V</u>ertical.
4. To rotate an object or shape, select Free Ro<u>t</u>ate, Rotate <u>L</u>eft, or Rotate <u>R</u>ight.

■ By selecting Free Ro<u>t</u>ate, you can turn any object or shape around. When you select Free Ro<u>t</u>ate, the object or shape will have green dots at its corners. To rotate the object or shape:

1. Click on a green dot and the mouse pointer will change to a rotate symbol .
2. Drag the green dot.
3. The shape or object will rotate until you release the mouse button.

Exercise 2a
Order, Nudge, Flip and Rotate

1. Create a new document.
2. Use the default margins.
3. Click A<u>u</u>toShapes. Click the moving handle [▬▬▬▬▬▬▬▬] at the top of the AutoShapes toolbar and drag the toolbar into the document window.
4. Use the Isosceles Triangle, Oval, Explosion 1 (found in the Stars and Banners submenu) and Fill Color buttons to create an ice cream cone. Follow the example shown below, or create your own.
   a. Use the Isosceles Triangle tool to draw a triangle. Flip and rotate the triangle as shown. Click the Fill Color button and select Fill Effects. Choose the Pattern tab and click a pattern for the cone.
   b. Use the Oval tool to draw the ice cream scoop and select a fill color and/or pattern. Send the ice cream scoop behind the cone (Draw, O<u>r</u>der, Send to Ba<u>c</u>k). Nudge the scoop into place.
   c. From the A<u>u</u>toShapes toolbar, select the Stars and Banners button. Select Explosion 1 and use the same fill color and/or pattern as the ice cream scoop. Position it below the ice cream scoop and send it behind the scoop. Nudge the Explosion into place.
5. Use the Select Object tool and group all the shapes together.
6. Save the file; name it **CONE**.
7. Print one copy.
8. Close the document window.

Exercise 2b
Nudge and Rotate

1. Create a new document.
2. Use the default margins.
3. Click AutoShapes. Click the moving handle [_____] at the top of the AutoShapes toolbar and drag the toolbar into the document window.
4. Use the Isosceles Triangle, Oval, Heart, Right Bracket [ ] , Scribble, Fill Color, and Line Style buttons to create a mouse. Follow the example shown below or create your own.

   a. Use the Isosceles Triangle tool to draw a triangle. Rotate the triangle as shown. Click the Fill Color button and select Black.
   b. Use the Oval tool to draw a circle and select a Black fill. Nudge the circle into the triangle as shown.
   c. Use the Curve tool (AutoShape Lines button) to draw a tail.
   d. Use the Heart tool and draw a small heart. Add Black fill. Rotate the heart and nudge it into position for the ears.
   e. Use the Right Bracket tool for the legs. Draw one leg and copy it. Nudge each leg into position.
   f. Use the oval tool for the eye, with no fill.
5. Use the Select Object tool and group all the shapes together.
6. Save the file; name it **MOUSE**.
7. Print one copy.
8. Close the document window.

Exercise 2c
Use All Draw Features Learned

1. Create a new document.
2. Use the default margins.
3. Click AutoShapes. Click the moving handle [_____] at the top of the AutoShapes toolbar and drag the toolbar into the document window. Click the Basic Shapes submenu and use the Oval, Isosceles Triangle, Moon and Fill Color buttons to create a dog. Follow the example shown on the next page or create your own, using the shapes you wish.
Note: Choose a high percentage Zoom to work with the spots on the face.

4. Use the Select Object tool and group all the shapes together.
5. Save the file; name it **DOG**.
6. Print one copy.
7. Close the document window.

- You may wish to add text to a drawing shape. To do this:
  1. Select the shape.
  2. Right-click the shape.
  3. Select <u>A</u>dd Text.
  4. Type desired text.

- If you have already typed text and want to change it:
  1. Select the shape.
  2. Right-click the shape.
  3. Select <u>E</u>dit Text.
  4. Make desired text changes.

Exercise 3a
Add Text to a Shape

1. Create a new document.
2. Use the default margins.
3. Insert the Folded Corner AutoShape anywhere on the page.
4. Size the shape to approximately 2" horizontally and 3" vertically. (If the ruler is not visible, click <u>V</u>iew, <u>R</u>uler.)
5. Right-click the shape and select <u>A</u>dd Text.
6. Use a sans serif font, 28 point.
7. Type the following text in the shape: Turn the Page to find out the end of this exciting story!
8. Save the file; name it **TEXT**.
9. Print one copy.
10. Close the document window.

Turn the page to find out the end of this exciting story!

LESSON 32

Exercise 3b
Use All Draw Features

Note: To complete this exercise, you will use the following features: AutoShapes, Fill Color, Line Color, Line Style, Rotate and Flip, Nudge, Order, Group and Add Text.

1. Create a new document.
2. Use the default margins.
3. Create the pig shown below (any size) using the necessary shapes and fills.
4. Group all parts of objects forming the pig.
5. Add a Bevel AutoShape around the pig. Send the Bevel AutoShape to the back.
6. Add text to the Bevel AutoShape. Type the word PIG using a sans serif font, 8 point.
   Note: Type the word PIG a few times, pressing the spacebar after the last time. Copy and paste the words until the box is filled. If necessary, select the text and center align it.
7. Save the file; name it **PIG**.
8. Print one copy.
9. Close the document window.

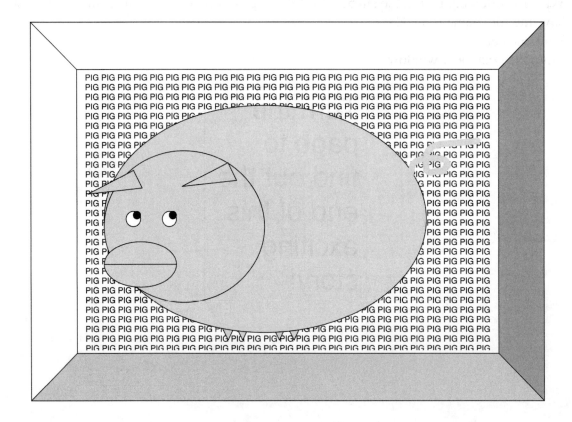

Timed Writing

1. Create a new document. Use the default margins.
2. Change font to Courier New, 12 point.
3. Take a 5-minute timing on the entire document.
   a. If you finish before the time is up, press the Enter key twice and start again.
   b. Do not correct errors. If you make an error, continue typing.
   c. To calculate your WAM speed, find the total number of words you typed and divide that number by 5.
4. Press the Enter key 4 times.
5. Take another 5-minute timing on the entire document, following the same instructions in Step 3 above. Calculate your WAM speed.
6. Compare your speeds.
7. Save the document as **L32TIME**.
8. Print one copy.
9. Close the document window.

	WORDS
The outside surface of the earth we live on is made up of a	12
crust of rock that ranges anywhere from 3 miles to 35 miles	24
thick. The low parts of the crust hold the water--oceans,	36
lakes, etc. The high parts of the crust are the continents.	48
It is easy to analyze the outer part of the crust but it is	60
not as easy to examine the inner core of the earth. Through	72
digging mines and drilling wells, it has been found that the	84
deeper the hole, the higher the temperature. If we go only	96
two miles below the surface of the Earth, it is hot enough	108
to boil water. Does this mean that the inner temperature of	120
the Earth increases rapidly by the mile? Scientists do not	132
think this is true. They believe that the center of the	144
Earth may not be more than 10,000 degrees Fahrenheit. Rocks	156
will melt at 2,200 degrees so the center of the earth must	168
be very hot!	170

....1....2....3....4....5....6....7....8....9...10...11..12

MOUSE/KEYSTROKE PROCEDURES

Group Shapes Into Objects

1. Click **Select Objects** button ![cursor].
2. Drag mouse pointer around all shapes you wish to group.
3. Do one of the following:
   a. *Right*-click mouse button.
   b. Click **Grouping** .... `G`
   c. Click **Group** .... `G`
   OR
   a. Click **Draw** on the Drawing toolbar .... `Alt`+`R`
   b. Click **Group** .... `G`

Ungroup Drawing Object

1. Select drawing object.
2. Right-click on the object.
3. Click **Grouping** .... `G`
4. Click **Ungroup** .... `U`
OR
1. Select drawing object.
2. Click **Draw** on the Drawing toolbar .... `Alt`+`R`
3. Click **Ungroup** .... `U`

Order Shapes

1. Select shape.
2. Right-click on the shape.
3. Click **Order** .... `R`
4. Make desired selection:
   - **Bring to Front** .... `T`
   - **Send to Back** .... `K`
   - **Bring Forward** .... `F`
   - **Send Backward** .... `B`
   - **Bring in Front of Text** .... `R`
   - **Send Behind Text** .... `H`

OR

1. Select shape.
2. Click **Draw** on the Drawing toolbar .... `Alt`+`R`
3. Click **Order** .... `R`
4. Make desired selection:
   - **Bring to Front** .... `T`
   - **Send to Back** .... `K`
   - **Bring Forward** .... `F`
   - **Send Backward** .... `B`
   - **Bring in Front of Text** .... `R`
   - **Send Behind Text** .... `H`

Nudge a Shape or Object

1. Select shape.
2. Click **Draw** on the Drawing toolbar .... `Alt`+`R`
3. Click **Nudge** .... `N`
4. Make desired selection:
   - **Up** .... `U`
   - **Down** .... `D`
   - **Left** .... `L`
   - **Right** .... `R`

OR

Press **Ctrl + arrow keys** to nudge a shape or object.

Flip and Rotate a Shape or Object

1. Select shape.
2. Click **Draw** .... `Alt`+`R` on the Drawing toolbar.
3. Click **Rotate or Flip** .... `P`
4. Make desired selection:
   - **Free Rotate** .... `T`
   - **Rotate Left** .... `L`
   - **Rotate Right** .... `R`
   - **Flip Horizontal** .... `H`
   - **Flip Vertical** .... `V`

OR

1. Click **Free Rotate** button ![icon] on the Drawing toolbar.
2. Click on green dot.
3. Drag to rotate.

Add Text to a Shape

1. Select shape.
2. Right-click on the shape.
3. Click **Add Text** .... `X`
4. Type desired text.

Edit Text Within a Shape

1. Select shape.
2. Right-click on the shape.
3. Click **Edit Text** .... `X`
4. Make desired text changes.

LESSON 33

- Create Tables
- Enhance Tables with Table AutoFormat Feature

Warm-up

1. Create a new document.
2. Set the left and right margins to 1".
3. Type each line twice, trying to type faster when you repeat a line. Press the Enter key twice after the second line.
4. When you see the vertical lines between phrases, say the phrase to say to yourself as you type. Do not type the vertical lines.
5. If you make an error, continue typing.
6. If you have time, repeat the exercise.
7. Save the document as **LES33**.

---

1 a;sldkfjghfjdksla; a;sldkfjghfjdksla; a;sldkfjghfjdksla;
2 ;p0p;/?; lo9ol.>l ki8ik,<k ju7ujmj jy6yjhjnj ;-;=;[;];';

3 fur fun gun gum guy buy but hut jut vug jim dim kid red cue
4 my, lot sit wet tex co. fat pat zip qt. s2l9 d3k8 f4j7 f5j6 ;0

5 now been ever which show through from enjoy last year
6 those there become became once come across name as an

7 last year|last year|now been|now been|once was|once was|
8 You can buy your gum from Jim McVug at the Little Red Hut.

LESSON 33

GOAL 1: Create Tables

- The **Table** feature allows you to organize information in rows and columns.
- A table consists of horizontal rows and vertical columns. The rows and columns cross to form boxes, which are referred to as table cells. Note the example below of a table with two rows and four columns:

Table with two rows and four columns

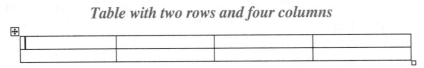

Note: You should be in the Print Layout view when working with tables.

- Information is entered into table cells after you have defined how many rows and columns are to be in the table. There are many ways to define the size of the table, but we will do it the easiest way.
- A title is usually typed before the table is created. Press the Enter key twice after the title.
- Click the **Insert Table** button 🖽 on the Standard toolbar and drag the mouse to select the desired number of columns and rows.

Insert Table

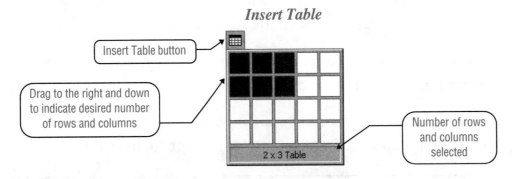

- The column widths adjust automatically so that the table fits between the left and right margins and the columns are of equal widths.
- After the table is created, you are ready to enter table text. The insertion point moves in a table the same way it moves in a document. You may use the mouse to click in the desired cell, or you may use the Tab key to move to the next cell. Shift + Tab will move your insertion point back one cell. When the insertion point is in the last cell of the last column, pressing the Tab key creates a new row.
- As you enter text in a table cell, the cell expands vertically to make room for all of the text.

- Pressing the Enter key in a cell expands the cell and the entire row vertically. You can vertically expand every row of the table and change the width of the table by dragging the **table resize handle** ☐. Rest the pointer on the table until you see the table resize handle appears in the lower-right corner of the table. Rest the pointer on the table resize handle until it turns into a double-headed arrow; then drag the table boundary until the table is the desired size.

- The Tab key, not the Enter key, will move the insertion point to the next cell.

- If the table is alone on a page, you may want to center it vertically. This is accomplished by centering the document page in the Page Setup dialog box.
  1. Click File menu.
  2. Click Page Setup.
  3. Click Layout tab.
  4. Click Center in the Vertical Alignment drop-down list box.

- You may also place the table anywhere on the page. Rest the pointer anywhere in the table until the table move handle ⊞ appears on the upper-left corner of the table. Click on the table move handle until a four-headed arrow ✛ appears and then drag the table to the new location. It will be easier to judge the table location if you change the zoom to Whole Page.

Exercise 1
Create a Table

1. Create a new document.
2. Use the default margins.
3. Center the title in all caps using a serif font, 16 point, bold. After typing the title, deselect the Bold option.
4. Press the Enter key twice after the title.
5. Change the alignment to left and the font size to 12 point.
6. Use the Insert Table button to create a table with 3 columns and 6 rows.
7. Enter the table text shown in the illustration. Bold the text in the first row. Do not press the Enter key in any cell; let the text wrap around to the next line.
8. Change the vertical alignment to center (<u>F</u>ile, Page Set<u>u</u>p, Layout tab, Center).
9. Save the document as **PRESIDENTS1**.
10. Preview the document.
11. Print one copy.
12. Close the document window.

FIRST FIVE PRESIDENTS AND THEIR FAMILIES

President	Wife's Maiden Name	Children
George Washington	Martha Dandridge Custis	None
John Adams	Abigail Smith	Abigail, John Quincy, Susanna, Charles, Thomas
Thomas Jefferson	Martha Wayles Skelton	Martha, John, Lucy, Jane, Maria
James Madison	Dolley Payne Todd	None
James Monroe	Elizabeth Kortright	Eliza, James, Maria

GOAL 2: Enhance Tables with Table AutoFormat Feature

- Once a table has been created, you can use the **Table Auto_Format** command to enhance its appearance.

Table menu

- Any or all of the options in the Table AutoFormat dialog box may be selected. To access the Table AutoFormat dialog box:
  1. Place your insertion point anywhere in the table.
  2. Click Table menu.
  3. Click Table AutoFormat.

Table AutoFormat dialog box

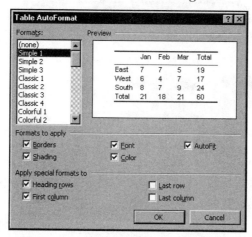

- There are 42 pre-defined formats that can be used to add a variety of borders, shading, font styles and/or colors to a table. You can add these pre-defined formats to the entire table or to the heading rows, first column, last row or last column.

- Column widths can be adjusted to automatically fit text by choosing AutoFit in the AutoFormat dialog box.

- To select any of the AutoFormat options, click the option check box so that a check mark (✓) appears.

- In addition to enhancing the table with the AutoFormat command, you may want to center the table horizontally across the page. To do this:
    1. Place your insertion point anywhere in the table.
    2. Click Table menu.
    3. Click Table Properties.
    4. Click the Table tab.
    5. Click Center in the Alignment section of the dialog box.
    6. Click OK.

Table Properties dialog box

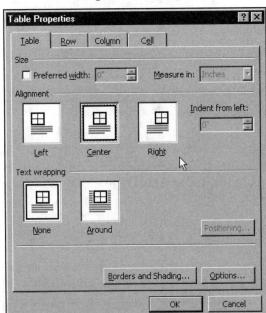

Exercise 2a
Table AutoFormat

1. Create a new document.
2. Use the default margins.
3. Center the title in all caps using a serif font, 18 point, bold. After typing the title, deselect the Bold option.
4. Press the Enter key twice after the title.
5. Change the alignment to left and the font size to 14 point.
6. Use the Insert Table button to create a table with 3 columns and 10 rows.
7. Enter the table text listed in the illustration below.
8. Center the heading row text.
9. Use the Table AutoFormat feature and select the List 8 format
10. In the Table AutoFormat dialog box, click Formats to apply: Borders, Shading, Font, Color (if you have a color monitor and/or printer) and AutoFit.
11. To apply special formats to the heading row, click Heading rows.
12. Change the table alignment to center (Table, Table Properties, Table tab, Center).
13. Change the vertical alignment to center (File, Page Setup, Layout tab, Center).
14. Save the document as **THANK1**.
15. Preview the document.
16. Print one copy.
17. Close the document window.

ALWAYS SAY THANKS!

Language	Thank you	Pronunciation
Chinese (Cantonese)	do jeh	daw dyeh
Chinese (Mandarin)	zie zie	syeh syeh
French	merci	mare-see
German	danke	don-kah
Hindu	sukria	shoo-kree-a
Italian	grazie	gra-tsee
Japanese	arigato	ahree-gah-tow
Korean	kamsa hamnida	kahm-sah ham-nee-da
Spanish	gracias	gra-see-us

Exercise 2b
Table AutoFormat

1. Open **PRESIDENTS1**.
2. Save the file as **PRESIDENTS2**.
3. Place your insertion point in any table cell.
4. Use the Table AutoFormat feature and select the List 8 format.
5. In the Table AutoFomat dialog box, click to apply: Borders, Shading, Font, Color (if you have a color printer) and the AutoFit feature.
6. To apply special formatting to the header row, click Heading rows.
7. Center the column headings in row 1.
8. Resave the file.
9. Print one copy.
10. Close the document window.

FIRST FIVE PRESIDENTS AND THEIR FAMILIES

President	Wife's Maiden Name	Children
George Washington	Martha Dandridge Custis	None
John Adams	Abigail Smith	Abigail, John Quincy, Susanna, Charles, Thomas
Thomas Jefferson	Martha Wayles Skelton	Martha, John, Lucy, Jane, Maria
James Madison	Dolley Payne Todd	None
James Monroe	Elizabeth Kortright	Eliza, James, Maria

Exercise 2c
Table AutoFormat

1. Create a new document.
2. Use the default margins.
3. Use a sans serif font, 14 point.
4. Center the title in all caps and bold.
5. Press the Enter key twice after the title.
6. Change the alignment to left.
7. Using the Insert Table button, create a table with 2 columns and 7 rows.
8. Enter the table text shown in the illustration below.
9. Use Table AutoFormat to apply borders, shading, font, color (if you have a color monitor and/or printer) and the AutoFit feature to the heading rows. Select any format.
10. Bold and center the column titles in row 1.
11. Change the table alignment to center (Table, Table Properties, Table tab, Center).
12. Center the table vertically on the page.
13. Spell check the document.
14. Save the document as **SUFFIXES**.
15. Print one copy.
16. Close the document window.

COMMON INTERNET DOMAIN SUFFIXES

Suffix	Type of Domain
.com	commercial institution
.edu	educational institution
.gov	government site
.mil	military site
.net	network organizations and service providers
.org	private organization

Timed Writing

1. Create a new document.
2. Use the default margins.
3. Change the font to Courier New, 12 point.
4. Take a 5-minute timing on the entire document.
    a. If you finish before the time is up, press the Enter key twice and start again.
    b. Do not correct errors. If you make an error, continue typing.
    c. To calculate your WAM speed, find the total number of words you typed and divide that number by 5.
5. Press the Enter key 4 times.
6. Take two 1-minute timings.
    a. Type as fast as you can for the first 1-minute timing.
    b. Type as accurately as you can for the second 1-minute timing.
    c. Do not correct your errors. If you make an error, continue typing.
    d. Press the Enter key four times between the timings.
    e. Calculate your WAM speed.
7. Take another 5-minute timing on the entire document following the same instructions in Step 4 above. Calculate your WAM speed.
8. Compare your speeds.
9. Save the document as **L33TIME**.
10. Print one copy.
11. Close the document window.

WORDS

Sunglasses are now worn throughout the year. This was not   12
always true. Some people wear sunglasses because they look   24
cool. If you are smart, you will wear sunglasses to protect   36
your eyes.   38

When the sun is out and shining brightly, sunglasses that have   50
dark lenses will screen out most of the sunlight. Screening   62
out sunlight is not enough. The sunglass lenses should also   74
protect against ultraviolet rays.   81

UV rays cannot be seen but pose a danger to the eyes. If you   93
spend a lot of time in the sun, the UV rays can irritate and   105
inflame your eyes. Over the years, exposure to UV rays can   117
cause cataracts. Cataracts cause the lens of the eye to   129
become clouded. Surgery must be used to correct this.   140

When you buy sunglasses, read the label to make sure you are   152
getting 100 percent UV protection. Your eyes are something   164
you want to protect.   168

....1....2....3....4....5....6....7....8....9...10...11...12

MOUSE/KEYSTROKE PROCEDURES

Create a Table

1. Click **Insert Table** button 🏢 on the Standard toolbar.
2. Drag to right and down to indicate desired number of columns and rows.

Move from Cell to Cell in a Table

- Press **Tab** to move one cell to the right .... `Tab`
- Press **Shift + Tab** to move one cell to the left............. `Shift` + `Tab`

Table AutoFormat

1. Place insertion point anywhere in table to format.
2. Click **Table** menu.............. `Alt` + `A`
3. Click **Table AutoFormat**............ `F`
4. Select desired style from list of **Formats**.................. `Alt` + `T`
   Click any or all of the following **Formats to Apply** to turn check boxes on or off:
   - **Borders** .... `Alt` + `B`
   - **Shading** .... `Alt` + `S`
   - **Font**............................. `Alt` + `F`
   - **Color** .... `Alt` + `C`
   - **AutoFit** .... `Alt` + `I`
5. Click any or all of the following to **Apply Special Formats To** specified parts of the table:
   - **Heading Rows** .... `Alt` + `R`
   - **First Column** .... `Alt` + `O`
   - **Last Row**..................... `Alt` + `L`
   - **Last Column** .... `Alt` + `U`
6. Click **OK**.............................. `Enter`

Center Table Horizontally

1. Place insertion point anywhere in table.
2. Click **Table** menu.............. `Alt` + `A`
3. Click **Table Properties** .... `R`
4. Click **Table tab**. .... `Alt` + `T`
5. Click **Center alignment** option . `C`
6. Click **OK**.............................. `Enter`

Move a Table

1. Position insertion point ⌶ anywhere inside table until table move handle appears ⊕.
2. Position pointer ⊕ over table move handle until move arrow appears ✛.
3. Drag table to new location ⊞.

Resize a Table

1. Position insertion point ⌶ anywhere inside table until table resize handle appears ☐.
2. Position pointer over table sizing handle ☐ until sizing arrow appears ↘.
3. Drag to size table as desired.

LESSON 34

- • Insert and Delete Table Columns and Rows
- • Add Borders and Shading to Tables

Warm-up

1. Create a new document.
2. Set the left and right margins to 1".
3. Type each line twice, trying to type faster when you repeat a line. Press the Enter key twice after the second line.
4. When you see the vertical lines between phrases, say the phrase to yourself as you type. Do not type the vertical lines.
5. If you make an error, continue typing.
6. If you have time, repeat the exercise.
7. Save the document as **LES34**.

---

1 `a;sldkfjghfjdksla; a;sldkfjghfjdksla; a;sldkfjghfjdksla;`

2 `aq1qaza sw2wsxs de3edcd fr4rfvf ft5tfgfbf fr45rftfgfbfvf`

3 `fur fun gun gum guy buy but hut jut vug jim dim kid red cue`

4 `my, lot sit wet tex co. fat pat zip qt. s2l9 d3k8 f4j7 f5j6 ;0`

5 `many the like or more now use these who still one knows`

6 `sure for even could some in that time this of while new`

7 `knows for sure|knows for sure|there are|there are|in or|in or|`

8 `Buy the guy standing near the vug a pair of red kid gloves.`

LESSON 34

- **Rows** and **columns** can be inserted or deleted in a table.
- To insert a new row above or below the insertion point:
  1. Click Table menu.
  2. Click Insert.
  3. Click Rows Above or Rows Below.
- To insert more than one row at a time, highlight the number of rows you wish to insert and then follow the three steps listed above.
- To insert a row at the end of the table, place the insertion point in the last cell of the table and press the Tab key.
- To insert a column to the left or right of the insertion point:
  1. Click Table menu.
  2. Click Insert.
  3. Click Columns to the Left or Columns to the Right.
- To insert more than one column at a time, highlight the number of columns you wish to insert and then follow the three steps listed above.
- To delete a row or column:
  1. Place your insertion point in the row or column you want to delete.
  2. Click Table menu.
  3. Click Delete.
  4. Click either Rows or Columns.
- To delete more than one row or column at a time, highlight the number of rows or columns you wish to delete and then follow the four steps listed above.

Exercise 1a
Insert Rows

1. Open **THANK1**.
2. Save as **THANK2**.
3. Insert the following three new rows in alphabetic order according to column 1:

Indonesian	termi kasih	t'ree-ma kas-she
Russian	blagodaryu	bluh-guh-da-r'oo
Swahili	asante	ah-sahn-the

4. Place the insertion point in the table, click T**a**ble, Table Auto**F**ormat and OK to apply formatting.
5. Resave the file.
6. Print one copy.
7. Close the document window.

ALWAYS SAY THANKS!

Language	Thank You	Pronunciation
Chinese (Cantonese)	do jeh	daw dyeh
Chinese (Mandarin)	zie zie	syeh syeh
French	merci	mare-see
German	danke	don-kah
Hindu	sukria	shoo-kree-a
Italian	grazie	gra-tsee
Japanese	arigato	ahree-gah-to
Korean	kamsa hamnida	kahm-sah ham-nee-da
Spanish	gracias	gra-see-us

Exercise 1b
Insert Rows

1. Open **PRESIDENTS1**.
2. Save the file as **PRESIDENTS3**.
3. Delete the last column in the table.
4. Insert a column between the first and second columns and type the column text shown in the illustration below.
5. Use the Table AutoFormat feature and select the Grid 8 Format.
6. In the Table AutoFormat dialog box, click Format to apply: Borders, Shading, Font, Color (if you have a color printer) and the AutoFit feature.
7. To apply special formatting to the heading row, click Heading rows.
   Note: After applying special formatting, the alignment of the column heading row may change.
   If necessary, recenter the column headings.
8. Resave the document.
9. Print one copy.
10. Close the document window.

FIRST FIVE PRESIDENTS AND THEIR FAMILIES

Insert this column

President	Time in Office	Wife's Maiden Name
George Washington	4/30/1789 to 3/3/1797	Martha Dandridge Custis
John Adams	3/4/1797 to 3/3/1801	Abigail Smith
Thomas Jefferson	3/4/1801 to 3/3/1809	Martha Wayles Skelton
James Madison	3/4/1809 to 3/3/1817	Dolley Payne Todd
James Monroe	3/4/1817 to 3/3/1825	Elizabeth Kortright

GOAL 2: Add Borders and Shading to Tables

- You have learned to add **borders** and **shading** to a **table** by using the AutoFormat feature to select a format that has shading in specific areas. For example, the Elegant format adds a double-line border around the table; the Columns 5 format adds shading to every other column.

Table AutoFormat dialog box

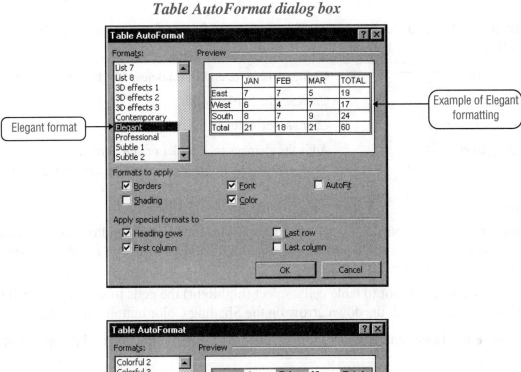

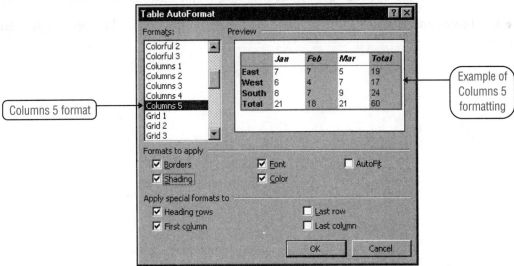

- You can customize table borders or shading using the **Tables and Borders** button 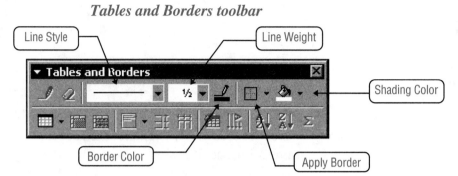 on the Standard toolbar. When you click the Tables and Borders button the Tables and Borders toolbar automatically appears on the screen and floats in the document window.

Tables and Borders toolbar

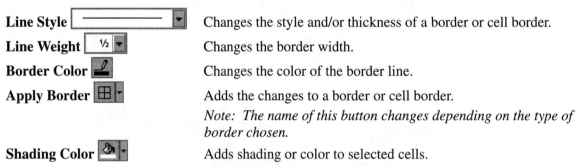

- To add borders and shading to a table, you can use five of the buttons on the Tables and Borders toolbar.

Line Style	Changes the style and/or thickness of a border or cell border.
Line Weight	Changes the border width.
Border Color	Changes the color of the border line.
Apply Border	Adds the changes to a border or cell border. *Note: The name of this button changes depending on the type of border chosen.*
Shading Color	Adds shading or color to selected cells.

- To change the table border, click on the Line Style, Line Weight and/or Border Color buttons to make selections. To apply your selections, click the down arrow on the Border Apply button and select Outside Border.

- To add shading or color to table cells, select (highlight) the cells to which you wish to add the shading or color, click the down arrow on the Shading Color button, and make your selection.

- To close the Tables and Borders toolbar, click the **Close** button [X] in the upper right-hand corner of the toolbar.

Exercise 2a
Table Borders and Shading

1. Create a new document.
2. Set the top margin to 2" and the left and right margins to 1".
3. Type the report shown on the next page using a serif font, 12 point.
4. Set the line spacing to double.
5. Center the report title in all caps using a serif font, 14 point and bold.
6. Press the Enter key once after the title.
7. Press the Tab key once at the beginning of each paragraph.
8. After typing the third paragraph, press the Enter key once before creating the table.
9. Use the Insert Table button to create a table with 2 columns and 7 rows.
   Note: Because spacing has been set to double, the table will appear double spaced. After the report is completed, you will change the table spacing to single.
10. Select the first row. Change the text alignment to center (click the Center alignment button on the Formatting toolbar).
11. Select the first column. Change the text alignment to center.
12. Enter the table text shown in the illustration on the next page.
13. Use Table AutoFormat to apply borders, shading, font, color (colors other than black, white and gray will print only if you have a color printer) and the AutoFit feature to the heading rows. Select the Contemporary Format.
14. Use the Tables and Borders button on the Standard toolbar to open the Tables and Borders toolbar.
15. Select the table (T<u>a</u>ble, Sele<u>c</u>t, <u>T</u>able). Use the Line Style button to choose a fancy border (your choice) around the table. Use the Border button to select the outside border.
16. Select the heading row and use the Shading Color button to add a gray fill. Select a fill darker than the gray fills already used.
17. Change the table alignment to center (T<u>a</u>ble, Table P<u>r</u>operties, Table tab, Center).
18. Place your insertion point below the last line of the table.
19. Complete the report.
20. Select the table and change the table to single space (F<u>o</u>rmat, <u>P</u>aragraph, Indents and Spacing tab, Li<u>n</u>e spacing, Single).
21. Spell check the document.
22. Save the document as **E-MAIL**.
23. Print one copy.
24. Close the document window.

Desired Result

ELECTRONIC MAIL

Electronic mail, also known as e-mail, is one of the most widely used features of the Internet. Everyone knows about sending and receiving paper mail. People who use the Internet call this type of mail "snail mail" because it is so much slower than e-mail.

Electronic mail consists of messages that you send and receive without having to use paper, a pen or pencil, an envelope, or a stamp. You can communicate with anyone on the Internet who has an e-mail address. You can send and receive e-mail 24 hours a day. To receive e-mail all you have to do is connect to your Internet provider and download and read any messages that have been sent to you. To send e-mail, you compose it in the e-mail program, address it (using an e-mail address) and your Internet provider e-mail server uploads the message and sends it to the correct e-mail address. The e-mail can be sent to one or more e-mail addresses. The e-mail can arrive at its destination within seconds.

Many people add emoticons to add a touch of humor to the e-mail. Emoticons are facial expressions that are made by typing a series of keystrokes that create an image of a sideways face. Below are some common emoticons:

EMOTICON	TRANSLATION
#:-o	Shocked
}:-[	Angry
:~/	Confused
:-)	Happy
:-(	Sad
:-O	Surprised

See if you can develop your own set of emoticons to use when you send e-mail.

Exercise 2b
Table Borders and Shading

1. Open **SUFFIXES**.
2. Select the table (Table, Select, Table).
3. Add any triple border around the table.
4. Add a gray fill to the first row.
5. Resave the file.
6. Print one copy.
7. Close the document window.

Timed Writing

1. Create a new document.
2. Use the default margins.
3. Change the font to Courier New, 12 point.
4. Take a 5-minute timing on the entire document.
   a. If you finish before the time is up, press the Enter key twice and start again.
   b. Do not correct errors. If you make an error, continue typing.
   c. To calculate your WAM speed, find the total number of words you typed and divide that number by 5.
5. Press the Enter key 4 times.
6. Take two 1-minute timings.
   a. Type as fast as you can for the first 1-minute timing.
   b. Type as accurately as you can for the second 1-minute time.
   c. Do not correct your errors. If you make an errror, continue typing.
   d. Press the Enter key four times between the timings.
   e. Calculate your WAM speed.
7. Following the same instructions in Step 4 above, take another 5-minute timing on the entire document. Calculate your WAM speed.
8. Compare your speeds.
9. Save the document as **L34TIME**.
10. Print one copy.
11. Close the document window.

LESSON 34

Did you ever wonder why you may like the taste of a certain   12
food and a friend of yours dislikes the same food? That is   24
because our food likes and dislikes are learned.   34

If there is a food that members of your family did not like,   46
you will probably not like the food either. You may never   58
have tasted the food, but you know you don't like it.   69

Another reason you may dislike a certain food is that you may   81
have once gotten sick while eating that food. You now think   93
of that food as getting you sick and you now do not want to   105
eat it. The food may not have been the thing that got you sick   117
but you associate it with the sick feeling.   126

The same way you learned to dislike foods, you can learn to   138
like them. Try to associate pleasant things with the food.   150
Try it when you are really hungry. If you try the food when   162
you are in the right mood, you may change your mind about it.   174

....1....2....3....4....5....6....7....8....9...10...11...12

350

MOUSE/KEYSTROKE PROCEDURES

Insert a Row

1. Place insertion point in row below or above desired new row.
2. Click **Ta**ble menu............. Alt + A
3. Click **I**nsert I
4. Click **Row** selection.

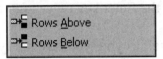

AS THE LAST ROW

1. Place insertion point in last cell of table.
2. Press **Tab** key .... Tab

Insert More than One Row

1. Position mouse pointer to left side of rows.

   Mouse pointer becomes black arrow.

2. Drag mouse pointer up or down to select number of rows to insert.
3. Click **Ta**ble menu............. Alt + A
4. Click **I**nsert I
5. Click **Row** selection.

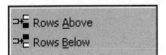

Insert a Column

1. Place insertion point in column to the left or right of desired new column.
2. Click **Ta**ble menu............. Alt + A
3. Click **I**nsert I
4. Click **Column** selection.

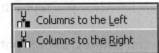

Insert More than One Column

1. Position mouse pointer above columns.
2. Mouse pointer becomes black arrow ↓.
3. Drag mouse pointer right or left to select number of columns to insert.
4. Click **Ta**ble menu............. Alt + A
5. Click **I**nsert I
6. Click **Columns** selection.

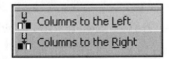

AS THE LAST COLUMN

1. Position mouse pointer above and to right of last column.
2. Mouse pointer becomes black arrow ↓.
3. Click mouse to select short tab to the right of each row.
4. Click **I**nsert .... I or 🔧
5. Click **Column** or **Row** selection.

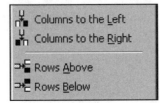

Delete Rows or Columns

1. Select column(s) or row(s) to delete.
2. Click **Ta**ble menu............. Alt + A
3. Click **D**elete............................. D
4. Click **R**ows............................... R
   OR
   Click **C**olumns C

Table Borders and Shading

1. Click **Tables and Borders** button 🗗 on the Standard toolbar.

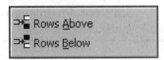

2. Select part of table to apply a border or shading.
3. On the **Tables and Borders** toolbar, select:
   - **Line Style** button
     [_____ ▾]
   - **Line Weight** button [½ ▾]
   - **Border Color** button ✎
   - **Apply Border** button ⊞ ▾
   - **Shading Color** button 🪣 ▾

LESSON 35

- Create WordArt Objects
- Format WordArt Objects
- Create a Letterhead Template

Warm-up

1. Create a new document.
2. Set the left and right margins to 1".
3. Type each line twice, trying to type faster when you repeat a line. Press the Enter key twice after the second line.
4. When you see the vertical lines between phrases, say the phrase to yourself as you type. Do not type the vertical lines.
5. If you make an error, continue typing.
6. If you have time, repeat the exercise.
7. Save the document as **LES35**.

---

1 a;sldkfjghfjdksla; a;sldkfjghfjdksla; a;sldkfjghfjdksla;

2 ;p0p;/?; lo9ol.>l ki8ik,<k ju7ujmj jy6yjhjnj ;-;=;[;];';

3 fur fun gun gum guy buy but hut jut vug jim dim kid red cue

4 my, lot sit wet tex co. fat pat zip qt. s2l9 d3k8 f4j7 f5j6 ;0

5 each when on and see all the have been only who in with

6 is than do knew to say they give does not if you be but

7 have been|have been|who is|who is|does not|does not|

8 Kids and gum don't mix! Lots of ducks sit in wet places.

GOAL 1: Create WordArt Objects

- The **WordArt** feature allows you to add graphic effects to your text. Use WordArt to enhance flyers, newsletters, letterheads or logos.

- WordArt can create striking text effects using additional text option features, such as Rotation, Flip, Stretch, Shade, Shadow, Border and/or Color.

- Here are some examples of WordArt:

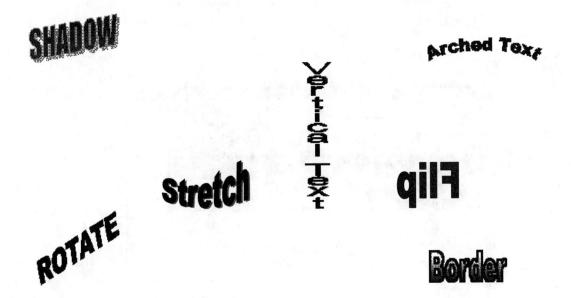

- Follow these steps to create a WordArt object:
  1. Click the Insert WordArt button ◢ on the Drawing toolbar.
     *Note: If the Drawing toolbar is not displayed, click *V*iew, *T*oolbars, Drawing.*
     OR
     a. Click *I*nsert menu.
     b. Click *P*icture.
     c. Select *W*ordArt.

2. Select a WordArt style from the WordArt Gallery, shown below.

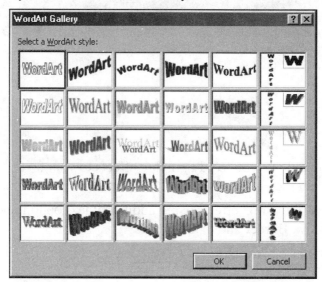

Note: Use the WordArt Gallery to begin your design. You can add changes later.

3. Click OK.
4. Type your text in the Text box, as shown below.

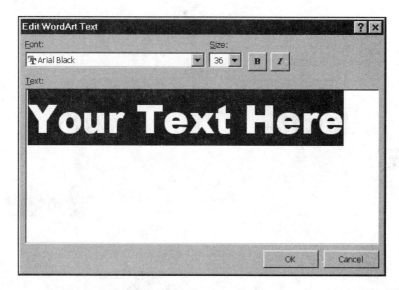

5. Change font, font size and/or font style.
6. Click OK.

- WordArt text objects are not considered document text; they are drawing objects and cannot be spell checked or seen in Outline View.

- In order to move or resize WordArt text objects, you need to display the handles. To resize the WordArt object, place the mouse pointer on a handle to display a double-sided arrow pointer ↔ and drag the object to the desired size. To move the object, place the mouse pointer on the center of the WordArt object to display a four-sided arrow pointer ✛, and drag the object to the desired location.

Exercise 1
Create WordArt Objects

1. Create a new document.
2. Click the Insert WordArt button on the Drawing toolbar.
3. Select the third WordArt style in the first row.
4. Click OK.
5. Type your first name in the WordArt text box.
6. Use the default font, font size and font style.
7. Click OK.
8. Place the mouse pointer on the center of the WordArt object.
   Note: The mouse pointer shape will change to a four-sided arrow.
9. Move the WordArt object to the top right of the screen.
10. Place the mouse pointer on the middle left handle and stretch the WordArt object to the left margin.
11. Click the Insert WordArt button on the Drawing toolbar to create another WordArt object.
12. Select any desired option in the WordArt Gallery. Do not use the same option as in Step 3.
13. Click OK.
14. Type your last name in the WordArt text box.
15. Change the font, font size, and font style as desired.
16. Click OK.
17. Place the mouse pointer on the center of the new WordArt object.
18. Move the object to the left margin, directly under the existing WordArt object.
19. Place the mouse pointer on the middle right handle and stretch the WordArt object to the right margin.
20. Delete both WordArt objects.
21. Close the document window.
22. Do not save the changes.

LESSON 35

GOAL 2: Format WordArt Objects

- To make changes to your WordArt text object, you will need to select it to display the handles. Once the object is active, the following floating toolbar displays.
  Note: A floating toolbar can be moved by dragging the Title bar.

WordArt toolbar

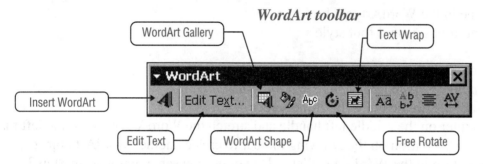

- You can make changes to a WordArt object by choosing one or more of the buttons on the floating toolbar:

	Insert WordArt	Click to insert a new WordArt object.
	Edit Text	Click to open the Edit WordArt Text dialog box.
	WordArt Gallery	Click to display the Gallery to change the style for an existing WordArt object.
	Format WordArt	Click to change WordArt options such as color and lines, size, position and text wrapping.
	WordArt Shape	Click to show WordArt Shape options.
	Free Rotate	Click to activate the Rotate feature. Drag a green handle to turn the object.
	Text Wrapping	Click to access the text wrap options.
	Same Letter Height	Click to make upper- and lowercase letters equal size.
	Vertical Text	Click to change text to vertical alignment.
	Alignment	Click to open alignment menu. Select desired alignment.
	Character Spacing	Click to open character spacing menu. Select desired spacing option.

- In addition to the buttons on the floating WordArt toolbar, you can use a number of buttons on the Drawing toolbar to enhance your WordArt object. You can add color, shadow, outline and 3-D effects by using the following buttons, (make sure the WordArt object is active before using these buttons):

	Fill Color	Click to change the inside color of the text.
	Line Color	Click to change the outline color of the text.
	Line Style	Click to change the line style.
	Shadow	Click to select a shadow style.
	3-D	Click to select a 3-D style.

- Once a WordArt object is created, you can move and copy it as you do a drawing object. The handles must be displayed before it can be moved or copied. The best way to move a WordArt object is to drag it using the mouse. To copy it, hold down the Ctrl key as you drag the object.

Exercise 2
Format WordArt Objects

1. Create a new document.
2. Access WordArt.
3. Use the first WordArt option in the first row of the WordArt Gallery.
4. Type your first and last name in the WordArt dialog box.
5. Click OK.
6. Place the insertion point on the WordArt object.
7. Move the object to the top-left corner of the page.
8. Make the following changes to the WordArt text using buttons on the floating toolbar:
   a. Click the Edit Text button and change your name to your initials in all caps and periods.
   b. Click the Rotate button and turn your initials on a diagonal slanting down from left to right.
   c. Click the WordArt Shape button and choose the second box in the first row.
9. Make the following changes to the color and lines using the Drawing toolbar buttons:
   a. Click the Fill Color button to change the fill color to yellow.
   b. Click the Line Color button to change the outline color to red.
   c. Click the Line Style button and change the size of the line to 2 ¼ point.

10. Copy the object and move it so there is a copy in each of the four corners and in the middle, as shown in the illustration below.
    Hint: Change the Zoom factor to Whole Page so you can see where to place the object.
11. Change the color, line color, shape and rotation of each object as desired. Feel free to be creative.
12. Save the document; name it **INITIALS**.
13. Print one copy.
14. Close the document window.

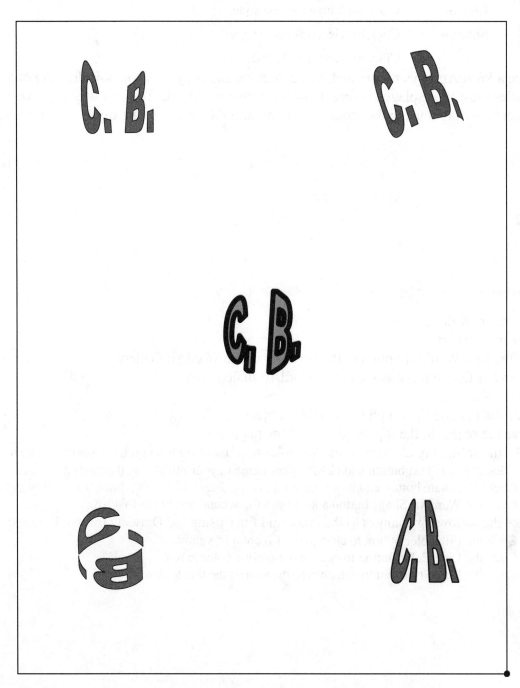

GOAL 3:   Create a Letterhead Template

Create a Letterhead Template

- You can create a letterhead as a **template**. A template is a predefined document that can be used over and over again without losing the original. For example, the blank document that appears every time you create a new Word document is a blank template. Its format is defined with preset margins, font, font size, line spacing, etc. All you have to do is type or insert text or other elements. When you save a document based on a template, the document is saved, but the original template is not affected.

- When you create a new document based on a letterhead template, all the features of the letterhead (formats, text, graphic objects, etc.) are available. Just type in the letter text and save as you would normally save any document. The original letterhead template remains unchanged, ready to be used again for future letters.

- Follow these steps to create a letterhead template.
    1. Click File menu.
    2. Click New.
    3. Click the General tab, shown in the illustration below.
    4. Click Template.
    5. Click OK.
    6. Design the letterhead as desired.
    7. Save the template.
    8. Close the document window.

New dialog box

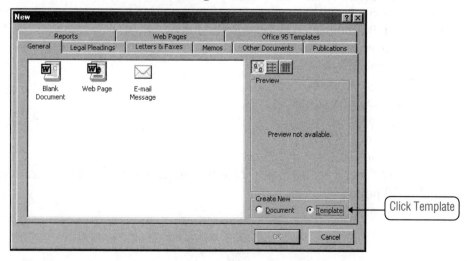

Exercise 3a
Create a Letterhead Template

1. Create a new template document. Click File, New, Template.
2. Set top and bottom margins to .5".
3. Set left and right margins to 1".
4. Click the Insert WordArt button on the Drawing toolbar.
5. Select the fourth style in the fourth row.
6. Type the following text in a decorative font: SCHOOLSTORE
   Note: Do not space between SCHOOL and STORE.
7. Use the default font size and style.
8. Click the down arrow on the Fill Color button on the Drawing toolbar and make the following changes:
   a. Click Fill Effects.
   b. Select the Gradient tab.
   c. Select Preset.
   d. Select the first Rainbow from the Preset Colors drop-down list.
   e. Select the From Corner option.
   f. Click OK.
9. Click the 3-D button on the Drawing toolbar and select the third style in the fourth row.
10. Move the WordArt object so it is within .5" from the top of the page.
11. Resize the WordArt object so it extends from the left to the right margins.
12. Create a text box and place it below the SCHOOLSTORE heading, as shown in the Desired Result illustration on page 362. Format the text box as follows:
    a. Type the following text in the text box: One-Stop Shopping for All Your School Supplies
    b. Center the text using the same font in 12 point, bold.
    c. Choose yellow for the font color. If you are not using a color printer, choose white.
    d. Click the Fill Color button and choose No Fill.
    e. You may have to remove the text box border. Follow these steps to remove the border:
       • Select the text box.
       • Click Format menu.
       • Click Text Box.
       • Click Colors and Lines tab.
       • Click Line Color.
       • Select No Line.
13. Create a footer and type the footer information, as shown in the illustration. Use the same font as in Step 12 in 12 point.

14. Click the Line button on the Drawing toolbar and draw a line above the footer, as shown in the illustration. Format as follows:
    a. Click the Line Style button on the Drawing toolbar and select a 2¼ point line.
    b. Click the Line Color button on the Drawing toolbar and select violet for the line color.
15. Compare your work with the book.
16. Make any necessary adjustments to duplicate the illustration as closely as possible.
17. Save the template document; name it **SCHOOLSTORE**.
18. Print one copy.
19. Close the document window.

Desired Result

**One-Stop Shopping for All
Your School Supplies**

123 School Street
Image, NY 12345

Phone: 1-800-555-3541   Fax: 1-800-555-8973

Exercise 3b
Create a Letterhead Template

1. Create a new template.
2. Use the WordArt feature to create a letterhead for your personal use.
3. Use as many tools as you need to make the letterhead attractive.
4. Make sure the letterhead does not take up more than 2" at the top of the page.
5. Be sure to include one or more of the following items of information in your letterhead:
   - Your name
   - Address
   - City, State and Zip
   - Phone and/or Fax Numbers
   - E-mail Address
6. Save the template; name it **STATIONERY**.
7. Print one copy.
8. Close the document window.

Timed Writing

1. Create a new document.
2. Use the default margins.
3. Change font to Courier New, 12 point.
4. Take a 5-minute timing on the entire document.
   a. If you finish before the time is up, press the Enter key twice and start again.
   b. Do not correct errors. If you make an error, continue typing.
   c. To calculate your WAM speed, find the total number of words you typed and divide that number by 5.
5. Press the Enter key 4 times.
6. Take two 1-minute timings.
   a. Type as fast as you can for the first 1-minute timing.
   b. Type as accurately as you can for the second 1-minute timing.
   c. Do not correct your errors. If you make an error, continue typing.
   d. Press the Enter key 4 times between the timings.
   e. Calculate your WAM speed.
7. Take another 5-minute timing on the entire document following the same instructions as in Step 4. Calculate your WAM speed.
8. Compare your speeds.
9. Save the document as **L35TIME**.
10. Print one copy.
11. Close the document window.

WORDS

When you think of your first job, you think of something you	12
may do in addition to going to school. There are laws that	24
do not allow any children under the age of 16 to be employed	36
during school hours. Years ago, when children worked, there	48
were no laws like this. To make money to help out the rest	60
of the family, many children worked from morning to night.	72

Child labor laws were written so children would not be taken	84
advantage of by the employers. Many children had to perform	96
duties that their bodies could not handle. As a result of	108
the Industrial Revolution, children were asked to work long	120
hours under conditions that were sometimes dangerous. They	132
worked in factories and mines. They never had time to play	144
or go to school.	147

Though child labor is not a problem in the United States, it	159
is still a problem in many of the underdeveloped countries.	171
We all hope there will be a time when child labor will not	173
be a problem anywhere in the world.	180

....1....2....3....4....5....6....7....8....9...10...11...12

MOUSE/KEYSTROKE PROCEDURES

Create a WordArt Object

1. Click the **Insert WordArt** button `◀` on the Drawing toolbar.
   OR
   a. Click **Insert** menu .... `Alt`+`I`
   b. Click **Picture** .... `P`
   c. Click **WordArt** .... `W`
2. Click desired WordArt design.
3. Click **OK** .... `Enter`
4. Enter text in the **Edit WordArt Text** dialog box.
5. Make any of the following changes:
   - Click **Font** menu .... `Alt`+`F`
   - Click **Size** .... `Alt`+`S`
   - Click **Bold** button `B`.
   - Click **Italic** button `I`.
6. Click **OK** .... `Enter`

Move WordArt Object

1. Click WordArt object.
2. Place mouse pointer over object to display four-sided arrow.
3. Drag WordArt to desired location.

Resize WordArt Object

1. Click WordArt object.
2. Place mouse pointer on any handle.
3. Drag to desired size.

Delete WordArt Object

1. Click WordArt object.
2. Press the **Delete** key .... `Del`

Format WordArt Object

1. Click WordArt object.
2. Click one or more of the following buttons on the WordArt toolbar:
   - **Edit text** `Edit Text...`
   - **WordArt Gallery** `▦`
   - **Format WordArt** `✎`
   - **WordArt Shape** `Abc`

- **Free Rotate** `↻`
- **Word Wrapping** `▨`
- **WordArt Same Letter Heights** `Aa`
- **WordArt Vertical Text** `Ab bↄ`
- **WordArt Alignment** `≣`
- **WordArt Character Spacing** `AV ↔`

OR

Select one or more of the following Drawing toolbar buttons:
- **Fill Color** `◇▾`
- **Line Color** `✎▾`
- **Line Style** `≣`
- **Shadow** `▣`
- **3-D** `▱`

Create Letterhead Template

1. Click **File** menu .... `Alt`+`F`
2. Click **New** .... `Alt`+`N`
3. Click **General** tab.
4. Click **Template** .... `Alt`+`T`
5. Click **OK** .... `Enter`

LESSON 36

• Format Two-Page Reports • Use Headers and Footers to Insert Page Numbers in Multiple-Page Reports • Use Thesaurus Feature • Create a Report Cover

Warm-up

1. Create a new document.
2. Set the left and right margins to 1".
3. Type each line twice, trying to type faster when you repeat a line. Press the Enter key twice after you repeat the line. When you see the vertical lines between phrases, say the phrase to yourself as you type. Do not type the vertical lines.
4. If you make an error, continue typing.
5. If you have time, repeat the exercise.
6. Save the document as **LES36**.
7. Close the document window.

---

1 a;sldkfjghfjdksla; a;sldkfjghfjdksla; a;sldkfjghfjdksla;

2 abcdefghijklmnopqrstuvwxyz abcdefghijklmnopqrstuvwxyz

3 fur fun gun gum guy buy but hut jut vug jim dim kid red cue

4 my, lot sit wet tex co. fat pat zip qt. s2l9 d3k8 f4j7 f5j6 ;0

5 few was say yes saw who off for run net who too out the

6 own can now web big get try yet two old due eye end did

7 off for|off for|who was|who was|now the|now the|run for|run for|

8 Sit with Tex Vug. Go to the hut to buy Guy 5 packs of gum.

366

GOAL 1: Format Two-Page Reports

- By default, Word's standard document page size is the same size as a standard sheet of paper measuring 8.5" x 11". When you reach the end of a page, Word automatically begins a new page. This is called a **soft page break**. In Print Layout View, you will see the actual end of the first page and beginning of the second page. In Normal View, Word inserts a dotted line across the screen to separate the pages.

- When you begin a new page, note the Status bar. The **Page Indicator** displays Page 2 and the **At Indicator** displays At 1" (unless you have changed the default top margin).

- You can create a page break before reaching the bottom of a page by inserting a **hard page break**. To insert a hard page break:
  - Press Ctrl + Enter

  OR

  1. Click Insert menu.
  2. Click Break.
  3. Click Page break.
  4. Click OK.

- You can delete a hard page break to combine text contained on two pages. To delete a hard page break, place the insertion point at the top of the second page and press the Backspace key once.

- **Widows** and **orphans** are single lines of a paragraph that appear at the top or bottom of a page. A widow is the last line of a paragraph appearing at the top of a page, and an orphan is the first line of a paragraph appearing at the bottom of a page. Widows and orphans should be avoided when working with multiple-page documents.

- The Widow/Orphan control feature prevents widows and orphans from occurring. Follow these steps to eliminate widows and orphans:
  1. Click Format menu.
  2. Click Paragraph.
  3. Click Line and Page Breaks tab.
  4. Select Widow/Orphan control, if it is not already checked.
  5. Click OK.

■ When previewing a multiple-page document, select the **Multiple Pages** button 🔳 to display more than one page on the screen. Note the following illustration of a multiple-page document in Print Preview:

Print Preview window

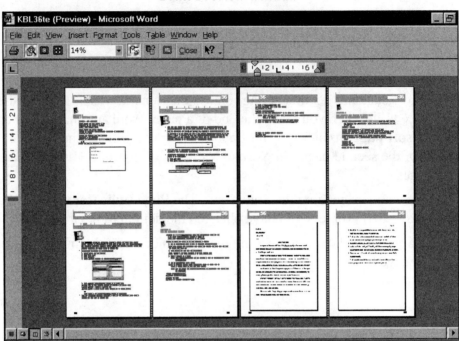

■ Most school reports follow the MLA (Modern Language Association) style. This style specifies the following format for reports:

• One-inch margins all around
• Double spacing
• Serif font, 12 point

■ In addition, the MLA style requires specific identifying information on the first page of the report. This identifying information includes your name, the teacher's name, the course name, the date and a centered title. This information appears at the top of the first page. Note the sample below:

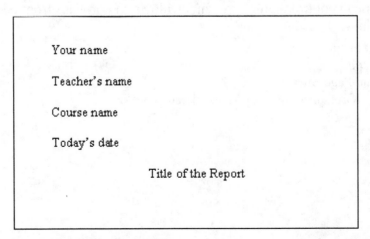

Exercise 1
Format a Two-Page Report

1. Create a new document.
2. Set the left and right margins to 1".
3. Change the line spacing to double.
4. Use a serif font, 12 point.
5. Use widow and orphan control.
6. Type the first-page report identifying information, as shown below.
7. Center the title.
8. Press the Enter key once after the title.
9. Change to left alignment.
10. Save the document; name it **STRESS**.
11. Do not close the document window.

Stu Dent

Mrs. Beldemsky

Futures 101

Today's date

Coping with Stress

LESSON **36**

- You have used headers and footers throughout this book to identify your documents. You have placed your name and the date field in the header and the Filename field in the footer.

- You will use headers and footers in multiple-page reports as well. As mentioned in the last section, you need to place specific identifying information on the first page of a report. In addition, the MLA style requires that you insert your last name and the page number at the right margin on every page, starting with the second page. Note the following illustration of the second page of a multiple-page report.

Dent 2

- After you create the header for the second and following pages, you will need to instruct Word not to print the header on the first page.

- Follow these steps to place the information in the header and give the instruction to start the header on the second page:
  1. Click <u>V</u>iew menu.
  2. Click <u>H</u>eader and Footer (the Header and Footer toolbar displays).

Header and Footer toolbar

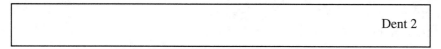

  3. Click the document's header area.
  4. Press the Tab key twice to right align the text.
  5. Type your last name.
  6. Press the Spacebar once.
  7. Click the Insert Page Number button ![#] on the Header and Footer toolbar.
     Note: When you click the Insert Page Number button, Word automatically numbers each page in the report.

370

8. Click the Page Setup button 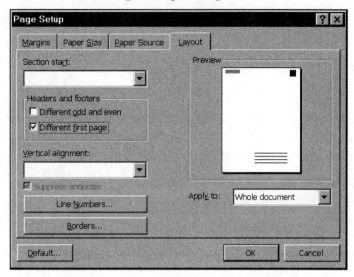 on the Header and Footer toolbar.
9. Click the Layout tab to access the following Page Setup dialog box.

Page Setup dialog box

10. Click the Different first page check box.
11. Click OK.
12. Click Close button on Header and Footer toolbar to close the Header/Footer window.

Exercise 2
Use Headers and Footers to Insert Page Numbers on Multiple-Page Reports

1. Place your insertion point at the top of the **STRESS** document. (If you closed the document, you will need to open it.)
2. Create a header.
3. Press the Tab key twice in the header to right align the text.
4. Type your last name in a serif font, 12 point, and press the Spacebar once.
5. Click the Insert Page Number button on the Header and Footer toolbar.
6. Click the Page Setup button on the Header and Footer toolbar.
7. Go to the Layout tab of the Page Setup dialog box and choose Different first page.
8. Click OK.
9. Click Close.
10. Resave the file.
11. Do not close the document window.

- The **Thesaurus** feature is a helpful tool to use when writing a report. By using the Thesaurus, you can avoid using the same word repeatedly in a document. It provides synonyms (words with the same meaning), antonyms (words with opposite meanings) and related words for selected text.

- Follow these steps to use the Thesaurus feature:
  1. Select the word you want changed.
  2. Click Tools menu.
  3. Click Language.
  4. Select Thesaurus to display the following dialog box:

Thesaurus

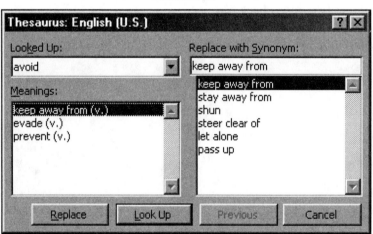

  5. Click Meanings to display different meanings for the selected word.
  6. Click Look Up to get additional meanings and synonyms for the selected word.
  7. Click Previous to go to a preceding list.
  8. Click Replace to replace the word in your document with the selected synonym.
  OR
  Click Cancel to close the dialog box without changing the selected word.

- The key to using the Thesaurus correctly is to make sure the replacement word agrees in number and tense with the original word.

Exercise 3
Use the Thesaurus Feature

1. Within the **STRESS** document, place your insertion point under the title. If you closed the document, you will need to reopen it.
   Note: Your insertion point should be at the left margin.
2. Type the report that appears on the next two pages. Format the report as follows:
   a. Use the first-line indent feature to indent the first line of each new paragraph.
      Note: Click Format, Paragraph, Indents and Spacing tab, select First line from the Special drop-down list.
   b. Type the report text in a serif font, 12 point.
      Note: All parts of the report should be in the same font and size.
   c. Create a numbered list as shown.
      Note: After ending the numbered list, you may need to reset the First line indent for the last paragraph.
   d. Use the Widow/Orphan control feature.
   e. Use the Thesaurus feature to replace the highlighted words. Be sure the tense and number of the new word is the same as the one it replaces.
      Note: The line endings will change depending upon the replacement word chosen from the Thesaurus.
3. Spell check the document.
4. Resave the document.
5. Print one copy.
6. Close the document window.

Desired Result

Stu Dent

Mrs. Beldemsky

Futures 101

Today's date

Coping With Stress

Have you ever been stressed? Some of the characteristic signs of stress are

stomachaches, insomnia, irritability, and the inability to concentrate. Stress is a normal part of

life and people of all ages experience it.

Whenever you are exposed to change, you will experience some degree of stress. This is

especially true at your age since everything is changing--from your body, to your feelings, to

how people react towards you as you grow up. Add to these changes any one of the following: a

bad day at school, fights with friends or family, report card time, and you have a lot of *STRESS!*

Not all stress is bad. Sometimes pressure urges you to do a little extra and achieve a goal

you might not have reached if you didn't push yourself. For example, if you are pressured, you

may study harder to get a better grade or earn the winning goal for your team.

You can't lock stress out of your life, but you can learn to cope with it. First, realize you

are not alone and that everyone is stressed at one time or another. Second, find an outlet for the

stress. You must let off the "steam," otherwise the kettle could explode. Exercise and talking

are all ways to vent to ease your stress.

There are a number of ways to help you conquer stressful situations. Choose one or more

of the following guidelines to reduce the stress in your life.

Dent 2

1. Don't take on more responsibilities than you can handle. Learn to balance school work with after-school activities or a part-time job.

2. Try to solve the problems you can and go to someone else if you find you're having trouble. Talk to a counselor, clergyman, or someone you can trust.

3. Make sure to exercise. Exercise is a sure-fire way to get rid of excess tension.

4. Realize that "this too shall pass." One thing in life is certain—everything changes; nothing stays the same. The high emotions you feel now will calm down. Be patient.

5. Keep your head and don't take risks that can have dangerous consequences. Don't endanger yourself.

Try to remember these methods when you are feeling stressed. They might not eliminate your problem, but they will help to get you through the crisis.

LESSON 36

GOAL 4: Create a Report Cover

- A **report cover** adds a finishing touch to the document. You can use many of Word's tools to enhance a cover. These may include one or more of the following features:
  - Pictures
  - Borders
  - Lines
  - WordArt
  - All Drawing toolbar options

- A report cover should include the title, your name, the class and the date. Note the following example:

```
                    TITLE



                  Your Name
                    Class



                     Date
```

- Make sure all parts of the cover are equally spaced. Remember to format the title of the report so that it is the most outstanding part of the cover.

- Follow these steps to create a report cover.
  1. Create a new document for the report cover.
  2. Set the top margin to 2".
  3. Type the report name in a large font and format attractively.
  4. Press the Enter key until the insertion point is approximately 3" below the title. You can use the vertical ruler on the left side of the screen to estimate the space.
     Note: When you press the Enter key, the size of the space you create depends upon the currently selected font size. Pressing the Enter key 5 times in 24 point creates more blank space than pressing the Enter key 5 times in 14 point.
  5. Type and center your name and press the Enter key.

6. Type and center the class name.
   Note: Your name should be in a slightly larger font than the class name.
7. Press the Enter key as many times as necessary to space the date equally from the class name. The distance between the title and your name should be approximately the same as between the class name and the date.
8. Type or insert the date.
9. Center the date.

Exercise 4a
Create a Report Cover

1. Create a new document for a cover for the **STRESS** report.
2. Set the top margin to 2".
3. Create WordArt text for the main title as shown in the illustration on the next page.
   a. Choose the fourth style in the top row of the WordArt Gallery.
   b. Type the title in a decorative font, 24 point and italic.
   c. Stretch the WordArt box horizontally so it aligns with the left and right margins.
   d. Press the Enter key several times to leave approximately 3" of empty space after the title.
      Note: The title will move down as you press the Enter key. You will have to move the title back to the top of the page. Check the Status bar to make sure you move the title to 2" from the top of the page. It should read At 2".
4. Center your name in a serif font, 16 point and bold.
5. Press the Enter key once.
6. Center the name of the class in the same serif font, 14 point.
7. Press the Enter key several times to leave approximately 3" of empty space after the name of the class.
8. Insert today's date and use the same font and font size as in Step 6.
9. Create a graphic page border for the cover. The illustration shows the lightening border in 16 point.
10. Compare your results with the illustration.
11. Save the document; name it **STRESS COVER**.
12. Print one copy.
13. Close the document window.

Desired Result

COPING WITH STRESS

Your Name
Futures 101

Today's Date

Exercise 4b
Create a Two-Page Report and Report Cover

1. Create a new document.
2. Type the report shown on the next page.
3. Be sure to format the report according to MLA style using proper margins, fonts and font sizes.
4. Include the first-page heading information as follows:

> Your name
> Mr. Arturo
> Multimedia102
> Today's date

5. Double space the report.
6. Create a header to begin on the second page.
   Note: Make sure the header does not appear on the first page.
7. Include page numbering in the header.
8. Use the Thesaurus feature to replace the highlighted words.
   Note: Be sure the tense and number of the new word is the same as the one the Thesaurus replaces.
9. Spell check the document.
10. Save the report; name it **DESIGN**.
11. Print one copy.
12. Create a cover for the report.
13. Format the cover attractively.
14. Save the document; name it **DESIGN COVER**.
15. Print one copy.
16. Close all document windows.

Tangled in Web Design

With the Internet reaching into more and more homes, many users are interested in creating Web pages. Whether these sites advertise a business, provide information or just serve to announce your presence on the Web, they must be attractive and readable or people just will not stay on your site.

Initially, it was very difficult to create a Web page. You needed to know HTML (Hypertext Markup Language) which is a computer language written in text and code. Your Web browser then interpreted the code so your computer could view the Web page. However, there are programs on the market that have simplified creating Web pages. Anyone who has worked with a word processing program can now create a Web page. You just type in your text, format your layout, insert your graphics and then mount the page on the Web--nothing to it. The one drawback is that these programs do not design the page, and many novices create pages without any attention to the design and layout. However, there are rules of design you can follow that will help you develop an attractive Web page. Artists have been following them for years, even before the advent of computers. These rules of design, along with some new ones, can be applied to the Web. Remember, you want your page to be eye catching and easy to read, especially if it's a commercial site designed to sell a product.

Here are some definite do's.

1. Know your audience and design the site to appeal to them.
2. Choose a concise title that easily identifies your page.
3. Contrast text with the background.
4. Use only one or two fonts per page.
5. Keep file sizes small so they don't take too long to load.
6. Provide a navigation bar that includes a link back to the home page.
7. Use tables to organize your content.
8. Check accuracy of spelling, information and grammar.
9. Test your page on different browsers.
10. Make a standard footer to include the following identifiers: author's name, e-mail address, and the date the site was revised.

Here are some definite don'ts:

1. Don't use blinking elements.
2. Don't overuse animations.
3. Don't use a very busy background as it can clash with the text.
4. Avoid excessive use of sounds.
5. Don't use multiple fonts and font styles.
6. Avoid placing links in the middle of paragraphs.
7. Avoid using frames.
8. Don't use counters.
9. Don't use all caps other than in a title.
10. Don't have one long page. Use multiple short pages instead.

You do not have to be a graphic designer to create interesting Web pages. Equip yourself with the rules of Web design before you begin to develop your Web page. You can find examples and information about Web design on the Internet and in numerous books and magazine articles on the subject. Using these guidelines can make the difference between an amateur Web page and a professional one.

Timed Writing

1. Create a new document.
2. Use the default margins.
3. Change font to Courier New, 12 point.
4. Take a 5-minute timing on the entire document.
    a. If you finish before the time is up, press the Enter key twice and start again.
    b. Do not correct errors. If you make an error, continue typing.
    c. To calculate your WAM speed, find the total number of words you typed and divide that number by 5.
5. Press the Enter key 4 times.
6. Take two 1-minute timings.
    a. Type as fast as you can for the first 1-minute timing.
    b. Type as accurately as you can for the second 1-minute time.
    c. Do not correct your errors. If you make an error, continue typing.
    d. Press the Enter key four times between the timings.
    e. Calculate your WAM speed.
7. Following the same instructions as in Step 4, take another 5-minute timing on the entire document. Calculate your WAM speed.
8. Compare your speeds.
9. Save the document as **L36TIME**.
10. Print one copy.
11. Close the document window.

WORDS

The cat family contains 36 different species. The members of   12
this family include lions, tigers, leopards, cheetahs, jaguars,   24
and the common domesticated cat.   31

No matter what size the cats may come in, they all have many   43
features in common. One of the features common to all cats is   56
their eyes. Cats are good at hunting because of the way their   67
eyes are constructed. The eyes are adapted for seeing in the   30
dark since the cat does most hunting at night. A cat's eyes   92
are large with vertically split pupils. During the day, when   104
it is light, the pupils become very small slits. At night the   117
pupils open wide in order to let in as much light as possible.   129

If you look at a cat in a dark room and shine light into its   140
eyes, you will notice how the eyes light up. The backs of the   152
cat's eyes are coated with a material that reflects every drop   164
of light that comes into the eye and causes the eyes to glow   176
in the dark.   179

....1....2....3....4....5....6....7....8....9...10...11...12

MOUSE/KEYSTROKE PROCEDURES

Widow and Orphan Control

1. Click **Format** menu .... `Alt`+`O`
2. Click **Paragraph** .... `P`
3. Click **Line and Page Breaks** tab .... `Alt`+`P`
4. Click **Widow/Orphan control** .... `Alt`+`W` check box to turn Widow/ Orphan control off or on.
5. Click **OK** .... `Enter`

Thesaurus

1. Select word to be replaced.
2. Click **Tools** menu .... `Alt`+`T`
3. Click **Language** .... `L`
4. Click **Thesaurus** .... `T`
5. In the **Meanings** .... `Alt`+`M` list box, click desired meaning.
6. Click desired item in the **Replace with Synonym** list .... `Alt`+`S`

   Note: Use up/down arrows to see more.

7. Click **Replace** .... `Alt`+`R`

   OR

   Click **Cancel** button `Cancel` to exit without replacing.

Page Numbering (without Header/Footer)

1. Click **Insert** menu .... `Alt`+`I`
2. Click **Page Numbers** .... `U`
3. In the **Position** drop-down list .... `Alt`+`P`
4. Click **Bottom of Page** (Footer)

   OR

   Click **Top of Page** (Header)
5. Click **Alignment** .... `Alt`+`A`
6. Select desired alignment.
7. Click **OK** .... `Enter`

Add a Page Number to a Header

1. Click **View** menu .... `Alt`+`V`
2. Click **Header and Footer** .... `H`
3. Press the **Tab** key twice to right align text.
4. Type your last name.
5. Press the **Spacebar** once.
6. Click **Insert Page Number** button `#` to insert page numbering.
7. Click **Close** button `Close`

Suppress Header on Page One

1. Double-click header on page two.
2. Click **Page Setup** button `📖`.
3. Click **Layout** tab .... `Alt`+`L`
4. Click **Different first page** .. `Alt`+`F`

LESSON 37

- Create a Personal-Business Letter Using Letter Wizard
- Type Letter Text • Copy Letter to Letterhead
- Create an Envelope

Warm-up

1. Create a new document.
2. Set the left and right margins to 1".
3. Type each line twice, trying to type faster when you repeat a line. Press the Enter key twice after the second line. When you see the vertical lines between phrases, say the phrase to yourself as you type.
4. If you make an error, continue typing.
5. If you have time, repeat the exercise.
6. Save the document as **LES37**.
7. Close the document window.

```
1  a;sldkfjghfjdksla; a;sldkfjghfjdksla; a;sldkfjghfjdksla;
2  aqaza swsxs dedcd frftfgfbfvf jujyjhjnjmj kik,k lol.l ;p;/;

3  fur fun gun gum guy buy but hut jut vug jim dim kid red cue
4  my, lot sit wet tex co. fat pat zip qt. s2l9 d3k8 f4j7 f5j6

5  ax fax fix tax taxi exit exist axis six sixty sixteen
6  breeze sneeze buzz buzzer dizzy fizzy plaza prize prized

7  if you will|if you will|but I may|but I may|go to|go to|
8  Fax the order for the red and blue cue balls to Pat Zip.
```

GOAL 1: Create a Personal-Business Letter Using Letter Wizard

- Letters are used for business and personal communications. You write letters to communicate with friends or organizations with whom you have dealings. A business letter is sent from one company or organization to another, while a personal-business letter is sent from a private individual (such as yourself) to a company or organization.

- For the purpose of this book, you will learn to create and format a personal-business letter. You might send a personal-business letter for any of the following reasons or situations:
  - To apply for a job.
  - To ask for information about a product or service.
  - To complain about a product or service.
  - To request a brochure from a college or school.
  - To request a bumper sticker from a radio station.

- Most personal-business letters contain the following parts:

  - **Date:** The date the letter was created, or, if you use the Date feature, the date the letter is printed or modified.

  - **Inside Address (or Delivery Address):** The name and address of the person or company who is receiving the letter.

  - **Salutation:** The greeting line. Follow these guidelines for the correct use of a salutation.
    * Use Ladies and Gentlemen if the letter is addressed to the entire company.
    * Use Dear Mr. Lastname or Dear Ms. Lastname if the letter is addressed to a specific individual.

  - **Body:** The content of the letter. There should be at least three paragraphs as follows:
    * The opening paragraph which introduces the subject of the letter.
    * The middle paragraph which provides most of the information.
    * The final paragraph which usually provides where and when you can be reached.

  - **Closing:** The complimentary close. Some common closings are: Sincerely, Yours truly or Cordially. Note that the second word in two-word closings is in lowercase.

  - **Signature Line:** The name of the person sending the letter.

  - **Return Address:** The sender's address. This is typed in personal-business letters or it may be contained in a letterhead.

- You can type a letter from scratch, or you can use the Letter Wizard to help you format your letter. We will be using the Letter Wizard to help us create our personal-business letters.

- A wizard allows you to customize a document by guiding you step-by-step through the creation of a document.

- The Letter Wizard allows you to choose the style of the letter, the information you want in it and the various parts you want included.

- The Letter Wizard offers you many options. Select those that fit the style of the letter you chose.

- Once the letter is created, the Letter Wizard provides placeholder text where you will type your own wording for the letter.

- Follow these steps to create a letter using the Letter Wizard:
  1. Click File menu.
  2. Click New.
  3. Select Letters & Faxes tab.
  4. Double-click the Letter Wizard
  5. Click Send one letter.
     Note: The Office Assistant appears. If you cannot see the entire Letter Wizard box, drag the title bar until it is clearly in view.
  6. Click Letter Format tab to display the following dialog box:

Letter Wizard dialog box - Step 1

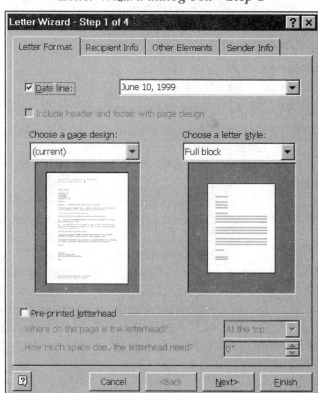

7. Make the appropriate selections from the following features:

- **Date line**: Click drop-down arrow to choose the formal date style (January 1, 2000).
- **Choose a page design**: Select the desired style and check the preview window.
- **Choose a letter style**: Select the full-block style; it's the easiest to use.
- **Pre-printed letterhead**: Do not select. Use only if you are printing on ready-made stationery.

8. Click <u>N</u>ext to display the Recipient Info tab.

Letter Wizard dialog box - Step 2

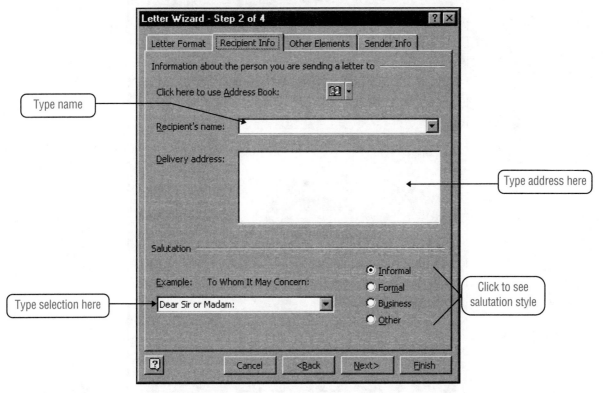

9. Provide the following information:

- **<u>R</u>ecipient's name:**   Type the recipient's name in the text box.
- **<u>De</u>livery address:**   Type the address of the party to whom you are sending the letter. Press the Enter key after each line of the address.
- **Salutation:**   Type your salutation in the text box. Click the option buttons to see different salutation styles, such as Informal or Formal.
  - ∗ Use Ladies and Gentlemen to address an entire company.
  - ∗ Use Dear Mr. Lastname or Dear Ms. Lastname if you know the person to whom you are writing.

10. Click Next twice to display the Sender Info tab.
    Note: For the purposes of this book, we will not use the Other Elements tab.

Letter Wizard dialog box - Step 4

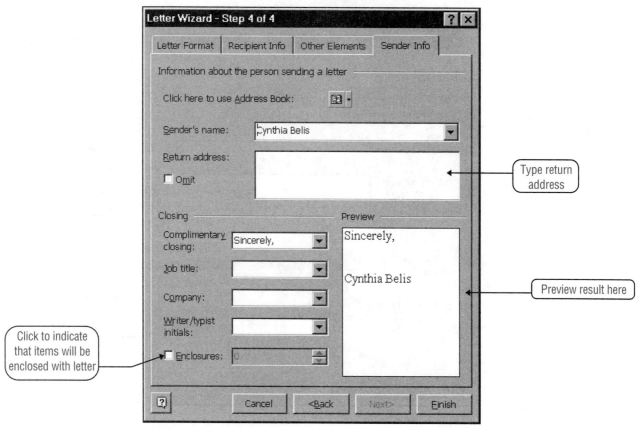

11. Provide the following information:

- **Sender's name:**   Type your first and last name.
- **Return address:**   Type your home address. Click Omit if you are using personalized
                              stationery that contains your address.
- **Complimentary closing:** Type your own closing or select one from the drop-down list.
- **Enclosures:**   Click to place a check in the check box when sending additional items
                              with the letter. Click up or down arrows to select number of enclosures.

12. Preview your closing.

13. Click Finish when done.

Exercise 1
Use the Letter Wizard to Create a Letter

1. Click File menu.
2. Click New.
3. Click Letters & Faxes tab.
4. Double-click Letter Wizard.
5. Follow the wizard to add the following parts to your letter.
   - Date   use today's date
   - Recipient's Name   Ms. Dee Jay
   - Address   WVUG Radio
     135 Broadcast Drive
     Musik, NY 11560
   - Salutation   select Business
   - Sender's name   Stu Dent
   - Return address   870 Cypress Drive
     New Meadows, NY 11554
   - Closing   select Sincerely
6. Save the document; name it **WVUG**.
7. Do not close the document window.

GOAL 2:   Type Letter Text

- Once you have created the letter, cancel the Letter Wizard.

- At this point, position the insertion point at the top of the page and press the Enter key until the insertion point is approximately 2.5" from the top of the page. The letter is now more attractively centered on the page.

- Try to leave the same amount of empty space on the top and bottom unless you are printing the letter on letterhead stationery. If you are not using letterhead, you may vertically center the letter on the page.

- The Letter Wizard uses a 10-point font, which is much too small for a letter. Change the font size to 12 point. Don't change the font size of the return address in the text box.

- Select the placeholder text and type the text you want in the body of the letter.

- At this point, you may want to make changes to the letter.
    - Traditional letter formats contain 3 blank lines after the date and after the complimentary closing. This requires that you press the Enter key 4 times after the date and closing.
    - Traditional personal-business letters require the return address to be above the date or below the sender's name. Since we are using the Letter Wizard, the return address will be placed in a text box at the bottom of the page. If you wish to be more traditional, you may move the return address from the text box and place it directly above the date or below the sender's name.
    - If you want to add your phone number, locate your insertion point at the end of the sender's name and press the Enter key once. Type the phone number directly under the sender's name.

- When you are finished, save or resave the letter.

Exercise 2
Type Letter Text

1. Place your insertion point at the beginning of the **WVUG** letter.
2. Press the Enter key until the Status bar reads At 2.5".
3. Replace the placeholder text with the text provided in the illustration on the next page.
4. Select all the text in the letter and change to a serif font, 12 point.
5. Spell check the document.
6. Check the Print Preview to see if the letter is placed attractively on the page.
7. Place the phone number below the sender's name.
8. Make any necessary adjustments to duplicate the illustration on the next page.
9. Resave the file.
10. Print one copy.
11. Do not close the document window.

Desired Result

May 26, 1999

Ms. Dee Jay
WVUG Radio
135 Broadcast Drive
Musik, NY 11560

Dear Ms. Jay:

I am a fan of your radio station and listen to your "Chart Toppers" every day. I think you are an awesome disc jockey and especially like when you have fans call in with their requests.

I would like a bumper sticker for my parents' car. They know how much I like your program, and they said I could put it on the car. Please send a bumper sticker to my home address listed below. I really would appreciate it.   Also, if you could play "Larry on the Slide with Donuts" this week, you would make my day.

You have a devoted fan in New Meadows.

Sincerely,

Stu Dent
(516) 555-2333

870 CYPRESS DRIVE
NEW MEADOWS, NY 11554

LESSON 37

GOAL 3: Copy Letter to Letterhead

- You can copy a letter created by the Letter Wizard to a letterhead template or document.

- If you are copying a letter to letterhead that contains a return address, make sure the return address does not appear in any other part of the letter. The Letter Wizard places the return address in a text box at the bottom of the page unless you choose to omit it.

- If there is a return address in the text box and your letterhead contains one as well, you must delete the return address from the text box. When you make a reference to the address or phone number in the letter text, make sure you point out the correct location. For example: *Please send a copy to my home address listed **above**.*

- Once the letter is copied to the letterhead template, save the document.
  Note: If you copy your letter to a letterhead that is not a template, make sure to save it under a different file name, otherwise you will overwrite the letterhead.

- Follow these steps to copy a letter to the letterhead.
    1. Open the letterhead template or document.
    2. Open the letter.
    3. Select the text in the letter.
    4. Click Edit menu.
    5. Click Copy.
    6. Click Window.
    7. Select the letterhead.
    8. Place the insertion point where you want the letter to begin. You may need to press the Enter key a number of times to position the insertion point under the letterhead.
    9. If the letterhead shifts down, select the letterhead and move it back to the top of the page.
       Note: You may need to group the various parts of the letterhead so they will move as one unit. Click the Select Objects button [cursor icon] on the Drawing toolbar. Using this tool, draw a box around the items in the letterhead, click Draw on the Drawing toolbar and click Group.
    10. Click Edit menu.
    11. Click Paste.
    12. Save the new document.
        Note: Use a file name that is different from the letterhead.
    13. Print the new file.
    14. Close all document windows.
        Note: Do not save the changes to the original letter file.

Exercise 3
Copy Letter to Letterhead

1. Create a new template.
2. Create a letterhead for Stu Dent using any of the formatting features you have learned (WordArt, Drawing objects, Clip Art).
3. Include the address in the letterhead, as shown on the next page.
4. Save the template; name it **DENT**.
5. Do not close the document window.
6. Switch to the **WVUG** document.
7. Copy the letter. Do not copy the return address at the bottom of the letter.
   Note: Since the return address is in the letterhead, you do not need to have it at the bottom of the letter.
8. Switch to the **DENT** document.
9. Use the Click and Type method to position the insertion point where the date is to begin.
10. Paste the letter onto the **DENT** letterhead template.
11. Go to the Print Preview window.
12. Make sure the letter is attractively placed on the letterhead.
13. Compare your work to the illustration on the following page.
    Note: Your letterhead will differ from the illustration.
15. Save the document; name it **RADIO**.
16. Print one copy.
17. Close all document windows.

Desired Result

870 Cypress Drive   New Meadows, NY 11554

May 26, 1999

Ms. Dee Jay
WVUG Radio
135 Broadcast Drive
Musik, NY 11560

Dear Ms. Jay:

I am a fan of your radio station and listen to your "Chart Toppers" every day. I think you are an awesome disc jockey and especially like when you have fans call in with their requests.

I would like a bumper sticker for my parents' car. They know how much I like your program, and they said I could put it on the car. Please send a bumper sticker to my home address listed below. I really would appreciate it.   Also, if you could play "Larry on the Slide with Donuts" this week, you would make my day.

You have a devoted fan in New Meadows.

Sincerely,

Stu Dent
(516) 555-2333

GOAL 4: Create an Envelope

- Once the letter is finalized, you can create a personalized envelope to go with it.
- Open the letter for which you wish to create an envelope and select the inside address.
- Follow these steps to create the envelope:
  1. Click <u>T</u>ools menu.
  2. Click <u>E</u>nvelopes and Labels.

Envelopes and Labels dialog box

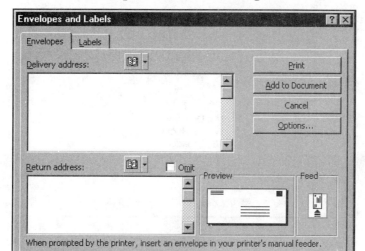

  3. Select the <u>E</u>nvelopes tab.
  4. Type the <u>D</u>elivery address if it does not appear in the text box.
  5. Type a <u>R</u>eturn address.
     Note: Leave this option blank if you are using preprinted envelopes.
  6. Click <u>O</u>ptions to select an envelope size.
     Note: Word uses a #10 envelope as the default. Make sure you are using the correct envelope to match the selected envelope size.
  7. Click OK.
  8. Click <u>A</u>dd to Document.
  9. Save the file.
  10. Print the file.

- When you send the envelope to the printer, the printer will prompt (ask) you to insert an envelope.

Exercise 4a
Create an Envelope

1. Open **RADIO**.
2. Select the delivery address. Click <u>T</u>ools, <u>E</u>nvelopes and Labels and select the Envelopes tab.
3. Type a return address if you are not using preprinted envelopes.
4. Print one copy of the letter and envelope.
5. Resave the file.
6. Close the document window.

```
Stu Dent
870 Cypress Drive
New Meadows, NY 11554




                                    Ms. Dee Jay
                                    WVUG Radio
                                    135 Broadcast Drive
                                    Musik, NY 11560
```

Exercise 4b
Use Letter Wizard to Create an Envelope

1. Use the Letter Wizard using your name and address for the sender and return address to create the following letter. Format the letter attractively.
   *Note: You may print this letter on the **STATIONERY** template (this is the personal letterhead you created in Lesson 35). If your letterhead contains your return address, do not place your address in the return address text box.*
2. Check the Print Preview window and make any necessary adjustments.
3. Spell check the letter.
4. Create an envelope and make sure it contains your return address.
5. Save the document; name it **PRODUCT**.
6. Print the letter and envelope.
7. Close the document window.

Desired Result

October 29, 1999

Mighty Shirts
4500 West Nylon Drive
Silk Screen, CA 93513

Ladies and Gentlemen:

I am writing this letter to tell you how disappointed I am with your product. I recently bought a T-shirt manufactured by your company at Funky Tees in the Cotton County Mall and attempted to return it.

I washed the T-shirt following the instructions on the label and all the printing ran onto the shirt. The shirt is unusable. I tried to return the shirt to the store, but they would not give me a refund saying I washed the product incorrectly. I paid $25 for this shirt and it should be of higher quality. You need to stand by your products so that the retail stores will willingly give refunds when there is a problem.

I am requesting a refund of $25 from your company and have enclosed a copy of my receipt. Please send the refund to the address listed below. Thank you for your cooperation in this matter.

Sincerely,

Your Name
(area code) (phone number)

Enclosure

YOUR STREET ADDRESS
CITY, STATE ZIP

Timed Writing

1. Create a new document.
2. Use the default margins.
3. Change font to Courier New, 12 point.
4. Take a 5-minute timing on the entire document.
   a. If you finish before the time is up, press the Enter key twice and start again.
   b. Do not correct errors. If you make an error, continue typing.
   c. To calculate your WAM speed, find the total number of words you typed and divide that number by 5.
5. Press the Enter key 4 times.
6. Take two 1-minute timings.
   a. Type as fast as you can for the first 1-minute timing.
   b. Type as accurately as you can for the second 1-minute timing.
   c. Do not correct your errors. If you make an error, continue typing.
   d. Press the Enter key 4 times between the timings.
   e. Calculate your WAM speed.
7. Following the same instructions as in Step 4, take another five-minute timing on the entire document. Calculate your WAM speed.
8. Compare your speeds.
9. Save the document as **L37TIME**.
10. Print one copy.
11. Close the document window.

	WORDS

There are many different superstitions around the world that   12
people hold onto. One such superstition is the fear of the   24
number 13. The fear of the number 13 is one of those fears   36
that are not just local. There are hotels around the world   48
that skip the number 13 when numbering the floors. These   60
same hotels may not have a room 13. Some people will not   72
stay with a group if there are only 13 people in it.   83

You, along with many other people, probably wonder how this   95
fear of the number 13 started. There does not seem to be one   107
single answer to this question. Some people say the number   119
13 was unpopular from the beginning since people could use   131
ten fingers and two feet to count, resulting in a total of 12.   143
Therefore, the number 13 was unknown and people are usually   155
afraid of the unknown.   160

Though most people still have a fear of the number 13, the   172
ancient Chinese and Egyptians felt that this number was good   184
luck.   185

....1....2....3....4....5....6....7....8....9...10...11..12

MOUSE/KEYSTROKE PROCEDURES

Use the Letter Wizard

1. Click **File** menu............... `Alt`+`F`
2. Click **New**.................................. `N`
3. Click **Letters & Faxes** tab.
4. Double-click **Letter Wizard**.
5. Click **Send one letter**.
6. Supply the necessary information in the dialog box.
7. Click **Next** .... `Alt`+`N` to move to the next dialog box.
8. Repeat Steps 6 and 7 until you have completed the Wizard.
9. Click **Finish**...................... `Alt`+`F` when done.
10. Place insertion point before the date.
11. Press Enter key until dateline is At 2.5".
12. Select placeholder text and type desired text.
13. Check the Print Preview window and make adjustments to letter placement as needed.

Copy Letter to Letterhead

1. Open the letterhead document.
2. Open the letter.
3. Select the letter text.
4. Click **Edit** menu .... `Alt`+`E`
5. Click **Copy** .... `C`
6. Click **Window** .... `Alt`+`W`
7. Switch to the letterhead document.
8. Place insertion point under the letterhead.
   Note: You may have to press the Enter key several times to place the insertion point at the proper location. You may have to adjust the vertical placement of the letterhead.
9. Click **Edit** menu .... `Alt`+`E`
10. Click **Paste** .... `P`

Create an Envelope

1. Open desired letter.
2. Select the delivery address.
3. Click **Tools** menu .... `Alt`+`T`
4. Click **Envelopes and Labels**...... `E`
5. Click **Delivery Address** .... `Alt`+`D`
6. Type different Delivery address, if needed.
7. Click **Return address** .... `Alt`+`R`
8. Supply return address, if needed.
9. Click **Options**................... `Alt`+`O`
10. Change envelope size as needed.
11. Click **Add to Document** .... `Alt`+`A`
12. Click **File** menu .... `Alt`+`F`
13. Click **Print** .... `P`
14. Supply envelope when prompted by printer.

Warm-up

1. Create a new document.
2. Set the left and right margins to 1".
3. Type each line twice, trying to type faster when you repeat a line. Press the Enter key twice after the second line. When you see the vertical lines between phrases, say the phrase to yourself as you type. Do not type the vertical lines.
4. If you make an error, continue typing.
5. If you have time, repeat the exercise.
6. Save the document as **LES38**.

---

1. `a;sldkfjghfjdksla; a;sldkfjghfjdksla; a;sldkfjghfjdksla;`
2. `aq1qaza sw2wsxs de3edcd fr4rfvf ft5tfgfbf fr45rftfgfbfvf`

3. `fur fun gun gum guy buy but hut jut vug jim dim kid red cue`
4. `my lot sit wet tex co. fat pat zip qt. s2l9 d3k8 f4j7 f5j6 ;0`

5. `summer fall winter spring north south east west yes no`
6. `isn't doesn't won't aren't can't hasn't didn't couldn't`

7. `in which|in which|which has|which has|which will|which will|`
8. `You can buy anything from gum to zippers at Red's Web site.`

LESSON 38

GOAL 1: Create Drop Caps

- A **drop cap** is a large capital letter that creates a point of interest and draws the reader's attention to the text. The drop cap is aligned with the top of the first line of a page, section or paragraph.

- The dropped letter starts at the top of the first line and extends to the bottom of the third line. The remaining text on those lines is indented to make room for the dropped capital letter. Word allows you to adjust the height of the dropped letter. Note the illustration below of a paragraph containing a dropped cap.

> Drop caps are large decorative letters often used to mark the beginning of a document, section, or paragraph. Drop caps are set to a much larger font than the remaining paragraph text and span the height of three or four lines. If you are using a decorative font for the drop cap, make sure that it coordinates with the remaining text in the paragraph.

- Follow these steps to include a drop cap in your text:
  1. Place the insertion point anywhere in the paragraph to contain a drop cap.
     Note: There must be text in the paragraph or the feature will not work.
  2. Click F̲ormat menu.
  3. Click D̲rop Cap to display the following dialog box.

Drop Cap dialog box

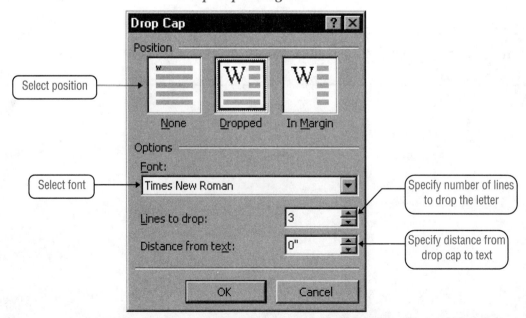

4. Click the desired position for the drop cap.
5. In the Font drop-down list, click the desired font for the drop cap.
6. In the Lines to list box, specify how many lines you want the letter dropped into the paragraph.
7. In the Distance from list box, specify the distance from the drop cap to the text.
8. Click OK.

■ A drop cap should be coordinated with the paragraph. If the paragraph text is in a serif font, the drop cap should also be in a serif font. However, you may choose a different serif font for the dropped cap. The same is true if the paragraph text is in a sans serif font. It is important not to mix serif and sans serif within the same paragraph.

Exercise 1
Type a Short Report with Drop Caps

1. Create a new document.
2. You will use the MLA format for this one-page report as follows:
   a. Set the left and right margins to 1".
   b. Use the default top and bottom margins.
   c. Set the document for double spacing.
   d. Use a serif font, 12 point, for the heading and paragraph text.
3. Type the following heading in the top-left corner of the page.
   • Your name
   • Mr. David Russell
   • Study Skills 102
   • Date
4. Center the title "How to Study Effectively" in the same serif font in 18 point, bold.
5. Press the Enter key once after the title.
6. Type the body of the report.
7. Use a drop cap at the beginning of each new paragraph. Format the drop cap as follows:
   a. Select the Dropped position.
   b. Select a different serif font.
   c. Drop the cap two lines.
   d. Allow no distance between the drop cap and the text.
8. Spell check the document.
9. Compare your result with the illustration on the next page.
10. Save the document as **STUDY1**.
11. Print one copy.
12. Close the document window.

Desired Result

Your Name

Mr. David Russell

Study Skills 102

Today's date

How to Study Effectively

There is so much for young people to learn, but are they being taught how to learn it? Students learn study and organizational skills in the primary grades; however, these skills need to be reviewed and further developed as students move on to middle and high school.

How do you study? If your studying consists of reading the material over and over again, you are **NOT** studying effectively. In order to get the most out of your studying, you must become actively involved in the process. Reading alone is passive involvement. To actively study, you should use as many senses as you can: sight, sound, and touch, if possible. This means that in addition to reading the material, you should be writing, speaking, and thinking about what you are studying.

It takes time and practice to develop good study skills—they don't happen overnight, but the wait is worth it. Good study skills not only help you to achieve good grades in school, but they are lifelong tools that will allow you to be more productive in both your personal and professional life.

GOAL 2: Review Text Wrapping Options

- In Lesson 28, you learned to insert graphics and integrate them with text.
- You can place text around a picture, shape or text box to create an interesting design.
- By default, clip art and other graphics are inserted with the **In line with text** wrapping style. You can change this format to other options. These include:
  - <u>I</u>n front of text option—where the graphic is placed in front of the text.
  - S<u>q</u>uare option—where the text surrounds the graphic on all four sides.
  - <u>T</u>ight option—where the text is closer to the image.
  - <u>B</u>ehind text option—where the graphic is placed behind the text.
- Follow these steps to wrap text around a graphic object.
  1. Click the object to display its handles.
  2. Click F<u>o</u>rmat menu.
  3. Click Pi<u>c</u>ture, Aut<u>o</u>Shape or Text B<u>o</u>x.
  4. Click the Layout tab to display the following dialog box:

Format Picture dialog box

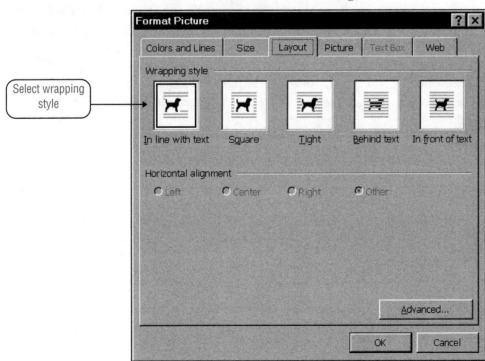

5. Choose the desired wrapping option.
6. Choose the desired alignment option.
7. If you need a more precise format, click the Advanced button to display the following dialog box:

Advanced Layout dialog box

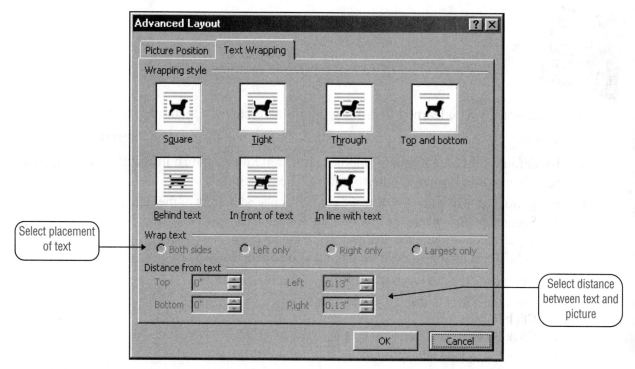

a. Select one of the Wrapping styles.
b. Select one of the following Wrap text options for the Square, Tight and Through styles.
  * **Both sides**   Wraps text around the left and right sides of the graphic object.
  * **Left only**   Wraps text around the left side of the graphic object.
  * **Right only**   Wraps text around the right side of the graphic object.
  * **Largest side** Wraps text around left or right side depending on which is wider.
c. Select the distance you want between the text and the graphic object.
d. Click OK.

8. Click OK.

Exercise 2
Apply Text Wrap to a Graphic Object

1. Open **STUDY1**.
2. Save the document as **STUDY2**.
3. Insert an appropriate graphic from the Clip Gallery as follows:
   - Do a search for either "triumph" or "victory."
   - Select an appropriate graphic.
   - Place it in the second paragraph of the report, as illustrated on the next page.
4. Click the picture to display the handles and scale the picture to 25% of its original size.
   Hint: Click Format, Picture, click the Size tab and change the scale percentage to 25%. Make sure the Lock aspect ratio and Relative to original picture check boxes are selected.
5. Select the Square text wrapping style.
6. On the Advanced Text Wrapping tab, set the graphic .13" from the text.
7. Change alignment to justify.
8. Compare your result with the illustration on the following page.
9. Resave the document.
10. Print the document.
11. Close the document window.

Your Name

Mr. David Russell

Study Skills 102

Today's date

How to Study Effectively

There is so much for young people to learn, but are they being taught how to learn it? Students learn study and organizational skills in the primary grades; however, these skills need to be reviewed and further developed as students move on to middle and high school.

How do you study? If your studying consists of reading the material over and over again, you are **NOT** studying effectively. In order to get the most out of your studying, you must become actively involved in the process. Reading alone is passive involvement. To actively study, you should use as many senses as you can: sight, sound, and touch, if possible. This means that in addition to reading the material, you should be writing, speaking, and thinking about what you are studying.

It takes time and practice to develop good study skills—they don't happen overnight, but the wait is worth it. Good study skills not only help you to achieve good grades in school, but they are lifelong tools that will allow you to be more productive in both your personal and professional life.

GOAL 3: Add Captions to Graphic Objects

- A **caption** is text in a text box that helps identify a graphic or illustration and aids in locating it within a document.

- Captions can be added from a list of ready-made captions or you can create your own. Captions can contain a label and number or text to identify the graphic. For the purposes of this book, we will use text to explain a graphic.

- Follow these steps to add a caption to an existing graphic:
    1. Select the desired graphic to display the handles.
    2. Click Insert menu.
    3. Click Caption to display the following dialog box:

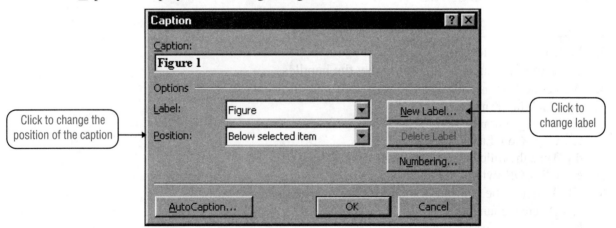

    4. Click New Label and type explanation text.
    5. Click OK to exit the New Label dialog box.
    6. Click OK to exit the Caption dialog box.
    7. Click inside the caption box and edit the text as desired.
    8. Click outside the caption box when you are finished.

- You may need to make adjustments to the text inside the caption box. Edit and format the text in the caption box as desired. If you do not want the graphics numbered, delete the number from the caption box.

- In addition to editing the text, you may want to resize or move the caption box. Select the box to display the handles. Adjust the size and placement as desired.

- If you have selected a text wrapping option for the accompanying picture, then you will need to apply the same text wrapping option to the caption box.

- Follow these steps to wrap text around a caption box:
  1. Click the caption box to display the handles.
  2. Click Format menu.
  3. Click Text Box.
  4. Select the Layout tab.
  5. Select the desired Wrapping style.
  6. Click OK.

Exercise 3
Add a Caption to a Graphic

1. Open **STUDY2**.
2. Save the document as **STUDY3**.
3. Click the Triumph picture to display the handles.
4. Add a caption as follows:
   a. Click Insert menu.
   b. Click Caption.
   c. Click New Label.
   d. Type the following: Study Skills Pay
   e. Click OK twice.
5. Click inside the caption box and format the text as follows:
   a. Delete the number 1.
   b. Center the text.
   c. Bold the text.
   d. Resize the box to fit all the text.
6. Click outside the caption box.
7. Make any adjustments to the size, place and text wrapping option of the caption box as needed.
8. Compare your work with the illustration on the next page.
9. Resave the document.
10. Print one copy.
11. Close the document window.

Desired Result

Your Name

Mr. David Russell

Study Skills 102

Today's date

How to Study Effectively

There is so much for young people to learn, but are they being taught how to learn it? Students learn study and organizational skills in the primary grades; however, these skills need to be reviewed and further developed as students move on to middle and high school.

How do you study? If your studying consists of reading the material over and over again, you are **NOT** studying effectively. In order to get the most out of your studying, you must become actively involved in the process.

Reading alone is passive involvement. To actively study, you should use as many senses as you can: sight, sound, and touch, if possible. This means that in addition to reading the material, you should be writing, speaking, and thinking about what you are studying.

Study Skills Pay

It takes time and practice to develop good study skills—they don't happen overnight, but the wait is worth it. Good study skills not only help you to achieve good grades in school, but they are lifelong tools that will allow you to be more productive in both your personal and professional life.

LESSON 38

GOAL 4:   Create Newsletters Using Columns

- A **newsletter** is a publication that is used to communicate information in an interesting format. Depending upon the organization, it can be used for announcing company news, events, products or articles of general interest to the readers. For example, a company or school can publish a monthly newsletter giving information about the achievements of its employees or students.

- Newsletters contain several sections described below:
  - **Banner**   Includes the name of the newsletter and the organization's name and logo (a symbol representing the company). This section should be eye catching and the focal point of the newsletter.
  - **Dateline**   Includes one or more of the following: the date, issue and/or volume number. This information appears under the banner and is in a substantially smaller font size than the banner text.
  - **Headline**   Provides the title of each individual article. It appears before each article and may be in bold. Usually headlines are in a larger font size than the article itself.
  - **Byline**   Follows the title of the article and gives the author's name. The byline is in a smaller font size than the title and can be in italics.
  - **Body text**   Includes the main text of each article.

- The top section of the newsletter containing the banner, date, issue number, etc., can be created using any of the features learned in this book. You can use WordArt, color, borders and shading, graphics, as well as any elements from the Drawing toolbar to enhance the attractiveness of the text.

- A newsletter combines text and graphics in a column format. You can have a two- or three-column newsletter. The Columns feature allows text to flow down one column and begin again at the top of the next column. This is known as **snaking columns** or **newspaper columns**.

- You can create the columns before or after the text is typed.

- You can have the entire document formatted into columns, or you can specify that the columns start at a certain point. For a newsletter, begin the column layout after the top section of the newsletter has been formatted.

- Follow these steps to create columns:
  1. Place insertion point where you want columns to begin.
  2. Click F_ormat menu.
  3. Click _Columns to display the following dialog box:

412

Columns dialog box

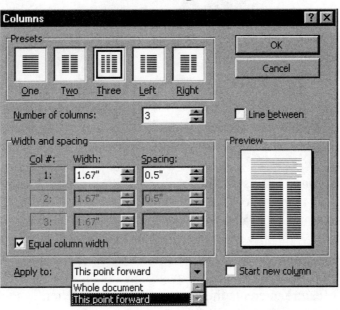

4. In the Presets area, click the number of columns.
5. Click Line between if you want a vertical line between the columns.
6. Click Equal column width if you want each column to be the same width.
   OR
   Specify the Width and spacing for each column.
7. Select This point forward in the Apply to drop-down list.
8. Check the Preview window to see how your document will appear.
9. Click OK.

■ To return to a single column, select the columns and select One column in the Presets area of the Columns dialog box shown above. Select This point forward in the Apply to drop-down list.

■ You may justify the columns. Justification uses even left and right margins and gives a crisper look to the column layout. To justify the columns, select the column text and click the **Justify** button ▤ on the Formatting toolbar.

■ Newsletter documents are long and involved. Therefore, you should save often to prevent loss of data.

Exercise 4a
Create a Newsletter Using the Columns Feature

1. Create a new document.
2. Set the top and bottom margins to .5".
3. Set the left and right margins to 1".
4. Save the document; name it **CYBERNEWS**.
    Note: Remember to frequently resave the document to avoid loss of data.
5. Press the Enter key 8 times to move approximately 2" down in the document.
6. Place the insertion point at the top of the page.
7. Use the WordArt feature to create the banner for the newsletter. Use the following options to duplicate the banner shown on the illustration on page 416:
    a. Use the second option in the last row.
    b. Use the default font and font size.
    c. Stretch the WordArt frame to the left and right margins.
    d. Click the Fill Color button on the Drawing toolbar and select Fill Effects.
    e. Click the Gradient tab and select Preset color.
    f. Select Chrome II as the color and From Center as the Shading style.
    g. Make any necessary adjustments to duplicate the illustration.
8. Select the WordArt object and drag to within .5" of the top of the page.
9. Click under the WordArt object and press the Enter key once.
10. Insert a text box for the dateline and type the following information at the left margin in a serif font, 11 point, bold:
    a. A Publication of Cybernaut, Inc.
    b. Press the Tab key seven times and type December, 1999.
    c. If the date runs over to the next line, delete a tab. If there is too much space on the right, add another tab.
    d. Remove the border around the text box.
        Hint: Click the text box, click Format, Text Box, click Lines and Color tab, click No Line.
11. Drag the text box under the WordArt object, as illustrated.
12. Insert a line from the Clip Art folder and place it between the title and the dateline as shown. If you do not have access to this feature, use a line from the Drawing toolbar. Format attractively.
13. Click under the dateline. Position your insertion point one blank line after the text box.
    Note: Click Show/Hide ¶ to show the number of blank lines between the text box and the insertion point. Press the Enter key if you need to add a blank line.

14. Create the columns as follows:
    a. Format the remainder of the document for two columns.
    b. Insert a line between the columns.
    c. Choose the This point forward option.
15. Type and format the body text as follows:
    a. Set the line spacing to 1.5.
    b. Set the body text to a serif font, 11 point.
    c. Justify the text.
16. Create a drop cap in a different serif font and drop it three lines.
17. From the Clip Gallery, insert the *debates* graphic from the People category, or, if you have access to the Internet, find a suitable replacement from Clips Online. Format as follows:
    a. Scale the picture to 50%.
    b. Make sure Lock aspect ratio and Relative to original size are checked.
    c. Select Square as the Wrapping style and Both sides as the Wrap text style.
18. Create a caption and change the label to say: What did I say wrong?
19. Format the caption as follows:
    a. Delete any numbers in the label.
    b. Select the same wrapping options as for the *debates* picture.
    c. Center the text in a serif font, 8 point, bold.
    d. Remove the border around the text box.
20. From the Clip Gallery, insert the *handshakes* graphic from the People at Work category, or, if you have access to the Internet, find a suitable replacement from Clips Online. Format as follows:
    a. Scale the picture to 30%.
    b. Make sure Lock aspect ratio and Relative to original picture size are checked.
    c. Select the same wrapping options as for the *debates* picture.
21. Create a caption and change the label to say: Be Courteous!
22. Follow Step 19 to format the caption.
23. Spell check the document.
24. Preview your work and make any necessary adjustments to duplicate the illustration on the next page.
25. Resave the document.
26. Print one copy.
27. Close the document window.

Desired Result

A Publication of Cybernaut, Inc.   **December, 1999**

People interact according to the unwritten rules of etiquette that have been handed down from generation to generation. Behaviors we take for granted are instilled in us at an early age. Take a moment and think about all the social customs we follow (or should follow) when we interact with others whether it be in person, on the phone, or driving a car.

Now comes the age of cyberspace with the arrival of the Internet and on-line services. Millions of people are using their computers to communicate in ways never thought possible. The information highway is an exciting place to find information and perhaps make new friends, but we do this in a vacuum. We don't hear the voice or see the facial expression that has traditionally helped us to convey our messages. Now we have only the written word, and we may sometimes forget that we are communicating with real people who have real live feelings. This could lead to a lapse in manners. As a result, there have been

Be Courteous!

books and magazines written on the proper way to conduct yourself when communicating on-line. One of the key points to remember when using a service or bulletin board is that there is a person at the other end of the computer, and we should apply the same standards to our on-line behavior that we follow in our daily lives. Ask yourself if

What did I say wrong?

your message is acceptable and if you would say this to someone in a face-to-face situation. Try to envision the person you're writing to so that the communication becomes more "human." Remember that anything you write takes on a life of its own. It can be saved and later forwarded to other users.

Be ethical, courteous, sensitive to others, and remember that your written word is your representative. If we all adhere to these general guidelines, then cyberspace will be a more pleasant place to visit.

Exercise 4b
Create a Newsletter Using the Columns Feature

1. Create a new document.
2. Set 1" margins all around.
3. Save the document; name it **HEALTH**.
4. Type the newsletter text shown in the illustration on the next page, using a columns format.
5. Make sure you include the banner, dateline, graphic elements and captions.
6. Format the text attractively using some of the following features:
   - font
   - font styles
   - font color
   - drop caps
   - alignments
   - line spacing
   - paragraph indents
   - WordArt
   - borders and shading

7. Insert appropriate graphics and format them using some of the following features:
   Note: Your graphics may differ from those in the illustration.
   - resize
   - wrapping options
   - wrapping styles
   - wrap text styles
   - alignments

8. Make sure your newsletter fits on one page.
9. Make necessary adjustments to format the newsletter attractively.
10. Your solution may differ from the illustration.
11. Resave the file.
12. Print one copy.

Desired Result

Healthy Computing

| Volume 15 | Official Publication of Computer Health | October, 1999 |

Are your eyes bothering you? Does your neck feel a little stiff? Have you experienced pain in your arms and wrists? Chances are good that your computer environment needs an adjustment. The following articles describe steps you should take to insure that you are working under the best possible conditions.

Have a Seat

First, let's take a look at the chair. You should invest in a comfortable and well-designed chair. It may be a little more expensive, but it can save on doctor's bills.

Make sure there is neck and head support as well as support for the lower back. These support options are adjustable in better chairs. You must also be able to adjust the height of the seat. Your feet should be able to reach the floor, but if that is not possible, use a footrest. Good chairs also have arm supports.

Try out the chair and make sure it's appropriate for you.

The Key to Healthy Wrists

Position the keyboard directly in front of you so you are centered over the **g** and **h** keys. The keyboard should be resting on a surface that is approximately 26" high. If you are using a traditional desk, attach a keyboard shelf that places the keyboard lower than the desktop.

To reduce the risk of injury to the wrists when typing, make sure your wrists are even with the keyboard. Do not type with your hands resting on the frame of the keyboard or on edge of the desk. Also, avoid bending your wrists in an upward position. Make sure the *feet* of the keyboard are opened so your keyboard slopes. Use a keyboard rest to keep your wrists at a good angle as you type. Take breaks and stretch out your fingers and arms periodically.

Keep the mouse close to you and not too far from the keyboard. Don't hold the mouse too tightly. If you are having problems with the mouse, you may try other pointing devices.

Shed Some Light

The monitor is a key factor in maintaining healthy posture. Make sure the monitor is on an adjustable base. The top of the screen should be even with your eyes. If you, or someone you know, wear

bifocals, the monitor must be adjusted so you are not bending your head back to look through the bottom of the glasses. See your eye specialist and get a set of glasses specifically designed for computer use.

Reduce eyestrain by adjusting the brightness and contrast, and if your monitor flickers, get it checked.

You need to rest your eyes at periodic intervals. Take breaks and focus on a distant point every 15 minutes or so.

If you follow these tips, you should be on your way to a healthy and happy computer experience.

Timed Writing

1. Create a new document.
2. Use the default margins.
3. Change font to Courier New, 12 point.
4. Take a 5-minute timing on the entire document.
   a. If you finish before the time is up, press the Enter key twice and start again.
   b. Do not correct errors. If you make an error, continue typing.
   c. To calculate your WAM speed, find the total number of words you typed and divide that number by 5.
5. Press the Enter key 4 times.
6. Take two 1-minute timings.
   a. Type as fast as you can for the first 1-minute timing.
   b. Type as accurately as you can for the second 1-minute timing.
   c. Do not correct your errors. If you make an error, continue typing.
   d. Press the Enter key four times between the timings.
   e. Calculate your WAM speed.
7. Following the same instructions as in Step 4, take another 5-minute timing on the entire document. Calculate your WAM speed.
8. Compare your speeds.
9. Save the document as **L38TIME**.
10. Print one copy.
11. Close the document window.

LESSON 38

Did you ever go to the store to buy a snack and have to choose   12
between many different brands? How did you decide which one   24
to buy? If they all cost about the same, you probably chose   36
the one in the package that caught your attention.   46

Packaging design is a big business. Companies hire people to   58
research how to get you to buy their product instead of a   70
different company's product.   76

The main purpose of a package is to hold the product. Today,   88
though, there is another purpose. That purpose is to sell the 100
product. Color is very important. Orange is supposed to make 112
you feel hungry. Red and yellow are supposed to attract you. 124
Blue is thought to make you feel calm. Green is supposed to 136
make you think about the healthy outdoors. Black is supposed 148
to be classy. Black and white plain packages are supposed to 160
make you think you are paying a good price. 169

Next time you go to the store, notice the packaging and see 181
what catches your eye. 186

....1....2....3....4....5....6....7....8....9...10...11...12

420

MOUSE/KEYSTROKE PROCEDURES

Drop Cap

1. Place the insertion point in the paragraph where the drop cap will appear.
2. Click **Format** menu .... `Alt`+`O`
3. Click **Drop Cap** .... `D`
4. Click desired position:
   - **None** .... `N`
   - **Dropped** .... `D`
   - **In Margin** .... `M`
5. Click **Lines to drop** .... `Alt`+`L`
6. Click increase or decrease arrows to set desired number of lines.
7. Click **Distance from text** .. `Alt`+`X`
8. Click increase or decrease arrows to set desired number of lines.
9. Click **OK** .... `Enter`

Text Wrap

1. Click the picture to display the handles.
2. Click **Format** menu .... `Alt`+`O`
3. Click **Picture** .... `I`
4. Click **Layout** tab .... `Ctrl`+`Tab`
5. Select one of the following Wrapping styles:
   - **In line with text** .... `Alt`+`I`
   - **Square** .... `Alt`+`Q`
   - **Tight** .... `Alt`+`T`
   - **In front of text** .... `Alt`+`F`
   - **Behind text** .... `Alt`+`B`
6. Select one of the following Horizontal alignment options:
   - **Left** .... `Alt`+`L`
   - **Center** .... `Alt`+`C`
   - **Right** .... `Alt`+`R`
   - **Other** .... `Alt`+`O`

7. Click **OK** .... `Enter`
   OR
   Click **Advanced** .... `Alt`+`A`
8. Select one of the Wrap text styles:
   Note: The following options only work with the Square, Tight, Through, Top or Bottom
   - **Both sides** .... `Alt`+`S`
   - **Left only** .... `Alt`+`L`
   - **Right only** .... `Alt`+`R`
   - **Largest side** .... `Alt`+`A`
9. Select one or more of the following to change distance from text:
   - Click **Top** .... `Alt`+`P`
   - Click **Bottom** .... `Alt`+`M`
   - Click **Left** .... `Alt`+`E`
   - Click **Right** .... `Alt`+`G`
10. Click increase or decrease arrows to change distance.
11. Click **OK** twice .... `Enter`, `Enter`

Add a Caption to a Graphic

1. Select the graphic to display the handles.
2. Click **Insert** menu .... `Alt`+`I`
3. Click **Caption** .... `C`
4. Click **New Label** .... `Alt`+`N`
5. Type new label.
6. Click **OK** twice .... `Enter`, `Enter`
7. Click inside caption box to edit text.
8. Resize or move caption box as needed.
9. Click outside caption box to continue working in the document.

Columns

1. Click **Format** menu .... `Alt`+`O`
2. Click **Columns** .... `C`
3. Click desired number of columns:
   - **One** .... `Alt`+`O`
   - **Two** .... `Alt`+`W`
   - **Three** .... `Alt`+`T`
   - **Left** .... `Alt`+`L`
   - **Right** .... `Alt`+`R`
4. Click **Line between** .... `Alt`+`B` to insert a vertical line between the columns.
5. Check **Equal Column width** .... `Alt`+`E`
   OR
   Click **Width** .... `Alt`+`I`
   - Click increase or decrease arrows to change width of the columns .... `⬍`
   - Click **Spacing** .... `Alt`+`S`
   - Click increase or decrease arrows to change spacing between columns .... `⬍`
6. Click **Apply to** .... `Alt`+`A`
7. Select one of the following:
   - **This point forward**
   - **Whole document**
   - **Selected text**
   - **Selected sections**
8. Check results in Preview box.
9. Click **OK** .... `Enter`

Justify Column Text

1. Select columns to justify.
2. Click **Justify** button ▤ on the Formatting toolbar.

LESSON 39

• Internet Basics • Create a Web Page Using a Template
• Format the Page • Use Styles in a Web Page
• Add Pages • Add Hyperlinks • Add Graphics

Warm-up

1. Create a new document.
2. Set the left and right margins to 1".
3. Type each line twice, trying to type faster when you repeat a line. Press the Enter key twice after you repeat the line.
4. When you see the vertical lines between phrases, say the phrase to yourself as you type. Do not type the vertical lines.
5. If you make an error, continue typing.
6. If you have time, repeat the exercise.
7. Save the document as **LES39**.

```
1 a;sldkfjghfjdksla; a;sldkfjghfjdksla; a;sldkfjghfjdksla;
2 aq1qaza sw2wsxs de3edcd fr4rfvf ft5tfgfbf fr45rftfgfbfvf

3 fur fun gun gum guy buy but hut jut vug jim dim kid red cue
4 my, lot sit wet tex co. fat pat zip qt. s2l9 d3k8 f4j7 f5j6 ;0

5 check costs learn about forget near far put around about
6 some very his her my mine much help felt just until sell

7 pay for|pay for|but much of|but much of|some very|some very|
8 If you want to have lots of fun, sit with Pat and Tex Vug.
```

GOAL 1:   Internet Basics

- Word 2000 provides tools to help you create Web pages. A Web page is the presence of a company, organization or individual on the Web.

- Web pages are written in a programming language known as HTML, which stands for Hypertext Markup Language. However, Word 2000 allows you to use basic word processing features to create a Web page. As you type and format your text, Word 2000 automatically translates it into HTML code "behind the scenes."

- Here's a list of a few terms you should know when writing Web pages.
  - **ISP**—Internet Service Provider. This is the company that gives you access to the Internet.
  - **Browser**—Browsers allow you to view the Web pages. The most common browsers are Microsoft Internet Explorer and Netscape Navigator.
  - **URL**—Uniform Resource Locator. This is an Internet address. Each page has an address so people can easily find the site on the Internet. Here's an example of a URL: **http://www.ddcpub.com** and an explanation of its parts.
    - * **http or Hypertext Transfer Protocol**—A set of standards computers use to transfer Web pages over the Internet
    - * **www**—The World Wide Web
    - * **ddcpub**—A company on the Web
    - * **.com**—a suffix that identifies a business

- Web pages may include any of the following elements: text, graphics—pictures, lines, animation, sounds, bullets, tables, videos and links to other sites.

- In this lesson, we will learn to create and format Web pages; however, the exercises in this lesson do not include publishing the page to the Web.

LESSON 39

Exercise 1
Internet Basics

Option A

Note: Option A requires Internet access. If you do not have access to the Internet, complete Option B.

1. Create a new document.
2. Center the following title: WELL DESIGNED WEB SITES
3. Format the title attractively.
4. Press the Enter key twice after the title.
5. Save the document; name it **GOOD WEBSITES**.
6. Do not close the document.
7. Access the Internet.
8. Search the Web and find 3 Web sites that you think are interesting and well formatted.
9. Place the insertion point in the URL and press Ctrl+C to copy the address.
10. Press Alt+Tab or click the document's button on the Taskbar to go back to Word.
11. Press Ctrl+V to paste the site address in the Word document.
12. Place your insertion point after the URL and press the Enter key twice.
13. Type a description of the site and what you like or dislike about its design.
14. Press the Enter key twice after each description.
15. Repeat Steps 8-14 for 2 more Web sites.
16. Spell and grammar check the document.
17. Resave the file.
18. Print one copy.
19. Close the document.

Option B

1. Follow Steps 1-6 above.
2. Read through this lesson to learn about proper Web design.
3. Create a numbered list containing 5 elements of a well-designed Web page.
4. Double-space the list.
5. Spell and grammar check the document.
6. Resave the file.
7. Print one copy.
8. Close the document.

424

GOAL 2:   Create a Web Page Using a Template

- You can create a Web page by using the Web Page Wizard or a Web Page template. In addition, any Word 2000 document can be converted into a Web page.

- In this book, we will use a template to create a Web page. Follow these steps to create the Web page.
  1. Click File menu.
  2. Click New.
  3. Click the Web Pages tab.
  4. Select Simple Layout template.
  5. Click OK.

  Note: If you do not see the Web Pages tab or files, the Web page authoring tools are probably not installed. To install, you must run the setup and select the Web page authoring components.

- Note the illustration of the Simple Layout template below.

> # Main·Heading·Goes· Here¶
>
> ### Section·1·Heading·Goes·Here¶
> Select·text·you·would·like·to·replace· and·type·over·it.·Use·styles·such·as· Heading·1-3·and·Normal·in·the·Style· control·on·the·Formatting·toolbar.¶
> ¶
> The·quick·brown·fox·jumps·over·the· lazy·dog.··The·quick·brown·fox·jumps· over·the·lazy·dog.··The·quick·brown·fox· jumps·over·the·lazy·dog.··The·quick· brown·fox·jumps·over·the·lazy·dog.·· The·quick·brown·fox·jumps·over·the· lazy·dog.¶
>
> ### Section·2·Heading·Goes·Here¶
> The·quick·brown·fox·jumps·over·the· lazy·dog.··The·quick·brown·fox·jumps· over·the·lazy·dog.··The·quick·brown·fox· jumps·over·the·lazy·dog.··The·quick·

- Templates provide a structure for the page. All you need to do is replace the placeholder text.

- The Simple Layout provides a three-column table. You can adjust the column widths as needed. The divider lines are only guidelines and will not appear in the actual Web page.

- Once the document is created, you will need to save it as a Web page. You should be aware of the following naming guidelines for saving Web pages:
  a. The first page of a Web site is usually named index.htm. Other names are home.htm or main.htm.
  b. Use lowercase for all file names and folders in your Web project. File names are case sensitive. Therefore, consistently naming your files in lowercase will avoid any problems.
  c. When saving the index file as a Web page in Word, the .htm extension is automatically added.
     Note: To display the .htm extension, you need to turn on the file extension option. Follow these steps:
        a. *Open My Computer or Windows Explorer.*
        b. *Click View menu and select Folder Options.*
        c. *Select the View tab.*
        d. *Clear the check mark from the Hide file extensions for know file types check box.*

- Every Web site you create should have its own folder. This folder should contain the main page (index.htm), additional pages, graphics and sounds included in that site. Follow these steps to save the file:
  1. Click File menu.
  2. Click Save as Web Page.
  3. The Save As dialog box appears, as shown below.

Save As dialog box

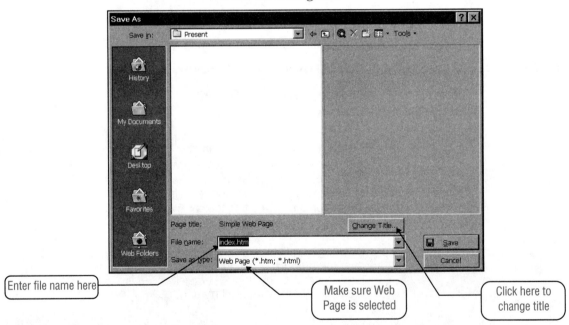

4. Click Save in box to select a folder for the page.
5. Click Change Title and provide a descriptive title for the page.
   Note: The title appears at the top of the Web site, in the Bookmarks or Favorites menus, and in the Title bar of the Browser.
6. Type a file name in the File name text box.
   Note: First pages of a Web site are commonly called index, but may also be called home or main.
7. Click Save as type box and make sure it displays Web Page.
   Note: Make sure your file extensions are turned on.
8. Click Save.

LESSON 39

Exercise 2
Create a Web Page Using a Template

1. Click File menu, New.
2. Click the Web Pages tab. Select the Simple Layout template. Click OK.
3. Click File menu, Save as Web Page.
   Note: When you save a document as a Web page, the Save as type text box automatically displays the Web page extensions (*.htm, *.html).
4. Click Change Title and change the title to Presenting Presentations.
5. Click in the File name text box and type **index** as the file name.
   Note: Web page file names should be in lowercase.
6. Click Save.
7. Do not close the document window.

GOAL 3: Format the Page

- The main reason for creating a Web page is to get people to visit your site. Therefore, the site should be well organized and attractively formatted.

- Word provides a number of features to enhance the appearance of the page.

- When formatting a page, it is important to follow some basic rules of design. Some of the more common ones are:
  - Your text and background must contrast. For example, use a dark text on a light background.
  - Do not use a busy background as it detracts from the message.
  - Break down the text into small paragraphs.
  - Use appropriate graphics sparingly. Too many graphics cause confusion and increase the time it takes for the page to load.
  - Use bullets or numbering to emphasize important items.
  - Make sure the hyperlinks are easy to find so the reader can easily navigate through the site.

427

- Word 2000 provides themes to format your page. These themes provide a look for your Web page by coordinating a number of elements, such as color, fonts and font sizes, styles, bullets, hyperlinks and graphics. Some schemes are conservative, while others are more entertaining. You can preview the themes and choose one that is appropriate to the message you wish to convey.

- Follow these steps to choose a theme:
    1. Click Format menu.
    2. Click Theme.
    3. The Theme dialog box appears, as shown below.

Theme dialog box

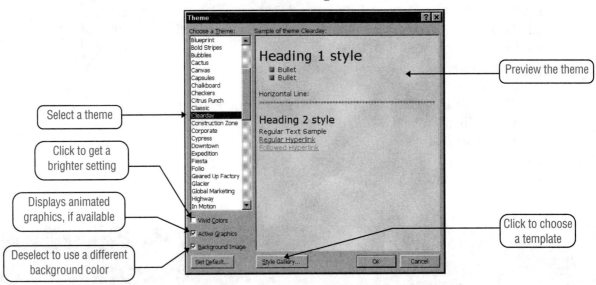

4. Using the Theme dialog box, make appropriate selections from the following options:
    a. Choose a Theme—Select a theme that is consistent with the "look" you want for your site.
    b. Vivid Colors—Click the check box to brighten the colors used in the theme.
    c. Active Graphics—Automatically displays animated graphics if they are available.
    d. Background image—Deselect if you wish to use a different background.
    e. Style Gallery—Choose a template for your page.
    f. Check your selections in the Preview window.
    g. Click OK.

Exercise 3
Format the Page

1. Continue working in the **index.htm** Web page document.
    Note: Open the index.htm document if it was closed.
2. Click Format menu.

3. Click Theme.
4. Select the Clearday theme.
5. Click Vivid Colors.
6. Click OK.
7. Resave the file.
8. Close the document window.

GOAL 4: Use Styles in a Web Page

- The Word template comes with placeholder text. Note that the different levels of text, headings, subheadings and paragraph text are each in a different font, font size and font style.

- Select the placeholder text that you wish to replace, and then observe the Style drop-down list on the left side of the Formatting toolbar. The style of the selected text is displayed. Note the following illustration of the Style drop-down list.

Style drop-down list

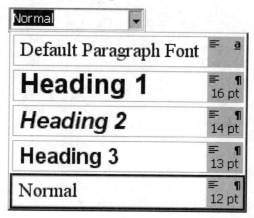

- When you replace placeholder text, the new text appears in the style of the original text. If you want to add other headings, subheadings or body text, make sure that you keep the format consistent with existing text and select the correct style for each level.

Exercise 4
Use Styles in a Web Page

1. Open the **index.htm** document from within Microsoft Word 2000.
2. Select placeholder text and replace with the text shown in the illustration below.
3. Center the title.

H1	# Presenting Presentations
H2	Introduction
Normal	Multimedia Presentations are a unique way to convey information. They combine text, graphics, movies and sounds in a slide show. Successful presentations follow certain rules of design. This site will acquaint you with these guidelines and help you create a show-stopping slide show.
H2	Follow these Do's
Normal	Click this Do's link to see a list of the top five design tips.
H2	Follow these Don'ts
Normal	Click this Don'ts link to see a list of the five worst presentation mistakes.
H2	Delivery Tips
Normal	Click this link to discover delivery methods for your presentation.

4. Format additional text using the same styles as the placeholder text.
   Note: Make sure the headings, subheading and text are formatted consistently.
5. Spell check the document.
6. Resave the file.
7. Print one copy.
8. Do not close the document.

GOAL 5: Add Pages

- You can add pages to your Web site. Web pages should be short so the reader does not have to scroll to see the information.

- You can add a page in the same way you created the first page.
  1. Click File menu.
  2. Click New.
  3. Click Web Pages tab.
  4. Select a template.
  5. Click OK.

- Even though you may have a number of different pages, they should all be formatted consistently. This helps readers identify that they are still on the same site. For example, if you chose the Clearday theme for your first page, all subsequent pages should use that same theme.

- Save additional pages using a file name that is descriptive of the page. Make sure, however, that you use lowercase and save it as a Web page.

- In addition, make sure you save all the pages in the site in the same folder. The folder name should also be in lowercase.

Exercise 5
Add Pages

1. Create an additional page to contain the Presentation Do's as follows:
   a. Click File menu, New.
   b. Click Web Pages tab.
   c. Select Simple Layout.
   d. Click OK.
   e. Click Format, Theme.
   f. Select the Clearday theme.
   g. Select Vivid Colors.
   h. Click OK.

    i.   Select the placeholder text and replace it with the text in Illustration A for Do's page, as shown.

    j.   Center the title.

Illustration A

Five Top Do's

Use These Sure-Fire Tips

- Use a contrasting color for the text.

- Use a font size that can be seen from the back of the room.

- Use bullets to emphasize key points.

- Include only key points in your text. Save the details for the oral portion of the presentation.

- Use separate backgrounds for different sections. This helps to visually organize the topics.

    k.   Start the bulleted list after the subheading. Press the Enter key twice after each line. Delete extra bullets between lines.
        Note: Use techniques learned in previous lessons to create, format and delete bulleted lists.

    l.   Make sure all formats for headings, subheading and text are consistent.

    m. Spell and grammar check the document.

2. Save the file as a Web page document; name it **dos**.
3. Print one copy.
4. Do not close the document window.
5. Create another new page to contain the Presentation Don'ts.
6. Follow Steps a-m above.

   Note: Use the text shown in Illustration B for the Don'ts page.

7. Save the file as a Web page document; name it **donts**.
8. Print one copy.
9. Do not close the document.

Illustration B

Five Top Don'ts

Avoid These Design Bloopers

- Using too many sounds.

- Using more than three fonts on a page.

- Cluttering the page with too much text.

- Using a difficult-to-read font or a font that does not contrast with the background.

- Using unrelated graphics.

GOAL 6:   Add Hyperlinks

- Hyperlinks connect the pages in your Web site. When you click a hyperlink, it's as if you are turning to a different page in a book. Hyperlinks are usually underlined and in blue, but they may be formatted differently depending upon the theme or color scheme you select.

- It is important to place hyperlinks in convenient locations so that the reader can move easily to another page or site.

- Each page should have a hyperlink to the home (first) page. It is also helpful to have links to all other pages within the site on each page.

- Follow these steps to create a hyperlink:
  1. Select the text you wish to use as the hyperlink.
  2. Click Insert, then click Hyperlink.

     OR

     Click the Insert Hyperlink button ![icon] on the Standard toolbar. The following Insert Hyperlink dialog box appears.

Insert Hyperlink dialog box

Insert Hyperlink	? ✕
Link to:	Text to display: Follow these Do's ScreenTip...
	Type the file or Web page name:
Existing File or Web Page	s39dos.htm
	Or select from list: Browse for:
	metacrawler File...
Place in This Document	Recent Files http://www.nba.com/ http://www.mtv.com/ http://www.sfballet.org/ Web Page...
	Browsed Pages
Create New Document	Inserted Links Bookmark...
E-mail Address	OK Cancel

Click to select file to link to

Click to search Internet for Web page you want to link to

3. Click in the "Type the file or Web page name" text box and type the correct file name. If you need to browse to the file or page, click the File button to access the file you wish to link to.
   Note: If you wish to link to a document on the Web, click Web Page. To use this option, you need a connection to an Internet Service Provider.
4. Click OK.
5. Click on the link to make sure it connects to the correct page. When you click on the link, the Web page should open in the default browser (Netscape or Internet Explorer). Viewing the Web page in the browser allows you to see how the page would appear if it were published to the Internet. In this way, you can see if any adjustments need to be made. Be aware that Web pages may display differently in another browser or in different versions of the same browser. Try to format the Web page so it will display accurately in both Netscape and Internet Explorer. Click the Close button on the browser to return to Word.

- You must test out your hyperlinks to make sure they work.

- If a link doesn't work, you need to correct it. Errors can occur for many reasons. Make sure that the hyperlink exactly matches the file names and folders of the files you wish to link to. Follow these steps to correct the link.
  1. Right-click the hyperlink.
  2. Click Hyperlink.
  3. Click Edit Hyperlink.
  4. Enter the correct location of the hyperlink, or select the file you want to want to link to.
  5. Click OK.

- You may need to remove a link. Follow these steps to remove a hyperlink.
  1. Right-click the link to be removed.
  2. Click Hyperlink.
  3. Click the Remove Hyperlink.
  4. Click OK.

Exercise 6
Add Hyperlinks

1. Click Window menu and select the **index.htm** document if it is not currently the active document.
2. Select the text "Follow These Do's."
3. Click the Insert Hyperlink button on the toolbar to create a hyperlink to the **dos** page.
4. From the Insert Hyperlink dialog box, click the File button and browse to the **dos.htm** file.
5. Select the **dos.htm** file and click OK.
6. Click OK.
7. Click the hyperlink to see if it works.
   Note: When you click the link, the Web page opens in the default browser (Netscape or Internet Explorer). View the link, then click the Close button to return to Word.
8. Repeat Steps 1-7 to create a hyperlink to the **donts** page.

9. Resave the **index.htm** file.
10. Click <u>W</u>indow menu and select the **dos** page to make it the active page.
11. Place your insertion point at the end of the last line and press the Enter key twice.
12. Type HOME using the same font as the previous paragraph.
13. Select the word HOME and create a hyperlink to the index.htm file.
14. Resave the file.
15. Click Window menu and select the **donts** page.
16. Repeat Steps 11-14 for the **donts** page.
17. Check to see that the hyperlinks are working properly on all three pages.
18. Edit any hyperlinks that do not work properly and resave the documents.
19. Close all document windows.

GOAL 7:   Add Graphics

- Graphics enhance a Web page if they are used appropriately.

- You insert and resize graphics on your Web pages as you did in regular documents.

- To move a graphic freely once it is inserted, you will need to change from an In line with text graphic to another wrapping style.

- Format, move and resize the graphic as you did before; however, some format options are not available in Web pages.

Exercise 7
Add Graphics

1. Open the **index.htm, dos.htm** and **donts.htm** files.
2. Create a new Web page by using the Simple Layout template and name it **delivery**.
3. Type the text shown in Illustration A on the next page.
4. Create a link to the home (index) page.

5. Create links to the **delivery** page in all other pages.
6. Check all of the links to make sure that they work.
7. Refer to Illustration B and choose relevant graphics for each of the pages.
8. Resize and move the graphics as needed.
9. Resave each file.
10. Print one copy of each page.
11. Close all documents.

Illustration A

Delivery Tips

Tips on How to Give the Presentation

- Rehearse the presentation again and again.
- Call ahead and see if you need additional equipment.
- Make eye contact with the audience.
- Involve the audience by asking questions.
- Have Notes Pages readily available.

HOME

Illustration B, pages 1-4

Presenting Presentations

Introduction
Multimedia Presentations are a unique way to convey information. They combine text, graphics, movies and sounds in a slide show.

Successful presentations follow certain rules of design. This site will acquaint you with these guidelines and help you to create a show-stopping slide show.

Follow these Do's
Click this Do's link to see a list of the top five design tips.

Follow these Don'ts
Click this Don'ts link to see a list of the five worst presentation mistakes.

Delivery Tips
Click this link to discover delivery methods for your presentation.

Five Top Do's

Use These Sure-Fire Tips

- Use a contrasting color for the text.

- Use a font size that can be seen from the back of the room.

- Use bullets to emphasize key points.

- Include only key points in your text. Save the details for the oral portion of the presentation.

- Use separate backgrounds for different sections. This helps to visually organize the topics.

HOME

Five Top Don'ts

Avoid These Design Bloopers

- Using too many sounds.

- Using more than three fonts on a page.

- Cluttering the page with too much text.

- Using a difficult-to-read font or a font that does not contrast with the background.

- Using unrelated graphics.

HOME

Delivery Tips

Tips on How to Give the Presentation

- Rehearse the presentation again and again.

- Be enthusiastic and use gestures to emphasize a point.

- Make eye contact with the audience.

- Involve the audience by asking questions.

- Have Notes Pages readily available.

HOME

LESSON 39

Timed Writing

1. Create a new document.
2. Use the default margins.
3. Change font to Courier New, 12 point.
4. Take a 5-minute timing on the entire document.
    a. If you finish before the time is up, press the Enter key two times and start again.
    b. Do not correct errors. If you make an error, continue typing.
    c. To calculate your WAM speed, find the total number of words you typed and divide that number by 5.
5. Press the Enter key 4 times.
6. Take two 1-minute timings.
    a. Type as fast as you can for the first 1-minute timing.
    b. Type as accurately as you can for the second 1-minute timing.
    c. Do not correct your errors. If you make an error, continue typing.
    d. Press the Enter key four times between the timings.
    e. Calculate your WAM speed.
7. Following the same instructions as in Step 4, take another 5-minute timing on the entire document. Calculate your WAM speed
8. Compare your speeds.
9. Save the document as **L39TIME**.
10. Print one copy.
11. Close the document window.

	WORDS
Over 20 million people, from all parts of the United States,	12
celebrated the first Earth Day on April 22, 1970. The purpose	24
of this event was to learn about environmental concerns and	36
issues. Earth Day was a way to make people aware of the many	48
environmental issues. Some of the issues were the poor air	60
quality, the pollution of rivers and lakes, and the chemical	72
toxic waste sites in many parts of the country.	82
Even though the Earth Day movement began in the United States,	94
it grew to be an international celebration. In 1990 more than	106
200 million people from 141 countries took part in Earth Day.	118
It is now an annual event celebrated every April. The people	130
participating in the event represent all nationalities and	142
cultural groups.	147
The Earth Day activities provide a chance to address global	159
environmental concerns as well as community concerns. Some	171
activities are clean-ups, art and essay contests, fairs, and	183
conferences. These activities are organized by thousands of	195
volunteers.	197

....1....2....3....4....5....6....7....8....9...10...11...12

MOUSE/KEYSTROKE PROCEDURES

Create a Web Page Using a Template

1. Click **File** menu............... `Alt`+`F`
2. Click **New**............................. `N`
3. Click **Web Pages** tab .... `Ctrl`+`Tab`
4. Select **Simple Layout**.
5. Click **OK**............................. `Enter`

Saving a Web Page

1. Click **File** menu............... `Alt`+`F`
2. Click **Save as Web Page** .... `G`
3. Click **Save in**.................. `Alt`+`I`
   and then select a folder.
4. Click **Change Title** .... `Alt`+`C`
5. Type a title.
6. Click **File name** .... `Alt`+`N`
7. Type a file name.
8. Click **Save as type** .... `Alt`+`T`
9. Select **Web Page**.
10. Click **Save**....................... `Alt`+`S`

Formatting the Page

1. Click **Format** menu .... `Alt`+`O`
2. Click **Theme** .... `H`
3. Select desired theme.
4. Click **Vivid Colors**............. `Alt`+`C`
5. Click **Active Graphics** ...... `Alt`+`G`
6. Click **Background Image** .. `Alt`+`B`
7. Click **OK**.............................. `Enter`

Add Hyperlinks

1. Select text to use as hyperlink
2. Click **Insert** menu .... `Alt`+`I`
3. Click **Hyperlink**......................... `I`

   OR

   Click the **Hyperlink** button [icon] on the Standard toolbar.
4. Click **File** .... `Alt`+`F`
   to browse for file to link to.
5. Select the file.
6. Click **OK**............................. `Enter`

   OR

   Type file name in **Type the file or Web page name** text box.
7. Click **OK**.............................. `Enter`

Editing a Link

1. Right-click the hyperlink.
2. Click **Hyperlink**................ `Alt`+`H`
3. Click **Edit Hyperlink** .... `Alt`+`H`
4. Click **File**......................... `Alt`+`F`
   to browse for file to link to.
5. Select the file.
6. Click **OK** .... `Enter`

   OR

   Type correct file name in **Type the file or Web page name** text box.
7. Click **OK** .... `Enter`
8. Resave the file.

Remove a Link

1. Right-click the hyperlink.
2. Click **Hyperlink**................ `Alt`+`H`
3. Click **Remove Hyperlink** .. `Alt`+`R`

GOAL 1:   Practice Specific Letters

Exercise 1
Specific Letter Practice

- The exercise on the following pages provides practice for each individual letter of the alphabet. There are 10 lines of practice for each letter. The lines contain:
  - Three-letter words.
  - Four-letter words.
  - Five-letter words.
  - Six-letter words.
  - Sentences which consist mostly of words that stress the specific letter.

- Practicing this exercise will build both speed and accuracy on specific letters of the alphabet.
  1. Create a new document.
  2. Use the default margins.
  3. Change the font to Courier New, 12 point.
  4. Select a specific letter you wish to practice.
  5. Type each line one time.
  6. Press the Enter key twice after every two lines as shown.
  7. Check your work for errors.
  8. Repeat the exercise if you feel you need additional practice.
  9. If you make a lot of errors on a particular letter, practice the drill for that letter.
  10. Save the document; name it **L40EX1**.
  11. Print one copy.
  12. Close the document window.

LESSON 40

"A"

1 ace act add ado age ago aha aid ail aim air all amp and ant
2 any ape apt arc are ark arm art ash ask ate awe awl axe aye

3 able ache acid acne acts adds afar aide airy ajar also aqua
4 arch area arms arts asks atom atop aunt auto away axes axis

5 about above acted actor added admit adult after again album
6 alike alive allow alone along among angry apart asked attic

7 abduct aboard abound absorb accept actual adding agreed
8 aiming allege apiece armful assume atomic avenue awards

9 Actors acted and ate atop Aunt Anne's Attic at Arch Avenue.
10 Alan and Abbie allege angry adults abound aboard area arks.

"B"

1 bad bag ban bar bat bay bed bee beg bet bib bid big bin bit
2 boa bob bog bop bow box boy bud bug bum bun bus but buy bye

3 baby back band bank bare beam beat beef best bike bill bird
4 bite blue boat body boil bomb born brew bulb bunk busy buys

5 birth black blame blank blend bloom boost bored boxer brace
6 braid brain brawl break bring broke brown bumps buyer bytes

7 babies ballad barely barked basket bazaar beggar behave
8 belong binary blanch blouse blurry breath browse bumper

9 Big boys blame bored brainy boxers before betting big bills.
10 By buying big boats, Bob Brown brings Betty Blue's best buy.

LESSON 40

"C"

1 ace act arc cab cad cam can cap car cat caw cay chi cob cod
2 cog con coo cop cot cow coy cry cub cud cue cum cup cur cut

3 cafe cage cake calf call calm came camp cash cell cent chef
4 chip city clam clip club coat coin comb corn cozy crab cube

5 candy cargo catch cause chain chaos chose civil claim class
6 clean clear clone cocoa color crazy cross crush curry cycle

7 camera cancel cannot carpet carton celery chance choice
8 choose cinema classy coarse comply course crease crunch

9 Corn cobs and crab cakes can create a classy cafe combo.
10 Can a cloned cow cry? Clip Carlotta's cute cat's claws.

"D"

1 add aid and bid dab dad dam day den dew did die dig dim dip
2 doe dog dot dry due dug duo dye end hid mad odd pod red sad

3 damp dare dark data date daze dead deal dean dear deny desk
4 dial dime dirt does down draw drop dual duck dull dump dust

5 daily daunt dealt death decay delay dense devil diary digit
6 disco dizzy dozen draft drama drawn dream drink dwarf dwell

7 damage dazzle debate debris deject delete dialer diesel
8 differ divert divest donate double dragon drudge during

9 Do David Dean's dainty drawings dazzle dazed disco dancers?
10 Dear Danielle dialed Darrin Drudge's date during dense dew.

LESSON 40

"E"

1 are ate beg den ear eat egg ego elf elk elm end eve ewe eye
2 gel hem hen her jet leg ore pie red see the tie vie wed woe

3 anew each earn ease echo edge else emit envy epic even ever
4 evil exam exit eyes file fine gaze hate have late mile tree

5 eager early ebony edits eight eject elbow empty ended enjoy
6 enter entry equal equip erase essay event excel exist extra

7 echoes edging edited editor effect eighth ejects eleven
8 emblem emboss empire employ enable enamel ending energy

9 Ed Elephant emphatically emphasized environmental efforts.
10 Eloise expected Elizabeth every evening except Easter eve.

"F"

1 elf fad fan far fat fax fed fee fen few fey fez fib fig fin
2 fir fit fix flu fly foe fob fog for fox fry fun fur off oft

3 face fail fair fall fare fast fate feel felt find fine fire
4 fish five flat flip flop foil fold font form four from fund

5 faint faith false fatal fault favor feast fifty fight final
6 first flame flash float focus found fresh fully funny fuzzy

7 family famous farmer fasten feisty fellow fewest fiasco
8 figure finish fleece floppy fondue forgot fought freeze

9 Fran and Frank fix fancy faxes for feisty foreign fellows.
10 Fresh fruit, fish, and fondue are featured at Foxy Flip's.

444

"G"

1 age egg ego gab gad gag gal gam gap gas gel gem get gnu got
2 gum gun guy gym hug jog leg nag peg pig rig rug tag tug wig

3 gain game gang gasp gate gave gaze gene germ gift girl give
4 glad glow glue goal goes gold gone good gray grew grow gulf

5 gauge gauze geese ghost giant given glare glass glaze gleam
6 glide glory going grace grand grant great group grown guest

7 gadget gallon galore gamble gazebo gender gentle giggle
8 giving global glitch golden gossip greedy grouch grumpy

9 Gregory George gave grumpy Gilda Greco giant golden geese.
10 Graceful ghosts galore giggle. Give greedy guests gossip.

"H"

1 had ham has hat hay hem hen her hew hex hid him hip his hit
2 hob hoe hog hop hot how hub hug huh hum hut the thy who why

3 hair half hand hang hard hate have haze hear heel held help
4 here hero hers hide high hire hold home hope hour huge hurt

5 halve handy happy hardy hasty hazel heard heart heavy helix
6 hello honey horse hotel hound house human humid humor hurry

7 hammer handle hangar hanger harbor harden hardly heaven
8 height helium helmet herbal hiccup horror hotdog hungry

9 Hip Hazel Hardy had happy Harry Hum handle her heavy horse.
10 Hungry Harold, Harriet's human horse, had horrible hotdogs.

LESSON 40

"I"

1 big him his hit ice icy ilk ill imp ink inn ins ion ire irk
2 its ivy kid lie mix oil pie pin sir six ski tie win wit zip

3 aide airy iced ices icon idea idle idly idol ills inch into
4 iris irks iron isle itch item kind king kiss life lion live

5 icing icons ideal idiot image imply incur index inert infer
6 inlay inlet inner input inset irate irony isles issue items

7 icicle ignore iguana immune impair impede impish impure
8 indent indoor infant infirm influx inform inning insect

9 Iris Iller ignored Ivy Imperato's impish independent iguana.
10 Ira's Imperial Insurance, Inc. indemnifies infamous infants.

"J"

1 jab jag jam jar jaw jay jet jib jig job jog jot joy jug jut
2 ajar jabs jack jade jail Jake jamb jams Jane jars Java jaws

3 jazz jeep jeer Jeff jerk jest jets jigs Jill jobs jogs join
4 joke jolt John jots jowl joys jugs jump junk jury just raja

5 jaunt jeans jeeps jeers jelly jests jewel joins joint joist
6 joker jolly jolts joust judge juice juicy jumps jumpy juror

7 jabbed jackal jacket jaguar jalopy jargon jaunts jersey
8 jewels jicama jingle jogger joyful joyous juggle jungle

9 Jackie and Jane joined Jill jumping jackels and jaguars.
10 Jumpy Johnny Johnson juggles jewels, jicamas, and jeeps.

"K"

1 ark ask elk ilk ink irk keg ken key kid kin kit oak sky wok
2 hike kale keel keen keep kelp kept keys kick kids kill kind

3 king kink kiss kite kits kiwi knee knew knit knob knot know
4 lake make okay okra poke seek skew skid skim skin skip take

5 keeps kicks kills kinds kings kinks kites kitty kiwis knack
6 kneed kneel knees knife knobs knock knoll knots known knows

7 karate kayaks keenly keeper kennel keypad kicked kidder
8 kidnap kidney kimono kindly kitten knight knocks koalas

9 Kenneth Kennedy kept kayaks, kites, and kimonos at Kitty's.
10 Katherine Kelsey Kellerensky's kittens keep knocking knees.

"L"

1 all gal gel lab lad lag lap law lax lay lea led lee leg let
2 lib lid lie lip lit lob log lop lot low lox lug lye owl pal

3 lace lady lake lamb lamp land last late lazy lead lean left
4 lend levy lick lied lieu life lift like line long look luck

5 label labor large laser later laugh least leave level light
6 limit linen lists lobby local loose lower lunch lurch lyric

7 landed larger lately latest lawyer leader league learns
8 legacy lenses lesson lethal lineup linger locker locket

9 Lillian Levy loves lavish local legumes for light lunches.
10 Let lethal local leagues learn long light lessons loosely.

"M"

1 aim emu gym him imp jam mad man map mar mat may men met mew
2 mid mob mod mom moo mop mow mud mug mum ram rim sum vim yam

3 made mail main make male many mark mass math maze meal mean
4 meet memo mild mile milk mind mock mold more most much must

5 macro madam magic major march maybe mayor medal media merge
6 meter might mimic minus modem money moral month mural music

7 manage manual margin maroon mascot meadow medium melody
8 memory meteor method minute moment mostly mother myself

9 Marilyn Marion Madison mixed many melons mainly on Monday.
10 Mr. Manfred Manley merrily married Ms. Meredith M. Miller.

"N"

1 and any can end ink nab nag nap nay nee net new nib nil nip
2 nix nod nor not now nun nut one own pan ran sun ten van win

3 nail name navy near neat neck need neon nest news next nice
4 nine node none noon norm nose nosy note noun nova nude numb

5 naive named nasal nasty naval needy nerve never newer niece
6 nifty night ninth noble noise noisy north notch novel nurse

7 namely narrow nature nearby needed nephew nestled newest
8 nibble nicely nickels ninety nobody noodle normal number

9 Norton N. Nelson normally never nixes Norma Neveton's nouns.
10 Neurotic Ned Norton is notorious for never noticing numbers.

"O"

1 ado ago box duo for hot job lot oak oar oat obi odd ode off
2 oft ohm old one ooh orb ore out owe owl own too two who zoo

3 oath obey odds odes odor oily okay omen omit once ones only
4 onto ooze opal open oral ours oval oven over owls owns oxen

5 oasis obese occur ocean oddly offer often olive onion oozed
6 opera optic orbit order organ other otter ought ounce owner

7 object oblong occupy octane offend office omelet online
8 onward oppose option oracle orange orchid ordeal oxygen

9 Oscar Orlando ordered oranges, octopus oreganato, and orzo.
10 Opportunity occurs and one often overlooks those occasions.

"P"

1 pad pal pan par pat paw pay pea peg pen pep per pet pew pie
2 pig pin pip pit pix ply pod pop pro pry pub pug pun pup put

3 page paid pail pain pair pale pass past path pear pick pier
4 pink pint plan play plus poem poor port pour prom pull pure

5 paint panel paper pasta pause peace peach penny phone piano
6 pixel pizza place plain point power price prior proud pupil

7 papaya parent pastry patent pebble pencil people period
8 permit phooey phrase plenty poetry prefix puddle python

9 Perhaps Peter picked a peck of pickled peppers purposely!
10 Paula probably picked a package of parched purple prunes.

"Q"

1 boq IQS IRQ qat QKt QMC QMG QMS qn. qq. qr. QSO PDQ qt. qua
2 Que qui quo QVC sq. SQL SQR qua qui quo qt. IQS IRQ QMC QMG

3 aqua Esq. Iraq qaid quad quai quay quey quid quip quit quiz
4 quod SPQR aqua qaid quad quai quay quey quid quip quit quiz

5 quack quail quake quart quash quasi queen queer quell query
6 quest queue quick quiet quill quilt quite quits quota quote

7 equate equity liquid quaint qualms quarts quartz queasy
8 queued quiver quorum quotas squash squeak squeal squirm

9 Quentin Quigley quickly and quite quietly quit quarreling.
10 Quiselda quietly quivered when Queen Quiq quelled queries.

"R"

1 are car far rag rah ram ran rap rat raw ray red rex rib rid
2 rig rim rip rob rod rot row rub rug run rut rye sir try war

3 race rage rang rare rate read real redo rely rent rest rich
4 ride ring rise rock roll roof room rose ruin rule rush rust

5 radar radio raise rapid ratio razor reach ready refer relax
6 relay renew rerun revue rinse risky robot round route rumor

7 random reason recede recent recess recipe redial reform
8 regard region reject relief ribbon rocket rodent rubble

9 Ralph Rye regularly requests reviews regarding revisions.
10 Revisit Ro's Ranch regarding rejuvenation and relaxation.

"S"

1 sad sat saw sax say sea see set sew sex she shy sip sir sit
2 six ski sky sly sob son sow sox soy spa spy sty sue sum sun

3 safe said sale save seat seem seen sell sent show side slow
4 smug snow sold some soon sort spin spot stay stop such swim

5 saint salad scene seize serif shall short sight silly sixty
6 sleep small snail solar sport squid start sunny sweet syrup

7 scream second select shadow simple sitcom skinny sleepy
8 smooth sneeze speech square steady summer switch symbol

9 Surely she shall suggest something sophisticatedly smart.
10 Since Shirley sat so still, Steve said she slept soundly.

"T"

1 ate but get jet let tab tad tag tan tap tar tax tea tee ten
2 tic tie tin tip tom ton top tot tow toy try tub tug two yet

3 take tale talk taxi tear tell term test text than that them
4 time tiny tire told took toss tree true tune turn twin type

5 table taste teach tease thank their there these thing think
6 third those three title today toxic train tried tutor twice

7 temper tennis though thrash threat thrown timing tiptoe
8 tomato toward trauma tuneup tunnel tweeze twelve twenty

9 Tina Tali tried to top Tom Tano's terrific time tying twine.
10 The teacher tried to take the train to the theater Thursday.

"U"

1 bud bug bum bun bus but buy cue due fan fun gut gum guy hue
2 hut mud nut our pun put rub sue sum sun ugh ump urn use you

3 club clue ecru faux foul glue guru lieu loud menu much quit
4 tofu ugly undo unit unto upon urge urns used user uses your

5 ulcer uncle under undid undue unfit unify union unite unity
6 untie until upper upset urban usage usher using usual utter

7 bureau deduct enough squish umpire unfold unique unisex
8 unison unpack unsure update uptown utmost visual yogurt

9 Uncle Uriah Uro used unwashed utensils under the umbrella.
10 Ulysses understood Ulee's urge to upstage Unna was untrue.

"V"

1 eve ivy van vat vet vex via vie vim vin von vow vug eve ivy
2 rave save vain vale vane vans vary vase vast vats veal veer

3 veil vein vent verb very vest veto vial vice vied vies view
4 vile vine visa vise vita void volt vote vows wave wavy wove

5 valid value valve vapor vault venom verge versa verse vexed
6 video vigor virus visit vital vivid vocal vogue voice vowel

7 advice advise avenue evolve overdo vacant vacate vacuum
8 valley vanish velour velvet vendor violet visual volume

9 Victoria Vixen views various venues of very vicious vices.
10 Vanessa Velasquez-Verlis visits and vexes venomous vipers.

"W"

1 how low new now owe own sew tow two wad wag wan war was wax
2 way wen wet who why wig win wit woe wok won wow wry vow wow

3 wage wait walk want warm week well went were what when whiz
4 whom wild will wind wise wish with wool word work worn wrap

5 waste watch water wedge weigh weird whale wheat where which
6 while woman women world worry worse worst worth would wrong

7 walnut walrus wander warmup weight weirdo wheeze whoosh
8 widely window within wonder wooden worthy wrench writer

9 Wednesday, Waldo Wodwistle whistled wistfully while waiting.
10 Wet Willy whined while watching window washers wash windows.

"X"

1 axe box cox fax fix fox hex lax lox mix nix pax pix pox rex
2 sax sex six sox tax tux vex vox wax xii xiv xix xvi xxi xxv

3 apex axes axis axle axon coax exam exec faux flax flex foxy
4 hoax jinx lynx maxi next onyx oxen pixy sexy taxi text waxy

5 affix helix index latex relax axiom boxer epoxy exact excel
6 exert extra exude faxed fixed maxim oxide sixth sixty toxin

7 duplex exceed except excess excite excuse exempt exotic
8 expand expect expert expose extend outbox surtax tuxedo

9 Xenia sent exactly six x-rays by taxi and fax to Xaviar.
10 Xerxes faxed X-mas cards to Xiphoide, Xavier and Xyster.

453

LESSON 40

"Y"

1 any boy bye cry day dye eye fly gym hay icy joy key lye may
2 nay pay rye say try way yam yaw yea yen yep yes yet yew yon

3 baby body byte cyan deny envy gray hymn jury myth pray type
4 yank yard yarn yawn yaws yeah year yeas yell yelp yoke your

5 angry cycle gypsy loyal maybe mayor rayon thyme worry yacht
6 yards yarns yearn years yeast yelps yield yokes young youth

7 anyhow anyone anyway beyond canyon crayon enzyme joyous
8 keypad oxygen voyage yawned yearly yelled yonder youths

9 You search Yahoo for: Yokohama, Ypsilanti, and Yellowstone.
10 Yuletime, Yoyna Yosemite yearns for yogurt, yucca and yams.

"Z"

1 adz biz fez Liz oz. Roz zag zap Zak Zen zig zit zip Zoe zoo
2 buzz cozy czar daze doze faze fizz fuzz gaze haze hazy jazz

3 laze lazy maze ooze oozy quiz raze razz size whiz zany zaps
4 zeal zebu zero zest zinc zing zips ziti zoic zone zoom zoos

5 bezel czars dizzy dozen fazed gizmo hazel jazzy ozone pizza
6 unzip zebra zeros zesty zings zippy zonal zoned zones zooms

7 bazaar dazzle enzyme gazebo wizard zebras zeroes zigged
8 zigzag zinnia zipper zircon zither zodiac zombie zygote

9 Zealous zoos in Zuni have zippy zebras and zooming zebus.
10 Zechariah zestfully flew zigzagging zeppelins over Zaire.

GOAL 2: Practice Balanced-Hand Words

Exercise 2
Balanced-Hand Words

- Balanced-hand words are words that are typed by alternating left- and right-hand fingers.

- The words are arranged alphabetically. Every letter of the alphabet is covered except X, Y and Z.

- Practicing these words will build your speed and accuracy.
    1. Create a new document.
    2. Use the default margins.
    3. Change the font to Courier New, 12 point.
    4. Type one line of each of the following words.
    5. Press the Enter key at the end of each line.
    6. Repeat any word if you feel you need additional practice.
    7. Save the document; name it **L40EX2**.
    8. Print one copy.
    9. Close the document window.

1 air	and	antique	auto	big
2 bit	blend	born	both	bow
3 bus	busy	but	city	civic
4 coal	cob	cocoa	cork	corn
5 cow	cozy	cub	cue	cut
6 dial	did	die	dig	digit
7 dish	disk	do	dock	dog
8 dorm	dove	down	duel	dug
9 dusk	duty	duty	dye	eighth
10 element	fib	fight	fire	fish
11 fit	five	fix	foam	for
12 fork	form	formal	fowl	fox

13 foxy	fuel	fur	fury	girl
14 go	hair	half	ham	hand
15 hay	heir	held	hen	is
16 it	jam	jamb	jay	kale
17 key	lair	lake	lame	laud
18 laugh	laughs	lend	lens	make
19 man	mantle	map	may	men
20 name	ox	paid	pair	pale
21 pane	pang	pans	papa	pay
22 pen	pep	problem	profit	quay
23 quantity	rid	rig	right	risk
24 rite	roam	rod	rot	row
25 rub	rug	rush	rut	sight
26 sir	sit	slam	slap	soap
27 social	sofa	sow	sue	than
28 the	their	then	they	tick
29 tie	tight	title	to	toe
30 tofu	tow	town	tug	turn
31 tusk	tutor	us	usual	vie
32 visible	visit	visitor	vivid	vow
33 when	widow	wit	with	world

GOAL 3: Practice Double-Letter Words

Exercise 3
Double-Letter Words

- The words in this exercise all contain double letters.
- The exercise is arranged alphabetically. It begins with words containing double As and ends with words containing double Zs.
- Double letters for every letter of the alphabet are included except Q and Y.
- Practicing double-letter words will build your speed.
  1. Create a new document.
  2. Use the default margins.
  3. Change the font to Courier New, 12 point.
  4. Type each line one time.
  5. Press the Enter key twice after every 2 lines as shown.
  6. Check your work for errors.
  7. Repeat the exercise or practice specific words if you feel you need additional practice.
  8. Save the document; name it **L40EX3**.
  9. Print one copy.
  10. Close the document window.

---

1 aardvark Aaron baa Baal bazaar salaam Isaac laager NAACP
2 bubble quibble hobby lobby nibble pebble stubborn rabbit

3 soccer zucchini hiccup moccasin accept occasion broccoli
4 embedded fiddle griddle huddle middle odd sudden toddler

5 three agree deed fee heel meet need street between wheel
6 differ effect coffee graffiti affix jiffy traffic layoff

7 baggy foggy rugged jagged clogged toggle giggling wiggle
8 highhanded hitchhiking withheld roughhousing withholding

9 genii Hawaiians coniine skiing taxiing aalii waterskiing
10 hajji hajjis hajji hajjis hajji hajjis hajji hajji hajji

11 bookkeeper jackknife stockkeeper chukka knickknack Vikki
12 all zillion ill ball follow cell yellow dull fall scroll

13 gimmick dimmer grammar mommy common commit dummy shimmer
14 winner bunny inn cannon annex dinner skinny penny tennis

15 door oodles floor took raccoon good yahoo balloon noodle
16 floppy happily rapped zipper yuppy oppose pepper applied

17 terrible worry correct quarrel sorry purr arrange horror
18 missing asset kiss tissue boss cassette scissors discuss

19 settle better matter attach chatter kitten letter hotter
20 continuums muumuus vacuum vacuumed vacuums vacuum-packed

21 chivvy chivvied chivvying revved revving divvied divvies
22 glowworm glowworms yellowweed hollowware bowwows powwows

23 xx xxi xxii xxiii xxiv xxv xxxvii lxxx mxxv cxxvii xxxix
24 dizzy buzz frizzy jazz pizza nozzle sizzles razz quizzes

GOAL 4:   Practice Word Families

Exercise 4
Word Families

- Each line contains a different word family. All the words appearing on one line contain the same group of letters (the word family) within each word.

- For reading ease, the exercise lines are arranged in groups of two. Before each group of two lines, the word families are introduced (i.e., day/way).

- Practicing word families will build your speed and accuracy.
  1. Create a new document.
  2. Use the default margins.
  3. Change the font to Courier New, 12 point.
  4. Type each line one time. Do not type the centered lines which indicate the word families you will be typing.
  5. Press the Enter key twice after every 2 lines as shown.
  6. Check your work for errors.
  7. Repeat the lines with which you had difficulty.
  8. Save the document, name it **L40EX4**.
  9. Print one copy.
  10. Close the document window.

---

day/way

```
1 Sunday Monday Tuesday Wednesday Thursday Friday Saturday
2 way sway highway anyway doorway driveway getaway halfway
```

air/are

```
3 chair pair hair flair dairy despair eclair fair aircraft
4 care fare area aware share apparent prepare rare careful
```

ire/ore

5 acquire esquire require haywire impaired inquire inspire
6 anymore bore censored chore sore deplore explore restore

ie/oy

7 allies movie copied anxiety society armies babies belief
8 ahoy enjoy joy ploy soy coy annoy boy destroy employ toy

oe/ow

9 aloe banjoes canoe coed does shoe echo gooey toe mangoes
10 show brow know owns brown chowder clown snow drown scowl

our/ncy

11 four mourn pour ourselves course fourth your tour devour
12 agency bouncy tendency currency efficiency fancy vacancy

er/ab

13 after power whomever another quicker never other deliver
14 crab dab gab jab lab blab flab slab drab grab table stab

ib/ob

15 bib fib glib nib rib crib bribe tribe describe prescribe
16 cob job hob lob blob slob mob knob snob squab robe throb

ack/ark

17 back jack hack lack black clack slacks knack snack quack
18 ark bark dark hark lark mark park sparkle aardvark quark

ake/eck

19 bake cake fake hake lake flake make quake rake take wake
20 beck check deck freckles wreck fleck neck speckled gecko

oke/ink

21 awoke coke evoke joke woke smoke poke spoke broke invoke

22 ink kink link blink think mink pinky wrinkle brink drink

unk/ces

23 bunk skunk chunk junk hunk clunk flunk punk spunk shrunk

24 aces balances chances coerces dances enhances faces ices

atch/ound

25 batch catch hatch latch match patch scratch watch thatch

26 bound found hound mound pound round ground sound wounded

ip/ed

27 skip chip dip hip lip blip clip flip slip nip snip strip

28 bed fed led fled sled sped bred shred shed wed died fled

old/end

29 old bold cold scold fold gold hold mold sold told unfold

30 end bend fend lend blend mend spend trend send tend vend

ag/ig

31 bag gag jag lag flag nag snag swag rag brag drag tag wag

32 big dig jig pig rig sprig wig twig beige align sign sigh

age/ale

33 age cage page stage wage engage enrage image eager usage

34 ale bale kale scale hale male pale sale tale stale whale

ine/ang

35 fine line mine ninety pine spine shine tine diner shrine

36 bang fang gang hanger clang slang pang range sprang sang

ing/ape

37 king ding cling fling sling ping wring ring bring spring
38 ape cape nape scrape drape grape shape tape escape lapel

imp/ice

39 imp skimpy chimp limped blimp crimp primps shrimp scrimp
40 dice lice splice slice mice nice spice rice price advice

ush/ight

41 gush hush lush blush flush plush slush rush brush thrush
42 height light blight flight might right sight tight night

oat/out

43 oat boat coat goat bloated float gloat moat throat loath
44 out bout scout doubt gout clout flout snout pout drought

ict/uct

45 evict strict district restrict verdict predict constrict
46 duct deduct induct product conduct instruction construct

ilt/ent

47 built guilt jilt lilt quilt silt tilt stilt rebuilt wilt
48 bent dent lent spent rent cent sent scent tent went vent

ept/est

49 kept slept wept concept exception accept intercept inept
50 best guest jest nest pest question rest crest test chest

ust/ost

51 dusty gust just lust must rust crust trust thrust robust
52 cost host lost most post roost utmost frost accost boost

eve/ave

53 eve peeve grieve believe relieve reprieve retrieve sieve

54 cave gavel knave pave raven brave crave grave save shave

ive/ose

55 chive dive five jive hive live drive strive thrive alive

56 chose lose close nose pose rose prose those arose choose

GOAL 5:   Practice Home-Row Words

Exercise 5
Home-Row Words

- All the words in this exercise are made up of letters contained in the home row only.
- Practicing home-row words will build your speed and accuracy.
  1. Create a new document.
  2. Use the default margins.
  3. Change the font to Courier New, 12 point.
  4. Type each line three times.
  5. Press the Enter key twice after repeating each line 3 times.
  6. Check your work for errors.
  7. Repeat the exercise if you feel you need additional practice.
  8. Save the document; name it **L40EX5**.
  9. Print one copy.
  10. Close the document window.

1 ad ads ah as ash ask sad sag shad shag skald slag dash

2 fad fads flag flags flak flash flask gad gads gal gals

3 gas gash glad ha had half has jag la lad lads lag lash

LESSON 40

GOAL 6: Practice First Alphabet Row Words

Exercise 6
First Row (Alphabet Row) Words

- All the words in this exercise contain letters from the first alphabet row on the keyboard.
- Practicing these words will build your speed and accuracy.
  1. Create a new document.
  2. Use the default margins.
  3. Change the font to Courier New, 12 point.
  4. Type each line twice.
  5. Press the Enter key twice after you repeat a line.
  6. Check your work for errors.
  7. Repeat the exercise if you feel you need additional practice.
  8. Save the document; name it **L40EX6**.
  9. Print one copy.
  10. Close the document window.

```
1 query quiet quip quire quirt quit quote quite we wet wire
2 wipe wipeout wiper wept wit woe wore writ write wrote wry
3 equip equity erupt riot rip ripe rite roe re rope rot row
4 rote route rue rut rye tie toe tier tip tire to top toque

5 torque tour trip tow tower toy trio tripe troupe true try
6 two type yep yet yew yip yore you your up ire it outer or
7 ore our out owe opt per pert pet pew pi pie piety pit poi
8 pity poet pore port pier pour pout pique purity power put
```

GOAL 7:   Practice Third Alphabet Row Words

Exercise 7
Third Row (Alphabet Row) Words Plus Vowels

- All the words in this exercise contain letters from the third alphabet row on the keyboard plus vowels from the other alphabet rows.

- Practicing these words will build your speed and accuracy.
  1. Create a new document.
  2. Use the default margins.
  3. Change the font to Courier New, 12 point.
  4. Type each line twice.
  5. Press the Enter key twice after you repeat a line.
  6. Check your work for errors.
  7. Repeat the exercise if you feel you need additional practice.
  8. Save the document; name it **L40EX7**.
  9. Print one copy.
  10. Close the document window.

```
1  zinc zombie zone azoic ox oxen axe axiom exam cab cabin
2  cam came cameo can cane canoe acne acumen cave cine ice
3  icon cinema coax convex cob coin coma comb combine come

4  ocean con cone cove cub cube cue cumin ace acme van vex
5  oven vane vein venom via vice vicuna vie vim vine vixen
6  voice vain bacon ban above bane be beacon beam bean bin
7  beau beaux bemoan benzoic boa bounce bovine box bum bun

8  buxom bone nab one naive on once ounce name nib nice no
9  nix income ion nub nova novice en an anemic anomie numb
10 imbue em emu aim am amen amino ma mace main man mane me
11 manic mauve mine maze mean men menu move mice movie mix
```

GOAL 8: Practice Vertical Reaches

Exercise 8
Vertical Reaches

- All the words in this exercise require finger reaches from the following locations:
  - Home row up to the first alphabet row.
  - Home row down to the third alphabet row.
  - First alphabet row to the third alphabet row.
  - Third alphabet row to the first alphabet row.
    1. Create a new document.
    2. Use the default margins.
    3. Change the font to Courier New, 12 point.
    4. Practice the following sentences to improve your reaches from one row to another.
    5. Type each line twice.
    6. Press the Enter key twice after you repeat a line.
    7. Check your work for errors.
    8. Repeat the exercise if you feel you need additional practice.
    9. Save the document; name it **L40EX8**.
    10. Print one copy.
    11. Close the document window.

Home Row to First Alphabet Row/Home Row to Third Alphabet Row

aq/az/za

1 aqua aquatics aqueous aqualungs aquanaut aquanauts aquariums
2 aquaplanes aquamarine aqueducts aquiline aquatically aquiver
3 azo azoic azide azonal azure azalea dazes mazes faze blazing
4 topaz ablaze bazaars dazzle dazzles frazzled zag zany zapped

sw/ws

5 swab swabs swims swam swat swill swear sweats sweater sweeps
6 sweet switch sweeter swelter swagger swindle swivels swizzle
7 paws grows laws cows sows sews rows flaws thaws slows browse
8 crows draws flows glows stows throws curfews browsed browser

de/ed

9 den deem deed dead deer dear deck deft deters defray deleted

10 abide abode accedes cadet evades indents order stride traded

11 edit edits edited edged edging edible edict educate educates

12 fed federal reduce pedal sedan hedonist learned loved needed

fr/rf

13 fro fry from free fray frame friar frost frail fragile front

14 fruits froth frump frumpy freight friends fructose frustrate

15 airfares carfare forfeits interfere perfumes perform perfect

16 serfs surf surfs afraid affronts curfews carfares proofreads

ju/uj

17 jug jugs jut juts judo jury juries jurist juice jump jumping

18 junked juke jute jujube juntas junket jungles judges judging

19 jumbo jumble junior judgment juggle juggled judicial jujitsu

20 injure injured injuries perjure perjury injustice hallelujah

ki/ik

21 kids kill king kiss kick kink kite kiwis kilts kind kindness

22 kindly kinship kindred kidnap kidney kilter kinetic kilobyte

23 asking faking khaki luckily networking skid pumpkin rekindle

24 alike hike hiking tikes bike like dreamlike sheiks turnpikes

lo/ol

25 lob loll loan look lock lofts loads lodge logic loose losing

26 local lonely lookup logical lonesome logistics closet clones

27 old older oldest olives olivary olympiad oligarchy olfactory

28 blob bloat boolean cloak collect floats follow halos armload

ft/tf

29 after gift left loft raft rift shift soft nifty often bereft

30 fifth swiftly fifteen airlift aircrafts chieftains afternoon

31 fitful hurtful tactful zestful flatfoot heartfelt delightful

32 artful tactful basketfuls doubtfully regretfully forgetfully

hu/hy

33 hum hug hut hue hues huff hull huge hung hunt hurl hurt husk
34 chunk hued exhume ketchup shuns shunned thud thumb brochures
35 huh pushup shut thug thus thumb thump rhumba typhus shutdown
36 hype hymn rhyme rhythm hydrogen hybrid hyphen apathy empathy

gr/rg

37 grab gray grad grid grit gross grow grain grieve grill great
38 grace growth ground grouch gravity grammar gridlock gradient
39 argon argue argyle barge bargain burger charge energy merges
40 agrees angry degrees diagram egress surgeon allergy allergic

---

First Alphabet Row to Third Alphabet Row/Third Alphabet to First Alphabet Row

ce/ec

1 cell cells cent cease census center deceased descend deceive
2 balance chance dances decreases precedes preface since vices
3 echo eccentric ecological economy economizes eczema ecstatic
4 beck affects becomes checks collects decades electric expect

nu/un

5 nub nuclear nudge nullify numb number nurse nurture nutrient
6 avenue bonus cleanup continue enumerates gnu minute revenues
7 unable unaligned unbalanced uncertain unzipped undo undelete
8 account amount announce chunk fauna functions punctual young

yn/ny

9 lynx lynch dryness dynamo dynast keynote larynx idiosyncrasy
10 shyness cynicism laryngitis polynomial cynic slyness coyness
11 many botany bunny colony corny crony ebony funny irony peony
12 penny loony felony pony rainy runny skinny sunny thorny tiny

tb/bt

13 basketball cutback outbid frostbite catbird fastback setback
14 tidbit hotbed meatball textbook football softball heartbreak
15 obtain obtuse obtrusion subtopic subtly undoubtedly subtract
16 debt doubts bobtail obtrusive indebted subtle redoubt obtund

um/mu

17 forum autumn costume bum bumble bumbling bumpers chums human
18 medium clumsy quorum glum slum jumble thumb jump number plum
19 amuck amuse demure emulate formula gamut immune much minimum
20 museum smuggled mud muzzle simulate musical commuter maximum

rv/vr

21 observant preserve reserve survey marvel undervalued unnerve
22 carving curve deserve swerved harvest interval nervous verve
23 woodcarving larvae intervention overviews conservative nerve
24 marvelous pervasive observe dwarves chevrons d'oeuvres vivr

GOAL 9: Practice Left-Hand Words

Exercise 9
Left-Hand Words

- All the words in this exercise use the fingers on the left hand only.
- Practicing these words will build your speed and accuracy.
  1. Create a new document.
  2. Use the default margins.
  3. Change the font to Courier New, 12 point.

4. Type each line twice.
5. Press the Enter key twice after you repeat a line.
6. Check your work for errors.
7. Repeat the exercise if you feel you need additional practice.
8. Save the document; name it **L40EX9**.
9. Print one copy.
10. Close the document window.

1 ace acerb acre acres acted ad ads adz after age aged arc are
2 art as aster at ate adverb awe axe saber sacred sad safe sag
3 sage sat save saw sax scab scar scare scarf scat screw stade
4 seat sect serf set sew sex stab stag stage star stare starve
5 stave stead swear sweat stew steward strafe straw strew swab

6 swag swat sea sear dab date daze deaf dear daft dare drafted
7 deft drab drag drat draw dart dregs drew dwarf dew debt face
8 facet fact fad fade fades far farce fare fast fasted fat fed
9 fate faxed faze fazes fears feast feat few frets gabs graced
10 gazes grads garb gates gave gear gets grabs great grad grade

11 grades graft grafted grated graves grazed grew gad gated gas
12 wad wade waders wafers waft wafted wag wager wages war ward
13 ware wars warts was waste wasted waters wave waxes we wrest
14 wear waves webs wed weft west wet ear east eat egad era erg
15 ersatz exact ears extras raced raft rafted rag rage rat red

16 rate raved raw raze re react rawest reads recast redact rex
17 ref rest tab tags tar tare taxed tea tear trace trade tread
18 zebras zed zest cab cad cadet cadgers cadre cafe caged care
19 cards caret cars cart car carves case cast caste caster cat
20 cater cave cawed cedar crabs crafted crags crate crave crew

21 craws craze crest crazed czars vase vast vat verbs vest vex
22 vets bad bade badge barest badger badges bags bar bard bare
23 barge bars bravest base based baste bat bate be beads beard
24 beast beat begs berg best bear beta brace brews brads brags
25 brat bed brave braze bread breads bet breast bred brew bats

GOAL 10:   Practice Right-Hand Words

Exercise 10
Right-Hand Words

- All the words in this exercise use the fingers on the right hand only.
- Practicing these words will build your speed and accuracy.
    1. Create a new document.
    2. Use the default margins.
    3. Change the font to Courier New, 12 point.
    4. Type each line twice.
    5. Press the Enter key twice after you repeat a line.
    6. Check your work for errors.
    7. Repeat the exercise if you feel you need additional practice.
    8. Save the document; name it **L40EX10**.
    9. Print one copy.
    10. Close the document window.

---

1 him hip ho holy hominy hop hulk hum hunk hymn join joy jump
2 jumpy junk junky kiln kin limp link lion lip loin lop lumpy

3 up upon yolk yon you ilk imp imply ink ion oil oily oink on
4 only oh ohm in ply phylum pi pin pink pinky ploy plum plunk
5 phony pony puns punk puny milky mink monk mop my nil nip no

---

LESSON 40

GOAL 11: Practice Common Words

Exercise 11
Common Words

- The words in this exercise are grouped by the letter of the alphabet, from shorter words to longer words.

- Practicing these words will build your speed and accuracy.
    1. Create a new document
    2. Use the default margins.
    3. Change the font to Courier New, 12 point.
    4. Type one line of each word. Try to increase your speed as you repeat the word. By practicing these common words, your overall speed will increase.
    5. Press the Enter key twice after each alphabetic group.
    6. Check your work for errors.
    7. Repeat any word(s) if you feel you need additional practice.
    8. Save the document; name it **L40EX11**.
    9. Print one copy.
    10. Close the document window.

A

1 a	am	an	are	ask
2 any	also	able	away	about
3 above	among	actual	April	always

B

4 be	by	but	been	both
5 begin	being	bring	break	broke
6 before	become	better	because	between

C

7 can	cut	can't	copy	come
8 clear	could	chance	course	couldn't
9 common	control	correct	company	customer

D

10 do	day	did	date	dear
11 does	don't	done	down	drive
12 demand	depend	direct	develop	December

E

13 eat	end	each	edit	ever
14 every	equal	effect	except	expect
15 either	employ	enough	economy	expense

F

16 few	for	fact	feel	fill
17 find	firm	from	first	field
18 figure	follow	format	further	February

G

19 go	got	gave	give	glad
20 goes	good	grow	gain	grade
21 great	group	gross	general	gigabyte

H

22 he	had	has	her	his
23 half	hand	have	help	hide
24 high	hire	hope	heavy	human

I

25 I	if	is	in	it
26 ill	its	it's	into	isn't
27 income	inform	insert	increase	Internet

J/K

28 jet	job	join	July	June
29 judge	January	key	kid	keep
30 kind	know	known	keyboard	kilobyte

L

31 leg	let	low	less	life
32 like	line	load	look	love
33 large	leave	limit	laptop	layout

M

34 me	my	may	made	make
35 many	more	most	must	March
36 might	money	month	method	megabyte

N

37 no	net	new	not	now
38 near	need	next	name	note
39 never	notice	network	nothing	November

O

40 of	on	or	one	our
41 out	own	only	over	often
42 offer	other	office	October	otherwise

P

43	pay	put	page	part	plan
44	play	post	paper	place	price
45	print	proof	public	prefer	perhaps

Q/R

46	quit	quiet	quite	quick	quote
47	qualify	quantity	question	run	read
48	ready	right	rather	result	return

S

49	so	say	she	said	same
50	save	some	since	still	small
51	should	several	special	suggest	something

T

52	to	the	too	that	than
53	them	then	they	this	time
54	thank	their	there	these	think

U/V

55	us	up	use	upon	under
56	until	usual	via	vary	very
57	view	value	verify	variety	version

W-Z

58	we	was	web	why	who
59	week	were	what	will	with
60	whom	where	which	while	would

XYZ

61	yes	you	yet	year	your
62	x-ray	Xerox	zap	zip	zeal
63	zone	zipper	zero	zest	zebra

LESSON 40

GOAL 12: Practice Common Phrases

Exercise 12
Common Phrases

- The common phrases in this exercise are arranged alphabetically.
- There are phrases beginning with each letter of the alphabet except X and Z.
- Practicing these common phrases will build your speed and accuracy.
  1. Create a new document.
  2. Use the default margins.
  3. Change the font to Courier New, 12 point.
  4. Type one line of each phrase.
  5. Try to increase the speed as you repeat the phrase. By practicing these common phrases, your overall speed will increase.
  6. Press the Enter key twice after each alphabetic group.
  7. Repeat any phrase(s) if you feel you need additional practice.
  8. Save the document; name it **L40EX12**.
  9. Print one copy.
  10. Close the document window

1 after the	able to	about the	agree with
2 and the	are there	ask you	as far as
3 as much as	as soon as	as you know	all there is
4 be the	be able to	be sure	be sure to
5 because of	because of the	beside the	beyond the
6 but the	back and forth	be able to	by the way
7 can he	can she	can you	care for
8 car for the	care of	care of the	could it
9 could be	could be because	could have	could have been

10 date the	decide upon	decide when	deliver it
11 depend upon	despite the	differ from	disagree with
12 do it	do not	do so	do you
13 each of	each other	early decision	early on
14 end it	either or	enough of	equal amounts
15 each of these	except these	effect a change	end of the
16 feel free	for the	for you	from the
17 free from	from you	follow the	further than
18 fill in the	find out	find out the	first of all
19 gave to	go for	go to	go to the
20 good for	good enough	great idea	hands on
21 he is	he has	he has the	hope you will
22 I am	I am sure	I have	I will
23 I will be	if it is	in case	in fact
24 in the	is the	it is the	if you can
25 jet lag	job hunting	join the	join us
26 joint venture	judge the	kind of	know of
27 know the	know of the	known for	knowledge of
28 let us	less than	less than the	like the
29 look at	look over	lower than	listen to
30 limit the	long enough	let me know	let us know
31 many more	many times	may I	meet with
32 more of	more or less	most of the	must be
33 must be the	much of	much more	much more than

34 next week	next year	near the	near the end
35 need to	need to be	no longer	not quite
36 note the	nothing is the	now is	now is the
37 of the	on the	on the way	once again
38 out of	out of order	out of the	over the
39 over the year	over again	on our	on our part
40 pay attention	pay it	pay it to the	part of
41 part of the	please allow	please let me know	post it
42 put it there	proof of	prefer it	prefer it to be
43 qualify for	qualify for the	question it	question of
44 quit the	quite good	quite well	rather than
45 read the	read all of the	record of the	return it to
46 save it	save it to	save the	save the file
47 share with	so far as	so it is	so much
48 so that	so soon	some time ago	speak to
49 take charge	thank you	that is	this is
50 this is the	they are	they will	to be
51 to be sure	to be the	tear up	too much
52 unable to	unable to be	unable to do	under control
53 under the	until now	up and running	up for sale
54 up till now	use the	used to	used to be
55 varies from	very good	very much	we are
56 we will	whether or not	which one	with the
57 you are	you are the	you will	you will be

GOAL 13: Timings on Progressive Sentences

Exercise 13
Progressive Sentences

- The progressive sentences in this exercise are sentences that build in length from 2 standard words to 20 standard words. Each sentence increases by one word.

- These sentences are used to build your speed and accuracy.
  1. Create a new document
  2. Use the default margins.
  3. Change the font to Courier New, 12 point.
  4. Begin with the first sentence. Try to complete the sentence in 15 (or 10) seconds.
  5. Do one of the following at the end of the 15 (or 10) second timing:
     * If you did not complete the sentence within the time, type it again until you do complete it within the time.
     * If you completed the sentence within the time, go to the next sentence, which will be one word longer.
  6. Save the document; name it **L40EX13**.
  7. Print one copy.
  8. Close the document window.

```
....1....2....3....4....5....6....7....8....9...10...11...12

Just wait.                                                    2

Take their cue.                                               3

He can buy some gum.                                          4

Buy a red rose at Tex Co.                                     5

Watch the new kid at this zoo.                                6

Is there such a thing as a fun fur?                          7

....1....2....3....4....5....6....7....8....9...10...11...12
```

LESSON 40

```
....1....2....3....4....5....6....7....8....9...10...11...12

Jim sent a check to your aunt and uncle.                          8

Park your car in the lot next to the new hut.                    9

Please sit next to Pat when you go to the concert.              10

Rock vugs are formed as a result of many years of decay.        11

A water gun is something they should never fool around with.    12

Jim gave Pat his cue to come onto the stage and recite his
lines.                                                          13

Tex's uncle gave him a dollar to go to the store to buy a
qt. of milk.                                                    14

They had a lot of fun last month at the big game show held
in the new barn.                                                15

Look for the ads for the red tag discount sale on Zip disks
at the Computer Hut.                                            16

Have you seen Jim Vug's new Web page?  The words are in red,
but the graphic is dim.                                          17

The Zip drives will not work properly with the disks I have.
They are far too fat to fit.                                    18

The Red Fur Company requested a guy and a gal to model their
furs for a fashion show next week.                              19

Follow these typing rules:  sit up straight, keep your feet
on the floor, and don't look at the keys.                       20

....1....2....3....4....5....6....7....8....9...10...11...12
```

GOAL 14: Timings on Progressive Paragraphs

Exercise 14
Progressive Paragraphs

- The progressive paragraphs in this exercise are paragraphs that build in length from 15 standard words to 80 standard words. Each paragraph increases by five words.

- These paragraphs are used to build your speed and accuracy while typing for one minute.
  1. Create a new document.
  2. Use the default margins.
  3. Change the font to Courier New, 12 point.
  4. Begin with the 15 WAM paragraph. Type the paragraph for 1 minute, trying to complete as much as you can before the minute is up.
  5. If you finish the paragraph before the minute is up, press the Enter key twice and begin the same paragraph again.
  6. Once the minute is up, do one of the following for the next one-minute timing:
     * If you did not complete the paragraph within the time, type it again until you do complete it within the time.
     * If you completed the paragraph within the time, go to the next level paragraph, which will be 5 words a minute faster.
  7. Save the document; name it **L40EX14**.
  8. Print one copy.
  9. Close the document window.

15

```
Try to type by touch.  Do not look at the keys and soon you      12
will type fast.                                                  15
....1....2....3....4....5....6....7....8....9...10...11...12
```

20

```
Try to eat healthy foods as best as you can.  This might be      12
difficult if you have a busy schedule.                          20
....1....2....3....4....5....6....7....8....9...10...11...12
```

LESSON 40

25

It is very easy to type fast, but like any other skill, it   12
takes time and effort to develop. As with any sport, you   22
must practice.   25
....1....2....3....4....5....6....7....8....9...10...11...12

30

Dogs make wonderful pets. There are dogs for all types of   12
people. The key in selecting the best dog is to match the   24
breed with your personality type.   30
....1....2....3....4....5....6....7....8....9...10...11...12

35

When typing for accuracy, slow down your speed. If you make   12
too many mistakes, slow down your reading. Focus your eyes   24
only on the word you are typing and do not read ahead.   35
....1....2....3....4....5....6....7....8....9...10...11...12

40

The latest word processing programs do more than just insert   12
and delete text. They offer desktop publishing and graphic   24
options also. You can create a newsletter, draw a picture,   36
or type a letter.   40
....1....2....3....4....5....6....7....8....9...10...11...12

45

Colors affect your moods. Blue is a cool color and can calm   12
you, while red is a warm color that can excite you. When   24
you decorate, consider the purpose of the room. Once you   36
make the decision, choose an appropriate color.   45
....1....2....3....4....5....6....7....8....9...10...11...12

50

Have you given any thought to a career? How do you find out   12
what you want to do? First, find out what areas interest   24
you, then research the careers in that field. Your guidance   35
counselor may be able to help you and point you in the right   48
direction.   50
....1....2....3....4....5....6....7....8....9...10...11...12

55

Exercise is very important, and to get the health benefits,   12
it must be done regularly. Make sure to choose an exercise   24
you enjoy so you will continue to do it. Exercises that   36
involve walking, running, dancing, or jumping are very good   48
for your heart and help your bones.   55

....1....2....3....4....5....6....7....8....9...10...11...12

60

When you search the Internet, you become a world traveler   12
without ever leaving your home. A wealth of information is   24
available on any subject. All you need to do is type in the   36
specific topic you wish to find, and within minutes you will   48
get a list of Web sites where you can locate the information.   60
....1....2....3....4....5....6....7....8....9...10...11...12

65

A good friend is someone with whom you share similar values   12
and interests. You can talk freely to each other and share   24
each other's inner secrets. When you are having problems, a   36
good friend will listen to you and be there for you in times   48
of need. It is so important to have a good friend and to be   60
a good friend in return.   65
....1....2....3....4....5....6....7....8....9...10...11...12

LESSON 40

70

It is important to have very good job skills. However, even	12
though you may know how to type or operate a computer, you	24
could be weak in personal skills. Personal job skills are a	36
must for success in any career, from medicine to teaching	48
skiing, for example. Those employees who are reliable and	60
get along with others usually do succeed on the job.	70

....1....2....3....4....5....6....7....8....9...10...11...12

75

Since people need to operate computers either at home or at	12
work, good typing skills are completely necessary. If you	24
cannot type, you may find it difficult to enter information	36
into the computer. It is wise to take a keyboarding course	48
so you learn to type without having to look at the keys.	59
Future technology may make typing obsolete, but until then,	71
move those fingers.	75

....1....2....3....4....5....6....7....8....9...10...11...12

80

It is most important to have interests outside of school or	12
work. These interests and hobbies help to make you a more	24
interesting and interested person. In addition to keeping	36
you alert and involved, hobbies provide an escape from your	48
daily routines. They permit you to take a break and regroup	60
your energies. No matter what type of hobby you choose, it	72
will help your mental and physical health.	80

....1....2....3....4....5....6....7....8....9...10...11...12

484

INDEX

INDEX

INDEX

INDEX

489

NOTES

NOTES

NOTES

NOTES

NOTES